HOW I LOST MY KIDNEYS IN CHINA

A TWENTY-FIVE YEAR OVERINDULGENT ODYSSEY

RANDALL FLORES

A MEMOIR

How I Lost My Kidneys In China: *A Twenty-five Year Overindulgent Odyssey*

Printed in the United States of America

Hardcover ISBN: 978-1-959096-30-6
Paperback ISBN: 978-1-959096-31-3
Ebook ISBN: 978-1-959096-32-0

**Canoe Tree
  Press**

4697 Main Street
Manchester Center, VT 05255

Canoe Tree Press is a division of DartFrog Books

CONTENTS

Introduction xi

1. Beijing: It Begins. 1

2. Taiwan: I'm Back (sort of) 53

3. Hong Kong: Livin' On a Shoestring 109

4. Kaiping: Roller Skating. 117

5. Nanjing: That Confounded Bridge! 124

6. Dongguan: Capitalism At Play 134

7. Putian: I'm a Shoe Dog. 140

8. Qingdao: Beer Capital 172

9. Fuan: Bagels and PBR 183

10. Putian: Raging Bull 199

11. Shanghai: Exiled. .210

12. Huaiyin: Bull Peanuts. 235

13. Suqian: Graduation 255

14. Qingdao: Legend .266

15. Taiwan: We Are All Friends Here 274

16. Shanghai: Things Are Looking Up 281

17. Putian: The Wedding 299

18. Zhejiang: Deer Dong 320

19. Shanghai: Lobster and Champagne 336

20. Moscow: Just Give Them Money 363

21. Shanghai: Down But Not Out 373

22. Hong Kong: Time For Me To Fly 401

23. Shanghai: It Had To End Sometime. 425

Epilogue. 476

Map. 477

The Code 478

Glossary. 480

To My Wife
I would have never made it out
without you

"Don't Try"

Headstone of Charles Bukowski

INTRODUCTION

I'm standing outside in the bitter cold on a January morning, still drunk, wearing boxers, a windbreaker, and flimsy slippers. I feel a powerful urge to rid myself of the yellow stomach acids in my belly. Currently, I am on the front line of a battle with a factory in central China, and my hotel is on fire. It's only Tuesday, the second of a three-day bender through the valley of hard-drinking miners. There will be another trip a few days later: the further, the better. It was my job, but I fed off the adventure, going to the edge without falling over.

For almost twenty-five years, I lived and worked in the Greater China Region and threw back swimming pools full of alcohol. I drank wine (red, white, yellow, and rice), whiskey, vodka, gin, sake, Chinese firewater (*baijiu*), Jager, beer, and anything else they served me. Why did I drink so much? Seventy percent was work-related, while the rest was the boozer in me. However, my life wasn't only about the liquor. I had other roles to play, such as a high-flying executive, a nuts-and-bolts factory guy, a road warrior, a family man, a boss, an adventurer, a gastronome, a teacher, a human resources manager, a fixer, an accountant, a runner, a tour guide, and an extremely ill person. I juggled all this while often not in the best state of mind.

The tale begins with my introduction to Mandarin and progresses with my career. Although the book follows the original timeline, some chapters overlap because of my long-standing relationships with factories in various cities. As China has changed immensely during the past three decades, most places no longer exist. I altered some names of people involved, and the prices and travel times are relative to the period. To be clear, I did not write this memoir to criticize China.

I owe the country and its citizens a lot. Instead, I wanted to leave an eyewitness account of the tumultuous transformation from my front-row seat. I tried to remember everything, but anyone who drinks knows you are lacking several evenings (years) of memories. They're gone like they never happened. But some recollections never go away. They are the best (or worst). I have included those stories here.

After twenty-five years, I had ample tales to fill a few volumes.

This one is long enough.

So grab a glass of your favorite tipple and enjoy the ride.

This is how I lost my kidneys in China.

CHAPTER ONE

BEIJING: IT BEGINS

"**M**andarin? Why do you want to learn Mandarin?" It was a reasonable question. I didn't plan on studying it. In 1987, I spent summer break at a prep school on the East Coast. I considered taking trigonometry or accounting.

My counselor said, "Take something fun."

She was right. Why would I spend a summer crunching numbers? Instead, I picked a course not offered at my Suburban Chicago high school. I chose Russian because I worked vacations at a factory alongside coworkers from Poland with relatives in Russia. In the shop, I was one of the few native English speakers and the youngest worker. It was a labor-intensive and tedious job:

- Load raw pieces of steel.
- Wait for them to be cut.
- Remove the finished product.
- Do it for eight hours.

Meanwhile, half of the plant heat-treated metal and giant furnaces cooked steel day and night. The temperature inside surpassed a hundred degrees.

When we punched out at 3:30 in the afternoon, most guys went home or to the corner bar to drink hard. I befriended a young Polish guy named Christof, who spoke English enough for us to comprehend each other. My carefree American lifestyle fascinated him, so he invited me to hang with the old fellas.

After work, we dropped by the neighborhood market and grabbed a fresh, uncut loaf of rye, sliced ham off the bone, and a liter of vodka. It was a simple spread and a welcome change from my usual routine of drinking American swill with a late-night run for sliders.

My coworkers were tough guys in their fifties and sixties. They had big, meaty fingers like sausages, and I could tell they had been through harsh times by the road maps of wrinkles on their faces and hands. They worked to wire money to their families and shared a desolate apartment that resembled the type of place someone on suicide watch would live in. It was an ideal spot to finish a hard day at the bottom of a bottle.

We sat around a cheap Formica kitchen table while one guy poured vodka into glasses the size of jelly jars. Everybody's cup held about four shots. I gained a taste and growing tolerance for booze before I should have. It wasn't always excessive; more like I trained for my future. In Suburban Illinois during the '80s, drinking, smoking, and getting into trouble were things kids did. But I wasn't ready to throw back exorbitant amounts of vodka, so I tore off chunks of bread to soak it up. To them, I was a novelty. They didn't know any other Americans besides this seventeen-year-old kid consuming their alcohol. I felt as if I had discovered an underground network of immigrants, which expanded my world. All this Eastern European influence persuaded me to take Russian, to speak with my newfound boozing buddies. I sent in my selection, and they notified me after dropping the course. Apparently, nobody my age imbibed with Russian-speaking Polish.

It left me with my second selection—Mandarin.

I studied for two months and got hooked. My addiction drove me to become fluent and learn as much as possible about China. It wasn't easy. Stores seldom carried books on learning Chinese, and few even sold guidebooks. My local video store only stocked Japanese classics such as Akira Kurosawa's *Seven Samurai* and the miniseries *Shogun*, but nothing in Mandarin. On weekends, I caught campy kung fu films on TV or a Taiwanese cooking show on one of the fuzzy UHF channels. But things improved when the film *The Last Emperor* was released. Before the movie, I had only seen pictures of The Forbidden City. Now, there was a three-hour motion picture shot on the palace grounds, breathing life into my history books. My desire to explore the palace and everything else China offered inspired me to search for a means to get there. At seventeen, the only jobs I qualified for paid a minimum wage of $3.35 an hour or slightly higher at the machine shop. Once they deducted taxes, I barely had anything left. If I wanted to travel to China, I needed someone to transport me over.

My initial consideration was the military. It seemed an attractive two-for-one deal: I could test my physical limits and request to be stationed in a Chinese-speaking location. One problem with that plan was that the United States did not have bases in Mandarin-speaking countries. I was clueless, but at least I found out before I enlisted.

Next, I thought about joining the Peace Corps or teaching ESL (English as a second language) in a remote village. It would be the ultimate immersion situation. That sounded fantastic, but I would speak fluently after a year and be broke.

College seemed to be the better option. At university, I would improve my Mandarin while earning a degree in business. Once I better understood the language, I could apply to study abroad. This was my intention when I searched for schools. Outside Yale and Stanford, only a few universities offered a degree in Mandarin. I applied and got admitted to two with Chinese language programs: a large state college in Illinois and a private university in Upstate New York. I leaned towards NY because I wished to visit. Upstate was not NYC, but it was still New York. Until then, I had lived most of my life in the Midwest. I aimed to travel, so I chose The Empire State.

After visiting the school in my senior year, I realized I had made the right decision. It was Pre-Frosh Weekend. I'm not sure if they planned it, but it was also the culmination of Greek Week. Half the students engaged in Greek games such as the pony keg chug or the drunken chariot race.

A fraternity president hosted me, and I stayed at the frat house for two nights. He signed up to entertain a pre-frosh, the last thing he wanted to do while the campus was in full *Animal House* mode.

He picked me up at administration and did a quick tour, identifying the library, financial services, and other essential buildings.

The tour ended at his fraternity house, where he gave me an enormous plastic mug.

"Take this. Do you drink beer?"

"Yeah."

"Good, the keg is over there. I will be busy all weekend. You can crash in my room, and someone is always ordering pizza. If anybody gives you trouble, say you are with me."

That was it. I roamed the frat quad for the rest of the day, drinking an abundance of alcohol and watching the drunken Greek games. This felt like heaven.

Sure, it became easier to purchase alcohol back home, but some nights, we did not score. And we tried hard (fake mustache, sunglasses, and an overcoat). The most accessible places to buy were the liquor stores in the rougher neighborhoods near the South or Westside of Chicago. We chose Richards Wild Irish Rose, Mad Dog 20/20, Brass Monkey, and malt liquor. Other times, we drank less harsh stuff, such as Milwaukee's Best, MGD, and St. Pauli Girl.

At college, they handed out all sorts of fruity cocktails loaded with booze, jello shots, and endless beer for free. I didn't even need to worry about getting robbed. All I had to do was walk by a house and extend my hand.

I knew I would do well here.

Mostly, university life was a ball except for the time spent in Chinese class from 6 to 8 p.m., five days a week. After class, I endured four hours a night in the library stacks, completing other classwork and learning how to write characters in simplified and complex forms, pronouncing the specific tone for every character (there are four tones), and understanding the English meaning. China uses a streamlined version of characters not used in Hong Kong or Taiwan, and it is best to learn both. As a result, I wrote them until I had deep pen impressions on my fingers. Then I returned to the dorm to unwind with the people drinking and smoking until the early morning. It was a great way to live if your parents paid for you to party.

I lacked that luxury.

I had to graduate with two degrees and find a pathway to China.

Mastering Mandarin turned into a lengthy process that thinned out the number of people—two weeks in, Chinese 101 shrunk from fifty to ten. With my head start, the first few weeks were easy. I surprised everybody when I announced I had a Chinese name, Luo Landi, derived from my English name by my prep school teacher from Taiwan. My university professor hailed from Beijing and said my name sounded similar to a girl's because the last character meant "younger brother," as in, "This child is a girl, but the next one will be a younger brother." She shocked me. Was I the equivalent of "A Boy Named Sue?" This wasn't good, but I had to own it for now.

In the spring of 1989, there were democracy protests in Beijing. I worked shifts at the gear factory and the Museum of Science and Industry while maintaining an active partying schedule with coworkers at both places. I had little time for news, but I visited a friend who had CNN. When I saw the mass demonstrations, I realized my chances of going looked slim. All inessential foreigners left, and nobody knew when things would return to normal. Fortunately, the situation eased during the second semester of my sophomore year in 1990. It was time to apply.

The study abroad program admitted individuals from universities around the U.S. and placed them in three colleges. I desired to go to Beijing but didn't care where they sent me. I applied and took the language efficiency test. Sadly, my listening skills lacked fluency, and I missed questions while struggling to work out the previous ones. They only accepted less than fifty applicants.

What chance did I have of getting in with a lousy listening score?

Next came the torturous wait for something to arrive in my student PO box. The only other applicant at my school was my girlfriend. What if I got in and she didn't? What if she got in and I didn't? I tried not to let it weigh me down.

Towards the end of the school year, we swung by the PO and stopped by our boxes. On that day, I received a large, thick, white envelope from the program.

It meant only one thing.

They had accepted me.

I looked over at my girlfriend, and she held the same envelope. Incredibly, they took both of us.

But when she opened her letter, it said she was accepted to Nanjing University. I still had not opened mine, but I wouldn't mind going to Nanjing. However, my letter said they welcomed me at Beijing University (Peking University or Beida in Chinese). I devoted hundreds of nights in the stacks and finally got what I wanted. Without my girlfriend, I could focus on my studies and get the most out of the experience.

It would be just fine.

I filled in the forms and waited.

A couple of months had passed since I sent my passport, but I had heard nothing. No information meant trouble. Maybe they denied my visa application or lost it in the mail. All kinds of thoughts ran through my mind as I labored in the factory.

Every day I returned, I checked the mail. Still nothing. The closer it got to the middle of August, the more I braced myself for bad news. Something was holding up my application. It shouldn't be taking this long.

Then, a week before I needed to fly out, I found a FedEx envelope waiting for me. Inside was my royal blue passport with a single stamp—a China visa and flight tickets.

It was official.

I packed an army duffle and a backpack.

A few days later, I got dropped off at O'Hare Airport to begin my adventure.

II

On the trip over, I flew on a Japanese airline (slippers and Japanese ale) and had an overnight stopover in Tokyo (Narita). I welcomed the good fortune, but it took time to gather the other sheep, taking the hotel transportation. My visit wound up being a shower, a brief nap, and another shower to wake up. I wanted to stay longer, but Japan would have to wait.

The following morning, I saw the people I would study with at the flight gate. I didn't talk to anyone, but was in the right location.

Upon arrival at Beijing Capital Airport, the scene shocked me. Besides character slogans and posters praising government policies, there were few advertisements. They painted the walls a greenish-yellow halfway up and white on the rest. The place lacked cafes or restaurants, and the duty-free section only sold cigarettes and alcohol. I detected a strong medicinal odor. It smelled sterile like they doused the building in it. Most gates were shut, and the seats remained empty as if the airport was closed.

"Doesn't anybody fly?"

My reaction revealed how little I knew about the country. There were 1.1 billion people, most of whom had never flown. Over the years, I would experience the repercussions of those passengers taking their first flight. It was not as thrilling for me.

Our group had twenty-five students from the same number of universities. We followed a chaperone, who greeted and led us through customs. China was not quite what I expected. I prepared for the historical side but not for the socialist part, such as the coldness of the customs agents. They gave me the impression I burdened them. In addition, everybody gawked at us without turning away.

As we waited for our luggage, I spotted a pair of soldiers standing at attention. They wore the same baggy olive uniform, one-size-fits-all belts, hats too big, and cheap tennis shoes. From what I could tell, they did not carry guns and seemed ill-prepared.

After about a half-hour, a loud bang started the sluggish baggage conveyor. We retrieved our bags and had them investigated for subversive items before we headed out through the sliding doors to the outside world. Once out, we saw a sea of people, and nearly all smoked. It was what I imagined it felt like to be a movie star. Everyone stared at our assortment of "*laowai*" (translated as "old outsider," occasionally derogatory), pointed, and talked about us as if we didn't understand.

Some curious souls petted us (especially those with arm hair) when we moved through the crowd.

"Look at that *laowai!*"

"That *laowai* is so tall!"

"Look at the clothing that *laowai* is wearing!"

Even if you didn't understand Mandarin, you would still hear the repeated usage of "*laowai.*" I had to get used to it because it was the first thing locals said when they saw me.

The university was in the northwestern section of town, but the city lacked a direct link from the airport: We had to go south, west, then north. The only path was via a two-lane country road. It took an hour to reach downtown, fifty miles away.

While the bus chugged along the road, I glanced out the window.

"Man, there are A LOT of bicycles!"

I read about China being the land of the bicycle, but seeing the army of cyclists in action was mind-blowing. It resembled the starting position of a competitive race at every corner, with elderly men struggling to corral the cycles into lanes. Staring down from the bus window, I had a bird's-eye view and couldn't wait to join the masses.

I presumed we would proceed across town on Changan Jie (Eternal Peace Street), the military parade avenue passing by The Forbidden City. As we drew nearer, I cross-checked the few hotels on my map, getting ready for the colossal picture of Mao. Suddenly, the moment arrived. It was splendid, but only for a few seconds. I swore to return.

Thirty minutes later, we drove through the west gate of Beida and halted at Shao Yuan, the dormitory for foreigners. We were distant from the Chinese dorms, perhaps by design. They could visit but needed to show their ID and receive a grilling from the ladies in charge. Images of the protests lingered, and registration made visitors apprehensive.

Once off the bus, we reunited with our luggage and gravitated towards our foreign director, a Ph.D. candidate with superior language skills. He told us to partner up for the rooms and to meet in an hour for a welcoming lunch. Beijing street life distracted me from connecting with anybody on the ride here. Now, I waited to be picked and watched the friendlier folks find roommates while I got left with the last guy. David seemed reasonable enough, meaning there was nothing wrong with him that a couple of nights out drinking wouldn't fix.

Our room was two doors down from the entrance. Although smaller than my place in the States, it had enhancements such as a ten-inch color TV, a boom box, and a fan. Beijing was hot and humid. I preferred the dry heat from the factory furnaces, but nothing could dampen my spirit.

My roommate was not as enthusiastic.

"You may have a single. I made a mistake and might go home."

He considered packing it in on the first day. I didn't know if I should talk him out of it or celebrate.

He opened his suitcase, and the likelihood of him remaining decreased further. He brought paper towels, toilet paper, cleaning gear, and chopsticks! His mom thought American cleaning products were unavailable (true). We had toilet paper, but it had the texture of low-grade sandpaper. Everyone envied the fluffy stuff from the U.S.

After showing me his stockpile of sanitation products, he sought our director to discuss a departure strategy. Virtually as soon as he left, he returned, announcing he would try it for a week. Scheduling flights and signing up for classes back home would be problematic, so I suspected this added to his decision to remain.

We assembled in front of the dorm and walked outside the university walls, deep into the Zhong Guan Cun neighborhood. It had to be the most startling phenomenon in a long time: a procession of *laowai*. What a magnificent display of foreign devils! Bikers on both sides stopped in their tracks while slamming into the cycle in front. Movie stars, indeed!

Some school officials spoke before lunch and welcomed us. Then, they served authentic food with heads, eyes, tails, and feet. We washed it down with the main banquet drink, Yanjing Beer, presented in large green bottles. The ale was a slight solace for not being fed Peking Duck. Only restaurants that specialized in duck offered it.

Once the meal ended, they gave us the next three days off to acclimate. That was what I desired—freedom to explore.

When we began the parade back to the dorm, I split from the others and started down an offshoot lane. I intended to learn Mandarin. If I remained with my classmates, I would speak English and not get the language exposure I wanted. I needed to make friends with locals.

The alley I ventured down had old guys sitting on tiny stools a foot from the ground. They smoked cigarettes while their birds in wooden cages hung from the trees. Some of them held pet crickets, producing a pleasant chirping sound. It reminded me of summer in Illinois.

Next to the seniors stood young guns shooting pool on a table with a worn surface—the shop behind blasted Chinese pop music. In the early nineties, China looked untouched, but I detected the harbingers of change. People had caught the capitalist bug and liked it. Bikes, TVs, and fridges remained out of reach for the majority, but not for much longer. I felt fortunate to witness this China before modernization erased it.

I found a restaurant that looked like the perfect location to observe Beijing life with a cold one. The venue where we ate lunch handed out room-temperature drinks. Little did I know, everybody consumed lukewarm beverages. Refrigerated liquids were not a thing. That's why ice-cold mini bottles of Coke from a vendor on the street with a dry-ice cooler tasted so exhilarating, similar to the commercials. But now, I thirsted for a chilled brew.

As luck would have it, this shop kept a few big green bottles in the fridge.

A Korean-Chinese man named Han owned the joint and worked alone. Incidentally, I would learn that the word "*han*" meant Korea (*han guo*), Chinese (*han zu*), and moose, depending on the tone. I'm sure I called him Moose a few times before getting it right.

I sat at the lone outside table and ordered a beer. Han's diner served an unusual dish called *shuan yang rou*. It employed a unique brass pot filled with red-hot coals in the bottom cavity that heated a moat of water around a smokestack in the center. You dipped thin rolls of frozen lamb shavings into the boiling water. Few customers desired to eat this on a sweltering summer day. That was why the four small tables inside begged for customers.

Han also offered appetizers designed to stimulate drinking. It wasn't clear how long the food sat in the display case. Better not to risk it. In fact, to keep myself safe while overseas, I created a code I adhered to.

This brings me to the first rule.

Rule #1: Avoid the cold dishes.

While I read my guidebook, Han brought me three opened beers. I sought to keep the beer frosty and wanted to avoid paying for something I had never ordered. This occurred regularly, so I implemented a second rule.

Rule #2: Ensure no one pops open beverages I never ordered.

As I took swigs, I watched and listened to bikes whizzing through the alley. This was the real China, not Chinatown. I made it and could come here daily to drink with my neighbors while practicing Mandarin.

I declared this hotpot joint my *Cheers*, where everybody knew my name or at least Han did.

While I enjoyed visions of grandeur, I overheard a commotion coming my way. It sounded like English, but I escaped my classmates long ago. Somehow, they found me. I don't think they searched, but now my hidden spot was no longer a secret.

I never inquired if the joint had a name. Restaurant names lacked importance when the venues provided no-frills nosh. We referred to it as "The Hutong" or "Alley" restaurant. If you said, "I'm going to The Hutong," everyone knew the spot. It was economical, with tall bottles setting us back 1.2 RMB (about fifteen cents). A lamb hotpot meal with ten beers ran 25 RMB.

Most meals in the student cafeteria charged 20 FECs with a beer or a Coke, which was overpriced for what we received.

China circulated two currencies: RMB (the People's Currency) and FEC (Foreign Exchange Certificates, foreigner money). To purchase items from sanctioned stores, hotels, and restaurants, we paid with FECs. All locals used RMB. Foreigners were allowed to use RMB, but you couldn't get them from the Bank of China. The black market was the place.

The school issued 250 FECs weekly as our meal plan, equivalent to $30 or a month's salary. We felt super-rich with these monopoly dollars bursting out of our pockets. Since we could spend the money however we pleased, I ate at the cafeteria out of convenience. The food was often room temperature, with small rocks in the rice, a common problem— nothing worse than biting into a mouthful of rice and chipping a tooth (it happened to a classmate). Even though the Hutong sold delicious lamb, it took time for Han to fire up the coals. Some nights, he refused me when I was too anxious. He didn't want to waste the energy for a single plate of lamb. I still planned to have many drunken evenings at my favorite spot, and I made a friend.

If I wished to stay on campus, a basement bar operated within our dorm. It was a place to pick up travel tips and get loaded close to home. A group of fellow scholars convened here. They were the students I got along with best. We came from different backgrounds but enjoyed a few rounds together. The others broke into their own factions and did whatever they did. They weren't a heavy-drinking crowd.

The first time I hung out at the basement bar, someone identified a genuine star in our midst. He was a Canadian famous for his Chinese New Year's Eve Gala performance. Hundreds of millions of viewers watched this show—hundreds of millions!

In 1990, he was the most recognized foreigner. "Big Mountain," a name derived from a character he played on TV, had the level of Mandarin we all aspired to achieve.

Someone introduced him to our table, but he didn't want to hang out with rookies.

III

The following morning, I woke at the crack of dawn. Before I continued exploring, I needed something in my belly. The cafeteria served hot soy milk, plain congee, cold fried eggs, and large steamed buns with a small ball of meat or greens. The thought of drinking a glass of heated soy made me want to throw up, so I ate the buns with tea.

Next, I investigated the used bicycle market our director recommended. A new Flying Pigeon or Phoenix (no Schwinn here) would set me back $100, depending on how heavy I preferred the bike (heavier bikes required more steel). I had no idea why someone would crave a hefty ride with no gears unless they planned to crash into others. The cost made a bicycle a family's pride possession, similar to a car. Every cycle came with a pocket-sized, red booklet that contained an ownership title. In theory, I was supposed to carry it at all times.

On the way, I passed a group of men standing in front of a restaurant with two sheep. These guys had scruffy beards and Eastern European facial features. They also wore unusual embroidered square hats, making them look Middle Eastern. When I passed, they said something in a low voice, as if speaking a secret language. No one else seemed to hear what they uttered, nor did they acknowledge the dudes existed. They repeated, "*Huan Qian, Huan Qian. Sheesh, Sheesh.*" I translated the first part as "change money."

They came from the western region of China called Xinjiang. Our Chinese handlers cautioned us about them, but they looked nice enough. Often, they peddled fruitcake as a side hustle.

How sinister could a fruitcake vendor be?

However, the most important thing about changing cash (besides the exchange rate) was to identify counterfeits. This was easier if your monger operated out of a shop instead of on the street.

Rule #3: Check your money for forgeries, and do not accept tattered bills.

The other item they sold was hashish. I listened for Mandarin when they spoke accented English.

As much as I desired to inspect this "*sheesh,*" I refrained from doing a drug deal. I longed to live in the People's Republic but not in jail or on death row.

The secondhand bike bazaar was a few doors down from the Xinjiang dudes. I almost missed it when looking for a flea market. Like other storefronts, it was a couple of rows of bicycles. When I stopped to check them out, a crowd formed. Everybody squeezed closer to get a listen while lighting up smokes. I had difficulty negotiating with people gathering around to hear my alien tongue. They also wanted to know how much the sales guys swindled me. As I walked between the aisles to evade the mob, they followed, knocking over bikes like dominoes. It was no use. I left and planned to return in a few days to give it another go.

IV

On Sunday, I walked to a park to practice writing characters. The place was active with Beijingers singing opera and playing traditional musical instruments. Similar to the alley, old men with their birds sat around and played cards while the crickets chirped away. It seemed like the perfect environment to immerse myself in local life. So, I sat at a small stone table, laid out my books, and wrote characters.

Immediately, I became the star attraction. Old guys strolled by with their hands clenched behind their backs as they leaned over to see what I wrote. They said something in a thick Beijing accent my ears tried to equate to the Mandarin I had learned. It turned into such a disturbance that I hardly got any writing done, but I improved my listening skills.

An hour later, a young guy came and sat down, saying nothing. Every time I looked up, he smiled. I assumed he would leave, but that was not the case. Other parkgoers walked by, asking if he was my teacher.

Finally, I said, "*Ni hao ma*? (How are you?)"

"Oh, you speak Chinese. That's great. You speak so well."

That was a stretch. Obviously, I spoke some, or else why would I be writing characters? Like most locals, this guy had studied English since grade school, and now he had the opportunity to use those words with a real, honest-to-goodness foreigner, but he didn't try. I wondered how long he would've sat across from me, saying nothing if I hadn't spoken first?

His name was Wang Yi. He was twenty-eight, married, had a newborn son, and had never met a Westerner. We continued to hold a rudimentary conversation until lunchtime. I considered trying one of the few restaurants. Instead, my new friend invited me to his home. He kept insisting, begging me to join him. Initially, I wavered: I knew little about him, and he wanted to take me to his house? But why would I refuse an authentic, home-cooked meal?

"I live close, only a few minutes from here."

He pulled me towards the direction of his abode. It was hard to refuse. I was eager to learn about real Chinese cooking, which resembled nothing like the takeout back home. I just discovered China did not have fortune cookies, so I had a way to go.

His traditional Beijing-style accommodation was in the alley behind The Hutong. Once through the outside swinging doors, they had a washing station on the left and a kitchen shack on the right that five families shared. Each lived in their own twenty-square-foot "apartment," big enough for a bed and a folding table for meals. They lacked air-conditioning but had a fan they operated on summer days. In the winter, they fed pieces of coal, twice the size of a hockey puck, into the small furnace in the corner. The heater had an exhaust pipe for the toxic, black smoke, making winter a haze of deadly air.

He introduced me to his wife and told her I would eat lunch with them. I couldn't imagine what she thought when he came home with a foreigner. There was no time to warn her. The neighbors appeared curious but hesitant. They weren't sure if I would be trouble politically or if they would catch something from me. Being respectful but prudent seemed to be the best option.

His wife smiled and started preparing the meal while caring for their infant son. Wang Yi opened the eating table, absorbing the room's remaining space.

People presumably regarded him as upper-middle class because he lived in one of the finest neighborhoods, owned a bicycle, and worked for the government. Wang Yi also collected VOA (Voice of America) tapes. The United States operated a radio station off the coast of China, broadcasting world news in English. It was the best method for locals to study the language. Inside a briefcase cassette tape holder, he saved dozens of VOA recordings, all labeled with date and subject as if he had a collection of bootleg Grateful Dead concerts.

"It's going to take my wife an hour to make lunch. She will buy things at the market."

"She doesn't need to arrange something special."

"No, no, it's no trouble. It's no trouble at all."

He asked what I wanted to drink. His wife would walk to the market to buy. Again, I didn't wish to burden her with all these errands (and delay lunch). No way would he take a chance that I might wander off if he left me alone. He waited his whole life to meet a foreigner.

I said, "Let's drink beer."

Beer was the most accessible and cheapest to purchase. Every place sold the green bottles I grew fond of. In addition, I thought alcohol would work as a vaccine. It was nonsense, but it gave me the confidence to try new foods.

"Beer? Perfect!"

His wife disappeared and came back with half a dozen warm bottles. Wang Yi grabbed two and applied one to pop off the cap of the other, a technique I needed to learn. I told him I liked to drink out of the bottle. That way, I avoided using a cup. Most people did the same.

We finished the first six, and I went for a piss break to pick up more.

"Go out the entrance, make a right, and then . . ."

"I'm aware of the location. I visited yesterday."

Instead of going to the toilet, I walked to The Hutong and bought a half dozen bottles of cold brew. I now had the beverage I craved, but how to carry six bottles? You had to bring your own bag, not for environmental reasons, but because complimentary bags were a few years away. Han took out some pink plastic twine and weaved it in and around the bottlenecks, pulling them together. The result was a sturdy hauling strap. I worried they would fall when I picked up the lot, but the straps held. What a fantastic makeshift bottle transport method! It was another unique skill.

Since I took longer, Wang Yi waited for me at the entrance to his compound, like a worried mother who expected her lost child to return. He assumed I got disoriented in the alleys. When I showed up with the beer, I expected joy and an acknowledgment for finding cold stuff, but he appeared embarrassed and apologized. I didn't understand.

If a friend turned up at your door with a six-pack in America, there would be jubilation. China had social norms that people adhered to. I broke a rule by purchasing beer. He lost face for not having enough, and I think I shocked him with cold ones. Wang Yi was a room-temperature drinker. It never occurred to him that The Hutong sold beer because he had never eaten there.

Han said most customers shied away from his joint since he was not a "*lao Beijinger*" (born and raised in Beijing) but from the northern part, opposite North Korea. I could tell by the shortage of patrons.

Wang Yi opened a cold one, and I guzzled it. "Ahh," it was so refreshing. I needed a chilled beverage in the hot weather, and the beer went down like water. The alcohol content was less than the malt liquor I drank at home, so getting drunk took a significant effort and many piss stops.

Before traveling to China, I planned to be open to exotic foods without becoming sick. It was the adventure and the risk. My knowledge of Chinese food increased with the recent additions of *gong bao* chicken (*kung pao*) and *yu xiang rou si* (shredded pork with fish sauce). I had much more to learn. Let the education begin.

Unfortunately, this would not be a day of risk-taking. The fried salted peanuts, stir-fried cabbage, and white rice were fine. I drew the line when his wife brought out boiled lamb with the thick skin still on and her favorite dish, sliced pig head. The lamb tasted good once I removed the skin and dipped it in black vinegar, but I passed on the head when I saw the eyelashes. Nope, today was not a day for fortitude.

I tried to get his wife to sit and partake. She remained for a bit but rushed out. Wang Yi claimed she was nervous and would eat what we left behind. Lucky for her, there would be plenty. I had no intention of touching the pig's head. It would be clear of foreign devil germs.

I still felt awful as she ran around while we dined. He said she was happier this way. "Luo Landi, no problem." He said that about everything. I thought "No problem" meant, "Yes, it's a problem." His wife seemed to fear me. After all, I was a random foreigner her husband had picked up in the park and was now sitting in their bedroom, getting drunk. What's not to be afraid of?

Because I outperformed him on the drinking, he tried something to improve his chances.

"Do you enjoy *baijiu* (pronounced 'bye joe')?"

I presumed *baijiu* was white wine. It translated as white alcohol (red wine translated as red alcohol). I assumed they used grapes to concoct it. Never assume.

"Sure, I can drink a lot of white wine."

If I could down two jelly glasses of Russian vodka, a bottle or two of wine would be no problem. This made him happy.

"I'll be right back." He returned empty-handed.

"My wife will head to the market to buy a bottle."

Once again, I was sorry she had to run errands for us and because we would need two bottles. She would have to make more than one trip.

His wife returned five minutes later with a bottle of *Erguotou*. Those three characters caused people to wince, shudder, hide, or cry. *Erguotou* was the finest, low-end hard stuff (fifty-six percent alcohol). It came in a green bottle, similar to beer, but this was not ale. He popped it open, and a peculiar scent infused the room like a combination of cleaning fluid and licorice. It reeked of pure trouble. If you have tried *baijiu*, you never forget that fragrance. It haunted you, leaving a memory of something irrational you did while on a business trip to the People's Republic.

Baijiu was drunk from thimble-sized shot glasses, smaller than U.S. ones. Wang Yi didn't have the tiny glasses; he seldom drank *baijiu*. No worries. The larger cup gave the hootch room to breathe, and it breathed heavily.

I took his word on the glasses being clean despite noticing his wife squatting in the courtyard, washing them in a red plastic water basin. What else could I do? Drink the entire bottle (Yep)? I made an executive decision. When he poured, I said to myself, "This is not white wine, but perhaps the flavor will be sweet like schnapps. At least the liquor will kill the germs. What have I gotten myself into? I need to keep my head straight so I don't go too far and lose my shit."

He filled the cups, but his glass held beer while mine had cleaning fluid. Then, he wanted to *ganbei* (dry glass or bottoms up), the preferred method of drinking, to test your manhood. It also got people to consume more. If someone challenged you to a *ganbei*, you had little prospect of avoiding it unless you were in a higher economic, leadership, or social bracket.

If a woman asked a man to *ganbei*, that was an exception. Everyone agreed a man never drank less than a woman. If a woman finished her glass while the man drank half, they would mock him until he downed the rest.

Before we imbibed, I said, "Wait a minute, let me take a sip so I know what I'm getting ready to finish."

I put the glass to my lips and inhaled a mouthful. It burned; I choked, coughed, and grabbed my beer. They did not make this from grapes. I needed to shift gears.

We clinked glasses. "*Ganbei!*" I made the amateur mistake of stopping halfway through. A small amount got caught going down the wrong pipe, which caused another coughing fit and made my eyes water. Wow, what a harsh introduction. Wang Yi laughed and asked,

"Too strong?"

After the choking stopped, I lifted the glass and finished it. This time, it had no burn.

I learned everybody passed through stages when guzzling *baijiu*. The process was the same, whether it was your first or thousandth time.

First Shot: "That did not go down well. Let's try again."

Second Shot: "That was less harsh. The next one should do the trick."

Third Shot: "Hey, that was smooth. Someone should sell this outside of China."

Fourth Shot: "I don't want to get drunk. I better drink more beer and *baijiu*."

Fifth Shot: "No sweat, I can *ganbei* with everybody at the table. *Baijiu* isn't half bad if you consume enough."

Sixth Shot: "Did I just eat turtle or chicken? Who cares? Let's wash it down with another glass."

Seventh Shot: "We are in for a long night. Better strap in."

Eighth Shot: "We should order a few more bottles. We are low."

Ninth Shot: "What's my name, and what am I doing here?"

And so on until you woke up at noon, on the floor of your hotel (or dorm) if lucky. Another side effect was the *baijiu* burps, the gift that kept giving. Even after my last glass, the burps brought back the flavor. It was torturous. You needed a particular skill to consume *baijiu*. I had that ability. My tolerance enabled me to out-drink everyone and stand tall. This initiation to the devil's juice became my first step to transitioning into an Olympic-level *ganbei* master.

Wang Yi poured more, and we continued through the afternoon. I looked at the food again. Nope. The pig eyelash still faced me. Eventually, his wife took the dish away to eat. With the pig head no longer winking at me, I lifted the party to the next level.

"Do you listen to rock and roll music?"

"Rock ' n' roll?"

"Yeah, rock ' n' roll."

He took out his massive dictionary.

"Oh, *yaogun* (rock ' n' roll). Yes, Mao Wang (Cat King)."

"Cat King?"

Who the hell was Cat King? His dictionary did not have a definition. Later, I found out he meant Elvis— "The King of the Cats." Why was that his name? Nobody knew.

I brought my Walkman with two tapes: *Best of The Doors* and Chet Baker's *Let's Get Lost*. Since I drank *baijiu*, The Doors seemed more appropriate. I grew up listening to them and recalled hearing Jim Morrison wail and howl for the first time. This would be Wang Yi's introduction to Mr. Mojo Risin'. I slipped a tape into the boom box he tuned into VOA on, and the primal screams of the Lizard King filled his abode and the entirety of the compound. The more I consumed, the more I increased the volume. He turned it down to avoid upsetting his neighbors. I was insensitive but drunk on *baijiu*. We had a splendid time filled with drinking, conversation, language learning, and friendship.

After consuming all the booze, I made multiple trips to the local outhouse. It was easy to find a restroom in any neighborhood. As Toucan Sam said, "Follow your nose; it always knows." The odor increased in strength the closer I got until I almost passed out.

Most alley commodes were stone rooms with a wall separating the men and women. They had no stalls, only rectangular holes in the floor to squat over. Some holes had stone platforms to step on to give you better footing. I already visited this toilet when drinking at The Hutong. Even though I walked in twice, I saw no one. Perhaps I used the "bad" bathroom.

I strolled in and whizzed into the nearest rectangular hole while disturbing the flies from their feast. When I stood on the platforms, I urinated into the hole. I lacked focus while struggling to breathe and splashed my shoes when I missed—years of waste brewing up an eye-watering concoction of fumes made me want to cry. The worst port-a-potty at the busiest music festival did not compare. If not careful, you might find yourself up to your knee in excrement. No thanks. Standing on the poop shoot platforms was not a good idea.

On my third visit, I ran into my first squatter. He was busy when I met him, but he still had time to say hello. He read a newspaper while perched on the platforms, like an acrobat or a ski jumper. I figured I might splash him, so I opted to pee in the corner.

Another guy strode up but refrained from entering. He used a trough out in the open. I felt foolish for using the dump room. Next time, I would use the pee canal.

Even the trough came with issues as random guys squeezed next to me in the three-foot-wide stall. I took a longer time, sharing the space with a couple of guys, shoulder to shoulder, each taking glances at what I worked with. There was no privacy or shame.

We drank and listened to music until nighttime. Wang Yi's face was as red as a ripe apple, and he was ready for me to depart. We had a wonderful afternoon, maybe too exciting. Not every day could he pick up a Westerner in the park.

He offered to walk with me, but that would be more trouble than walking alone. Wang Yi had more than his limit. His wife agreed he should not escort me. He would lean more on me than I would on him.

I had a half-hour stroll to the dorm and needed to return before the small gate closed. If not, I would have to enter through the main entrance. Beida contributed a substantial number of students to the democracy protests. As a result, they enhanced security. I wanted to avoid the hassle of the guard reviewing my ID, which listed my birth year as 1990. Anybody could see I wasn't born in 1990, but inconsistencies induced hiccups in China.

On the way back, the streets looked desolate except for a few bikes and the occasional bus. Some people kept their doors open as a relief from the heat, and I observed families going about their regular activities. As I navigated the alleys, I listened for the odd bike bell signaling when someone wished to pass me.

"This is just my third day. I'm going to have an excellent five months."

I reached the dorm in time to continue drinking at the basement bar while sharing my local experience with my classmates. It was a good day.

V

As potent as it was, *baijiu* didn't provoke a hangover like tequila or whisky. The problem was the beer. Every morning, I needed to intake fluid, but not from the faucet. The school warned only to drink boiled water and never eat fruit with the skin on. Disregarding either of these orders would lead to severe bodily repercussions, making your stay unpleasant.

I couldn't recall having boiled water as a beverage before I landed in China. It never occurred to me as a go-to refreshment when dehydrated. It may be a fluid, but it didn't stop the sensation of being expunged of liquids and even made it worse. In addition, the water had a rusty aftertaste. The weak tea bags they gave us did nothing to hide it.

Compared to the Chinese dorms, our dorm seemed luxurious. Instead of dark holes, we had porcelain ones and a proper sit-down toilet with no seat (a squatter on higher ground for those with no fear of heights). Western legs did not suit these toilets: we lacked some squatting muscles. I "held it" as long as conceivable before surrendering and bending the knees.

It took balance and aim to squat. You wanted to ensure you released your business in the right spot, or you splashed yourself. I developed a technique where I used a piece of tissue and gripped the bottom of the stall door. That prevented me from falling back, but it looked odd for anybody wandering in and seeing four fingers clutching the door.

Apart from the toilet situation, washing clothes became an inconvenience. In my American dorm, we had industrial-sized washing machines. We didn't have a machine in China (some of us chipped in to buy one, but it was useless and expensive); everything had to be hand-washed. Have you tried to clean a pair of jeans by hand? Try wringing out the excess water, and your forearms resembled Popeye's. When your muscles froze, you either waited or quit and took your soggy garments back to your room to hang over your bed.

Our class schedule was from Monday to Friday, 8 a.m. to 11:30; afternoons free. We had two older instructors with experience teaching foreigners and a twenty-eight-year-old female teacher who taught newspaper Chinese. The trouble with introducing American students to something political was we challenged things. Local students wouldn't have asked questions. Anytime the conversation shifted into a sensitive area, Ms. Wen held her finger up to her lips and pointed to the ceiling to suggest someone listened. I don't know if that was true, but they canceled the course. The two other teachers refused to discuss it. They knew how to toe the line.

Before class, the school arranged for a famous Tai Chi Master to instruct us at 6:30 in the morning. It was an opportunity to learn the moves I saw the seniors at the park practicing. The teacher was old school and accustomed to receiving a hundred percent respect from his followers. He no longer accepted new pupils and taught us at a special request from the university we pressed for.

During the first week, everybody turned up early, ready. When jet lag began to wear off in the second week, half the group showed up late. The teacher got angry, yelled at everybody for being disrespectful, and threatened to go home. By the third week, he canceled the course. We failed our first test.

In the afternoon, most students hung around the dorm, speaking English. I remained in my room, writing characters and memorizing vocabulary. At night, I went drinking to use what I had learned. I found my method worked well.

I waited a few days before returning to The Hutong to avoid bumping into Wang Yi. We were fine, but if he saw me, it might compel him to treat me, which he could not afford. I also wanted to hang around different people, so I searched for alternative places to dine.

Besides hotpot, we had a Sichuan (Szechwan) restaurant. I didn't realize how unusual it was to have something not local. Most places served Beijing staples. To me, it was all Chinese food. Only later did I recognize the specialties of each provincial type of cuisine. Now you can enjoy any kind of food in any city. Modernization!

The Sichuan place had three round tables, each accommodating ten customers on short stools. If I arrived when it was packed, I had to stand behind someone almost finished to intimidate them and commandeer their seat. It was as cutthroat as a game of musical chairs.

When I sat down, the owner cleared away the dirty dishes and wiped the table with a grimy rag while throwing down the flimsy, one-page menu. Then, she lingered over me until I decided.

They had the favorites such as *gong bao* chicken, pork with fish sauce, sour and spicy shredded potatoes, and *shui zhu* beef or fish (in a numbing chili oil soup). The ingredients were smaller but heavier in flavor. These dishes became my golden standards.

Like most things, the food was dirt cheap ($1.50 a plate). I enjoyed it so much that I broke my cold dish rule. They had an appetizer called "strange flavor chicken" (*guai wei ji si*), which rose to the top of my list.

It had shredded chicken with a spicy peanut and garlic sauce poured on top. They boiled the chicken after I ordered it and then cooled it, making it safer.

Another first for me was tofu. The restaurant concocted a tofu dish that would convert any non-believer. They cut two flat pieces of fried tofu the size of a matchbook, stuffed a pork mixture inside, dipped them in egg, and sautéed them. Next, they poured a thick, soupy broth on the cooked squares. Wow, what an excellent hangover meal. It took longer to make, so they would not sell it during busy periods, but it was worth taking a trip during off-peak hours.

The backup dish was "sliced pork and vegetables over sizzling rice" (*guo ba rou pian*). First, they fried rice cakes and arranged them on a sizzling hot plate in front of you. Then, they dumped a bowl of sliced pork and vegetables over the cakes. The rice crackled and popped when the soup soaked it. This dish needed to be devoured before the cakes became soggy.

My American friends and I often talked and drank too long while avoiding eye contact with the irritable customers expecting to take our stools. The owners wanted our business because we ordered lots of drinks and pricey plates while locals came in for a bowl of noodles. We also provided entertainment. People never got enough of the *laowai* eating their food. They watched as we ate. How did we use chopsticks? What did we enjoy eating? What were we doing in China? In the beginning, it felt amusing. After the hundredth time, it was annoying.

Across from the Sichuan joint was Mao Mao's with the sheep. They provided Qing Zhen, halal for the Muslim people in Western China, and served lamb hotpot, but I had a favorite hotpot place. Mao Mao's was less attractive because of the filthy bike repair shop in front and the pusher men slanging tea and fruitcake. I stayed away but monitored those sheep to see how long they lasted.

There was a delicious government dumpling and noodle house nearby. I didn't know dumplings were a significant part of Beijing cuisine. Little balls of minced pork and leeks were enclosed in a dough pocket and boiled to perfection. They prepared them fast and cheaply.

The menu was an indecipherable bunch of characters scribbled on an old chalkboard. I studied the situation and deduced they made one type of dumpling, one type of noodles, and a combination of rice and pork belly in a bamboo steamer. I walked up to the first window to purchase and picked up a strip of paper to hand over to the food window; one for dumplings and another for noodles.

They sold dumplings by the weight. This confused me. I expected to buy by the piece or the dozen. The locals used the Chinese weight measurement, *liang* (equal to 1.8 ounces), to order. Most customers said, "I'll have *er liang* (2 X 1.8 ounces or 3.6 ounces, equivalent to a quarter-pound)."

Liang also stood for the number two, so I heard, "I'll have two orders of two dumplings."

Four seemed too few. I ordered twelve *liang*, thinking I purchased 12 X 2 or twenty-four, but I bought 1.4 pounds—a massive amount. They looked at me with respect.

"Wow, twelve *liang*! You foreigners can eat."

I procured all those dumplings with a beer for only three dollars. The afternoon burps of garlic and leeks were free. I had to remember never to select these on a date.

Of course, it wouldn't be Beijing without Peking Duck. The most famous duck restaurant, Quanjude (QJD), has made ducks for over 150 years. The original owner paid a retired chef from the Imperial Kitchen for the recipe. He wanted to serve it to ordinary citizens. To cook, they roasted the birds for several hours, basting a savory coating until they turned a gorgeous golden brown. Usually, the server pushed a carving cart over to your table with the finished product and sliced it with a bit of meat, a little fat, and a piece of skin—the perfect harmony.

After carving, you stuffed the meat in a crepe-like tortilla with plum sauce and shredded scallions. If done right, nothing compares.

While you speculated if they served this in heaven, the kitchen made duck soup out of the bones to be slurped up after you stuffed many "duck tacos" down your throat. Although the broth looked like dirty dishwater, it tasted amazing.

The local duck shop was less of a celebration, but I couldn't beat the price of 30 RMB ($6). My classmates were not as excited about eating duck, so sadly, I had it only twice during my first tour.

I never grew accustomed to the absence of napkins in all the restaurants. It seemed unnatural not to wipe my mouth when eating. Most places handed out single-use wooden chopsticks wrapped with a scrap of paper the size of a gum wrapper. That minuscule piece became our only napkin, and I employed it sparingly. If I got into a jam, I wiped my hands on the insides of my shorts. It was improvisation at its finest.

VI

I spent most of my time studying in the stacks at school in the U.S. It forced me to focus. Plus, the library had air conditioning.

When I attempted to enter the library at Beida, an elderly man blocked my entry. He pointed to my feet, saying,

"You can't come in with sandals."

Most local students wore leather sandals with sheer ankle socks, which were okay. My Tevas were not. The old guy refused to budge, so I had no choice but to return to obtain proper shoes.

On my second attempt, he let me in with Rockports.

In the library back home, I sometimes had an entire floor. At Beida, they had an enormous study room filled with students but no single cubicles embedded within the stacks. I searched for a vacant seat and squeezed in. They lacked A/C and only had ceiling fans circulating hot air. I never anticipated uncomfortable conditions such as this. However, I persisted.

I sat down, and nobody paid attention to me. Maybe their concentration would rub off, so I took my textbooks out and studied. Ten minutes later, someone let out a loud fart, breaking the silence. How could somebody be so brazen? I was the only person to poke my head up. Everybody else continued reading as if nothing had happened. If this was the type of riff-raff I had to contend with, then I had better study in my dorm.

I never visited again.

As I walked on campus, students (male only) approached me to make friends. It felt strange to have someone sneak up and ask,

"Hello, can I help you?" or "Hi, are you an American?"

The longer I stayed, the less I approved of this method, but in the beginning, I didn't mind.

At the end of my first week, a guy came up to me and introduced himself as Xiao Zhang (Little Zhang). I was on my way to purchase a bike again. If I intended to remain in China, I required wheels. Xiao Zhang walked up at the ideal moment. He hoped to start a conversation and make an American friend. Done. Now, his new American acquaintance needed a favor,

"Can you walk with me over to the bicycle market and get a reasonable price?"

Xiao Zhang was happy to accommodate.

He could share this adventure with his seven other roommates (they packed them in over in the Chinese dorms) and would receive an hour of free conversation with an English speaker.

This was priceless, considering there were no native English language instructors on campus.

Prior to arriving at the market, I told him,

"After I stop to look at the bikes, keep walking like you don't know me. Once I have made my choice, I will meet you a few stores down and tell you which one to buy."

No way would I be able to bargain. They saw me coming long before I arrived. All the guys in the business promptly stood up and followed me.

"Friend, you want to buy a bike?"

"Hello, how about this one? Cheap, Cheap."

"What kind do you like?"

"How about this one? Very good."

They pushed me towards the new bikes at prices above 500 RMB.

Soon, a crowd formed as I snaked through the rows of cycles, outrunning the sales guys with lit cigarettes dangling from their mouths. When my eye caught the one I wanted, I escaped and parted the group of bystanders.

I informed Xiao Zhang, and he bought it for 115 RMB ($14).

"Make sure they give you the ownership papers. I prefer a bike with a title."

He returned, and I asked,

"Did you get the title?"

"*Mei you.*"

That meant he neglected to ask, or they didn't have. Either way, I owned a "hot ride." He saved about 50 RMB or two weeks of dumplings. The best part was outwitting the sellers.

It was my first bargaining victory, but I knew I would lose the war.

I couldn't wait to tell my classmates about the fast one I pulled until another student stole my thunder. He picked up a cycle for 10 RMB less. What? Xiao Zhang was not the tough bargainer I thought he would be. Next time, I would have to start with a low price and not budge. If I wanted to do that, I needed to clear my afternoon. Killer shopping skills require lots of effort and perseverance.

Since I owned wheels, Xiao Zhang sought to bring me to his favorite place.

"Meet me at the main gate at 5 p.m."

I showed up, and once I saw him, he said,

"Follow me."

That was easier said than done. It had been ten years since I last rode on two wheels, and riding on the streets of Beijing took skill. There were too many cycles to count. "Bling, bling." "Bling, bling." Office workers, dudes with heavy items strapped to the back, and old ladies tried to overtake me. I pedaled harder to keep up.

When we set off, I assumed he was taking me to a drinking establishment, or perhaps he wanted to play "snook" (what people called eight ball). It was a long journey to get drinks. I yearned to turn back, but he was ahead and seemed excited to show me something, so I kept going.

After an hour, we arrived at a wide avenue I recognized as Eternal Peace Street. He brought me to Tiananmen Square. This was his favorite place? It was dark, and the lights shined on the big Mao picture. I hadn't expected this or would've taken my camera.

Here, I stood in front of the place that had led me to China. Xiao Zhang said that his friends had joined the protests, and possibly he did too. I didn't know what to say. Suddenly, things got real. I watched everything on CNN. Now, I was standing in the same square on the other side of the TV. It looked surreal to see people playing music, flying kites, and ballroom dancing in the same area where tanks rolled over. I thanked him for sharing his sacred spot, but I wished he had informed me beforehand. I would have prepared and slapped some Vaseline on my out-of-shape thighs. Man, I needed more exercise.

That would change after riding a bike everywhere.

VII

Our first school excursion took us to the Friendship Store and Silk Alley, an hour away on the east side. They told us the Friendship Store stocked the foods we desired from home. We needed to show our passports to get in, and they only accepted FEC. This exclusivity fooled me into thinking they had some excellent stuff. Nothing about imported clothes, preserved food, and goat's milk appealed to me. I missed milk, but not from a goat, and lacked a refrigerator. If I picked up something, it had to be dry goods. Who wants to buy a can of peas or sardines? I hoped for Doritos, but no such luck. Many of the shelves sat empty. Nevertheless, I felt I should buy something because the store sold products unavailable outside. So, I purchased a crusty loaf of bread—another rare item.

Silk Alley consisted of lanes hawking Chinese crafts, everything made of silk, and knock-offs like Tag Heuer watches, North Face backpacks, and designer bags. They traded all this contraband next to the U.S. Embassy. The market literally ended at the wall. They couldn't stop it, but it was ironic.

Silk Alley also turned into the ideal place to change money. As soon as you got within two blocks, people came up to you to beg for cash (sometimes mothers with children or just children holding infants) or wanted to exchange money.

"Change money", "Change money."

No matter the hassle, you relinquished a lot if you didn't do it. For example, when you swapped currency in a hotel, they handed over 4.7 FECs per $1. If you converted U.S. dollars for RMB on the street, you received a rate of 8.3 RMB to $1. The outside market rate for FEC to RMB was 125 RMB for every 100 FEC. They should have been equal, but FECs bought you a bottle of Johnny Walker, a carton of Marlboros, and a ticket out of China. In addition, locals could exchange FEC for U.S. Dollars, while RMB did not have that option. Thus, the thirst for FECs equaled the demand for greenbacks.

As you wandered down the alleys, any shop not servicing other customers would have someone in front ready to tempt you to change money. I liked to walk all the lanes to hear the rates on offer, and I avoided the trader with the best one.

There had to be a catch.

The rate also depended on how much you needed and no small or dirty bills. With FECs, this never became a problem because Beida issued brand-new fifties and hundreds. The money looked and smelled so fresh; I thought they printed them on campus, but it was because so few foreigners arrived to use them.

U.S. dollars had defects, such as words and pictures drawn on them, torn pieces, and even burn marks. The traders refused anything that wasn't perfect. If you brought less than impeccable bills, you took those home.

If you wanted to exchange a considerable amount, like $500, they led you through a maze of low-hanging bags and silk clothes to a different store, a bank with more cash. When swapping bills, you had to take a few precautions.

1. Always check every single bill (**Rule #3**).

2. Only hand over your dollars once you count and examine theirs.

3. WATCH YOUR BACK!

It was possible to have one guy distract you while another ran off with your bag or wallet. I also did not recommend walking deep into some stores. Tourists dropped their guard because they assumed nothing bad would happen in friendly China. Unfortunately, as society developed, so did the crime.

Once I figured out how to take the bus and subway to Silk Alley, I wound up going once a month to pick up more polka-dotted silk boxers and visit my bank. The silk underwear felt cool in the summer heat and was easy to wash, efficient, and cheap.

I had a new addiction.

VIII

My Chinese professor in the U.S. had family living in the Capital. Like other mainland scholars in the '80s, she studied abroad and remained. Her father lived alone, and she gave me his number. I called after I settled, and he came to see me.

The guards knocked on my door and said a visitor was waiting. I spotted a retired-looking, graying man slightly taller than me. He stood proudly with his hands on his hips and had a paunch, similar to Mao.

"Are you Luo Landi, the student of my daughter Xiao Miaor?"

He spoke in a voice deeper than most, with a standard Beijing dialect as recognizable as a Boston accent. I mimicked his pronunciation when I was with him because it was perfect.

"That's me,"

"Have you eaten?"

"No, I haven't."

I wasn't aware locals used "Have you eaten?" rather than addressing someone with greetings, such as "How are you?" or "What's up?" It was a courtesy. Instead of "No, I haven't," the correct response should have been, "Yes, have you?" When you reply no, the other person feels obligated to treat you. We had already planned to eat, so it didn't matter. But I made him chuckle with my straightforward answer.

"Do you own a bike?"

I was proud to reply, yes.

"Okay, meet me in front."

I walked into the dorm to grab my cigarettes and keys. I figured he must live nearby because he rode.

"Are you ready? Let's go."

He started, and we traveled north and took the road around the university grounds. Next, we hung a right and cruised alongside the Old Summer Palace (Yuanmingyuan). We continued until we took another turn and kept going. I enjoyed seeing a separate part of the city.

An hour later, we arrived at a housing project and headed to the last building. We locked up the bikes and hiked up three flights to his floor. He resided in a single room with a kitchen, TV, VCR, washing machine, and his own toilet. Compared to Wang Yi's apartment, this was ballin' (in a socialist fashion). While he pulled out a circular folding table, he asked,

"Do you enjoy lamb hotpot?"

He just said the magic words.

"Very much."

"Setting up the pot and coals will take time. You can watch a movie."

He worked (retired) at the Beijing Movie Studio and had access to films before they were released. I watched a flick about a farmer who discovered the Terracotta Warriors that protected the tomb of Qin Shi Huangdi, the first emperor of China. The warriors sprung to life to experience modern Middle Kingdom living but seemed unhappy. Halfway through the film, Lao Zhu finished preparing the feast with the right ingredients, including the proper dipping sauce. He knew his stuff. The burning coals in the center of the brass pot crackled, and tiny embers flew out of the cone. I wondered if something might catch fire, such as his bed, two feet away.

"Luo Landi, *Mei wen ti* (No problem)," he said in a slow drawl like a sage.

He assumed control of the meal and filled the boiling hot water moat with bright red, thinly sliced, frozen lamb, cabbage, tofu, and glass noodles. When cooked, he sent it to me.

To drink, he served me beer until he asked,

"Do you drink *baijiu*?"

"I'm gaining a taste for it."

He said, "I require a few thimble-sized shots to feel alive."

"I need an entire bottle."

He laughed when I told him about my first time drinking at Wang Yi's. He would look at me, hesitate for a couple of seconds, and then let out an "Ugh," then another "Ugh" or a "she she she" as if he tried to hold it back.

We had a wonderful evening, even though we came from different backgrounds and were separated by two generations. I wished I had a better vocabulary to talk more with him.

I stayed until I drank everything and ran out of smokes. He rode with me to the street, worried I wouldn't find my way. It wasn't hard; the main roads were straight. The small streets twisted in every direction. Stay on the big avenues. It was an hour, no matter what route I chose— nothing like a lengthy cycle ride to sober up.

During the semester, I ate with Lao Zhu three times. We dined out when he wanted to try something else. Hotpot looked easy, but a lot of work went into it. I attempted to pay when at a restaurant, but he informed the staff not to accept my money. They listened because he resembled their grandpa. People knew he was somebody by the way he spoke. He was genuine.

IX

If I wished to make a long-distance phone call, the Office of Telecommunications (an hour and a half away) was the place. Thankfully, Beida was so prestigious that they put a phone center on campus. It was operator-assisted: I gave her the number, fifty or a hundred RMB, and waited. She advised me what booth to enter and when I ran out of money.

I intended to visit my girlfriend, but I waited for a letter with her telephone number. In September, Beijing was hosting the Asian Games, the first major international sporting event. They gave everybody a holiday and encouraged citizens to stay home. It was an ideal time to head to Nanjing. First, I needed to apply. Beida preferred to keep close tabs on the students, including the foreigners. They required a confirmed hotel and flight ticket, which I did not have. Instead, I aimed to return before the school noticed. Besides, how would they know? We didn't have a roll call, and we all looked alike, right?

Nanjing was 700 miles away. Air tickets cost too much. I decided to take the train and rode my bike to the depot (over an hour away) to obtain a ticket. There was no guarantee of seats with a billion people.

As a foreigner, they allowed us to skip the sea of locals to use the FEC-only window with no line. I planned to remain in Nanjing for two days and needed to purchase a round-trip. But I could only buy a one-way. With the Asian Games opening, tickets to Beijing were unavailable. I would have to secure a return after I arrived.

It was risky.

For my departure, I purchased a top-bunk hard-sleeper for $15. Locals preferred the bottom bed with more height. They would sit, talk, drink tea, eat sunflower seeds, and smoke with the other bunkmates. If I had the bottom, I would have kicked them off, and they would be upset. A train ride was a big deal. People anticipated the chitchat. I would have made enemies if I stopped them from enjoying that segment.

Considering what it had taken to reach the station, I was exhausted. Most individuals placed their bags on the luggage rack and chained them. It didn't occur to me to carry a bike lock. Instead, I slept with my backpack.

Thank God I didn't have to drop a deuce. The toilet was the usual squatter, but instead of a dark hole, it was a hole emptying onto the tracks. The room stank even though the waste spread all the way to Nanjing. People missed the spot because of the rattling and left smeared stains for the rest of us to endure. I walked outside to brush my teeth.

I rode that rickety rail for seventeen hours. It halted in every town and stopped as if the engineer had fallen asleep, woken up, and slammed on the brakes. Then, the rear cabins banged into the cars in front. The inertia rolled my body to the edge of the bunk whenever we paused, but the safety straps prevented me from falling. It wasn't a great way to wake up.

My girlfriend met me at the terminal and took me to her dorm at Nanjing University (Nanda). They accepted backpackers, and it sounded perfect until I saw the dorms. The foreigners lived in the same building as the Chinese students, with fewer people. It was a language immersion situation, but the local students wished to speak English, and the Americans wanted to converse in Mandarin.

"This will not work. Do you know of any hotels?"

"The Jinling,"

Rooms there cost $150 a night. That felt like a fortune when I paid a dollar or two for my meals.

I saw a hotel near the university called the Zhong Shan. From the outside, it appeared to be my price range. We had to investigate further whether they would accept foreign devils.

First and foremost, I had to go to the travel agent to pick up a rail ticket. I would have purchased one at the station if I had found an FEC window. I wished to bypass the scrum and would pay extra. Foreigners paid nearly double for the same seat as locals, anyway. It was part of China's two systems. Occasionally, it worked to our advantage; other times, they gouged us.

The only ticket available was a hard seat for seventeen hours. How would I sit for that long? Overnight, too! It would not be a smooth voyage.

After I picked up the ticket, we visited The Jinling to change money. This place made me feel embarrassed about not being better dressed. I also wished I didn't wear shorts with oily Sichuan stains. The locals enjoyed the hotel from the street because a guard prevented them from getting closer. Even dressed as I was, foreigners had no problem entering (two systems).

Next, we checked out the Zhong Shan. They accepted Westerners for $20 a night, so I took it.

We ate lunch at a joint outside the university gate. The place had no name, but it hung promotional flags for Sprite on strings zig-zagging throughout the inside, so the students referred to it as the "Sprite Outlet." They served Sichuan dishes and foreigner-friendly items such as garlic stir-fried shoestring potatoes with green pepper (*qing jiao tu dou si*), sweet and sour pork (*tang cu li ji*), and stir-fried green beans with garlic and chili (*gan bian si ji dou*). Trust me, the food tasted great. They had a massive fridge for cold beer (a refrigeration charge per beer) and a menu with English translations. Although I primarily ordered *gong bao* chicken, fried rice, and dumplings, I desired to learn about other dishes.

During the next day and a half, we toured the Confucian Temple (Fuzimiao), Sun Yat-sen Memorial, and the Ming Tombs with the stone animal procession (identical to Beijing). Most sites had few tourists as local tourism had yet to take off, except for the Confucius Temple, which was located downtown. It turned into a hotbed of tourist and hawker activity. I think the Sage would have objected if he had seen it.

On the second day, we made the depressing trip to the terminal. While we waited, we experienced EVERYONE in the waiting room staring, pointing, and talking about us.

"Look at the Chinese woman (she was Korean) with the *laowai!*"

"How can she be with a *laowai?*"

Due to all this unwanted attention, I now looked forward to getting on the train.

Once on, travelers stood in any space possible. Seat numbers separated the benches, but more bodies squeezed on. Smaller stations sold standing tickets, and it got crowded. A conductor pushed a cart of snacks, warm beer, and hot tea down the walkway every half-hour to make matters worse. Everybody in the aisle leaned over the people sitting. I had the window seat with a small stationary table, giving me unblockable legroom, which helped.

When we left the depot, loud broadcasts and music continued until midnight. They started up again after sunrise. I listened to my Walkman to block out as much as possible, but they never turned off the lights the whole night. It was impossible to sleep under these conditions, and I was reluctant to leave my seat to return with someone else sitting there. I had a miserable ride.

Five minutes from Beijing Station, everybody jumped up to claim their luggage. Then suddenly, we came to a jolting halt just short of the platform, and the hot water tanks (Chinese trains had an abundance for tea) toppled over. The boiling water came splashing out like a river. I was sitting and lifted my feet. The individuals standing in the aisle with their bags scrambled to get out of the path of the scorching water. It was chaotic. People yelled and pushed while I enjoyed my music.

Rule #4: Never stand up early or rush for a plane or train exit.

I disembarked and was back into the crush of travelers leaving the terminal. Then, I squeezed through another narrow turnstile, got in line to wedge onto the subway, changed to the bus, and walked twenty minutes to the dorm. I returned in time before they locked up.

In the future, no hard seats.

Beijing has an unfathomable number of tourist attractions. It would take a considerable amount of time to see them all. Our school organized trips to The Forbidden City, The Great Wall (Badaling), Ming Tombs (Dingling), The Temple of Heaven, Long Qing Gorge, and both Summer Palaces. The spots were impressive beyond words, and I visited them multiple times. Besides the cultural sites, we took a tour of a humongous state-owned enterprise (SOE). If you worked there, your *danwei* (work unit) controlled every aspect of your life, from what accommodation you lived in (on the plant grounds), when you married and had "a" child, and when you could leave. The factory had its own schools, hospitals, and grocery stores. It was impressive and alarming.

Most aspired to do business with China. For this reason, our director arranged a meeting with the country rep of a U.S. bank. His company got permission to open an office in the '80s. He seemed to have the dream job. Not only did he work for a great firm, but he had a driver and lived in a villa he shared with his wife. Their abode was a reconverted Qing Dynasty courtyard within the ruins of the Old Summer Palace (Yuanmingyuan).

How could I not want that position?

But, he talked about broken contracts, deals not in your favor, and a poor business environment. His advice was to work elsewhere. It was an actual hardship posting in which you never won battles. If he had the dream job and felt miserable, I may have chosen the wrong path. I still had a few years to figure it out, so it didn't bother me.

In the meantime, I enjoyed Beijing's nightlife. Periodically I would eat at Wang Yi's house. If I planned to meet him, I rode to his house to tell him because he lacked a phone. It worked out until my plans changed. I had to cycle to his home to say I couldn't go to his home!

During the semester, I spent a lot of time at The Hutong and became a regular. I learned drinking games and wandered into the kitchen to observe Han managing the coals. Once, he invited me to have hotpot with the local police. I understood little about what they discussed, but we agreed on drinking *baijiu*. It partnered well with *shuan yang rou*.

When I started going to The Hutong, I used my bike. It was cooler and quicker. As I drank more, I lost balance and control. I wobbled as I peddled.

After I crashed, I opted not to use it while boozing.

I was too much of a liability.

If I stayed out late and missed the cut-off for the small south gate, I scaled the wall. I did it twice with no problem. But an old man who guarded the entrance spotted my friend Nick and me climbing over after a bender at Wang Yi's. He shouted to stop but refrained from pursuing. We kept walking until two People's Liberation Army (PLA) soldiers halted us at our dorm. They resembled grade school kids.

"Show me your IDs," said the more emboldened one.

"We're students and live in Shao Yuan."

"Did you see two guys scaling over the wall?"

"No." What proof did they have? I made small talk as one soldier glanced at our IDs.

"Have you been to America?"

They said nothing.

"How old are you guys?"

"*Er shi sui.*" (twenty)

"Do you know what you would do at an American college if you were twenty?"

They looked puzzled.

"You would join parties and have fun instead of strolling in the dark."

They didn't find the humor in it and instructed us to return to our rooms.

It was too late to wake up the grouchy man guarding our building. I had another idea. We walked alongside the dorm to my window. It had bars extending out with the top open. We climbed up the bars and over into the cage. The opening was wide enough to squeeze through, and I went first.

As I entered, I heard a scream. I thought I had the wrong room, but I saw my stuff. Evidently, my roommate hooked up a classmate, and they fell asleep. They locked the door and expected me to knock, not crawl through the window. The girl freaked out and ran to her room, wrapped in his sheets. I found the entire experience amusing. My roommate did not, and his anger turned my exuberance into fury because of the *baijiu* surging through my veins. We argued a bit in the hallway. Our classmates opened their doors and said shut up.

Making friends again!

XI

Not long after I returned from Nanjing, two events occurred: A fresh group of travelers arrived from California, and I provoked more trouble.

The newest arrivals moved into the older main building above the classrooms. Philip from our program established contact and brought me to a bash.

As soon as we reached the top of the staircase, I sensed the tootsie roll stuff the sheepherders pushed. I couldn't believe somebody had the gall to smoke that, but we continued.

The party room had yellow light escaping from under the door, seeping into the dark hallway. Philip knocked, and it swung open. They neglected to lower the music or care about the smoke from the sticky icky. These guys seemed fearless or thick.

Five people passed two spliffs in opposite directions as they swapped stories about Chinese peculiarities.

On a CD boombox, they blasted "The Girl from Ipanema" by Stan Getz. After a month of listening to cassettes on crappy headphones, I enjoyed hearing loud music.

But I assumed we would receive a knock on the door from the boys in green (PLA) about the noise and the sticky. No one else appeared worried.

"Relax, they don't know what the smell is. Besides, the staff took off at five," a guy said as the loaded cigarettes moved my way. Perhaps he was right, but I still felt edgy.

Although the Californians were cool, they had a different vibe from what I sought to get out of my China adventure.

Two weeks later, they left.

The problem I created for myself stemmed from my trip to Nanjing. While there, I drank with the students and revealed that people in our group had hooked up. The flings seemed quick, considering we arrived in China not too long ago.

I mentioned one girl who wouldn't stop talking about her beau back home. She planned their entire future. Three weeks into a study abroad program, she cheated with someone.

Because the dorm phone was in the hallway, I could hear the calls. I didn't care what others did, but the Nanda students were interested.

What was the harm of telling a story about people studying in a school 700 miles away?

"Is her name Amy?"

Oops, I had said too much. The guy who asked knew her fiancé. I forgot that only a few schools offered Mandarin so that they might recognize people from our class. I had hoped he would keep quiet until we returned to the U.S.

Right after I got back, the girl received a drama-free call. That was good news. A few weeks later (what it took to receive a letter from China), the shit hit the fan. She picked up her regular phone call from her fiancé. This time, she cried. She said she had made a mistake and begged him not to end their relationship.

After the call, she knocked on my door and yelled at me.

"Why did you say something? It's none of your business. I was going to tell him."

Yes, I stepped into some trouble. The girl gave me an evil look and avoided me after that.

Little by little, she no longer hid her new relationship, so it didn't matter.

Coincidentally, I ran into her again two years later in Taiwan.

By then, all was cool.

XII

With so much drama in the dorm, I craved comfort food. I needed KFC. The largest KFC in the world opened at the bottom edge of Tiananmen Square. I took the bus for forty-five minutes, the subway for twenty-five, and walked fifteen. Talk about a long trek for chicken.

Standing outside the towering three-story palace, I thought I had made a mistake. The line went down the street as far as possible. I asked individuals at the front how long they had waited.

"About two hours."

That was to get inside! There had to be a better approach.

I waved at a police officer guarding the exit to see if I could buy my way in.

"Do you have FEC?"

"Of course."

"Okay, please come in."

He confused me. Was he telling me to enter for takeout or squeeze into the sea?

Once inside, I understood. They operated a counter for FEC payers like me. It looked strange for a member of the staff to be standing at attention, waiting for a *laowai* while customers stood in line for four hours on the people's side. In addition, we received a ten percent discount. They gave me back the cash I would typically receive from the money mongers. I felt privileged and sorry for the masses. They appeared melted together, with no personal space. Not only did they fight to order, but they fought to escape as the crowd filled in any open territory.

The FEC register turned into a great benefit.

On my way here, I pondered all the items I would buy.

"I'll get two pieces of extra crispy and two pieces of original."

I didn't need to be creative. They served a set meal on a white, sectioned paper plate similar to the kind you would use at a picnic, with a piece of chicken (original), a scoop of mashed potatoes, a scoop of coleslaw, and a square of bread. The only choice was one piece or two. To drink, they sold beer, cola, or tea. The entire feast cost $2.00; multiply that by three (one-child policy), and you had an expensive family outing.

For me, ordering became the easiest part; finding a place to sit was challenging. As I turned to walk up the stairs, a guy dropped his tray. Man, that sucked. Just when he thought he would experience palatable heaven, his dreams spilled onto the ground that everybody had stepped on. I considered giving him my tray, but no need. As fast as his plate flipped, he got down, scooped it up, and kept moving.

Don't disrupt the flow.

I merged into the river, going floor after floor. It was futile. All the individuals on the human escalator were looking for seats, too. I needed to find someone almost finished and stand behind them. That usually worked, but people hung around at KFC to be seen.

"This is fast food. You eat, and you go!"

I nibbled on my chicken until I scored a chair. It felt relieving to bend my knees after standing for so long. Now I could enjoy the rest of my meal.

As I picked up a piece and took a bite, I noticed dozens of eyes watching me. They wanted to observe how I consumed the chicken. Did I hold it a particular way or swallow the bones? Their questions would soon be answered, but I would have disgusted them if I had followed the KFC motto and licked my fingers.

After finishing every morsel and having a lengthy rest, I started the journey back before I passed out from fatigue.

Over the next two months, I came back twice.

Pizza Hut was the only other American nosh available except for the Chinese attempts served in a handful of hotels. The sole McDonald's was 1,200 miles to the south in Shenzhen. There was no mention of Pizza Hut in my guidebook, so I couldn't believe my eyes when I spotted the logo. None of my classmates saw it or knew of its existence. Was it a mirage?

Pizza became a big part of my diet as a college student. While in China, I committed to sticking to local cuisine until I caved into my withdrawal symptoms. Besides, I had already relapsed at KFC. I might as well go all in.

Admittedly, Pizza Hut would not have been my initial choice in America. Now, I yearned for some and rounded up others to share the hour taxi.

Since I lacked an address, we drove until we found the sign. It was the first Pizza Hut in China. Although I desired some 'Za, I also hoped they had a salad bar. Raw vegetables were cold, crunchy, and not suitable for your stomach. That's why locals did not care for them. In Beijing, only one vegetable mattered: cabbage. In the fall, we ate cabbage, cabbage, and more cabbage. Trucks arrived from the countryside, dumped an entire load on the streets, and sold it there. Restaurants stocked gigantic heads outside like firewood and grabbed another "log" when needed. The cabbage grew dirty after a few weeks, so a salad with clean vegetables sounded fantastic.

Because they only accepted FEC, the joint sat empty. We could finally enjoy our meal without being on display, and they had a salad bar! But, because they flew most items up from Hong Kong, they limited the selection to a few things with Thousand Island or oil and vinegar to pour on top. They provided small bowls and allowed only a single trip. "All-you-can-eat" was not a service anyone provided. I didn't mind. I savored every bit. Years later, Pizza Hut expanded to other cities. They still only allowed one trip, but locals worked around this by piling their veggies sky-high. They used watermelon slices and potato salad to fortify their structures, a real art.

Every time I rode my bike, I looked for restaurants. I searched for "safe" places, but sometimes, I had to take a risk when I came across something special.

Beijing had a few alleys near a shopping district (Wangfujing), hawking street food, ranging from baby birds, squid, scorpions, bug larvae, and other creatures they threaded a wooden stick through and grilled. I avoided those proteins but tried "*xian bing*," a thick, doughy, round bread stuffed with pork and fried. It was oily, hot, and good, but don't bite into it right away, or you will receive a jet stream of boiling juices in your mouth.

Another snack I mustered up the courage to try was a breakfast food called "*jian bing*." The sellers of this delicious wrap had portable carts they set up at intersections. People on their bikes rode up to get one. I didn't discover *jian bing* until later (I ate breakfast on campus or not at all). At first, I hesitated because it broke my code. The pop-up culinary bikes had hygiene standards off the charts.

To make it, the seller dipped a ladle into a bucket of batter and spread it on a flat, round stovetop, creating a thin, crepe-like wrap. Then he cracked one or two eggs in the center and slapped a somewhat sweet brown sauce over the cooked egg layer. Finally, he added scallions, cilantro, chili sauce, a crispy deep-fried won-ton sheet, and he folded the packet of goodness into a paperback-sized egg marvel.

It blew rice gruel out of the water.

The bucket of batter was the problem. It had no cover, so dirt, rat droppings, or other things could have fallen in. But it tasted amazing, and I never caught the bug from those sandwiches.

I got it from someplace else, and it destroyed my world.

XIII

The university granted us another break for a few days, and I intended to travel to Nanjing again. My friend Nick wanted to visit Shanghai, so we pedaled our bikes to the station to purchase tickets.

Once we scored them, we searched for nosh to fill our stomachs. The station sold box lunches and noodles for the masses about to start their journeys. We sought something safe, but there weren't a great deal of restaurants in the whole city. I finally spied a hotpot joint. I considered hotpot the safest dish. How could we catch something from dipping raw food into boiling water? And the place served cold beer, so we parked, locked our bikes, and gave it a go.

Rule #5: Only eat at a restaurant near the train or bus stations if it is a KFC.

The absence of anybody else dining there should have been a warning sign. When we entered, the owner welcomed us like he hadn't seen a customer in a while.

I ordered two *jin* (pound) of frozen, shaved lamb and bottles of chilled beer.

A young girl brought the beers and glasses. I refrained from using cups as much as possible after noticing how people washed dishes. Most restaurants rinsed off the utensils in a plastic tub on the curb. Plus, I never encountered soap, even in the bathrooms. Nevertheless, these glasses seemed spotless, so I didn't stop the server from pouring. My gut said, "This is an awful idea."

Rule #6: Avoid using cups and utensils unless disposable.

We ate a decent dinner, paid our bill, and hopped on our bicycles to ride north before slipping into a beer and lamb coma. It took motivation to fight through an hour of bike traffic while digesting an enormous amount of food.

After a few days, I embarked on the seventeen-hour journey. I stayed for two nights and attended class. On the second day, I felt terrible. I had a fever, chills, muscle pains, etc. It was not a pleasant way to do an abundance of walking. I wondered if that cup caused my illness.

I should have listened to my gut.

The train ride was a hard one. Every jolt or sudden stop rattled my bones and weak body. I made it back to the dormitory and dropped by Nick's room. He appeared to be just as ill as me. I figured I contracted hepatitis when my skin and eyes turned yellowish. Every day, I shocked my classmates with my Simpson-ish tone.

Besides rice and apple slices, my mouth rejected other foods. My weight dropped, and my clothes were baggier. I stopped drinking.

It was serious.

A week later, my classmate turned the corner because of the gamma globulin shot he received before arriving in the East. I wasn't required to take the shot since I only stayed half a year, which made little sense. I should have gotten it anyway.

Our director suggested I head to the Sino-German Clinic in a socialist hospital close to the embassy district. I lacked an alternative, so I followed his advice. When I arrived, they directed me to the examination room. A German doctor walked in, speaking *Deutsch*. Then he tried some English. It surprised me he didn't speak Mandarin, and I speculated about how he communicated with the nurse. She couldn't converse in English or German.

He looked me over, applied pressure to my abdomen, and said he could do nothing. I had to wait it out.

"If things get rough, swallow these pills," then he handed me an envelope with "SOS" on the outside. I was clueless as to what they were.

This was my first encounter with health care in China, and I left unimpressed.

I required a month to recover. During that time, I did little but attend class and withdraw to my room. I lacked energy and was in pain. It was so awful that I wanted to depart China because I didn't have an idea how long it would persist. But since it took so much effort to get here, I kept pushing forward, hoping my misery would end.

Fortunately, I recovered just before Thanksgiving. My hunger was restored, but I made no preparations for the holiday. Locals did not eat turkey, mashed potatoes (only at KFC), corn (I never saw it), stuffing (no bread), and all the other traditional dishes. I prepared to skip it or go to KFC.

At the last moment, the banking executive we met invited those celebrating the holiday to his villa. He had purchased a frozen turkey and other items from Hong Kong while his wife gave birth there. She carried the food back with a newborn. Mike, the banker, cooked the large bird in his oven (one of the few in all of China) because he didn't trust his maid with the meal. Someone experienced needed to prepare it. The result was the most enjoyable Thanksgiving dinner I have ever had. We were truly thankful for this feast.

With two weeks left, I received a letter from my university telling me they had decided to discontinue the Mandarin program because of a lack of students. Can you imagine an absence of interest in today's China? In 1990, individuals fixated on Japan. The People's Republic was a sleeping giant. My school recommended continuing my studies in Beijing. They would do everything possible to help. What? I loved Beijing, but I prepared to leave. For a semester, I lived in a Chinese bubble. I had some catching up to do when I got home.

Another suggestion they proposed was to pursue an alternative major. I had already planned to declare two, but I had only claimed the Chinese one up to that point. They would have notified me of the closure if I had not done so. That would have been the end.

I would discuss the situation with the dean's office after I returned. There wasn't much I could accomplish in Asia by sending slow mail.

With my academic future in the air and my study abroad coming to a close, it was the ideal occasion to have some tea my friend Philip concocted. He bought the equivalent of six black film containers packed with the sticky icky he got from the sheepmen. Through curiosity, he brewed tea with the brown stuff and created a potent mix that set the scene for a lovely afternoon.

With classes over, he dealt out the spiked beverage to the remaining people. Before it kicked in, we moved to the government dumpling house for lunch. Nick arranged for a hired car (no taxis) to send him to the airport from there.

By the time we arrived at the restaurant, we had started to feel it. Everything was hilarious. Perhaps Philip had crafted a heavier dose. I thought the meal was going well until Nick said he couldn't stand. He had a long day of international travel ahead. This was a problem.

We picked him up and dragged him out because he was in dire shape. I asked Philip if one of us should go with him. It sounded like a lousy way to spend the rest of the afternoon, so we returned to the dorm instead. Nick escaped okay and had a hell of a story to tell if he remembered.

XIV

I planned to remain in Beijing until January and persuaded my girlfriend to fly up to see me instead of backpacking around the country in the winter for two weeks.

In order to save cash, I rode the bus to pick her up at the airport. The weather was sub-zero, but someone neglected to install glass in the windows. They were wide open. Even with my green PLA coat, I froze.

The bus had two ticket takers, but there were few passengers, probably because it turned into an icebox on wheels. The young attendant in the back started a conversation. No local girl had chatted with me like that before, giggling and smiling. As I got closer to my stop, she gave me her phone number. She wanted to meet up. The experience shocked me so much that I told my girlfriend. She refused to believe me.

I should have called the ticket taker to introduce them.

With a few students staying through the Christmas holiday, the dormitory remained open. My roommate departed long ago, and I had a single, but Beida was strict about letting visitors in. Since I had a student ID, I took my girlfriend's bag and handed her a Beida sweatshirt to resemble a local. They stopped me, but I was legit.

To get her into the dorm, I suggested we carry on a loud conversation in English. The guard would think she was just another American.

A few days later, we moved to a hotel to spend the last week in luxury with a bathroom. Few hotels in the entire city accepted foreigners, and most catered to people with expense accounts or tour groups. I booked a room at an old socialist place built in the fifties to shelter Soviet experts with multiple buildings spread throughout a gated block of land. It had a grand entrance, but foreign travelers resided in a guest house in the rear.

The problems started after I brought my girlfriend over. Around 11 p.m., the phone rang. The front desk spoke in English. That didn't work out well, so I spoke Mandarin. They demanded my guest leave. I assumed they thought she was a local, maybe a working one, but I informed them she was an American. Then they hung up. We received a second call thirty minutes later, and I explained the same. They cautioned that if we failed to come down, they would contact the police.

We let them know our displeasure and the gravity of the accusation. The staff confiscated our travel documents. We protested, but it seemed futile. It was best to fight it out in the morning.

The next day, I went down to complain. They admitted they had made a mistake and returned our passports. That was a positive step. For the week we stayed there, I expected another battle every time the phone rang. Luckily, they left us alone after realizing we were just tourists. However, they provided an additional reason to change my Chinese name when the hotel staff called me by my surname 'Luo' and 'Sir.' Together, 'Luo Sir' sounded like LOSER, with a Beijing accent.

Between visits to the major tourist sites, we ate a last supper with Wang Yi. He moved into a new apartment building during my illness and vacated the alleys. As I no longer used it, I gave him my treasured bike. We enjoyed several drinking sessions over five months and would have many more. I was glad he dared to approach me in the park.

Then we stopped at my favorite hangout, The Hutong. I tried to convince my girlfriend to converse with Han in Korean, but they avoided talking to one another. It seemed strange until I realized I wouldn't care to speak to random Yanks I met overseas.

Han became a friend, and I would return to his restaurant one day.

Finally, we arranged a meal with our teacher's father. I introduced her, but he and I were *baijiu* buddies. I would miss him the most. He represented Beijing's past, while Wang Yi and Han were the future. I had difficulty saying goodbye but felt confident I would find my way back.

I remained at the hotel until my girlfriend left for the U.S. on New Year's Eve. Her departure was perfect timing. I had something planned.

XV

On New Year's Eve, I arranged a last supper with two of my schoolmates. They stuck around for a second semester and planned a bash. I expected a long night of boozing, and it would be easier to stumble back to the dorm for my flight at noon.

Our venue of choice was Mao Mao's with the sheep. By now, only one stood outside. His chances of surviving did not look good.

Locals didn't celebrate NYE unless it was the Lunar New Year, so we had the place to ourselves. We ordered a couple of pounds of lamb, tofu, cabbage, and cilantro. I enjoyed the taste of cilantro, and they encouraged it as a condiment for the hotpot sauce.

Prior to our feast, the cook strolled out the front door with a cleaver and a red basin. His helper followed. I knew what would happen next, but I had to witness it. We grabbed our beers and walked out to watch. Mao Mao's sat smack-dab on the corner of an active intersection in the Haidian District. I couldn't imagine slaughtering an animal on the streets of Chicago, but no one cared here. People still found foreigners more interesting than the sheep slayers. We stayed until they drained the blood and completed the skinning. Then, we sat down for the freshest lamb hotpot meal I had ever eaten.

During dinner and after, we played Chinese drinking games. One of my favorites was "stick, tiger, chicken, worm." The game was similar to rock, paper, and scissors, where the winner guessed the more dominant choice. It went like this:

Stick beats the tiger.

Tiger eats the chicken.

Chicken eats the worm.

And the worm eats the stick.

The sloppier I became, the more I lost.

I also encountered trouble with another drinking game, where we counted in multiples of five, guessing if the combined total of fingers would be 0, 5, 10, 15, or 20. Both players opened and closed their hands at the same time. Some people turned passionate and did a version of jazz hands while trying to outguess their opponent. The more I drank, the more I got the numbers mixed up because my mind was slower than my hands. At my tipping point, I had to retire because I no longer made sense.

Towards midnight and after a lot of beer (I couldn't get my friends to drink *baijiu*), my companions hired a car to check out the sunrise at The Great Wall. This sounded like a fantastic excursion, but my flight to the U.S. was early. I didn't want to miss it.

They returned just before I left. I would have been on edge had I gone with them. Plus, they froze. The idea was better than the reality.

When my car to the airport arrived, I said my goodbyes and prepared to leave.

This period in Beijing was my favorite because the vibe differed from today's Middle Kingdom. It was a People's Republic with a smaller Western footprint and less cutthroat competition. It wasn't until Deng Xiaoping embarked on his tour of the South in 1992 that things accelerated. Despite getting deathly sick, I assumed my future would involve China. Somehow, I would return to travel or work. For now, I was going home.

CHAPTER TWO

TAIWAN: I'M BACK (SORT OF)

It felt like I had come out of the woods after a lengthy camping trip when I transited through Tokyo from Beijing. Japan marked a return to civilization. There were lines with no pushing, sit-down toilets with toilet paper, and no sounds of hawking up phlegm. They served chilled beer and drinkable water. Although I liked China, I didn't realize how far I had strayed from who I was. I had to reintroduce myself to social norms, like holding the door and washing my clothes.

On the fourteen-hour-long haul to Chicago, the people seated next to me were forced to endure my odor because I had worn the same clothes for most of December. It was too cold to worry about the stink when I walked around China. In the confines of a tight airplane cabin, I didn't have to ask who smelled. To make the situation more aromatic, I hand-carried a bottle of *baijiu*, leaking in my backpack (try carrying an open bottle of sixty percent hooch in your hand-carry today). I did everything to hold in my scent and found sanctuary at the rear of the plane—the smoking section. Passengers there didn't notice my perfume, but it was smokey even for a smoker.

Upon touching down in Chicago, the customs officer asked for my passport.

"Where are you coming from?"

"China."

"What were you doing in China?"

"Studying Chinese."

"Open your bags and take everything out."

The customs agent checked through my stuff and stopped at the bottle of *baijiu*.

"What's this? God, it smells awful."

"That's Chinese medicine. People told me it cured many ailments, like the flu or a cold."

He sniffed it, made a face, and jammed it into the bag.

"You can go."

I worked my things into my duffle in a Tetris way. Finally, I was free to head home, take a long shower, throw away my smelly clothes, and grab a new pair of silk boxers.

Not long after I returned, I flew to New York to begin the spring semester of my junior year. I concentrated on sorting out my Chinese degree, finishing my economics degree, and heading back to China. The university allowed me to create the classes to complete my degree. I crafted the courses, found a teacher, and published the lessons for others to take. Finding a teacher was the easy part. There were lots of Chinese graduate students who needed the cash. The difficulty was locating a vacant classroom. Twice a week, my class (two Chinese girls, my girlfriend, and the teacher, a Taiwanese female grad) strolled from building to building, looking for a room. The classes were loosely structured but suitable to maintain my fluency.

I focused on my goal from the get-go, which paid off with a light schedule during my senior year. To prepare for my next transit through Japan, I took Japanese.

What else do you do with free time in college? You get into trouble. I lived in a fraternity, and people were always ready to party. My alcoholic tendencies added fuel to the fire. *Baijiu* had heightened my tolerance, and everything went down easily now.

The only thing holding me back was a lack of cash, but I found ways around this problem. College bars had good deals if you showed up at the right time. My favorite place charged no cover until 10 p.m. and all-you-could-drink from ten to eleven.

I would show up with a couple of friends to test the limits of all-you-could-drink to see if they would kick us out. Other joints served cheap pitchers and well shots to keep the festivities going.

In between my turn at darts and foosball, I memorized Japanese and Chinese flashcards. I carried them to kill two birds with one stone.

As graduation neared, I hoped to find a way to Asia before settling into a job and moving on with life. I searched for positions in China, and nothing came up.

My Peking U drinking buddy told me securing a teaching gig in Taiwan would be easy. At least I could pay the bills until I discovered something better. That was my best option.

Subsequently, I purchased a round trip to Taipei a week after graduating. Once they gave me the visa, I packed the same duffel and rode out to O'Hare again.

I was going in for another tour.

II

I landed in Taipei on the morning of June 3, 1992. It looked like China, twenty years in the future, with advertisements for luxury hotels, restaurants, and shopping. It seemed more relaxed and less dreary. I couldn't wait to start this adventure.

A crowd waited outside of customs, but there were no shouts of "*laowai.*" The only individuals that paid attention to me were the taxi drivers. "Taxi, taxi. Which hotel?" I bypassed them and opted for the bus. Not knowing Taipei made things challenging, but I relied on my Lonely Planet. For shelter, it suggested a youth hostel on the campus of Taiwan University (Taida). If Taida turned into a bust, there was another college nearby called Shida.

I got dropped off at the entrance to Taida and zig-zagged through the university grounds with a duffel and a backpack weighing me down. By the time I located the correct building, my shirt looked as if someone had sprayed me with a hose. After I registered, they put me in a room with another American. He had recently graduated and needed employment, so he tagged along to find a job board I had read about.

It was impossible to elude the cavalry of 125cc motor scooters. They almost outnumbered the Flying Pigeon bikes in Beijing. When walking on the street, motorbikes zoomed past. They swerved enough to get by. Then they veered right back, barely missing the other scooter coming from the opposite direction. They played a coordinated game of chicken for madmen.

It was 10 a.m., and I hungered for Sichuan food. A year and a half had passed since I'd left Beijing, and I craved authenticity. As we walked longer than expected, I scanned every sign, but no Sichuan. Each restaurant specialized in beef noodles. I wasn't fond of noodles, but they should be fantastic with everybody selling them.

We stopped at one of the busier joints and ordered two bowls and two Cokes. Both turned out to be just what I needed—a yin and yang of flavors and temperatures. The soup came with fat chunks of stewed beef. They were flavorful but not enough to sustain me. I tried the noodles and committed the rookie mistake of losing grip and splattering red oil all over my white T-shirt. Any attempt to correct the problem worsened it. As a result, I avoided noodles until I worked out how to eat them without throwing away my shirt.

Around noon, the noodle place became crowded. The staff nudged us to pay the bill and surrender our table. It took a while, but I mustered up ample energy to drag my jet-lagged body off the stool. Then, we crossed the road to investigate the bulletin board. It was a letdown, but I had plenty of time to search elsewhere.

With fatigue setting in, we grabbed a taxi to our hostel. I felt drained and looked forward to crashing in the AC-cooled room. But I remembered I only had enough money to last a few months. I couldn't afford to sleep.

My Taiwanese teacher gave me the address of a school she knew. It sounded like a sure thing, so I ducked out when my roommate slipped into a coma. I wanted to avoid competition.

The address was located right outside the university gate. That had to be a promising sign. When I got close, I realized I had passed it. I walked back and spotted a small plaque for an English school outside a stairwell. The name was close enough, so I checked it out.

I climbed up the dark stairs and found the school, but it didn't appear to have a lot of business. I thought my teacher provided me with a solid reference. It turned out to be similar to the other "*bushiban*" schools. *Bushibans* were study centers operating on practically every street in Taipei. The term sounded like "bull shit" class (*ban*), and I reckoned many inexperienced teachers like me taught them.

My brain instructed me to return to the hostel, but my wallet said, "I need food." What's the worst that can happen? I pushed the glass door, setting off a chirping bird sound. I entered, and a young lady popped her head up enough to clear her cubicle wall.

"Can I help you?"

"I'm here to apply for a teaching job."

My Beida friend said my chances of snagging employment were excellent, even without a teaching degree. He told me about a preference schools had for specific teachers. Americans with blonde hair and blue eyes, or "The California Look," received the first offers. Next in line were Yanks with dark hair, then Australians, British, and other English speakers, depending on their accents. Younger teachers were always in demand. This put me in two categories and gave me a leg up. I didn't mind if those were the only reasons they hired me. I just wanted to get my foot in the door.

Not all schools followed this biased method of employing, but I saw a pattern.

"Have you taught before, or do you have a teaching degree?"

"No, but I have degrees in economics and Chinese. I also taught ESL."

I taught English as a second language to be matched with a Mandarin speaker. It didn't end out that way. Instead, they paired me with people from India and Mexico. I learned little, but now it sounded superb on my application.

"Let me get you a form."

While I waited, I noticed an impressive collection of textbooks on the shelves. That looked official and inspired me to fill in the application. I presumed they would call me at the hostel to interview since I wore a T-shirt, shorts, and Tevas, not appropriate business attire but suitable jungle wear. They at least wanted to ensure I owned decent clothes, right?

No need. She informed me I had a class the next day. Holy shit! Tomorrow? What will I teach? What will I wear? No way could I sweat it out on the bus wearing a shirt and tie. I needed to acclimate, but I said okay.

She handed me the address and asked if I had a motorbike. I'd literally just walked off the plane.

"No, I don't."

"It will take longer to get there by bus. Please don't be late."

"Wait, isn't there a teacher's handbook?"

"You will teach business English. They will give you the materials."

What the hell! Not only did I need to stand in front of a class, but I had to teach them something I had no time to prepare.

Despite the complications, I felt uplifted.

For instructing a two-hour session twice a week, they would pay me $240. I still planned on applying to other schools, but I had landed my first gig in a foreign land.

With a job set, I checked out the streets before heading back. My roommate slept the entire time. It filled me with pride to know I found work when I easily could have dozed off. The best way to conquer jet lag is to keep moving until your body clock adjusts. Don't sleep during the day.

I told him I planned to check out a bar across the street.

"If you don't get up now, you'll wake up at 2 a.m. when the bars are closed. There won't be anything to eat or drink. The joint I'm heading to is called Hot Lips. With a name like that, it has to be good."

I think the name got him up. We ran into two other travelers looking for a pub on the way out. Rich was a well-weathered Kiwi, surfing around Asia. John was a Canadian searching for employment but would teach English if necessary. Few people wanted to teach. Most preferred to work in an office with A/C and a steady salary.

I took the lead since I read Chinese and had a solid sense of direction. Taipei addresses were confusing with their lanes and missing street numbers. The pub would be easy to miss in a normal situation with no windows. This didn't look like the best location. Inside were a handful of individuals, including a bubbly, thirty-something Taiwanese woman with a poodle perm named Sugar. She ran the place with her less talkative husband.

"Hello, come on in. Hi, what do you want to drink?"

I had a tight budget and needed to stretch my cash, so I ordered a big brown bottle of Taiwan Beer for 55 TWD ($2). John said, "I heard Taiwan Beer uses formaldehyde. The more you drink, the more preserved your body gets." I didn't believe him, but it gave me another reason to consume it.

An older, bald foreigner sitting at the bar turned to us and asked, "So you guys are American?" Rich jumped in with his Kiwi accent and said, "Yanks? No way, bro."

"Obviously, I am." I had nothing to be ashamed of and needed to talk to anyone who would help me find a sponsor for a work visa. Otherwise, I was required to leave the island after sixty days. That meant flying someplace far and expensive. It wouldn't be worth staying if I had to make visa runs every other month.

Bill hung out at Hot Lips every night. He moved to Taiwan to escape something and start a new life, drinking full-time. He planned to live out the rest of his days at the bar or until he ran through his savings, whichever came first.

While we drank, Sugar brought Bill a sandwich. He said she seldom made food, but he taught her to cook something for him because he came in daily. "The Hot One" consisted of a layer of cheese followed by fresh Thai chilis called mouse shit peppers, onions, and another layer of cheese, grilled into a gooey mess. I had a better-than-average resilience to heat and loved a challenge, so I asked her to prepare one for me. It tasted damn good, but it set my mouth on fire. She used a layer of mouse shit peppers, not a few but a layer! For me, eating super spicy food was similar to drinking *baijiu*. Sometimes, the initial bite went wrong, and I coughed and shed tears. Then, everything adjusted to allow me to stuff countless amounts down my throat without complications until the following day. It was still wise to diminish the effects on my stomach and to cool off my mouth with more beer.

After I finished a few bottles, I searched for the loo.

"Sugar, where's the toilet?"

"In the room behind the black curtains."

I sat there for a while and neglected to notice they had a hidden room. A pool table, slot machines, and a few people were on the other side of the drapes. It was an illegal gambling den. I wanted to play pool, but the table barely fit. If you tried to shoot, you had to lift the end of your stick sky-high. As a result, I skipped the billiards and focused on drinking with my new friend, Rich. We had similar personalities and motivated each other to keep going. Our roommates were more concerned about dealing with a hangover while looking for a job.

They sipped their beers.

The next day, we hit the pavement, searching for employment. Finding a sponsor would be problematic. Most *bushibans* paid foreigners to work but refused to invest in a resident visa. Even though I assumed they made "contributions" to the right people to ward off random checks, I didn't dig this kind of unlawfulness and needed a sponsor.

We had little luck knocking on doors without teaching degrees. Our last option was an advertisement I stumbled upon for Mr. Andy's English. We found the building and rode the elevator up to the third floor. A handful of others were applying for jobs but were lower on the desirability scale. My chances looked decent, so I filled in an application. The guy running the show, Dave, said,

"Come back in two days, and we will have a schedule for you."

"Where are the classes held?"

"The student will choose a venue such as a teashop or a fast food joint. Talk with them for an hour or use their materials."

Dave promised to provide a resident visa if I stuck around for a few weeks to show my loyalty. That sounded solid, but I required a visa now.

More importantly, I had to instruct in a couple of hours and needed to change my sweaty clothes and put on new ones, which would be sweaty as soon as I wore them.

The location was more than an hour in rush hour traffic. As the bus traveled along Dun Hua North Road, I noticed tall glass towers on both sides. I presumed I would teach at a small office building, but I ended up at a large Taiwanese chemical company—a gigantic skyscraper with people dressed in business attire.

"I'm going in hot and sweaty and don't know what to say for two hours. This doesn't look good."

When I reached my floor, I passed through the glass doors into the office and said, "I'm the English teacher."

The receptionist led me to a conference room and instructed me to wait there. Despite being merely five minutes late, there were no students. Ten minutes later, one person showed up, and then another. I started a conversation, but I'm not outgoing, so it took a lot of effort.

"Hi, my name is Mr. Randall, and I'm your teacher," I said as I wrote on the whiteboard. It felt strange calling myself "Mr."

"Are there more students?"

"There are ten."

"Are they sick?"

"They assumed we didn't have a teacher or were busy. "

While we talked, another two slipped in thirty minutes late. I didn't care because I still got paid. If the students showed up late, they helped shave time off the clock. Ultimately, six arrived. I was relieved I didn't have a large group for my teaching debut.

"Is this the first class?"

"We have been taking it for a few weeks, but the teacher left."

The school told me I would teach them for six weeks.

"Can you tell me what you've been studying?"

They showed me the book and photocopied a few pages. I had the class introduce themselves. They replied with short answers like, "I am Tony. I enjoy baseball." Then I asked, "Why did you pick the name Tony?" and "What is your favorite baseball team?" This wasted the rest of the hour until I called for a ten-minute break. That left me with fifty minutes of "teaching" left. I tried everything to pass the time and struggled with the material they provided.

At 8 p.m., I ran out and hopped on the bus to Hot Lips. My friends waited to hear about my teaching experience. It was a miserable endeavor outside my wheelhouse, but I had no choice.

I had to pay the bills until I found something else.

III

My next task was to find an apartment. I noticed an ad in the daily for a double room on Roosevelt Rd, in the southern region of Taipei. Most bars in my guidebook were on the same street. It sounded like a choice place to live.

But Roosevelt Road ran across the southern boundary of Taipei, and the action happened near Sections One and Two. The flat was in Section Five, practically in the next town. How would I enjoy the bars if I lived off the map?

As our only option, my roommate and I checked it out. We rode the bus and got off at the closest stop. Then, we followed the street a little further before identifying the correct lane. The nearest 7-11 was three blocks away. That showed me how far we would be from the action. We would have to walk that distance to buy cold beer!

I rang the buzzer to get the landlord to open the downstairs security door. The apartment was on the third floor with no elevator, and the stairwells were unfinished concrete. When I knocked, a Taiwanese guy named Mike answered. He was the owner.

The flat had two bedrooms, no A/C, a kitchen built for one, and a bathroom with half a tub and no shower curtain. I wasn't aware that such bizarre setups existed. But our primary requirement was affordability, so we took the room and moved in.

With everything in motion, I hustled to Hot Lips to splurge and shoot the shit with Sugar and Bill. As the evening progressed, I found myself *ganbei'ing* beer and whiskey with the dudes addicted to the gambling machines. They invited me to join after I spoke Chinese. I had taken the time to learn Mandarin, and they respected that. Naturally, I felt elated to consume someone else's booze. I couldn't afford it on my own. My school loans required reimbursement in six months, so my hard alcohol habit needed to be satiated through the generosity of others.

Rich and John still stayed at the hostel, but Rich planned to relocate to Southern Taiwan to look for a job. Taipei didn't have surfing, and he disliked the atmosphere. His idea sounded fantastic, but I already had things set up. He asked me to hold on to his board as he traveled south. After he settled, he would return to collect it. I had no problem with that.

The following morning, the doorbell rang. It was Rich with a big-ass surfboard. It surprised me he would trust it with a guy who drank as much as he did. Perhaps he figured, where would I go with a nine-foot surfboard?

My other flatmate, Ricky from Missouri, showed up one day. He looked thirty, lived and worked in Taiwan for two years, and had everything figured out.

"Yeah, man, Taiwan is great."

"How did you get an office job and a resident visa?"

"You just have to do it, man. You know what I mean?"

No, I didn't. Thankfully, Ricky mostly slept at his girlfriend Sunshine's apartment. When he returned, he sat in his room in a leopard skin G-string with the fan blowing on his crotch, not reading, just sitting on the bed, staring at the mirror. The situation got worse when Sunshine came over. She was a cute girl with an annoying high-pitched laugh that did not match her petite size. Ricky would come back with her, say hi, then retreat to his bedroom, where the laughter turned into something sensual.

Meanwhile, my roommate and I hung out in the living room in our underwear (no G-strings), trying to survive the heat. It seemed hotter inside than outside. Ricky would step out to use the toilet and say, "What's up, dude," with a cheeky grin and his Southern twang before flashing his skinny, pale-white ass cheeks. I hoped this wasn't what I would become after a couple of years living abroad.

Not having A/C in the flat made life miserable. I struggled to fall asleep in the sticky weather and drank to doze off. It worked until 6 a.m., when the sun seeped into my room, turning it into a greenhouse. I woke up sweaty every morning, with a searing ray of light heating my bamboo bed. Waking up dehydrated and wet was a cruel type of punishment.

Most mornings, I relocated to the living room sofa to sleep. I spent most of my time in the lounge, drinking and listening to music. I didn't feel bored because everything was different, and I knew things would improve.

Even though I tried not to move to prevent sweating, I had to swat the cockroaches. Taiwanese roaches were fierce, about the size of my thumb, and could fly! No one told me they could fly. I would hear a fluttering sound and see an enormous sucker gliding through the air, landing on my back or head. Occasionally, they would come straight towards my face as if in 3D. I detested them.

When I awoke in the middle of the night with a cockroach on my cheek, I no longer considered them irritating pests. I had nightmares about them crawling into my orifices and laying eggs, and I checked often to ensure none were on my face or body. This part of Taiwan sucked.

Mike, the landlord, frequently slept in the living room, too. He didn't live in the apartment but crashed here when drunk. He knew I liked whiskey, and one night, he brought over a bottle of Chivas that we polished off with a dozen beers. My roommate called a friend, and we went for more whiskey and ale. It turned into a huge night.

During the evening, I kept increasing the boombox volume; the only entertainment besides alcohol, Sunshine, and Ass Cheeks Ricky. At one point, the neighbor told us to turn it down. We were good until the police arrived. Mike answered the door, and we were all in our underwear. I can't imagine what they thought with four guys in their skivvies, a collection of empty bottles, and the Grateful Dead on the radio. They gave us a warning, but we were out of booze.

The party ended after I flung one of the empty whiskey bottles towards the garbage can on the balcony. I'd lived in a fraternity for three years, and we habitually threw empties off the porch. That terrace had nothing below, but my Taiwan balcony was above the alley. The neighbors wouldn't be pleased about bottles dropping from the sky. Luckily, it didn't go over the rail.

Mike didn't get mad, but it was the wrong thing to do.

He invited me to a food festival with his girlfriend the next day. I tasted many Taiwanese snacks—a dehydrated, starving, hungover person's dream. As we walked, he said, "Don't do it again." I understood.

No worries, I planned to get out and widen my social circle. I didn't come to Taiwan to be holed up in a sweatbox, sitting in my underwear with other guys.

IV

I returned to Mr. Andy's, and they provided phone numbers for students all over town. The school motto was, "We will teach you anywhere, anytime." It felt like prostitution: I showed up at a meeting place, talked with a student for an hour (ninety percent were female), she paid for my drink or meal, handed over the golden ticket, and we went our separate ways.

Occasionally, things got weird. One student I taught at home answered the door in a silky nightgown. I didn't know if she was advertising something, but a fifty-year-old homemaker did not interest me.

When I was green, I accepted as many classes as possible. I walked and rode buses to earn a few extra bucks. They only paid $15 an hour, and I wasted too much time traveling, so I needed something better.

My contract lasted three months, and Dave held some of my earnings to prevent me from leaving. If teachers split, they left the customer high and dry. They kept a deposit to keep us in line. Dave stalled on the work visa, too.

Despite the hassle, I met some decent people through Mr. Andy's, like Wang Jun, a mechanic for a major American airline. Mr. Andy's suited him because his schedule revolved around the planes. He had to be flexible.

Wang lived in the eastern suburbs of Taipei, near the airport, and came into town for his lessons. He nearly gave up until they assigned me to teach him. We met a few times before he invited me to his house. One weekend, I took him up on the offer.

He greeted me at the bus stop despite my insistence that I could find his flat. It proved to be a positive thing: The address situation in the burbs seemed worse than downtown. We walked down a winding road for twenty minutes and up a hill to his place. Wang introduced me to his wife and then slipped out to buy more beer when I said I could drink a lot. He left me to sit in the living room with his baby son while his spouse cooked. Again, it shocked me that someone would invite a stranger into their home. I surmised my Mandarin gave them trust in me, or I found friendly people.

When Wang came back, we moved into the dining room. He unfolded a table, and we sat on stools, a tight squeeze. Wang's wife, Emily, worked as a fast food manager, but she possessed amazing culinary skills. She knew how to make a succulent three-cup squid (*san bei you yu*).

Three-cup was a Taiwanese cooking style where you cooked your protein (chicken, offal, or seafood) in a clay pot with healthy amounts of rice wine, soy sauce, and sesame oil (three cups). Add garlic, chili, ginger, and sugar, then caramelize it. Finally, throw in fresh basil for extra flavor. If done right, the result turned into a mouth-watering, spicy sauce.

I didn't care for squid, but three-cup squid was fantastic.

Wang saw me down a few cans at our previous sessions. Those meetings only lasted sixty minutes. This was noon on a Sunday, and I had nothing to do.

Soon, we ran out of beer. Wang had a limit of one and figured six would be enough. I didn't want to descend the hill for booze, so I asked, "Do you have other drinks?"

He pulled out an unopened bottle of *Jinmen Gaoliang*. I'd never heard of it, but I smelled an old friend—*baijiu*. After Beijing, I visited many restaurants seeking it. They all thought it was impressive that I spoke Mandarin, but none stocked the good stuff. I wanted rocket fuel, sixty percent alcohol, and here it was. I had no idea they made *baijiu* from sorghum ("*gaoliang*"), nor did I know what sorghum was. *Jinmen Gaoliang* was Taiwan's most famous version of *baijiu*. Wang, weighing ninety-eight pounds, sat out the jet fuel drinking. However, Emily was a healthy-sized woman and said she would join me. We drank and talked through the afternoon until we kicked the bottle, but I had to keep going. To appease me, they gave me a half-full one. That was all they had left.

Both Wang and Emily looked loaded and happy. Wang turned a dark red when he got drunk, Marlboro red. Someone told me it was a gene thing. I didn't seem to have it. When I finished the second bottle, I surprised them. I ate and drank almost everything in the apartment. But I needed to get on my feet before I had trouble walking. I stayed at their place all day, taking advantage of their generosity, but now it was time to leave.

I picked up a few tallboys from a mom-and-pop for the walk and bus ride. All that liquor was what I required to sleep off the heat and roaches. I put on my headphones and listened to The Doors while drinking on the bus.

During my stay in Taiwan, I traveled to Wang's house four times. I kept returning because of their warm hospitality and Emily's exquisite three-cup dish. She made it with the right combination of spices. They also supplied plenty of *gaoliang* for me to consume.

My biggest regret was not spending time with Emily to study her craft. I have been trying to replicate it ever since.

V

Towards the middle of the summer, I accepted an offer to instruct at a school with multiple locations and actual classrooms. Finally, I would teach inside instead of at shady places such as someone's home. They would sponsor me if I worked at least sixteen hours a week.

My other contracts were winding down, and I looked forward to dropping the business English class. The students often ditched, and I didn't receive payment. From the beginning, that job sucked.

Mr. Andy's kept me on a leash for another six weeks. I refrained from taking on new pupils and waited for my current ones to finish their tickets. I taught at all three schools for a month from 10 a.m. to 9 p.m. with travel breaks in between but stretching myself thin.

The new school wanted me to teach introductory-level courses because I spoke Chinese and moved things along. Those classes were harder than the advanced ones because the students seldom felt confident enough to speak. I did the talking and improved my Chinese.

I doubt they learned much.

Part of the problem was the boring teaching materials. I used them every day, month after month. I repeated, "Johnny goes to school, and April goes too," at one branch, then traveled to the next place and did it again. My brain shut down after instructing too many entry-level classes.

For the advanced, I used the *Economist* to keep it interesting. After some introductions, we talked about an article for forty-five minutes. Then, I took a ten to fifteen-minute break while determining what to discuss for the following forty-five. When I taught these classes, I kept a dictionary under the table to look up the words.

Making up a definition is really hard.

Teaching often became a joke and a popularity contest at the beginner level. I needed to entertain them. If I didn't, they walked out. They had no obligation to stay. If there was laughter coming from another classroom, I had pressure to make my students laugh, or they wandered over to the funny room.

Soon, I got great at talking about nothing for long periods. Six months in, I spent two hours taking roll call. Taiwanese selected their English names for how they sounded. Most picked off-the-wall monikers such as "Zero," "Human," "Catchup,"…, etc. (I liked "Long Gun"). Their names begged to be investigated.

I graded my performance on how much I made everyone laugh. Lots of laughter was reassuring. Soon, more wanted to join, and my class grew from five or six to forty after I learned how to entertain ("Are you not entertained?"). Periodically, the class got so big that people stood in the hallway. I was doing stand-up, but I wasn't a natural comedian. Occasionally, I told a joke, and it fell flat, or they didn't get it. The result was silence, with forty faces staring at me, waiting for what came next. It was exhausting, but I had to keep things moving.

Then, I ran off to another school to do the same, more or less.

Eventually, I worked at five branches and sometimes forty hours a week. I knew I was doing something right when I detected students traveling to other schools to join my class, stalker students. Nothing wrong with that. The school was similar to a gym membership; members joined any course at any branch. But if an elementary student joined advanced, they would disrupt the flow.

This school kept me occupied, especially as I completed my other contracts. They also honored their promise to sponsor me. They gave me an offer I couldn't refuse.

VI

My lease ended in August, so I started an arduous search for something better. Luckily, my roommate received a tip on a flat in the middle of town off Zhongxiao East Rd, one of the city's busiest shopping and entertainment areas. The person residing in this palace planned to return to the U.S. to earn an MBA. He invited teachers over to see if anyone was interested in taking over his lease.

The apartment was on the fourth floor (no elevator), but they called it the fifth (the number four sounded like "death" in Chinese). It was four bedrooms with polished hardwood floors, a kitchen the size of my living room, and an American washing machine (still no dryer). An industrial-sized Whirlpool washing machine! Are you freakin' kidding me? Whatever they paid the workers to carry that sucker up four flights of narrow stairs and wedge it into this tiny bathroom was worth it. I dreamed of washing two pairs of pants at the same time.

The bathroom came with a full tub and a shower curtain. My present place had the square tub, which was dangerous with the curved inner walls. Hastily turning could provoke a slip and a fall, but not with this regular-sized tub. I never expected I would become obsessed with bathroom facilities.

Most of the teachers at the schools I taught at were male. We shared info about job and club openings, visa regulations, stalker students, and girlfriends. Being new to the game, I didn't believe the tales of girls who waited outside apartments all night for their teacher-boyfriend to come home or attempted suicide because he wanted to break up. They sounded exaggerated. However, the longer I remained, the less embellished they seemed.

The other topic of the day was the mandatory HIV test. Teachers had the choice of becoming legit and taking the test or leaving. One teacher I knew departed because he didn't want to see the results. He had done many risky things, such as "sleeping with prostitutes on an excursion to Bangkok without protection." I could understand why he ran from the outcome.

Listening to the stories from the guys exiting made me feel as if I'd missed the boat. "The good times are over," and "The gravy train has left the station," is what they said.

Around town, I sensed the ghosts of preceding entrepreneurs and English drillmasters. Before they turned up, others left. It was a natural changing of the guard. When one guy took off, he made room for the newest arrival. Someone had to replace these spent soldiers of the English language. Otherwise, demand would have outpaced supply.

The dude with the posh pad paid $650 monthly for rent, while my roommate and I shelled out $250; gigantic cockroaches were on the house. We looked to rent two single rooms for $300 and find individuals to take the other rooms. The landlord agreed because we were low maintenance.

That was fantastic. Soon, I would have a significant upgrade in my digs. I still only had the duffle, so moving would be easy. But what to do with the surfboard? A few days turned into weeks. I told the landlord to expect a call and planned to leave it.

With my affairs arranged, I needed to figure out where to go for my visa trip. My time expired, and I had to dip my foot outside Taiwan for at least a day.

VII

The cheapest destination to reset my visa would be Hong Kong. When I checked the newspaper for a travel agent, I found an affordable price for a tour of Seoul. It was cheaper than buying a round-trip and hotel on my own, and it included meals. This was a fantastic opportunity to see a new country and fill my belly.

The tour group was Taiwanese except for one "big nose" (the Taiwanese phrase for foreigner meant big nose—it sure beats foreign devil). We went on a three-day excursion to the renowned spots in Seoul with lots of shopping. Everyone brought a friend or a spouse. Since I was alone, they gave me a single.

On the second day, people loosened up once they heard me speak Mandarin. Before that, I felt like an outcast. Most did not care for Korean BBQ or Kimchi. They packed instant noodles, and I ended up with a more significant portion of the food and alcohol. I was evaluating non-American beers and needed lots of samples to know if I enjoyed a particular one, which in this case turned out to be OB, the Korean Budweiser.

A guy from Southern Taiwan, traveling with his girlfriend, enjoyed watching me drink through the first day. Towards the end of the second, he asked me to join him. I cautioned I had little to spend. He looked loaded. Sure, we could go out if he picked up the tab.

The others carried pockets full of U.S. dollars. I held a booklet of traveler's checks, which some hotels did not take, nor did the bars. Lin had a bundle. He said he brought the dough for his girlfriend to buy cosmetics; either way, he would spend the money.

Because neither of us spoke Korean and Lin did not speak English (he used Taiwanese), it limited our decision. Our hotel was isolated but ran a nightclub in the basement with a $20 cover. That was past my budget; however, Lin whipped out a wad of greenbacks—the wrong thing to do. He looked flashy, decked out in a flowery silk shirt, expensive branded jeans, gold chains, and a fanny pack. His pinkie nails extended past his other fingers, representing that he made enough cash he didn't have to do labor. Lin played the part of a mobster tourist and said he was a member of "The Black Hand Party" (Chinese for the mob). He seemed okay, but now I knew he had a dangerous side. I had to stay alert.

The gentleman at the door sported a white tuxedo. I presumed he would deny me entrance with my backpacker attire. It was amazing how cash opened doors, especially when you had a club to fill. The tuxedo guy spoke some English, so I did the talking as he directed us to a leather sofa. Girls on stage danced in Vegas-style feathered dresses, and a guy sang in loud Korean. I spotted a few dark booths on both sides with dudes smoking away, and I got concerned they might jump us later. I had nothing of value except my life, but I kept my eye on them anyway.

Rule #7: Always negotiate in advance the price of anything you eat, drink, or anyone you sit with.

Lin wanted to start the party and urged me to tell the tuxedo guy he had a lot of money. Similar to many people I encountered, the host assumed I was one of the U.S. soldiers stationed there. My buzz cut and youth probably gave him that idea. He called me "G.I."

"We want to order some beer. Is there a minimum fee for the table?"

"$20 for five beers. No charge for the table if you order a fruit plate, G.I."

"How much is the fruit plate?"

"$50, G.I."

This was early in my Asian adventure. I did not understand the fruit and alcohol thing, but I translated for Lin. Then he pulled out the bills. I ordered more beers anytime we ran low. Lin told me to ask how much it is to have some girls sit with us.

"$50 for twenty minutes, G.I.,"

It seemed odd that every item cost fifty or twenty. There were no prices listed, but Lin threw down more bills.

Next, three ladies in full-feathered regalia strolled over from the stage and sat down. The host also hung around, drinking our beer. They remained as long as Lin doled out the ducats.

"Would you like some peanuts? $20."

"How about some dried squid? $20."

The later it got, the more I expected Lin's girlfriend to show up and kill him for partying with other women and spending her cosmetics money with "big nose." We stayed until the club closed, and Lin had used up all his funds, or they closed because he ran out. Lin dropped over $800. He told me there was plenty in Taiwan. If he didn't care, then I didn't.

We took the elevator to our floor, and Lin put me on the spot. He said it was too late to return to his room; he didn't want to listen to his girlfriend complain. Instead, he asked if he could sleep in my room. The guy had just spent money on me. I couldn't refuse—huge mistake.

Lin entered and showered for an hour. He somehow sprayed water everywhere. How did he drench everything, including the towels?

Rule #8: Do not share a hotel room with someone unfamiliar; if you do, shower first.

When we walked down for breakfast, the group was buzzing about how I tore apart the couple from the south. While we sat in the nightclub, his girlfriend knocked on doors, looking for him and telling everyone it was my fault he was out. She probably knew better, but it became a reason to rally others. After that, the women avoided me, but the men wanted to repeat the cycle. On the final night, we stayed at a place without a club and stuck to the lobby. The wives were happy: they rescued their duty-free funds.

We flew back to Taipei the next day, and I received a visa upon arrival. I needed to complete the work visa paperwork within sixty days before leaving again.

On my way out, I picked up a bottle of Chivas and a slab of smokes, then returned to my cockroach hut.

VIII

A few weeks after returning, I moved uptown. There would be no more roaches on my face, no more Ass Cheeks Ricky, and no more sizzling sun waking me in the morning. But I had a new problem: A vendor cart downstairs cooked stinky tofu (*chou doufu*). All day long, the stench drifted up to our balcony.

It was an annoying inconvenience but not enough to dampen my excitement about a better lifestyle.

On the bright side, the apartment was within walking distance of Pizza Hut, and they served all-you-could-eat lunch twice a week. What a comfort to have American fast food close for when hungover, but I avoided the pizzas with squid, shrimp, and corn.

The location of my new flat reduced my traveling time. In addition, I refrained from taking inconvenient classes, giving me more opportunities to stack them. On average, I taught six to eight hours a day, Monday to Friday, and six hours on Saturday. After doing so much standup, I looked forward to stopping at 7-11 and picking up a half dozen bottles of Taiwanese beer before heading upstairs to my apartment. My flatmate and I together would have a few dozen empty 20 oz bottles weekly. It was a necessary chore to make an empties run to get the bottle deposits back and stock up on more.

Soon, I fell into a teaching routine, running from place to place and drinking at home daily. I earned decent coin and met friendly people, but the entertaining aspect ran me down, especially when hungover. Saturdays were the worst. I hit it hard on Friday. Then, I struggled the next day. I woke up dehydrated and tired, but I had six hours of entertaining ahead. Every Saturday morning, I swore I would not drink again. But once I made it through the first four hours, my body began to recover, and I planned what bars to attack.

I got stuck in a vicious cycle of happiness and pain, but there wasn't much else to do besides listen to music and drink. In the new apartment, we had a TV, but we only received CNN, NHK, Wowow, and a bizarre Japanese channel with women playing rock, paper, and scissors. It seemed to be a gambling game: someone played while the rest of us watched. The women removed an item of clothing if the player guessed right. They never got naked, but it drew your attention, making you think this time it would happen.

It was more entertaining than CNN.

When we ran out of beer, I would coerce my flatmate to go to Spin and Roxy, two popular teacher hangouts. We dropped by three or four venues every Friday and Saturday. On the way, I played cassettes, like Red Hot Chili Peppers (*Blood Sugar Sex Magik* released in 1991), to pass the time in traffic. Taipei taxis had decent stereo systems, and I sat in the front and controlled the tunes. The drivers turned it down several times, but most enjoyed the music.

Almost every club charged a 200 TWD ($8) cover charge. I couldn't afford to squander my budget on covers, or else I went home to drink. I didn't mind that, but I wanted to be outside, too, so I had to be selective with my club choice. Whenever I scouted a new club, I kept an eye out for the closest 7-11. As I lived on a tight budget, I improvised: I paid the cover, got my hand stamped, walked to 7-11, bought some tallboys, and drank them on the street. This was the perfect way to get liquored up at an affordable price.

The numerous motorbikes on the sidewalk provided comfortable seating, too.

After Spin, we zig-zagged our way north to Shuang Cheng Jie, or the Combat Zone, as people called it. Shuang Cheng Street consisted of a couple of alleys with bars open late. Some were expat hangouts like The Pig and Whistle, pulling decent pints of ale and cooking Western food. Others were places with velvet curtains serving businessmen who found the advertisements in the Taiwan tourist magazine. The pictures in the ads showed a foreign bloke surrounded by three or four young, attractive girls. In reality, the scene was depressing, with a few mature women serving drinks and flirting with anyone who walked in. Usually, one or two foreigners sat in each joint. The places looked rundown and hung faded pictures of past glory or signed currency from around the world, mentioning the female boss or the fun time they enjoyed.

Peering into these places, I hoped I would never be the lonely guy, hemmed in by aging hostesses sporting outfits suited for girls twenty years younger and wearing make-up that tried to take your attention away from their age. Many guys wobbled out of these bars, dropping hundreds of duckets, not knowing what they had purchased. The hostesses specialized in detaching you from your money. Negotiate first (**Rule #7**).

We always hit up 7-11 to refuel before entering the bars of the Combat Zone. It was in the middle of the strip, making it convenient and a great location to watch people bar-hopping, looking for something better than the place they had just left. I walked out of the pub every thirty minutes and downed a few cans to ensure I kept the correct balance. It was my nightly routine.

My favorite place to drop in after refueling was called Farmhouse. They had a band and charged a cover, usually more than I had left. The best way to avoid the fee was to open the door forcefully and walk right in. This only worked with complete confidence, like I belonged and the bouncer should know me. Because I was lit when I arrived, I practically always walked in without paying. If you seemed out of place, they'd throw you out. It got easier the more often I showed up.

Rule #9: Take control of the situation; do not wait for someone to tell you what you can't do.

Similar to other businesses with a "Western" theme, Farmhouse had this horrible sawdust odor, which I guessed had something to do with barns. They put a foosball table on the second floor. Foosball and darts were staples of my college days, but I rarely played anymore. My 20 oz courage lifted my game, but there came a point where I was useless. That stage arrived when I strode into Farmhouse.

Next, we headed to B52s. Like many of Taipei's hot discos, B52s was a fire death trap. The government attempted to stamp out these clubs, but another opened as soon as one closed. B52s did not have a cover and was hopping until dawn.

Their band blared the hits of the day, such as "Hip Hop Hooray", "Rump Shaker", "Nuthin' but a 'G' Thang", "Jump Around", "Free Your Mind", "What is Love", "Here comes the Hotstepper", "All That She Wants", and "Informer." These songs played in constant rotation.

Once I squandered my cash, I took a taxi home at 2 or 3 a.m. Before heading up to the flat, I stopped at 7-11 to pick up a late-night treat: a 7-11 hot dog. The shriveled dogs rolled on the rollers most of the evening, making them resemble fat Slim Jims. With a steamed bun, they made a delicious snack. But don't think about what parts of the animal they used. That would spoil the meal. Actually, the heated bun was everything. Imagine finding none available. If that happened, another 7-11 was nearby. They often had buns but no dogs (some skipped the bun and ate a dog on a stick). Then, I would pull a bun "shiest." This entailed taking a bun and running it to the second store to complete the meal. I didn't consider it stealing as I paid in the end. Plus, the store workers never cared. Maybe it was too late to be concerned with someone acquiring a bun. Who knows?

One night, I had an epiphany when I sat in the living room eating my dog and listening to some drunken Tom Waits' ballads about Christmas cards from hookers in Minneapolis and pianos that had been drinking. This was the rest of my life, no longer a summer break. Sure, I had loads of fun, and waking up in Taipei felt like Beijing: There was no telling what the day would bring. I couldn't get enough of this sense of adventure. But there was also the other side that made me miserable, the part where I hustled every day and had no family or friends to fall back on. Even though I had completed school a few months ago, I never paused to realize that my tour of Taiwan would be a make-it-or-break-it moment. Now, it hit me: This was not a temporary study-abroad situation. I needed to build a complete life. I needed a better job and a group of friends who enjoyed living life to the fullest.

Right now, my only contact was my flatmate, but we moved in different directions. He disliked his job and Taiwan. I didn't want his mood to affect my plans, so I looked for fellow drinking companions. They had to be out there somewhere.

Initially, I tried a bar around the corner. If this place worked out, not only would I save cash on covers and taxis, but I would also require less effort to stumble home. Several neighborhood watering holes operated in the alleys, but this one stocked Taiwan's most extensive LP collection—a complete wall dedicated to the black vinyl. They carried music from almost any Western artist, and the DJ said he knew his stuff.

"C'mon, challenge me."

The song that came to mind was Chicago's "Saturday in the Park." I gave him a simple test, and he passed. After that, anytime I entered the bar, the next song the DJ put on was "Saturday in the Park."

I enjoyed having a theme song.

When it happened a few times, I realized I was the resident expat—a title with the perk of free drinks and invites to join drinking games with other drunks. I even got invited to the bartender's wedding. If just the DJ, bartender, and I hung out, we rotated buying drinks for each other, and I controlled the LP selection. Sometimes, I put on my CDs to enlighten the DJ further. The place began to resemble my living room, but I wished it had drawn more customers to make things more interesting.

Besides myself, another regular hung out, but he didn't drink. John was in his thirties and said he drank until something "terrible" happened. He swore never to do it again. I sensed he had done something worse than crashing a car, so I never asked.

As my friendship with John grew, he informed me the incident involved stabbing somebody. I did not need to know that. Still, I couldn't understand how he sat and sipped soda and lemon without a hint of vodka. Despite not having a boozing partner, it felt good to converse with someone in my regular, casual English and not the speed-adjusted, enunciated language I used in class. But he wouldn't go clubbing. John stuck to the neighborhood bar. That was as far as he trusted himself.

And so I ventured out again, searching for fellow inebriates.

IX

Before hunting for drinking buddies, I had to leave the island to retrieve my resident visa in Hong Kong. I had limited knowledge of the territory but would get a quick education. Since I needed to travel there, I planned to cross the border into China. I still had contact with my college girlfriend, and she returned to Nanda for graduate study. The relationship was on life support, but it provided me with an excuse to return. Nanjing wasn't Beijing. However, it held memories for me. I wanted to check out what had changed.

I couldn't get a visa for China in Taiwan or fly direct. British-controlled Hong Kong became the best location to process things. So, I arranged to take an hour and a half flight to Hong Kong, secure a cheap room, pick up my visa at the Taiwan visa office, go to the China visa office and apply for a visa, buy a ticket to Nanjing, fly two hours, stay for two days, fly two hours back to Hong Kong, stay a night, and fly to Taipei.

Usually, the airports were on the edge of town. Hong Kong's Kai Tak was in a densely populated area with row after row of buildings. Our plane approached in a direction that seemed like we had sailed between the high-rises. It turned into the coolest descent.

We touched down, and I rode a bus to the Tsimshatsui (TST) District.

My guidebook said TST was the spot to locate the cheapest housing. Individuals attempting to drag you to their hostel surrounded anybody who alighted along the main road (Nathan Rd.). I looked forward to rooming at Chung King Mansions (CKM) but disembarked at the wrong stop. A room sherpa talked me into staying at the Miramar Mansions down the street. The guy offered a single with AC for HKD 200 ($25), a bargain compared to $100 for the Holiday Inn. All I had to do was look at the cramped quarters and laundry hanging everywhere to know it was a dump, but it would suffice.

With my lodging set, I strolled down Nathan Road to the real CKM to see what they offered to eat. Chung King Mansions resembled no other housing project. It felt like a crossroads, a contemporary souk. Thousands from various countries lived and worked in the five building blocks. Outside stood Africans dressed in ethnic clothing, Indians with turbans and long beards, travelers from the Middle East, and random backpackers like me. With so many cultures, there had to be good food.

At first, the guys trying to draw me to their makeshift restaurants didn't bother me. I knew they hustled to make a living. But it got aggressive when I hit the first floor. The best way to deal with them was to plow through. I parted the flock and wandered the shops selling souvenirs, electronics, wholesale goods, clothing, and regional delicacies. I intended to find a sit-down restaurant, but no luck. They hid the places, so I returned to the entrance.

After four months in Taiwan, I required a break from Chinese food. The only other nourishment I splurged on was McDonald's. Now, I needed something radically different.

When I reached the entrance, sherpas besieged me again. I listened to each and selected the most persistent dude working for a kitchen called the New Delhi Indian Club. Once I agreed, he took off through the crowd to the last block. A long line waited for the lifts, stopping at each floor (seventeen floors). I did not look forward to squeezing in with a group as hot and sticky as me.

Luckily, my sherpa wanted to return to the front line.

"Forget about the wait. Follow me."

He led me out the exit to a dark alley. Then, we entered a dirty stairwell and hiked up three flights. In a few minutes, I transitioned from the famous streets of TST to a precarious situation. I prepared myself in case he turned around and pulled a knife. My years growing up in Chicago gave me "Spidey sense," which kept me protected.

We halted on the third floor, walked through swinging wooden doors, and stood in front of a flat. He opened the door, and inside was room for twenty diners, a kitchen, and a mini toilet. They ran a tight organization. I had discovered an affordable gem that smelled terrific on a hungry stomach. Not everybody appreciated the significance of a small restaurant churning out outstanding Indian cuisine, but I did.

The menu had all the standards, but I remembered the vindaloo the most. That shit burned. I conquered Mexican, Thai, Chinese, and Korean hot, but this vindaloo took me to the next level. It was the kind of hot that woke you up in the middle of the night with a massive pain in your chest. Fire going in and fire going out. It probably doesn't sound tantalizing if one had to pass through the pain. But something addictive about the thick, creamy sauce filled with spices and chili made you desire more suffering. The proper way to neutralize the volcanic mixture was to chug a few bottles of ice-cold Tsingtao or Kingfisher.

I picked up both visas and booked a flight to Nanjing the following day. In the evening, I headed back to the New Delhi Club before a Chinese diet on the mainland. This time, I marched through the hustlers to the alley and up the dirty staircase.

I stayed in Hong Kong for a day, but it felt like I had been here for ages.

Most flights into China were en route to Beijing or Shanghai. Planes to medium-sized cities were few. I got lucky as I found a round-trip that fit my schedule. The plane was almost empty—a big difference from when I rode the train as a student. Now, I have flown back in comfort with a job and more money than two years ago but was not a success yet.

The Nanjing Airport was fifteen minutes by taxi to the city center. Customs was a breeze once the agents bothered to get to their stations. My flight appeared to be the only international one. They opened and closed the airport with every arrival.

The regular scrum of taxi drivers waited to grab anyone who exited. As a foreigner, touts surrounded me, pulling my backpack towards their taxis. They thought my girlfriend was local and bargained with her to shuttle her prized *laowai*. It cost $2 to get into town, but the drivers demanded $10. Depending on how many travelers required taxis, I usually negotiated a lower price but not the local one.

This was my third trip, and it seemed like I had never left. I noticed few changes beyond a developing restaurant and bar scene outside the university gates.

It was a fun place.

After two days, I started my journey back to Taiwan as a resident.

X

Things fell into place after my visa run. I continued to improve at entertaining the students, sometimes teaching them something. The company I worked for also offered Japanese, so I took classes. I studied Chinese from textbooks I bought in Nanjing. I even discovered a gym. It looked like a high school weight room, but it served the purpose. Overall, the quality of my life improved.

One evening, I came home and discovered a letter in my mailbox. It read, "I'm sleeping in the park. Come get me."

That's it, no name. I suspected someone had mistakenly left it. The only park I knew was Sun Yat-sen Memorial, a fifteen-minute walk. That space was massive. How would I find who wrote the note? I blew it off and walked upstairs but I couldn't stop thinking about it.

"Perhaps the little, triangular sliver of grass, the neighborhood garbage dump, is a park?"

Just in case, I walked downstairs to investigate. I stepped around the corner and noticed a guy sleeping on a barrier wall with no shirt. It was my Kiwi friend, Rich. I thought he had left Taiwan. I would have been in China if he had shown up two weeks earlier. That's how he lived. He called my old apartment to retrieve his board, and Ass Cheeks Ricky gave him my forwarding address. On his return, he located my place and slept in the "park."

We continued up to my flat and raced to the bottom of a bottle of Chivas while catching up. He taught English and lived with an American gal in the middle of Taiwan. I knew little about the rest of the island but imagined taking a trip at some point. Rich gave me the motivation.

We finished the whiskey and prepared to take the party on the road. I only had a single class the next day starting at 2 p.m.

"No problem. I can have a huge night and be okay to teach."

We cleaned up the bottles and headed for the door when my flatmate returned. Rich did not dig him and was pleased he would not be joining our pub crawl.

"I wouldn't do that to you. We're presently not on favorable terms because I pulled a gag that went wrong."

My flatmate suffered from a fear of mice. There were just as many rodents as dogs, and stray dogs were everywhere: on the sidewalk, on the doorsteps of shops, inside shops, and any place they found space. People abandoned them, and they infiltrated Taipei. At least they remained on the streets, unlike the rats and cockroaches.

We should have taken our disposable 7-11 shopping bags stuffed with all our smelly rubbish (including "shit rags," toilet paper had to be thrown out, not flushed) down to the alley every evening. The trashmen collected the refuse in the morning. But we got lazy and avoided going down once we climbed four flights. As a result, we flung the tied bags onto the balcony and shut the patio doors. It would be okay because there were no mice on the fourth floor, right? We kept the garbage on the terrace until it grew into more bags than we could handle, or the stench became overwhelming. I neglected to consider rodents coming up through the pipes when drawn to decomposing rubbish.

One day, I detected bite marks on a loaf of bread sitting on the table. I set down a glue board, captured the sucker, and disposed of him. A week later, I awoke to a high-pitched scream and door slamming. When I got home the night before, I didn't catch my flatmate. I assumed he hooked up, and the girl realized she had made a mistake, screamed, and ran out. He took an early flight for a visa run, so I slept some more. Later, I saw his note. He said he attempted to shower, opened the door, saw a rat, screamed, threw his towel at it, slammed the door, ran to his room, and then slammed his door. It must have been a whopper. I needed an extra-large glue board.

I placed the trap and caught it, a mouse smaller than my hand. Chicago in the '70s had super rats the size of cats. They grew powerful enough to remove the steel lids off the garbage cans! Those were rats.

I decided I would help him get over his fear.

Instead of tossing this poor guy, I saved him on the balcony, still stuck, gradually dying. It was harsh, but his only other option was the rubbish heap.

I waited until my flatmate fell asleep, then I placed the sucker inside his room. The first thing he would look at in the morning was the mouse (barely moving) lying on the floor before his door. I realized I took it too far when I heard my name being called to remove it. It was worse than I had imagined. He couldn't even step over it. I had to cool it after that.

It wouldn't help the situation to have a drunk Rich take the piss out of him, so it was better he stayed behind.

I steered my friend to all my favorite joints and their relevant 7-11s from south to north and back south again. Towards the end of the evening, I lost him. We weren't far from my apartment, so I figured he had stumbled back. I got wasted enough that walking turned into an issue. I hated not having control of my legs, but I consistently found my way with my DPS or Drunk Pilot System. DPS directed me home if I drank to where I no longer made conscious decisions. I usually recalled how and when, too. Occasionally, I picked up souvenirs—like giant jungle plants. They helped to green up the apartment, and I had to replace them because we never watered them.

When I returned, I didn't see Rich, but I was in no shape to look for him. There was nothing to do except wait and enjoy my 7-11 hotdog. Ultimately, he would have to turn up to pick up his bag.

Around 9 a.m., I woke up groggy to the sound of the downstairs buzzer. I tried to piece together what had happened. Then it hit me. I lost Rich. The buzzer was still ringing, and I heard someone yell,

"Bro, wake the fuck up!"

It was Rich and, in one piece, sort of.

He got lost finding his way from the toilet in the last club, and I was nowhere in sight. He ordered another beer and wandered about looking for my flat. Tragically, he tripped and chipped off part of his front teeth on the metal handrail while leaving the club. His luck changed when he spotted an unlocked push-bike and "borrowed" it. He cycled around the city (population three million) until he recognized things.

I insisted that the story justified at least a shot, plus I wanted to make up for deserting him. Then we could grab food at the Thai restaurant downstairs before walking ten minutes to school for my 2 p.m. However, we drank too much, and I skipped lunch.

I made it to class as scheduled, but I was hot and sweaty from speed walking with an alcoholic cloud engulfing anyone within a ten-foot radius. When I passed, the students probably detected the vapors escaping into the atmosphere. I tried not to breathe out, but the liquor burst through my pores. There was no hiding it. Mentally, I was fine and had no other issues, such as slurring my words or running into the walls. I felt this way when I drank hard the day before. I rarely felt drunk the day after, but I was exhausted. Fortunately, the class only had six students, and they were regulars.

A pupil in front said to me during the break,

"Teacher, you smell like you drank a beer for lunch."

"Yeah, an old friend came to visit, and I drank one." (a beer, half a bottle of whiskey, but no lunch)

"Taiwanese businessmen are like that too."

That was good to know. I now had an excuse.

Once class wrapped up, I headed home. Along the way, I picked up some dumplings and devoured them before passing out. Rich left, but I planned to see him.

XI

Just when I felt good about my life, I woke up one morning with a killer toothache. The right side of my face swelled up, and my jaw became tight. I had an impacted wisdom tooth that acted up. I needed to see a dentist, but how would I arrange that? How would I identify a qualified person to rip out a giant molar from the rear of my mouth? I passed by a few dentist offices, but they looked cheap. Instead, I went to a leading hospital and got directed to the receptionist. She instructed me to wait for the dentist to evaluate whether he would take me as a patient.

Luckily, I was an acceptable case.

"How much is this going to cost?"

"About 5,000 TWD ($200)."

That was a fortune. I had sufficient funds, but this, on top of my recent trips to Korea and China, would set me back. On the bright side, I would no longer have the ache.

They pulled it a few days later, but the dentist had difficulty. He injected Novocain into my gums, but I sensed him drilling. One guy held my head while another wedged against the side of my mouth, tearing it open. It took so long that they gave me a second batch of Novocain shots. They required three hours to win the battle. My mouth was torn out of shape and numb, but I told them I wanted the tooth. It cost me this much money and trouble that I had to take it.

I got my head together, paid the bill, grabbed my tooth, and left the place with a massively swollen mouth plus an enormous gap. Blood poured out of the space like a river. It seemed odd to leave the fissure open. The dentist indicated it would close up, but the hole continued to bleed. My jaw tightened more, so I returned to complain. He said I had an infection—no shit!

"How do we fix it?"

"I can give you antibiotics. You'll be better after a few weeks."

"How do I eat?"

My jaw locked up and wouldn't open wider than an eighth of an inch. I drank soup from instant noodles to ensure something entered my stomach.

"Here, stack these wooden tongue depressors and wedge them in your mouth. Every day, try to add another to pry it open."

That was my remedy—tongue depressors. Meanwhile, I dropped pounds and got hungry, to where I was no longer hungry—on the other side. I sipped milk through a straw for nutrients until I propped my mouth open enough to fit a piece of bread in, but I couldn't chew.

Through all this, I never took leave. I may have appeared like I practiced to be a ventriloquist, but I kept going. My experiences provided material for my classes, and my students were all too happy to tell me I got ripped off. They said an extraction should cost 500 TWD ($50). I worried my jaw would not return to normal, but it bounced back before Christmas.

Just in time to make up for my absence.

XII

I often took the alleys in my neighborhood instead of sitting in a taxi or on a bus stuck in a jam. Zhongxiao East Road, the main road towards my apartment, constructed a subway line that blocked traffic, especially at night. I got off before hitting the worst part, ten blocks from my flat. The sidewalks were packed with shoppers, slow walkers, motorbikes, and dogs—too many obstacles. I just wanted to rush to the comfort of my home after a long day of Taipei life.

The alleys turned out to be the best way to travel and uncover exclusive shops. I discovered a bar with an open mic for performers to sing or play acoustic. I hung out here to break up the monotony of frequenting the same place.

One evening, a guy on stage played guitar and sang Taiwanese folk songs. After he finished, he came over, sat down, and asked me what tunes I liked.

"Everything."

Apache was an Indigenous Taiwanese with ancestors originally residing on the island. He was tall and had long black hair—like the Indians he got his name from. Apache spoke in short phrases and used facial expressions to say the rest. It shocked him that I spoke fluent Mandarin. He wanted to talk about music but needed to do something. It was well past midnight. What kind of errand did he need to run?

I thought little of it. When living overseas, I made temporary friends and never saw them again. It was society in motion. I lost many solid ones because we were on different paths.

Shortly after Apache left, he came back and said,

"Hey, man. I was lucky to meet you, so I planned to do my thing another time. Tonight, we drink and listen to music."

He sensed we should be friends. Many people wished to be my friend to speak English, but Apache wanted to learn about Tom Waits and Jim Morrison while consuming whiskey. The friendship was mutual.

As a musician, he appreciated different types of rhythms, and he drank hard. He bought a round of beers and shots, and I did the same.

Apache told me he had recently retired from a gang and tried to start a singing career, but he still had gang-related responsibilities. It surprised me they allowed him to quit, so I didn't believe him, but I knew he was tough. Some people look tougher than others. He was one of those, like Machete. We stayed until the bar closed. I drank enough not to care, so I invited him to my apartment to keep the party going. I remembered introducing Wang Yi to fantastic music and wished to do the same for Apache. First, I stopped for smokes.

At the convenience store entrance stood a gigantic promotional display for Camel cigarettes.

"That's a cool sign (I smoked Camels)." Apache paused.

"Do you want that?"

"Well, yeah, but..."

Before I finished, he turned, walked into the store, and took the display. The guy running the shop ran out and yelled, "Come back here. You can't take that!"

Apache halted and said, "What are you going to do?"

The clerk said nothing and returned to the store.

I didn't consider it wrong because I never told him to take it, but I neglected to stop him. It was just a promo, and it looked swell in my living room with the jungle plants.

We continued until 5 a.m. Suddenly, my flatmate opened his door to find me, Camel Joe, and a tall Indian-looking dude smoking something similar to crack while I changed tunes and drank Chivas with white noise on the TV (the rock-paper-scissors girls slept at night). Apache called his medicine "#4." He put it on tinfoil, lit the bottom, then inhaled the smoke.

It looked hardcore to the uninitiated.

My flatmate summoned me into his room to warn me not to party in the apartment. This sounded hypocritical, but I made peace. Besides, we had run out of booze, and I had to meet students at the National Art Museum for a Sunday of culture.

Apache offered to give me a lift on his bike, saving me a fortune in taxi fare. One of the most exhilarating things about Taiwan was riding a motorcycle on cleared streets. This was Sunday morning, and he rode fast. Apache said his medicine gave him clarity. It made sense in an intoxicated way.

We cruised down the streets at lightning speeds and arrived at the museum without trouble. I neglected to consider how the students would react to Apache (he resembled a rock star or a gangster) and myself showing up, smelling like cigs and hootch. I repeatedly forgot to separate my hard-drinking life from my good-natured teacher persona. This time, I had no choice.

The longer we stood there making introductions and waiting for the museum to open, the less enthusiastic I was about spending my Sunday surrounded by crowds. What was I thinking? I took a raincheck, and Apache sent me home.

Now that we were friends, Apache would call around midnight with an address. The first time, I met him at a karaoke next to a school I worked at. Inside were six large U-shaped booths, each filled with five or six guys (one or two girls) slamming Remy or Hennessy. Apache introduced me to all his "brothers." He was the elder and got mad respect.

We drank XO, and it burned when doing shots. The boys ordered lots of the stuff. Someone constantly showed up with a new burgundy-colored box and pulled out another pear-shaped bottle. My students informed me gangsters broke bottles of XO to show off their wealth to other gangs. I witnessed this with all the wastage and spillage of expensive Cognac, $160 a bottle.

I had never had much experience with karaoke until that moment, but I instantly learned the ropes. It was about giving respect and accepting it.

The karaoke specialized in Taiwanese and Mandarin ditties. They had two laser discs with old English numbers such as "500 Miles" and "Country Roads." I decided the most suitable tune for me was "In the House of the Rising Sun." It involved less singing and more reading. "My Way" was another easy one. I sang a few Mandarin songs by reading the characters. No matter how badly I butchered them, I always received the crowd's approval for trying. I figured they clapped because I was Apache's brother.

One night, I met Apache at a bar in a coastal town called Ji Long. It was at the dark end of the street with no windows. When the door opened, he waved me in from the other side of the room. The guy managing the door locked it behind me. I worried I got myself into a situation, but I had to play it off. Apache informed me we wouldn't leave until the party finished. I didn't want them to think I couldn't hold my own. Apache took a risk vouching for me. As long as I kept my cool, I would be all right. Ultimately, the sun would come up, and then we would depart.

Twice, we dropped by a construction site and drank a ghetto mixture of rice wine used for cooking and a Taiwanese herbal energy drink while watching the tattoo-covered brothers play cards for cash. The rice wine tasted nasty, but the energy drink neutralized it. The result reminded me of Mad Dog.

Like many of his brothers, Apache chewed betel nut (similar to chewing tobacco in the form of a nut the size of a pistachio). When I chewed betel nut, it sped up my heart rate, gave me a buzz, and turned my ears red. And similar to chewing tobacco, you had to spit. With betel nut, my saliva (and teeth) was bright red. When I first arrived, I thought the spit stains on the streets of Taipei resembled blood stains. Since it was a man's thing, they utilized young girls dressed in skimpy bikinis and high heels to sell them. His brothers handed me boxes. I usually found them in my pockets and other items I lifted.

My time with Apache was never dull. He showed me a side of Taiwan I would not otherwise have seen. I ran with him as much as possible without killing myself. Later, he developed liver damage and stopped consuming whiskey and *baijiu* but reverted to the rice-wine mixture full-time.

I knew him for about a year before he invited a girlfriend over. She was a big girl. I had never met a Chinese woman her size. She looked like she could beat the shit out of me but suited Apache. Whenever he brought her around, she would complain about his drinking, and he argued with her. Once, he left her at my apartment because she nagged him, but the next time, they were fine. Apache said her father wanted to kill him. It seemed like too much drama.

One thing I will always feel indebted to Apache is the new Chinese name he gave me. I said I hated having a "girl's name" and asked if he would pick a better one.

"Yeah, I don't like your name. It's not who you are. You must change it to something special, like a movie star."

"Maybe you can work with my Spanish name, Renaldo."

"Yeah, I can use that."

The next occasion I saw him, he had a name for me. From now on, I would be known as "Mr. Thunder." The other part translated as "peaceful promise," or the Chinese name for Arnold, as in Arnold Schwarzenegger. That added another level of coolness.

I thanked him for my movie star name, Thunder, Mr. Arnold Thunder.

XIII

Taipei nightlife thrived, with new clubs opening often. Usually, I heard through the teacher grapevine which hot club to hit and coerced my flatmates to scope out the scene (we found a graduate student to rent an empty room). Before Taiwan, I never clubbed much except when I frequented venues such as Medusa's in the Belmont area of Chicago.

But I grew tired of the rock-paper-scissors girls.

I needed to go out and find "**it.**"

"**It**" was instant gratification or a cure for the loneliness in my soul. "**It**" was where everything came together: the music, the atmosphere, the drinks, the people, and for a moment, I felt all right. Even when I found "**it**," it never lasted long, so I had to change the venue constantly. Places like Circus, Day and Night, Top, Doors, Kiss La Boca, Whiskey A-Go-Go, Absolute, BAM, DV8, Fubar, Tu Mambo, and more became my favorite haunts. Going out helped kill time and waste money, but it didn't ease my soul.

Hip-hop music was the main staple of most places, and I occasionally encountered dance battles in giant discos when a rap song came on. In the early '80s, I learned how to moonwalk and spin on my head to where a dance studio in our local mall paid me as a twelve-year-old to teach a breakdancing class until it faded. During that period, I tagged along with friends to battles on Chicago's South and West sides. But I quit back spinning eight years ago. I figured breakdancing was extinct—not in Asia.

When I strolled over to the dance floor, I noticed dancers crowding around a circle. I had a suspicion but had to witness it. Sure enough, a couple of locals battled against four black dudes. Although I was retired, I felt young and flexible, especially after a few drinks. I waited for an opportunity and jumped into the ring during a break between dancers. Then, I paced to mark my territory and expanded it before breaking into some top rock shuffling and doing the windmill. My body moved out of muscle memory, but my sense of balance and direction was off. Sometimes, I clocked bystanders with my feet while windmilling. Still, it amazed the crowd to observe a Teva-wearing foreigner breakdancing.

After the first round, everybody cheered for me to break out again, but the more I attempted to improve, the more I banged my head on the ground. The inertia kept me going, but something seemed wrong. Perhaps I shouldn't think I was twelve years old. At that point, I realized I had better go out on top. I left the circle with people patting me on the back. I even shocked my flatmates. "Who the hell was that guy?" It was my hidden talent. I hid it for a reason, like collecting comic books.

A group of massively built Chinese guys I recognized from the gym walked up to me. They paraded around in oversized Gold's Gym tank tops to show off their impressive muscles and worked as bouncers. Before they saw me break, they avoided me. Now, they came up to say hi or to spot.

Who knew breakdancing would be helpful so many years later?

Besides the muscle guys, I also befriended the African dudes. They were Igbo from Nigeria. The leader, Ramson, sported black turtlenecks, gold chains, and sunglasses similar to Cazals. I enjoyed hanging with him and his brothers because they were straightforward. They referred to me as "Randimoolah" because I reminded them of a person in a Nigerian soap opera. I liked the name. It sounded as if I had lots of moolah, but they never asked me for anything until once, Ramson called to see if I knew anyone who wanted weed.

"Not really, but how much are you talking about?"

"A garbage bag full."

I had visions of somebody tossing a hefty bag over the side of a boat and another guy rushing over to snatch it. That sounded like an execution-sized load. I declined.

When we club crawled, I sometimes dropped by my apartment for whiskey before moving to the Combat Zone. I had a bad habit of wanting to listen to specific songs during various parts of the evening. That was the quest for "**it**." I was anxious, never satisfied, and struggled to reach perfection before the clock ran out. I never had enough time and tried to squeeze too much in. It was a good thing my friends accepted my restless behavior. But the Nigerians had a low tolerance. I would page Apache to booze with; he got along with them well. If I planned to piss off my flatmates, I might as well make it worthwhile and invite the entire gang.

I downed a few shots at home and then led the party to the Combat Zone. At the Zone, we would switch between 7-11 and B52s.

One evening, I saw a fight between locals start in the corner of the club. It instantly escalated into a gang brawl, with beer bottles and chairs flying. You might get away with that if you are in a deserted bar. In a packed disco with only one exit, things escalated. My muscular Nigerian brothers cleared a path for us. Ramson pointed out blood on my shirt and recommended I remove it before someone thought I fought.

That was my cue to call it a night.

I looked for kicks and uncovered a full dose that evening.

XIV

Before I arrived in Taiwan, I was clueless about Taiwanese cuisine. I changed that through trial and error, especially at the night markets.

Besides the "three-cup" dishes, outstanding hot and sour soup and potstickers (dumplings steamed and sautéd to a crisp) were available. I had never tasted potstickers before Taipei and have never had better after. While in the U.S., I grew fond of hot and sour soup. I ordered it in China, but their soup included tripe or fish stomach, and the flavor resembled a weak broth instead of a thick soup. I happily gulped down the more familiar hot and sour in Taipei. They prepared snack foods with greater expertise than anywhere else. Visit a night market like Shi Lin and experience some of the best appetizers in the world.

Lu rou fan, an oily mixture of pork belly with fat and spices poured over rice and chicken leg rice (*ji tui fan*), became essential parts of my diet. I consumed them weekly.

Most of the time, I dined at *dai pai dangs*, a smorgasbord of various Chinese dishes similar to Panda Express restaurants. I chose two or three hot entrees with rice and seaweed soup. The food was decent and affordable, at 60 TWD ($2) a meal.

Even though I got upset about ruining my shirt on the first day, I warmed up to noodles. Downstairs from my flat was a phenomenal hand-cut noodle shop. A guy outside the entrance held a brick of dough and used a sharp cleaver to flick off razor-thin slices at an astonishing speed. The slivers flew into a massive pot of boiling water. I walked by this shop that burst with customers for an entire year. Eventually, I entered and figured out what everybody else knew: they made damn delicious noodles. And since the place was downstairs, I could pull a Clark Kent and change my shirt if required.

We had another place in the alley that cooked an amazing *gong bao* chicken. They used lots of shredded ginger and loads of chili. For safety's sake, they asked if you preferred a little, regular, or super spicy. By the time I left, I had conquered the extremely hot one.

You needed to be a professional to reach that level.

I tried other things, such as "stinky tofu (*chou doufu*)." They fried the tofu, producing a stench like dirty sweat socks that someone left in the bottom of a gym bag for six months. After that odor drifted into my window for weeks, I accepted the aroma and enjoyed the taste when doused with chili sauce.

There were many wonderful foods that I passed by, assuming I would have time until I ran out.

Naturally, the American in me missed nosh from home. Taipei had a restaurant called Dan Ryan's, named after the man who got expressways built in Chicago. They hung Windy City memorabilia and sold "American-sized portions," but not Chicago-sized. That was too much for most humans. I would have gone often if they had given me a Chicagoan discount. On Friday nights, TGI Fridays became the meeting point for the expat office crowd. It was entertaining to check out for a drink, but I recognized no one besides a guy who kept trying to pick me up. It gave my flatmates plenty of laughs whenever "my boyfriend" wanted to buy me drinks. They were jealous that someone showed me attention despite being the wrong sex.

Because Western restaurants charged too much, I learned to make my own food. First, I tackled Mexican. Some places served pseudo-Tex-Mex, but not authentic. I found all the ingredients except tortillas, so I rolled my own. Regularly, I made quesadillas for my flatmates to smooth over any differences. It opened my eyes to the power of food.

Nothing settled arguments better than decent Mexican.

XV

On Sundays, I looked for a change in pace. The two English papers were the best places to locate info about events. One weekend, I noticed an ad for bungee jumping at Wulai, a neighboring town famous for its waterfalls, seafood restaurants, and hiking. On every narrow street, the villagers sold dried seafood and hand-crafted items. Most of the stands sold wooden penises besides the Buddhas, and a few shops had a table full of erect phalluses. I couldn't figure out the connection, and the penises appeared out of place.

I had never bungee jumped before, but Wulai seemed suitable, and it cost nothing. A couple of American guys started a business. They required adventurous types to show the locals how to do it. That was why they didn't charge. We were the test dummies. They said they'd done jumps in New Zealand and had experience.

I sure hoped so.

I arrived in time to watch them set up on a bridge about forty meters (one hundred and thirty feet) above a dry river. If I had a malfunction, the trickle of water would not save me. It didn't seem high, but it was enough.

They secured the ropes and the platform, and then a guy operating the business prepared to leap. It looked like a piece of cake. My hangover from Saturday settled my nerves. I wanted to be ready for my turn, which came sooner than expected; I was first. They strapped the pro guy to his feet and gave me the option of doing the same or being connected to my chest. I chose the latter, which meant I would jump backward and not see the ground.

Better not to know.

As I strapped up and the guys checked the tightness of the cords, my fear and anxiety levels rose. My biggest concern was that I might freeze. If you jumped backward, you needed to jump away from the bridge. To help me, everyone counted down from five. When it reached zero, I would force myself to jump.

"Ready? Five, four, three, two, one."

Everything went silent except for the wind. The people on the bridge faded as I fell until I hit bottom. Then, the cord snapped me back up. I bounced until I came to a standstill. What a rush!

Another weekend, I caught an ideal ad in the paper.

"Are you a young, native English speaker? Do you enjoy drinking beer and talking to Chinese girls? Then join us on Sunday."

I thought there had to be a catch. Plus, the last thing I desired to do on a Sunday was teach, but curiosity kept nagging me to check it out.

It was a language club where members paid money to go on trips and converse with native speakers in our natural habitat—the bar. To entice foreigners to chat on their day off, they provided drinks at no charge. Being served free booze on a hungover Sunday seemed too good. On top of it, most were young ladies in their 20s. A few male patrons joined but had difficulty finding somebody to talk with. The pretty girls received the most practice. I joined a few events with a hundred students and about twenty "teachers." Everybody tried to get in on a conversation and surrounded each foreigner. I only needed to speak.

Unfortunately, with the free flow coming off a week of drinking, the party continued non-stop. I came home pretty lit a few times and hated life on Monday.

Thankfully, this club only held this party once a month. Otherwise, my Taiwan tour might have ended earlier with too much burning of the candle at both ends. Drinking hard, consistently, seven days a week, was aging me fast. I needed to slow down.

For a healthier option, students asked me to accompany them on trips. I happily joined these outings at the beginning of my tour to learn more about the island. Individuals took me to the coast to swim and the mountains to hike. The swimming was fine, but hiking up a hill in the humidity felt brutal. The possibility of cold brew and tasty food at the ultimate destination kept me going. I was disappointed to find only hot tea, peanuts, and playing cards.

During Christmas, my pupils drove me to the woods for a BBQ of many things I did not eat (squid, tofu on a stick, fish balls) but plenty of beer to drink. It would have been better if my jaw had healed properly.

Once, a student invited me to her house in the countryside. I tagged along, not knowing it was just her family and me. She planned to introduce me as a recent addition, but she sat in on only a few classes. I think she intended to corner me into a relationship.

She didn't know the way to my heart was through a bottle of Chivas.

After we returned, I ran into her before class. I rushed to prepare, so I brushed her off. Then she fled to the corner to sulk. Everything that happened in the lounge became public for all to witness. It didn't look good. I had an advanced session at that school with eight regulars. I was not aware she told them I dumped her. How could that be? I never dated her or gave her the slightest hint she interested me besides agreeing to join the trip. With all this drama, I moved my classes to another branch. For the next few months, I noticed her in my class from time to time. She replied with sarcastic answers. As a result, I stopped picking her and never saw her again.

I instructed her for a few weeks. I wondered to what extent of retaliation she would have gone through if we dated.

Rule #10: Be careful not to be too casual with students.

Yes, proceed with caution. Students often took a liking to their instructors. After hearing so many terrible stories, I avoided that route. My flatmates also had complications with their pupils. We received phone calls from them looking for us. The school made it easy by displaying our telephone numbers on our time cards in big black marker and placing them near the entrance.

Eventually, no one answered the phone, so I bought an answering machine to screen.

Listening to the messages made for an interesting end to the evening.

Rule #11: Regarding students with gifts, proceed with extra caution.

Students gifted me mooncakes, books, jewelry, and other items. The presents were great but a hassle to carry. Other times, they invited me to dinner. I needed to be careful with meals. I learned my lesson on my previous trip to the countryside.

Some hired me for private classes—similar to my job at Mr. Andy's. They paid for my meal while we talked in English and Chinese. One group of three middle-aged housewives invited me for tea and paid me $30 an hour to chat.

I heard about nightclubs that employed young men to sit, drink, and eat with wealthy women.

That sounded like what I did.

One woman I taught pro-bono was an attractive flight attendant (ten years older) who pursued me to start a conversation. She wished to hire me to correct her English, which I found odd since she spoke well.

"I want to speak the American way."

She had gotten engaged to an older American she met in a grocery store while on a layover in Los Angeles (like in the movies) and thought she needed practice in everyday lingo.

Sometimes she called me to go out with her friends. Why would I turn down dates with flight attendants? But it was a peculiar relationship where she flirted with me and asked if she should marry the guy. Occasionally, she drew me into her apartment, but I didn't want to get involved.

Three months later, she married him and invited me to the wedding. At Taiwanese weddings, they place a registration book at the entrance where you sign your name. As a foreigner, I stood out. They assumed I belonged to the groom's party and sat me with his family, who flew from the U.S. Everybody wanted to find out how I knew the groom. I had to clarify that I was friends with the bride.

That felt uncomfortable.

"I'm her English teacher" sounded strange when she spoke fluently.

These examples were inconvenient and mild, nothing compared to one student. She called herself Justine (among other names) and showed up in my primary lesson. Justine looked thirty-five and wore lots of perfume and designer clothes to the point of being gaudy. She seldom spoke because she didn't care to study. She was a stay-at-home wife with nothing to do. I had plenty in my day classes, and they seemed harmless. Justine liked that I used Chinese. Whenever I saw that students didn't understand, I translated.

She joined my classes on the north side and sat across from me, smiling. At first, Justine wanted to be entertained like the others. Then, she approached me to have English conversation sessions over lunch, but I moved away from those lessons while I worked in classrooms.

I made an exception when she paid me fifty for the hour and covered the meal, a generous offer I could not refuse.

Things were okay for a few months until she showed up at the other schools I taught at. Sometimes, she joined an advanced class but barely spoke enough for entry-level. Then she waited for me to walk to my next school. This annoyed me because I mentally prepared myself for the next two hours of entertaining on these walks. I also detoxed by walking fast and sweating out my hangover. Between my afternoon and evening classes,

I had a two-hour break and three kilometers to cover. She attempted to keep up, but I walked fast. I told her she shouldn't be waiting.

The following week, she gave me a motorbike. I presumed she hoped to ride with me, and I explained I enjoyed the walk. But I received her present. It was 250cc and had quite a kick. When I first got on, I accidentally turned the throttle; the bike shot out from between my legs and nearly crashed through a glass window of a bank. Luckily, I held tight until I unlocked my grip on the accelerator. I needed practice and got that training in Taipei traffic, like jumping into the deep end to learn how to swim. The motorbike saved me a lot of time. It also prevented Justine from walking with me, but she knew which days I took the bus for convenience; she knew my entire schedule. On those days, she showed up in her luxurious BMW with tinted windows. I had to admit that the new car was a better ride than the bus.

When my flatmates saw me get out of a BMW once, they asked, "Who was that?"

"That's the BMW woman." The car she drove was more reliable than her English name.

The longer I had sessions with her, the further she stalked me. She gave me gifts (**Rule #11**) like jade jewelry (not my style), clothes (definitely not my style), and an expensive watch (my type, but the first time I wore it, I caught it on a nail while going down the stairs in a club; I got down on my hands and knees to find it). If I refused the presents, she followed me until I accepted. The situation spiraled out of control. I had to keep the status quo and not make any abrupt maneuvers.

I instructed her for a year and a half, and she was a reason I left Taiwan.

XVI

I made my first trip to the U.S. after a year abroad. It felt weird being away for so long. When I ran into friends, they asked what I did and where Taiwan was.

"When are you moving back?"

I never considered that. I had a plan. First, I wanted to work at a Chinese company to learn how they managed. After two years, I would switch to an American firm operating in China. Lastly, I would work for a U.S. company that sent me back and forth.

Teaching English was the first step.

The machine shop I worked for in Chicago gave me a taste of international business, sourcing a factory to mass-produce a switch they made in Japan. It was an opportunity to earn experience. To find a manufacturer, I searched for contacts at the Taiwan International Trade Sourcing Library. Most were far away, but I found a plant nearby. I phoned them, put on my best business clothes, and rode to the next city. They turned out to be a trading company but had an onsite workshop. When I showed them the sample, they discussed the fees for opening the molds. They required me to pay $500 upfront, which I might not be reimbursed for, so I walked away from the project.

Meanwhile, I sent resumes to U.S. companies and anyone in the American Chamber of Commerce (AmCham) business directory. I checked the answering machine to see if prospective employers called. I also scanned the wanted ads, but there was nothing for entry-level. Most companies looked for general managers. There were jobs, but I didn't know the right individuals to connect me.

Fortunately, I stumbled onto an opportunity that fit my master plan—a trade job at a Taiwanese firm.

One of my flatmates had a friend visiting who had a short-term gig lined up at an engineering company. The owner needed somebody to contact overseas manufacturers to convince them to sign a license agreement. Two months later, the girl quit and introduced me to the boss. We hit it off, and he hired me.

The office was cramped with ten employees. The trading operation only had one—me. I impressed everybody with my Mandarin, which gave me credibility. It also caused the staff to use Taiwanese. As the token foreigner who added no value to the engineering projects, they didn't keep me in the loop. Despite the cold shoulder, I worked eight hours daily, mostly listening to my headphones and looking for another gig. Often, I spent time at the sourcing library, digging up addresses for companies I cold-called by typing up letters (no computer, just a typewriter), asking if they required a representative for their products. Most firms ignored me, while some signed agreements. Then I kept typing faxes to explain how soon the contract would be inked and what else was in the works.

I typed up faxes about nothing.

Some days, I photocopied all day. Instead of putting papers on the tray, I produced single copies. That way, I wouldn't fall asleep, a definite possibility on hungover mornings. I think the owner wanted me there, in case he brought clients. They would see a big nose, which meant we were international.

I still instructed English for two hours nightly and six on Saturday to adhere to my contract. I earned better money teaching, but the trade job fulfilled my grand scheme. It wasn't great, but everybody needed a start.

One day, the boss called me into his office and informed me that we had a crucial bid coming up. He wanted me to attend the meeting and said to wear a suit. They would introduce me as the company's foreign engineer.

"And if you have some older Western friends, tell them to come." I didn't have any, and my current friends would not help.

During the discussion, I tried to look interested. They used Mandarin. That was the reason I wouldn't talk during the presentation. I doubted the client thought I was vital, but they agreed to the plans and closed a deal.

When the meeting ended, I got invited to the dinner. Finally, I would enjoy some kick-ass Chinese food and drink for free.

"Sure, I can go."

"Can you drink? There will be a lot of drinking."

"Oh, I can hold my own."

They escorted us to a private room when we arrived. I never realized these rooms existed because I never dined at restaurants excellent enough for them. The private room gave the host space to entertain by any means. This room had a guy with a drum set and a synthesizer.

It seemed weird having him sit in the corner, smiling, wearing a vest and a fez hat, while he waited for my boss to start. I followed the boss's lead. He said a few remarks, we all toasted, and then the one-man band started playing synthesized Taiwanese reverb music. Next, the food arrived. We had ten people, three from our side. The guys informed me our boss drank heavily. I partied with the office staff, and they didn't drink past three beers. I wasn't sure what "heavily" meant to them.

For safety's sake, I, too, drank heavily.

The meal started with beer. Then, my boss asked the clients if they wanted to drink *baijiu*. Now, things were about to lift off. The customers toasted me with *baijiu*, assuming I would be an easy target. On the contrary, this was what I wanted. Since I avoided speaking Chinese, I couldn't warn them about my five months of training on the other side of the strait. The clients assumed they would put me away once I started—a mistake. This was my first time on the receiving end of *ganbeis*, but I fended them off.

About two hours into the dinner, the door opened, and a woman dressed in a skimpy dress with sequins and tassels entered. I sat with my back to the door and figured they brought in another dish (she sure was!). She guessed that as the lone foreigner, I was a VIP, so she came up from behind and covered my eyes. My mind raced to think, Who did I know here? When she removed her hands, she turned, sat on my lap, and pressed my cheeks as if to kiss me. No one else had a girl on their lap. Something was wrong. The other guys enjoyed it, but they waited to be next. Our boss told her to move to the right person. It still seemed she attempted to reach my side.

We continued for another hour. The boss looked wasted and Marlboro red, and we carried him out to a taxi. I didn't have a problem with the liquor, but I kept forgetting my role and spoke Chinese from time to time.

"You speak Chinese very well."

"Only a little."

I heard that many times. What people meant was, "You speak well for a foreigner." So few foreigners spoke Chinese that if you uttered "hello," people thought you spoke well. They set the bar low almost out of arrogance because most foreigners never took the time to learn it. That's why when I spoke fluent Mandarin, it shocked people, but not so much today.

My coworker and I accompanied the CEO home. He lived close to where I did. I planned to catch a cab from his doorstep. He was stone-cold passed out. My coworker, Jack, took the front while I sat in the rear, ensuring the boss stayed upright. Jack said,

"Reach into his pocket and grab his wallet to pay for the taxi."

"Excuse me?"

"Reach into his pocket and get his wallet."

The bill was $30, but I hadn't drunk enough to dig through his pockets.

"Sorry, I can't do that. You're essential. You do it when we get there."

After we arrived, I flagged down a taxi to take me home while enjoying the memories of my first blow-out business dinner. Little did I know I would join more than a thousand blow-outs over my career.

The next day, I said nothing to the other workers. Jack didn't show up, though he drank little. He used the cop-out excuse of being unable to down *gaoliang* to avoid the roulette round of *ganbeis*.

I took everything they had.

About noon, the owner appeared. As he walked in, looking disheveled, he told me to follow him and close the door. I assumed he would fire me for speaking Chinese. Who knows what etiquette I might have broken because of my inexperience and sloppiness? He asked me if I enjoyed myself. "Here it comes." But to the contrary, I impressed him with my *ganbei* skills. He wanted to use me at dinners to get others drunk. I could even come in late. That sounded fantastic. First, women were paying me to speak with them, and now a guy was going to pay me to drink for him. My luck was changing, and I gained a renewed interest.

XVII

I lived in Taiwan for a year and a half before taking off to the southern part to visit Rich. He told me his American girlfriend kept him on a tight leash, and he wanted to lower my expectations. I doubted he could stop if I continued.

I rode the bus, and once I discovered they had installed toilets, I bought a few Miller tallboys (a rare commodity) to continue where I ended the night before. They called these long-distance coaches "chicken buses" because of how the drivers drove. It was a dangerous game of bravery.

When I rode the chicken buses, I found it was better to do it sloshed.

I arrived at my destination four hours later, ready for another drunken escapade. After sitting on the bus for so long, I planned to hit the town running. Rich said he had promised his girlfriend we would drink at home. We had no choice but to pick up a couple of bottles of whiskey and head to his place. He lived on the outskirts, almost farmland, renting a two-story house.

I met his girl and could tell she suspected other Americans were too American. Some people living overseas had that attitude. To dilute my "American-ness," she invited over a couple from the kindergarten they taught at. They were Bohemian and looking for the "real Taiwan experience." I would not have expected Rich to hang with this crowd, but we all routinely readjusted.

He had lived on the edge for as long as I knew him (not long). It shocked me to see him tamed, but my arrival sparked something.

A few months prior, I alluded to the girl from whom I took the trade job that it would be amusing to dose in Taiwan with so many off-the-wall situations. One day, I received a letter with no return address. Inside were a few paper squares wrapped in tinfoil. This would be the perfect venue to experiment. Rich was game, but his gal abstained. She became upset with how I had disrupted their relationship. I knew things would get worse.

As the evening progressed and the whiskey bottles emptied, he argued with her, releasing pent-up aggression. I had that effect on people. They were yelling on the front lawn. I considered calming them down, but the other couple warned me it would not be a good idea.

They were fighting because Rich would not have returned to his old ways if I hadn't visited.

I passed out on the sofa in the early morning. But before that, I was a menace with the music. The other couple planned to stay but returned home instead. Two bottles of whiskey will do that. The neighbors phoned the landlord. In the morning, he walked in, looked at the scene, grabbed a large wedding photo hanging on the wall, and exited.

It was too much for his wedding picture to bear.

When I got up, I made plenty of apologies. Rich said, "Bro, no need. I don't like her friends, and the landlord is a prick. You broke nothing. No damage was done. Next time, we have to drink at your place."

I still felt guilty about causing a rift. I made up for it by cleaning. If Rich stayed with his girlfriend, it would be my last chance to hang with him.

Another brother lost to the sands of time.

XVIII

During my final six months in Taiwan, things came unglued. Someone was warning me my time had expired. Teaching and working at the trading company drained me of spirit. I approached my goal of a full year at the trade corp. when the boss skipped out on the Chinese New Year's bonus. That was the last straw. Although a critical bid fell through, I kept the suppliers at bay. I already accomplished what I set out to do. It was pointless to stay.

Inside look at a Chinese company: Done

An acting stint as a stereotypical silent foreign partner: Done

Business dinner and karaoke chops: Done

Then, somebody stole my motorbike from outside my apartment. I purchased a lock but got lazy. Even though I received the cycle as a gift, it devastated me.

When I walked into the police station to file a report, they said locating a stolen moped on an island with millions of them was not likely. But, once again, a student came to the rescue and lent me a scooter. She now assumed we were dating. I also felt obliged to hang out, which further misled her.

A few months after I reported my bike stolen, the cops found it one block over. Someone cut the wires. It needed to be repaired, but otherwise, it worked. I handed over the other motorbike, relieving me of the pressure.

Then, I got sick—just like my Beijing illness. I caught the bug sitting in a bar with Apache. A snack cart selling morsels that went well with beer stopped by. I recognized some food, but it was dark.

Rule #12: Trust your gut.

My gut advised me not to eat things off the wagon, but my belly, full of the *baijiu* I drank at dinner, said go ahead. I required food and ignored **Rules #1 and 12.** The spicy beef slices tasted great, and I continued to nibble on them. A few days later, I had chills and couldn't keep anything down or in. Apache called me to meet up, but I was deadly sick.

The illness put me out for two weeks and made teaching problematic. In the middle of class, I would sweat and have the impulse to rush to the toilet. I concentrated on keeping my shit together and attempted to hold it until the break when I searched for a safe bathroom. The unisex squatter at the school terrified me, and I prayed to make it through.

Rule #13: Always know where the best toilet is for peace of mind.

This rule served me well, and the people traveling with me who did not go through the tolerance buildup, I did. I had a few close calls, but never a disaster. This second battle did not help my kidneys, but I felt young. Nothing would stop me.

The realization that I was wrong came later.

Finally, the BMW woman pursued me more than before. I informed her I no longer had time for meals. She thought I had lied to her. In retaliation, she dropped on me the thing I dreaded:

"I want to tell my husband I like somebody else."

A chill ran up my spine, and my face froze. Her spouse was "involved in the black market." I didn't need this drama at twenty-four years of age. We had only met for lunch, and it should have been okay. But then she started showing up at the clubs with her sister. It concerned me her husband would follow them, and I informed her to stay away. However, that did not discourage her.

She said her *lao gong* (husband) didn't care. I wanted her to remain calm, so I had no choice but to keep meeting. The deteriorating situation caused me to be paranoid and edgy. I needed a way out because I couldn't sleep. Apache, my ace in the hole, disappeared, and I never saw him again. My Nigerian brothers departed as well. My best option was to take off, too.

It was easy to leave my job at the trade corp. I strolled in and said thank you and goodbye. For my English classes, I told them I had an emergency at home and had to resign. Next, I bought a ticket to Hong Kong and told my flatmates I would be back in thirty days.

I left Taiwan with mixed emotions. During my two years, I enjoyed massive fun and learned a lot. The newness stimulated me. But with no long-term prospects and the BMW woman closing in, it was time to leave.

I returned after a month to get the rest of my stuff, and my flatmates said the BMW woman had regularly called, trying to catch me picking up. Eventually, she gave up, so I figured the coast was clear. When I packed my stuff, I heard a buzz from downstairs. It rang again and again. It had to be her. Did she catch me by chance, or did she wait every day? Nevertheless, she had me cornered.

While I packed, I never turned on the lights. Now, it was dark, and I waited for the buzzing to stop. It did, but then the phone rang. The nearest pay phone was down the street, so it was my chance to escape. I hustled out and ducked down the alley without turning back. Later, I met up with my flatmate and hit the clubs until morning, then headed to the airport. Everything worked out, but I kept looking over my shoulder.

Thankfully, I made it out in one piece. I made many upstanding friends and enjoyed this tour. It seemed like the right amount of time.

Now, I took another leap of faith and vacated my high-paying teaching gigs for the unknown.

CHAPTER THREE

HONG KONG:
LIVIN' ON A SHOESTRING

After safely escaping from the clutches of the BMW woman and the other things that overwhelmed my Taipei life, I prepared to start fresh in Hong Kong. I had adequate funds to last three months and the tail end of a ticket to the U.S., expiring in August (1994). That gave me ninety days to snag a job. If unsuccessful, I would head back to the suburbs of Chicago. Nothing wrong with that; I just thought I had another destiny.

When I arrived, I had to live as economically as possible, which meant Chung King Mansions (CKM). Once I exited the airport bus, I singled out a less obtrusive room sherpa and followed him up on the elevator. I requested the cheapest accommodation until I found a short-term apartment. They gave me what I asked for—a bed for HKD 55 a night ($7). My room had sixteen bunks, and I filled the last slot, a foot below the massive air conditioner cooling the entire room.

Hong Kong was ninety-nine degrees Fahrenheit with ninety-nine percent humidity, but I froze and walked out to thaw.

The other guys were backpackers from around the world. They took a pit stop at the crossroads of Asia while I tried to start a career. I had nothing to gain from talking with them, so I kept to myself. Because I spoke little, someone said I was Greek, so people nicknamed me "The Greek." A couple of travelers inquired about visiting Greece, and I played along.

"Are you the Greek?"

"Yeah, sure," I replied in my best Zorba accent without saying much of anything of use for somebody wishing to head there.

No one knew me; I could be whoever they wanted me to be.

With my sleeping arrangements set, I visited the New Delhi Club for some tandoori and vindaloo, but no pub crawling. The following morning, I woke early and made my way to McDonald's. Taiwan McDonald's didn't serve breakfast, and I craved an egg McMuffin, hash browns, and coffee.

While I dug into my meal, I flipped through the paper, searching for apartment listings. The only flats available for my budget of $900 a month (HKD 7,000) were on another island named Lamma. I took the ferry out to investigate. The ride lasted longer than I expected. When I disembarked, I glanced at some listings and then got back on the ferry. It was too far to live and network at the bars while returning at the stroke of midnight like Cinderella.

The next day, I saw an ad for a room in a shared flat in Causeway Bay (CWB), an essential shopping district on Hong Kong Island. The area had multiple restaurants, movie theaters, and grocery stores. It was a convenient location, and I rushed to talk to the landlord. He divided the apartment into four singles and a communal toilet/shower. After asking about my background and photocopying my passport, he rented me a room at HKD 3,500 ($450) a month.

My flatmates were girls, which would have been an excellent opportunity (*Three's Company*), but being destitute, my sole focus was finding employment.

Now that I had an address and a contact number, I sent out resumes. The clock ticked; I needed to move fast. Americans could only work with a sponsor, while British and Australians got one-year work visas on entry.

We received tourist visas valid for thirty days.

My language skills made me stand out as a candidate for gigs on the mainland. Although locals spoke Cantonese and English flawlessly, I had better Mandarin than others. Plus, I desired to move to the mainland, but they didn't want to leave H.K.

In 1994, the local English newspaper, *South China Morning Post*, had over two hundred pages of wanted ads in the Saturday edition. Two hundred pages! It was the most significant part. However, the majority of the posts looked to fill finance positions or Country Manager—two hundred pages and not a single job for me.

Whenever I opened the paper, I hoped it would be my lucky day. I would go to McDonald's for breakfast and free coffee refills while I scanned their public copy of the newspaper to save a few coins. Every bit helped. I also gathered the addresses of American companies to send resumes.

These were the darkest days of my adventure. Looking for work discouraged me, and searching for employment behind the eight ball was worse. I refused to give up. Every day I lacked a career, I was closer to going home.

When not sending resumes and scanning the ads, I wandered the streets. It was the cheapest way to experience a city. I walked wherever the roads took me, like a nomad. I aimed to stay out so that when I came back, there would be a message. On every occasion I returned to no calls, I felt depressed.

For my meals, I bought instant noodles, even though I abhorred them. I used the extra cash to treat myself to healthy amounts of a bargain swill called Skol. It was palatable ice-cold, and I enjoyed every drop after walking miles in the heat.

I frequently patronized a live music bar called The Wanch, a venue for local bands that packed in customers until they flowed out into the street. The music ranged from covers to originals. Live music was a crucial change from the synthesized disco I attempted to exorcise from my soul. Because of my low cash flow, I only visited during happy hour or store fronted 7-11 for a few brews before returning to the pub.

I often drank with a young Australian cat named Pete. He labored on a job site with other Ozzies. They came from work, and they partied hard. Pete ran on the Wanchai Hash House Harriers (WH3) and persuaded me to join. I was not a runner, but he said,

"Don't worry, mate. It's a drinking club with a running problem."

When he put it that way, I had to join. It sounded like an opportunity to get my mind off the search and meet people.

At the Hash, individuals ran or strolled a path set by a Hare, who volunteered to lay the trail with flour, chalk, or hell money (fake money burnt at funerals). After an hour of cooling down and drinking, the designated Hash Master called for a circle to be formed. He/she would then lampoon runners with light jokes and insults while making them consume punishment beverages labeled "down-downs." The harshness depended on the group and the local culture. The Wanchai Hash had families, so things never went too far. As a group, they were more welcoming.

While I lived in Taiwan, I read about the Hash, but my flatmate convinced me they were hardcore runners. When Pete mentioned all-you-can-drink cold beer, I looked for my running shoes. The runs weren't impossible, but they would have been easier if I had quit smoking.

Once the Hash finished, I wound up at The Wanch, or a cheaper place named The Beer Castle, until I ran through my budget.

The Wanch occasionally held open mic night, and I drank with Pete when he got up to sing. He was alright. One of his signature songs was "American Pie," and he sang the entire song.

Pete knew I applied for jobs. A few times, I showed up in the middle of his set, and he asked over the mic, "Hey Randall, how's the job search?"

Patrons would turn to look, and I would shake my head no. Sometimes, I received a pity pint, which eased the pain.

I valued my time at The Wanch but left as soon as happy hour concluded. At $8, the pints were too much. It was back to my jail cell to drink swill and watch the two English TV channels. I had to stay steadfast and stretch my dough.

Once my thirty days expired, I left and returned after I had an entry stamp from another place. I headed back to Taiwan for my first excursion to retrieve the rest of my stuff while escaping the BMW woman.

On my second trip, I encountered an opportunity that nearly changed my future. Although I could come back the same day, I stayed to receive an injection of adventure. Most of the south spoke Cantonese, so I proceeded further inland to reach a Mandarin-speaking area. Guangzhou had a mixture of both dialects, so I moved in that direction. I rode the MTR (H.K. subway) to the KCR (H.K. Train) to the border and walked across. From there, I sat on a long-distance bus to Guangzhou Train Station (four hours). The station handled the massive influx of workers. It acted as the door to the future.

When I reached the city, I headed to the White Swan Hotel, the only five-star in town and the location of the U.S. Consulate. I read in my Lonely Planet that there were many cheap hostels outside the Swan, and I found one, but I shared a room with two guys.

Next, I roamed the city. There were motorbikes everywhere, similar to Taipei, and the air tasted heavy. I selected a restaurant popular with the backpacker crowd. They served foreigner-friendly Chinese dishes but nothing spicy. I hoped to discover a Sichuan restaurant, so I had a beer and explored more.

It was a good thing I waited; I spied a Sichuan joint away from the beaten path. Finally, I would dig into some flavorful dishes. The food brought back memories.

The following day, I accompanied my roommates for beers and talked them into going to the Sichuan restaurant for dinner. They had begun a three-month backpacking trip across China and didn't speak Mandarin. I was jealous. They followed their Lonely Planet to wherever looked interesting. It was a journey I needed to take. While we waited, they attempted to talk me into joining them. They needed someone to lead. Under the influence, I agreed, but then I wised up. The best thing was to continue my job search. I would've returned home after three months if I had traveled with them. Plus, the guys preferred to go cheaper than I wanted. Their budget did not include alcohol, which seemed insane.

It was now August, and I had thirty days left. I did a few interviews, but most businesses lacked operations on the mainland.

One company offered a position in Hong Kong with a starting salary on the low end of an expat benchmark, so low I could barely maintain my present pathetic life.

Then, while sitting at McDonald's, I noticed an ad that changed everything. It read:

"Are you a Native English speaker, preferably from North America? Do you speak some Chinese and have trade experience?"

It described the position of a 'Company Liaison' based in China for an importer of footwear. I was unaware of what a Company Liaison did, but I was qualified. Although I had never stepped foot in a shoe factory, I had worked in factories, and they should be the same, more or less. Even with my credentials, my age became a problem. Firms expected expats to be middle-aged. But the People's Republic was unique. Many Western businesses didn't know how to approach it. They needed young guys with no family willing to endure the hardships, even welcome them. I knew it, but the companies I applied to weren't keen.

Anyway, I sent my resume.

A couple of weeks later, I received a call asking me to come for an interview. I had forgotten about the company and prepared to move back. Two weeks was a long period for the unemployed. I assumed I didn't get the job and continued searching. The phone call was a welcome surprise.

I jumped at the opportunity.

The office was in the Sheung Shui District, on the Hong Kong/ China border. I underestimated the time it would take to get there. Plus, it was hot and sticky, and I was sweating. Since I didn't have a mobile phone (nobody did), I waited until I got off the train to call. I said,

"I'm an hour late. We should cancel the interview. I feel miserable about it, but nothing is working out today."

The guy on the other end told me to go to McDonald's. He would meet me there.

When I entered through the doors of the Golden Arches, a friendly-looking dude walked up and introduced himself as Bryon.

"Thanks for making the extra effort. Come on."

I followed him through the thick crowd to the kiddie area on the other side. At first, I thought he was joking, but he made a beeline for the open table. I squeezed into the miniature plastic chair with my suit and tie on. They secured the seats, and our knees bumped against each other, awkwardly close.

At least they had air-conditioning.

Bryon was the GM, and he questioned me about my background. But I really wanted to know, "What does a Country Liaison do?" Before he could answer, the meeting ended when the kids pushed us out, and he had another interview.

"Now that I can find the place, I will reschedule. After all, I am overstepping."

"Don't worry about it. We have time. The other candidate won't get the job. His chances aren't good," he said with a chuckle and a wink. It seemed I had the position. Yeah, forget about the other guy!

Bryon took me to the office, tucked inside a typical Hong Kong housing complex with rows of tall buildings arranged around a public area. The flat looked average-size (slightly bigger than a shoebox), nicely furnished, and modern. Bryon lived in one of the three bedrooms, much better than my present quarters. He had a two-person bar in the living room, and we sat there. The next applicant stood outside, waiting in the corridor. A neighbor with a small dog locked up inside made a ton of noise. The pup generated an annoying high-pitched "uurruurr, uuurruuurr" sound that echoed off the cool, marble slabbed walls, amplifying it. Just when I thought it had stopped, the dog started again.

It sucked for the dude in the hall, but it was a dog-eat-dog world.

Bryon noticed on my resume that I had joined a fraternity.

"Can you drink?"

"I'm pretty good at it and getting better."

"Can you sing?"

"I sang in Taiwan."

"Good, you will do a lot of drinking and singing. In China, YOU ARE THE MOVIE STAR."

Imagine that! I knew that feeling and had a movie star's name.

"What's the job?"

"You have to check on the quality of the shoes. Don't worry that you lack experience. It's easy. Act like you know. You also need to eat and drink with the trade companies and factories. Drink with everyone. Drink every night. You're the movie star."

"Sounds great. How much does it pay?"

"Well, there's bad news and good news. The bad news is the pay is low for expat standards. However, you'll live in a hotel, and your meals, telephone calls, and transportation will be covered. You can bank your salary."

Forget about the salary, PAY FOR MY MEALS? Free food seemed better than cash for a man living off instant noodles and canned soup.

Where do I sign up?

Before we finished, I asked, "What about the guy waiting?"

"Oh shit! I forgot about him. Hide in the back. I need five minutes. I want to be nice," he said with that characteristic grin.

After he finished, I prepared to leave. Bryon said, "The job is almost yours. I need to meet another person and will call you in two days."

That sounded wonderful, but it wasn't a sure thing. Why did he have to say, "Almost?"

So I waited, tick. . . tock. The date on my ticket approached. I regretted thinking I snagged the gig.

I went to the movies and strolled the malls, hoping to find a message when I returned. What was the hold-up? I was perfect. But I continued to wait.

On the second day, Bryon phoned.

"The position is still open. Do you want it?" He asked me like I had already passed.

"Of course I want it."

"Excellent. We're going to China the day after tomorrow. Gabriel, my assistant, will tell you where to get the visa. I'm looking forward to working with you."

That was it. After all the empty belly evenings, sleepless nights, and depressing times, I had locked down a position. I no longer needed to return, failing to fly. Finally, I reached the light at the end of the tunnel.

It was time to celebrate. I ate soup at a restaurant, not from a can—no more kimchi noodles.

My return was complete.

The adventure continued.

CHAPTER FOUR

KAIPING: ROLLER SKATING

I met Bryon at the China/HK Ferry Terminal. Since he did not provide guidance, I showed up wearing a suit.

"Why did you wear a suit? We're traveling to a factory. It's going to be hot."

I could have used that information beforehand, but I made the best of it, dropped the coat, and rolled up my sleeves.

Our destination was Kaiping, Guangdong. We took a slow boat, and I marked that off my list. The ride gave Bryon ample time to describe my role. He wanted to teach me the ropes of business in China. I paid attention while he unloaded his wisdom on me. He loved to reiterate,

"Remember, you are the movie star."

He said it so often I believed it.

We boarded the boat and sat in the VIP cabin. I thought, "We travel like movie stars, too." This was one of his secrets: pay the additional charge for the VIP cabin, and we had the whole place to "stretch out." I couldn't see the benefit of this. We never ate their complimentary meal; there were no tables to work on, and we waited for everybody to disembark. After a gigantic wave, I would roll off the sofa. The only advantage seemed to be a lack of noise.

The company driver met us on the other side of customs. As we drove away, I witnessed a group crowding a guy who had stolen a bike. He remained on the ground with the cycle around his neck while bystanders hit and kicked him. It was a trial by an angry mob.

Don't steal a bicycle here: Their neighborhood watch is killer.

My next impression was that the roads appeared worse than the most potholed streets in Chicago. It took two hours on bumpy trails to reach the hotel from Jiangmen Port. It didn't help that the toy truck we rode in had little matchbox wheels and no shocks. My bones ached as if I had just gotten off a rickety wooden roller-coaster by the time we reached the city.

Bryon proclaimed we had to visit the workshop tomorrow. It came down to those miserable roads. He said the journey would be too perilous in the dark. He had alternative plans. There was no telling where this adventure would lead. I had a similar feeling as a student; anything seemed possible. I could say the same about any place, but something magnetic about Chinese culture drew me in because it was unique and untouched.

According to Bryon, the hotel we arrived at was the only halfway decent one in town. He spent a year living in Kaiping before setting up a company. It was tall and run-down, similar to most guesthouses. The hallways were dim, as if the power got shut off. Bryon advised me to drop off my stuff and meet him downstairs.

When I found my room, my key didn't work. I returned to the lobby and saw him chatting with the front desk staff. He saw me and said,

"That was quick. I want you to meet some people."

I dropped my backpack and followed him through the corridors into the rear of the building. We wound up in a room with five young ladies reclining on bunk beds. The girls worked for the nightclub. They perked up when Bryon wandered in. While I speculated whether we were getting into trouble, he attempted to sweet-talk them to go out on the town. He persuaded three, and we headed out.

Kaiping and China as a whole had little entertainment. Expats (none here) drank heavily or found other ways to pass the time, such as drinking heavily. Bryon told me when he stayed in Kaiping, he dropped water balloons from the roof, freaking out the pedestrians. Yes, it was cruel, but later, I realized how tedious living alone in a small town would be. I took the drinking route to ease the boredom, but I had crazier moments.

We squeezed into the same sardine can truck, and Bryon gave directions while sitting in the back with the gals. I glanced out the window to look for something remarkable. Much of Guangdong resembled a continuous stream of storefront strip malls selling furniture or machinery. The avenues looked the same, with construction everywhere. The only thing that mattered was the building of more factories.

Guangdong had an extensive range of things they ate, including dogs. We saw entire streets specializing in canine cuisine. They kept the dogs in cages outside the restaurants for gastronomes to pick the one they desired, like the lobster tank at Red Lobster. Did a German Shepard taste different from a Labrador? Did a wild dog have a gamier flavor? I never found out.

We ate at a place with monkeys in cages instead of dogs. The primates reminded me of a video where they trapped one with its head above the table. Then, they cracked open the skull to eat the brains. I guessed the video was fake until now.

But dinner was a few hours away. Instead, we ended up at a colossal open-front building blasting repetitive European disco. When I exited the car, I realized we had arrived at a roller rink, yes—roller skating. Bryon and the ladies enthusiastically changed their shoes while I sat this one out. I couldn't believe I spent my first day watching my boss skate in circles with three girls. What was I doing? It felt as if they had transported me back to junior high, and I waited for them to do the hokey pokey. Bryon smiled and winked at me as he passed. This continued for an hour before the women returned to the nightclub, and we proceeded to dinner.

After eating, we relocated to the cabaret, where WE were the movie stars. The club was a banquet room with tables surrounding a dance floor. As the finest hotel, this had to be the first choice for wedding parties and over-the-top after-dinner festivities. Before deluxe karaoke rooms opened and locals had loads of cash to blow on Remy, Johnny, and fruit plates, bands and singers entertained. Listening to some characters sing in the karaoke, I decided more should have left it to the professionals.

Bryon walked in, leading the way. The hostess, wearing a velvet Chinese *qipao* with embroidered flowers, greeted him like someone famous. He flirted with her as she directed us to the front table while the show waited. This felt similar to the scene in *Goodfellas*, where they paraded through the kitchen while staff scurried to set a table for them. The other customers enjoying their fruit and drinks speculated about who these American movie stars were. Some Chinese said Bryon resembled Tom Cruise. He had five years on me but swaggered like someone older.

We sat, and the three roller girls, dressed up in some pretty awful satin prom dresses, came over to help eat the fruit plate, getting no love from the two of us. The girls wore badges with numbers to "purchase them" for a dance or have them sit with you and fill you with fruit. I grew accustomed to the fruit and drinking thing, but I was uncomfortable being fed.

For all his awkward mannerisms and unusual comments, Bryon knew how to work the system. He learned Chinese songs and sang them by heart. People rarely got up to sing with a professional singer, but foreigners were free to do as we pleased. We were strange souls who did the unpredictable. I was a novice, but he was a pro.

The master of ceremonies completed a few songs and turned to Bryon to ask him to sing. Everybody applauded. He smiled, waving like he didn't warrant it when strolling over to tell them what to play. He looked like Sinatra or Tom Jones. The band played "The Moon Represents My Heart." Bryon sang in better Chinese than he spoke while walking the floor. The crowd loved it, as did the cheering section at our table. He glanced at me and winked, implying, "This is how you do it." That was helpful advice. He taught me how necessary it was to perfect a few Chinese tunes.

After he finished, people showered him with flower baskets.

He set the bar high.

Rule #14: Learn local songs and dialects to create *"Guanxi"* and credibility.

Guanxi—I'm confident countless chapters and books are available on the subject.

Cultivating *guanxi* was an essential part of doing everything. You can translate it as, "You scratch my back, and when the time comes, I will scratch yours." Still, it went further with individuals doing things to have someone owe them—not much different from *The Godfather*.

Life in China revolved around your *guanxi* choices and calling in those favors when you needed help with the government, police, health care, or school. Without it, nothing got done, or it was done at a plodding pace. With it, you could accomplish anything.

Early the next day, we set off to conquer the dirt roads and stop by the factory. It was a government workshop acquired by a Hong Kong trading company. They made cheap canvas vulcanized shoes called CVOs. I swiftly memorized all the shoe terminology. It was imperative to seem like I knew what I was doing, or I would be unimportant.

Vulcanized shoe factories were loud, with an abundance of white powder to keep the raw rubber from sticking to the other sheets. The production line was a continuous conveyor belt in which the separate parts moved from one station to another. They put the shoes on racks at the end of the line, with the shoe last (shaped like a foot).

Next, they shoved the entire lot into a baking oven. When the product cooled, the workers threw the metal lasts into steel bins. "Clang!" "Clang!" It was a non-stop, ear-shattering clamor you could hear long before entering the workshops.

The process looked simple, but it required skill. Chinese factories applied vast swaths of glue around the shoe. They thought the consumer wanted to see plenty of adhesion, symbolizing quality. If they hid the glue, locals would not trust the product. We convinced them the opposite was true for Americans. This became tougher than expected, as the workers had no idea what a U.S. department store resembled. Most purchased their stuff from vendors, who peddled goods off a tarp spread on the floor. Try explaining to someone earning a dollar a day about ensuring white shoes stayed clean or why the shoe box needed to look new. They sat with blank stares.

We finished an introductory walk through the production lines and inspected the packaged products. The rest was small talk, cigarettes, and tea. This would become the pattern for factory visits: the joyous arrival, followed by the manager throwing cigarettes at me, some exceptional tea, and a stroll through the workshops. This plant had a boss who enjoyed smoking out of a tall bong. I thought he passed it around when visitors showed up, but he only smoked tobacco and kept it to himself.

After the niceties and goodbyes, we headed to the port to catch the ferry. Bryon booked the VIP cabin again, but a bride and groom party coming from the wedding joined us. The bride wore a puffy white wedding dress, and they all reeked of alcohol. We stuck it out, though they made plenty of noise.

The groom was boisterous and deep red, almost purplish. He glanced at us and reiterated, "Slorry, Slorry." He slurred his words and did not enjoy the ride. The waves hit the older boats much harder than the modern hydrofoils.

I mentioned to Bryon, "He's gonna lose his lunch. He has the look. We should prepare to leave."

Sure enough, a few waves later, the guy discharged the contents of his stomach onto the carpet. As his bride bent over to pick up their bags, the second round arrived and projected on her, making a horrible mess of regurgitated red wine on her dress. Without a word, we picked up our bags and moved to economy.

All in all, it seemed like an odd twenty-four hours with the company.

Upon returning to my apartment cell, I had a proper meal with my expense account. I could have gone to a fancy restaurant, but I needed a pizza. Coming from Chicago, I had high standards, but as with everything, I accepted what they had available. And so, I dug into the best cardboard-based pie sans the seafood and Thousand Island sauce while resting in my cave, wondering where this job would lead.

Over the next five years, I traveled to Kaiping to inspect the goods and train staff. The hotels and life improved, as in all of China's cities. I will never forget when the first three-star opened. They had a restaurant with something in the morning for a Western stomach. Not going to the factory hungover on an empty belly was good.

They also served wild animals. Near the Romanesque staircase to the second floor, they had more exhibits than the zoos of small towns. No joke. They had live chickens, birds with white plumed fur (think Dr. Seuss), ducks, and other birds I failed to recognize. There were numerous snakes to choose from. Civet cat? Whatever that was. (They blamed civet cat for starting the SARS outbreak.) Okay, but owl? Wasn't that illegal? The seafood selection also provided top-notch aquatic lifeforms such as groupers, gooey ducts, shellfish, and critters deep from the ocean. It was quite a spread of proteins. I assumed these gourmet delights were purely characteristic of Guangdong, but in the mid-'90s, I spotted the trend in most cities. Factories brought me to these unique restaurants, not underground but unmarked with no menus. SARS ended this business in 2003. Two years later, they returned more prevalent than before. It was expensive, and that was the point. They gave me the finest, which I appreciated even if I didn't want to eat it.

Kaiping grew fast once the infrastructure improved. Before, it would take hours to reach a factory fifty miles away. Once they paved the streets and the tugboats transformed into hydrofoils, these Pearl River Delta (PRD) cities took off. There was a strong Hong Kong influence, and everything in the PRD resembled H.K.

As the cost of living and wages increased, factory prices rose, pushing us further inland.

After the '90s, I never visited again.

CHAPTER FIVE

NANJING: THAT CONFOUNDED BRIDGE!

O ur next stop was a place I knew well: Nanjing. I returned a success, but I knew no one to tell.

We planned to visit a factory a hundred kilometers northeast in Yangzhou. Nanjing was the closest landing strip. Because of the travel time, we stayed a night prior to seeing the production lines. That was an excellent opportunity to stop by old haunts.

I met Bryon at Kai Tak Airport in H. K. He surprised me with an economy class ticket when I expected the VIP treatment. He said he avoided first class seating on short flights because pilots hitching a ride sat up front, snoring or abruptly moving the seats back. The rear of the aircraft remained vacant.

"Not many travelers fly to China."

I witnessed that on my last trip.

"Don't check in luggage. It takes too long to retrieve."

Again, it would have been better to have known this beforehand. I didn't have a chance to pick up a suitcase. Instead, I carried my oversized backpack.

"Always get on the plane first to take up the overhead space."

He already said few individuals flew, but I understood his point. Plus, I had my big-ass bag to store.

As a consolation for dragging my backpack through customs, Bryon got me into the VIP airline club he bought a membership in despite flying on a competitor airline.

"Buy the club membership, enjoy the fruits of first class, but endure economy seating on a state-run airline for an hour or two."

Yes, we had red carpet treatment. It opened my eyes to what life as a traveling manager could be like. It sure beat how I traveled before.

We landed, and modernization had yet to start. As we sat in a taxi, I flashed back to my twenty-year-old self cruising the same streets. Things changed unhurriedly in old China, especially in the second-tier cities and beyond. Nowadays, you might not recognize a town you left for a short period.

Bryon stayed at the top hotel to show the trade corp. he was the boss. In Nanjing, it was still The Jinling. Previously, I could only afford to grab something from the coffee shop. But now, I slept in the most refined luxury that China offered. It felt incredible exiting the taxi and pulling up to the registration counter to check in instead of changing money and leaving.

I concluded Bryon knew little about the city. Therefore, I recommended a restaurant. This was my fifth day working for the company, but I sensed I would be the person managing the arrangements. This wasn't part of my job description, but it seemed natural with my focus on the details.

Most travelers preferred to be informed about their destination or what to eat while in an exotic country. They went with the flow. That was not my nature. I seized control and ensured each trip was smooth.

Rule #15: From the choice of hotel to transportation, understand the full itinerary and who handles what.

Sometimes, agents focused on the wrong details, while I understood what people wanted. **Rule #15** saved me frequently. It benefitted not only the person I traveled with but me, too. Once things developed, keeping track of the best travel routes became harder, but traveling grew easier.

I met Bryon, and we walked to the restaurant. I picked a hotpot place, something I missed from my Beijing days, but I didn't expect authenticity. Close enough had to do. Hotpot ranked high on my favorite dish list, but Bryon didn't care for it. He liked steamed river fish, boiled prawns, and white rice.

After checking into my room, I confirmed the venue served the right dishes for him.

Rule #16: Scope out the area for the choicest eateries. Ensure the restaurant has items suitable for your companions. A good meal makes people happy. A bad one increases the tension.

Whenever I stopped by an unfamiliar city, I explored. I checked out as many restaurants and hotels as possible. Knowing where to get a decent club sandwich in Ningbo or the latest lodging in Hangzhou was the information I specialized in. I became obsessed with knowing each city's inside knowledge and trying all the unique places. But I met my match in the 2000s after an explosion of venues nationwide. I no longer maintained that high standard of identifying everything but kept trying.

After dinner, we decided to survey the nightlife. I recalled seeing a disco outside the hotel I stayed at two years ago, so we wandered in that direction.

Amazingly, we found the joint, and it still operated. Inside were all the bells and whistles you expected, such as flashing lights, smoke machines, and an over-talkative DJ. We strolled in and secured a hi-table facing the dance floor. We only drank a few pitchers with the food, but Bryon had a low tolerance and appeared buzzed. He tried to chat up the servers and anyone alone. Any girl in the club came with a pack of others. I detected a potential problem and kept my eyes open while Bryon attempted to dance with some girls in a circle.

Soon, a gang of guys filled in the space left by Bryon. I told them my friend would return, but they could remain until then. The locals outnumbered us, fifty to two. We did not need to cause trouble with those odds.

When Bryon came back, he told them to move. They slid over but pushed up against him. Bryon took it as encroaching and said, "Fuck off," among other things. They most likely did not comprehend everything, but they only needed to hear the word "Fuck" to figure out he had cursed them. I think all students of foreign languages want to learn the bad words. The "F-word" ranked at the top of the list. It was best to avoid using it in situations such as this.

Rule #17: If outnumbered, do not start a fight.

Bryon was ex-army but not a huge guy. He seemed oblivious to what was happening behind his back. I stepped in between him and the crowd to defuse things. There were five or six guys and more behind who would have relished the opportunity to stomp two foreigners. To avoid that, I offered to buy beers. They told me they had no problem with me. They wanted Bryon. I would not allow that; he'd just given me a job.

While I negotiated with the talkative one, another snuck around the table, grabbed a broken beer bottle, and sliced Bryon's arm. That escalated things. We got surrounded until security directed us to a space near the door. I complained, but they said, "You had better leave."

What? WE GOT KICKED OUT. What kind of justice was that?

I grumbled, but we took it as a sign and returned to the hotel to find the infirmary. He didn't require stitches, but it ruined his shirt, and he had a cut. China felt safe because most citizens stayed home at night. That changed as society developed.

The next day, our agent met us in the lobby to go to Yangzhou, four hours away by car. Historically, Yangzhou was a wealthy merchant city first settled during the Spring and Autumn Period from 770 to 475 BC. I recognized it for its most famous dish, Yangzhou fried rice. Other towns concocted their own, but eateries often served the Yangzhou one.

I enjoyed fried rice and perfected my own variant. This trip was the student meeting the master.

Yangzhou was also famous for its toy factories. On this inaugural visit, we arranged to inspect one of the largest in the country. Going to a toy factory was like visiting Santa's workshop except for the couple hundred Chinese worker elves, who questioned why someone bought the products they produced. How do you explain why shoppers spent their hard-earned cash on a pair of slippers shaped like bananas or dinosaur feet? The owners didn't care as long as the orders kept coming and they earned suitcases full of money.

Before starting off to Yangzhou, we had to leave Nanjing, which meant crossing the big Nanjing Bridge.

In 1994, Nanjing had a population of 3.5 million. I would have predicted a city of that size to have multiple arteries leading in and out, but it appeared the only one accessible to us was the Nanjing Yangtze Bridge. The bridge was 4,589 meters (2.8 miles), with two lanes in each direction but no shoulder for breakdowns. To be fair, China had almost no cars when they built it from 1960 to 1968. It seemed adequate.

When finished, it became the first significant bridge designed and constructed by the Chinese and the third to cross the Yangtze. In those respects, they created a marvel of engineering. However, it turned into a nightmare, as it was the ONLY bridge. Throw in ancient buses breaking down, and we had the makings for a disaster.

How bad? It took fifteen minutes to cross on a rare day without traffic in the early '90s. Usually, crossing the bridge in less than an hour was a success. But as the number of cars increased, bus lines got added, and the caravans of trucks arrived bringing building materials for the city, the average time grew to two hours, with possible three-hour crossings. Most of the cars I rode in had bad A/C. The only option to stay cool was to roll down the windows. Imagine being stuck on a bridge in the heat of a brutal Nanjing summer, with no A/C and no way to know when traffic would move. Then you get the picture.

With the windows down, I fended off the beggars. Once they spotted a foreigner, they swarmed and attacked. If that happened, the agent shooed them away. They didn't want me to witness this side of the PRC. If I gave them money, they would surround our car, thus further irritating my handlers to the point where **they** gave a dollar.

On one regrettable trip, it took five hours to cross. Five hours! Buses broke down in both directions, causing mayhem. Whenever a traffic jam formed, the appropriate measure would be to wait, and someone would clear up the problem. That's the rational thing to do. In China, cars squeeze in any space available, including the opposite side of the road. If they filled the street, there would be no way to pass—this should make sense to the other drivers. But, when crowd mentality set in, no one wanted to be caught waiting. As a result, vehicles piled up, causing gridlock for miles. One by one, the police pulled them back until they broke the bottleneck. Sure, I could suck it up and endure the hassle of crossing once, but when it happened three or more times a month, I began to hate that damn bridge.

Anyone living in a major city could attest to the growing traffic problems. The towns were densely populated and poorly equipped to handle the onslaught of automobiles. Towards the end of the '90s, new highways opened up, but they provided encouragement for people to buy cars, further clogging the roads. Five hours was a long time. That's what happens when a country sheds its skin.

Once we crossed the bridge, it felt as if we had achieved something, but it was only the beginning of the car ride. It would take an additional three hours over rugged roads. Because of the traveling time, we had to stay at the destination instead of rushing back.

When we reached Yangzhou, we advised the agent to skip downtown and head to the production lines. We continued to the outskirts, arriving at a massive gate. The agent said, "Here is the workshop, but we aren't making production here. Your orders are in another factory, a sub-factory. It is another hour."

Sub-factory, as in substitution or sub-par, was a term frequently used. It was an outside workshop that may or may not be affiliated with the plant we placed the order. Most of the time, we found out we had products manufactured in a sub-factory when we visited. No one told us because these workshops were small, full of hazards (fire, electrical, chemical, etc.), and hard to reach. They would not pass a social compliance audit and received orders through a compliant workshop. Sub-factories did not pay full benefits and had lower costs.

We often discovered kids playing in rural sub-factories while mom or grandma worked a sewing machine. They saw no problem with this, even when a foreigner arrived. The low-end factories got paid for the amount of items produced. That prompted the laborers to throw in as many pieces as possible and take a gamble no one would not find out. The factory argued to negotiate a better deal if the customer issued claims. Not a lot of loyalty existed between business partners at this level. It revolved around price and desperation. You only used sub-factories if all other options had been exhausted.

Naturally, when they said they produced the order elsewhere, we had to check it out. After spending half the day in the car, another hour wouldn't matter. We still had a few hours of daylight to check the production lines and finished products.

When we arrived, the manager took his time with the tea and cigarette formalities until we got up and searched for our production. We placed a few orders for plush animal slippers, like unicorns, monkeys, and cats. Each had a soundbox sewn in that produced an animal sound when someone pressed a patch. We entered a narrow warehouse building and found mountains of slippers waiting to be packed—magical white unicorns lying on the dirty floor.

I inquired about the dirt, and they said, "Don't worry. We will clean them before packing."

It started to get dark, and the lights were dim. I selected a few pairs from each mountain and laid them on the table. Some jammed too much stuffing into the neck and head, while others didn't have enough. They resembled a before-and-after unicorn weight loss ad. A couple left the stitching open with cotton candy stuffing hanging out. Several installed the wrong sound boxes, so a monkey made a horse sound.

Each slipper had a stitched-on patch the size of a quarter, which should have read, "Push Me." What they'd made said, "Pus Me." Right then, I knew we had to reject the product, and someone would lose money. We needed to stop this abomination from making more products until another agent led us to the same crappy sub-factory.

They agreed on the problems, knowing they would use the rejected product later.

"Let's go to dinner."

Let's go to dinner meant more than Let's eat dinner. The manager signaled that he:

1. Was tired of talking.

2. Has plans of using his staff to get you drunk, so you change your mind about the shipment.

3. Has reservations at a karaoke and wants to get the meal over with.

4. All the above.

They chose option two, my favorite.

The countryside lacked restaurants, and we preferred to avoid riding with the manager after drinking. Telling a boss he should not drive made him want to do it even more. It was best to choose someplace close to the hotel.

The manager had me ride shotgun to pick my brain. When we ate, I also sat next to him. He would toast me until drunk, then call in surrogates. Whiskey and wine existed in a handful of high-end hotels (in all of China), and there was only a type or two to choose from. People living far from the metropolises had never had those beverages. The majority downed warm beer. As individuals earned more and alcohol companies arrived, their tastes developed. Some bought expensive wines and whiskeys, while others doubled down on the national liquor, *baijiu*. In 1990, I paid $1 a bottle for my favorite rocket fuel, but in the 2000s, consumers spent thousands on top-shelf stuff when the only difference seemed to be better packaging.

It tasted the same to me.

We drank beer, which was not challenging. Bryon swallowed antibiotics for the cut, so he sat this one out. With him riding the bench, I did the boozing for the team. We had a few rounds of *ganbeis* in between plates. They gave us the first tasting of each dish as a courtesy. I tried everything, including "Drunken Shrimp." They placed live river shrimp in a glass bowl and doused them with *baijiu*. The alcohol put them into a state of euphoria.

Then, we watched them flopping around until they stopped. If I were a pro, I would put the entire shrimp in my mouth and suck the juicy bits out of the head while spitting the shell out of the left side of my mouth. I opted for the manual method of twisting the heads off and peeling the shell. Nobody told me the secret when eating live shrimp. When I twisted the head, it broke towards me instead of away. The digestive tract was fluid and squirted all over my white button-down shirt. I sat for the rest of the meal with the orangish liquid splashed across my chest like a Jackson Pollock painting.

The devil's juice was the only positive thing to come out of the ordeal. They didn't think I drank it, so they never offered it. Once I talked about my Beida experience, I earned their respect and a few extra *ganbeis*. Then, I mentioned I went to school at the same time as Big Mountain, and the manager took the liberty of doing a little thigh-slapping (my thighs). He called me a "*Zhong Guo Tong*," which loosely meant "I was Chinese-like." This was the first occasion I used the Big Mountain name-drop and realized how useful it would be. People perked up when I mentioned his name, and they congratulated me. I don't think they would have acted the same if I said I shook hands with Michael Jackson. Big Mountain was huge.

The other side could not match me on the liquor, and we finished within two hours. It was the start of my legendary run as Mr. Thunder, the *baijiu*-loving foreigner.

With no nightlife, they sent us to our hotel, the Yangzhou Guesthouse, a sprawling collection of buildings connected with long, empty hallways. Every second and third-tier city had a government guesthouse. They were the best places to stay. When the government held meetings, they booked out the joints. Business travelers would have to reside at lower-quality guesthouses. No matter where we stayed, they charged foreigners extra. By 1994, the dual currency system (FEC) ended, but the dual pricing system lingered.

Even at the best government housing, finding food challenged me. Often, I wandered the grounds searching for any place serving breakfast. Most guesthouse restaurants kept strict hours for mealtime. If you showed up to eat at 8 p.m., they might be out of rice and most dishes. It shocked me when I heard that a Chinese restaurant ran out of rice. How was that possible?

In rural areas, they offered noodles and rice porridge on the street for breakfast. A basic guesthouse meal consisted of watery congee, various cold dishes served all day, and fried eggs, almost deep-fried because of the amount of oil used. They cooked the eggs early and stopped service. After that, they read the paper and sipped tea.

With no hope of food and a rough journey ahead, we hit the road on an empty stomach. This became routine as I traveled more:

- Take off hungry.
- Make it to the following factory by 10 a.m.
- Conclude business before a three-hour lunch.
- Hit another factory with a three-hour dinner.
- Repeat.
- Go home.

This time, we had a flight to Hong Kong and settled for whatever TV dinner China Eastern served.

I would visit Nanjing and Yangzhou many times a year. After every season, I thought I would be out of Yangzhou until another agent dragged me back. I found it fascinating how people kept reinventing themselves.

Over the years, the roads and hotels improved, but the drinking got harder.

Next, we had to solve a problem in the future land of satisfaction, Dongguan.

CHAPTER SIX

DONGGUAN: CAPITALISM AT PLAY

With my second trip concluded, I anticipated taking my training wheels off. I had the movie star part perfected and the job I would pick up later.

Before I starred in the leading role in my own China drama, I needed to wait for Bryon to arrange a trip to accompany me.

When hired, I assumed he would provide my housing.

"No problem. You can stay in the office apartment. I have another flat in Shekou across the border that I stay at on weekends. In two days, take a ferry over. The factory agent will pick us up and drive two hours to Houjie in Dongguan," he said.

I assumed they called the area "Shekou" or "Snake Mouth" because of the girlie bars outside the dock. There weren't a ton of women hovering around at 10 a.m., but the idea seemed akin to a watered-down Wanchai. Bars such as these didn't exist in the north. Chinese Communist Party (CCP) rules were more flexible down south.

Bryon said Shekou became a home port for foreigners in the oil business, working on rigs in the bay. They attracted enterprising young ladies and heavy drinking establishments. He told me three months ago, an expatriate attempted to kill himself by turning on the gas in his apartment and lighting the fumes. He blew himself and his furniture onto the pavement in front of the bars. The sofa remained in the street for people to consume beers alfresco. It sounded like an improbable tale, but the longer I stayed, the more it made sense.

I met Bryon outside customs, and we waited for the agent to show up. The guy drove an American minivan like a soccer mom, but this was top-of-the-line luxury in China. Most people rode in Chinese hatchback taxis, kryptonite to foreigners with long legs. You would need someone to wedge you out if you contorted into the back seat. Minivans provided plenty of legroom. They didn't sell these cars on the mainland. It had to be imported in a container from the U.S. Regardless of how he secured the vehicle, it was nice to have good ol' American comfort for the two hours of rugged roads.

Louis (the agent) was a cunning guy who did his best to pamper customers—crucial when rough journeys broke people. Irritated purchasers seldom made concessions. Although he grew up in the PRC, he seemed Western-savvy and spoke excellent English. He previously worked for a U.S. company and knew what we demanded. Louis was the owner of the factory and the trade corp. boss, a helpful arrangement. If the order ran late or the quality was insufficient, he blamed the factory as if we didn't know he managed both.

On this trip, we planned to inspect the production of water shoes or "aqua socks." I recalled reading about malleable aquatic footwear and wanted to see how they produced them—maybe even get samples for myself. Louis exported to most stores and generated loads of cash, but I was hired because his product lacked suitable quality.

We arrived at the factory before lunch and had limited time to review production. The plant was small, with just six injection machines, but they produced and shipped nearly two million pairs yearly. The manufacturing process was simple.

- Stitchers stitched together a neoprene sock.
- The injection workers stretched the sock over a metal shoe last on a rotating machine, which sank into a shoe mold.
- They injected melted thermoplastic rubber (TPR) to form the outsole.
- After ten seconds, they pried it off and tossed it onto a table for price ticketing, quality control, and final packaging.

Quality suffered in this situation and a considerable amount of junk got thrown in. We had the job of finding the defective pairs.

This trip should have been a quick in and out, with four hours of driving and two on the ferry for an hour on the production lines. However, since they had to rework, Bryon wanted me to stay behind and do a final inspection. The plant had a history of complications, so Bryon suggested I might need to remain and should prepare. I didn't require a technical background in footwear to inspect these shoes.

When I joined the company, they began working with new agents on large orders of lower-end products. The recently established Hong Kong office did not have quality control inspectors (QCs) and relied on factory QCs. I was the first hired to check on production. This bothered the agents. Most overseas customers never inspected goods because of the traveling. I enjoyed it; the further, the better. The agents would soon find my arrival irritating. They just hadn't realized it yet.

After lunch, Bryon returned to Hong Kong while Louis rushed to another place he owned up north. They left me in the hands of the plant manager.

Mr. Wang looked for a place for me to stay. I preferred to be next door to come and go as I pleased. The closest place was a guesthouse called The Red Mansion.

This hotel was so rock bottom my room lacked a window. I had curtains but found just a wall, not even a frame! No worries, being fresh on the job, I wanted to spend as much time as possible in the factory. If I didn't reject the shoes now, I would reject them during the final inspection. Then, they had to rework (again) and discard the defective shoes. It slowed down production when line workers had to do the rework. I thought they would appreciate me helping them uncover defects, preventing charges on the American side. However, the longer I remained, the more the manager had to accompany me. I didn't need the companionship and enjoyed walking alone, learning things while removing shoddy products. I felt at home after laboring in a machine shop for four summers.

Although I liked Mr. Wang and got along with him well, he was ill-prepared for his role. We developed products with problems the factory had never considered. While he struggled, the manufacturing business in China was experiencing unheard-of growth. Factories needed to adapt.

Mr. Wang treated me to lunch and dinner daily, but we ate at the same restaurant in my hotel. It was the only proper one in the area. Around eating time, someone would send me back to get cleaned up. Then I waited in my windowless room until I received a call to come down.

Mr. Wang drank little, so we didn't have big benders during the day. That changed when his drinking friends came out to play at night. There was a network of Hong Kong managers and owners working in Houjie. They all took turns footing the nightly entertainment bills to keep the party going.

The first night foreshadowed what the next couple would be like. We had dinner and drinks at the hotel. I mentally prepared to head to my room when Mr. Wang asked,

"Do you enjoy karaoke?"

"Sure, I sang in Taiwan."

That relieved everybody. Taking care of this foreigner would be easier than they expected. He made phone calls, and then we piled into the car on the way to the karaoke. Presumably, because everyone had been drinking, a guy pointed out the "50 RMB" and "30 RMB" streets.

"What does that mean?" I asked, already guessing the answer.

"The worker girls come out at night, and that is what they charge for their services."

When did this start, and how did this activity fit with the communist doctrine? The workers earned about 300 RMB monthly; 50 RMB was a big deal. But what kind of sex would you get for 30 RMB ($8)? This new China had become more capitalistic than I had ever imagined.

Karaoke also differed from my experience in Taiwan. We sat in a private room, and they brought in trays of beer, Johnny Walker, and snacks. It looked marvelous, but they gave us a tray full of empty glasses; we only had four guys. That soon changed.

Somebody knocked on the door, and I expected another of Mr. Wang's friends or more snacks, but a parade of ten young ladies in long velvet dresses came in. A more confident woman dressed differently led the others. They lined up before us while we relaxed on the leather sofas, smoking cigarettes. Mr. Wang sat beside me with his hand on my thigh and said, "Pick any girl, and she will drink and sing with you."

Nothing like this existed in the north. It wasn't prostitution. The women peeled fruit, drank, and sang, or *"san pei"* (three functions). No matter how innocent it seemed, I had difficulty choosing. It looked demeaning. They stood, smiling or looking straight ahead. "Disgusting, a foreigner! He probably can't speak Chinese. Don't choose me," was what a few of them appeared to be thinking. How dreadful to walk into smoky room after room to be judged and rejected. I told the manager to pick the one that could drink the most. If someone accompanied me, she should know the quantity of booze involved. They assigned a girl from the middle of China, known for spicy food and *baijiu*. She drank with the other guys and girls to give me a break. She also opened pistachio nuts and attempted to hand-feed me, but I told her to set them in a pile. Never would I have expected an attractive girl to peel pistachios while I sipped Johnny Walker and beer. It would have been paradise if they had better music.

The longer we sang, the more thankful I was for the girls. They kept the party from turning dull. Otherwise, it would have been four guys getting sloppy and singing songs about heartbreak.

After three hours, I requested to be sent back. The evening ended when I tried to sing songs such as "Tie a Yellow Ribbon Round the Old Oak Tree." I had run through all my standards and dug deep.

The following day, I asked to change to a room with an actual window. Mr. Wang also put in a good word. He spent loads of money in the hotel and had some influence. Plus, I paid almost double in Hong Kong Dollars (many places in Guangdong, including Shenzhen, charged foreigners in HKD, not RMB). Shouldn't that earn a better setup?

When I returned for my noontime clean-up, they swapped my room. I opened the curtains to find I had a view of a brick wall. Then it occurred to me: I asked for a room with a window, and they gave me one. I should have asked for a window AND A VIEW. I should have been precise.

For the rest of my time, we followed the same routine: go to the factory, reject shoes, eat, drink, sing, and repeat. Mr. Wang thought I looked tired and offered to lend me a motorcycle to ride around town. The streets were dusty and dangerous, with over-loaded trucks barreling down the roads at high speeds. No thanks.

Instead, they took me out to see historical sites in Taiping. I refused to admit it, but leaving the hot factory felt good. With all the time I spent helping them, if they still had problems, they would need to work it out by themselves.

In the end, I did an inspection and rejected the order. Mr. Wang sent me to the ferry port and promised to remove the bad stuff. They neglected to do so and shipped anyway, instigating chargebacks. I did all I could to help them.

This was my first visit to Shekou and Dongguan. The next time I visited, the hotels, restaurants, and karaoke got more impressive. Shekou grew from a few girlie bars to a few streets with an expanding entertainment scene. Dongguan went even further.

From time to time, the government would "strike hard" to clean things up, but love (and greed) would find a way, and the police tired of enforcing it. Then, everything returned to normal until the next campaign.

It was China's "whack-a-mole" method of dealing with every problem.

CHAPTER SEVEN

PUTIAN: I'M A SHOE DOG

I completed two weeks of training and prepared to be escorted to my home base, Putian, in Fujian Province. The location was somewhere across from Taiwan. That's all I knew.

Initially, I felt disappointed I wasn't stationed near Beijing, Shanghai, or even Nanjing. But Putian turned into uncharted territory: I couldn't find anything about the town in my Lonely Planet. This would allow me to go off the beaten path and experience a China that most never would. Bryon informed me I would remain for at least thirty days and should pack as if I wouldn't be coming back. That was easy with just a backpack to my name.

The flight from Hong Kong to Fuzhou, the capital of Fujian, took an hour and a half. The airport was decorated with the same socialist flair as the others. It shared the runway and air space with the military next door, causing delays.

After we landed, the plane parked on the tarmac. We disembarked down a ladder car and walked into the customs building. This was the only flight. I realized how few people flew when I traveled more.

Our agent made the arrangements and informed us we had to stay in Fuzhou since the road was under construction. The hundred-kilometer (65 miles) journey would take four to eight hours. It was unsafe to travel at night for the usual reasons, such as no street lights and dangerously rough roads. I didn't mind staying an evening in Fuzhou, as everything was new.

The airfield was on the southern edge of town, but the decent hotels were in the northern part. Going from one end to the other took an hour, but not because of too many vehicles. The government came up with the idea of installing fences to separate the cars from the bike lanes as well as to prevent pedestrians from crossing in the middle. Now, the two-lane street became blocked at each opening. Also, individuals ran to the center and catapulted themselves in front of oncoming traffic so they didn't have to walk to the crosswalk.

As a result, a short journey became an unnecessarily long one.

We headed to the Hot Spring Hotel. It had all the requirements of a four-star, like CNN, room service, club sandwich, and a functioning business center, but the rooms were situated around an open-air lobby lounge. At night, performers sang opera, and the acoustics carried the sound to the top floors. It never thrilled me to hear amateur Pavarotti and Callas hitting the high notes when I arrived after eight hours on the road.

We checked in, and I went to my room to search for anything about Putian in my Lonely Planet.

"There has to be something I missed."

The next day, the agent rented a VW Santana hotel car to take us south. Santanas were high-end comfort compared to other vehicles on the road, such as the Jinbei "bread vans," hatchbacks, or tractors. "Lawnmower tractors" were wagons the length of an American pickup truck with a drive pulley engine exposed in the front. The driver steered with long handlebars attached to the axle. We also referred to them as "Mad Max machines" because they looked straight out of *The Road Warrior*. They made loud noises, belched smoke, and moved as if they had a mind of their own.

Fujian also had motorcycles, bicycles, farm animals, and pedestrians sharing the same highway as the cars. Drivers dodged these obstacles as if playing a video game. The streets lacked a median separating oncoming traffic. There was only a dotted yellow line. Cars veered back and forth to pass obstructions, often calling it close. Sometimes, individuals laid in the center. I thought they tried to kill themselves, but others said they were crazy. Both could be true, but what a painful way to die.

We arrived in Putian in the afternoon and drove to the trade corp. office. Bryon explained that I would inspect shipments and that they should help me as much as possible. After a quick meeting, smiles, and handshakes, we stopped by the best hotel to check in. As I filled in my registration forms, I noticed Bryon didn't complete his. I assumed he kept a long-term room like he had advised me to do. But as I picked up my bag, he said, "All right, I will see you in Hong Kong in thirty days. We will have production in many factories. Ask around. Everyone knows our company. When you find out where the orders are, let me know. Remember, **YOU** ARE THE MOVIE STAR. Eat and drink every night and meet people."

Bryon got back in the car and returned to Fuzhou. Even the Hong Kong agent left because Putian felt too rustic.

I wanted adventure, and I got it.

II

The best lodging in town was The Heavenly Concubine Hot Spring. The only thing it had in common with the Hot Spring in Fuzhou was no hot spring. Instead, there was a pond in front, from which people told me they had recently fished out a body.

They named it after Mazu, the Goddess of the Sea. She was a female shaman born on an island close to Putian in the tenth century. I understood the heritage they aimed to portray by naming the building in her honor, but the English translation was misleading.

The Heavenly Concubine amounted to a three-star. The original owner planned big things but fell short of money, which prevented the place from achieving its full potential. I was reminded of this every time I passed the doors that said "Western Restaurant," with a hefty steel chain entwined around the decorative handles. I assumed they only served dinner, but they never unlocked the chains.

They gave me a suite on the second floor, at the far end of the hall. Being a movie star, I owned the entire floor; they booked everyone else on the fifth and sixth levels. I presumed they protected the local customers by keeping me quarantined. And I could play music as loud as my shitty speakers would bear without worrying about other guests.

The hotel had two wings, and I often ran down the hall from one to the other when bored (instead of dropping water balloons). It felt similar to *The Shining*, with an empty resort. The only sign of life was a KTV (a mini version of karaoke) at the other end, frequented by a couple of drunks singing love songs as loudly as possible.

Despite this occasional infringement, I had an excellent setup for the price of 250 RMB a night ($30), fifty percent off the rack rate. That was a lot of bread locally (a month's salary). The hotel didn't take credit cards, and I paid cash. Bryon floated me $5,000 for expenses until I returned to Hong Kong to replenish and rejuvenate. That amount would go a long way in Putian, with little to spend it on besides my hotel bill.

Once settled, I explored the town. A row of old Chinese shops lined the street outside the hotel with large wooden plank boards they removed every morning and slid back into place in the evening. Everything was dark except for the factory across the road, the barber shack (suspiciously not cutting hair), and a disco.

I investigated the disco.

None of the shops had names, so I referred to the joint as "The Wooden Head Disco" (WHD) because of the head carved out of a tree stump at the entrance. The WHD hung a red velvety fabric at the door to block out whatever nefarious activity they were engaging in. Whenever I heard loud music coming from the other side of a curtain, there was most likely a combination of mirrors, poles, and dancers on the inside. The WHD had all that, but not how I imagined it.

The bar was dark, with a wall of mirrors and spotlights on the ceiling. They installed a disco ball, and Christmas lights decorated the DJ booth. In the rear corner was the toilet. The odor caught my attention when I entered.

Around the dance floor were several small, leather-like sofas. With almost no one inside, I had my choice of seating, but I picked a beat-up couch near the entrance—safety first. I strained my eyes to read the menu—another abused piece of laminated paper. It helped when someone peeked their head through the curtain, and I received a fragment of light. They sold beer by the pitcher, a welcome change, but I missed drinking room-temperature swill in large green bottles. Those bottles reminded me of my days at Beida and that China had begun to vanish. I swore to return to Beijing before I no longer recognized it.

I probably should not have used the cups, but my last illness in China happened four years ago. Things had improved since then, right? Mostly not, but at least they blanched the cups in boiling water. Putian beer glasses were twice the size of an American shot glass. I could down a glass in two gulps, making *ganbeis* easy.

The server brought my pitcher and a songbook in case I wanted to sing for an empty dance floor. No thanks. The disco played many Hong Kong love songs by Andy Lau and Jacky Cheung, but every thirty minutes, they stopped the slow songs and put on European disco (They loved a song called "Brother Louie."). Then, everybody rose and danced their best moves or did some stretching. The lucky ones stood in front of the mirrors and watched themselves attempt the latest dances learned from Taiwanese or Hong Kong karaoke videos. They also did a number called the three-step four-step, similar to the Cha Cha Cha. It seemed odd to watch the men ballroom dancing with other men and women doing the same. Rarely did the sexes mix.

The guys sported pagers and key chains jangling with keys on their belts. I think they thought it worked as an aphrodisiac; women would flock to them once they saw the enormous amount of metal dangling from their hips. Perhaps it was cultural because I never heard someone say, "I must meet that guy with the big key ring on his belt. He can open many doors!"

I didn't feel like a movie star as I sat in the dank club, drinking my warm pitcher of watery, foamy draft Snow Beer, watching the locals twirl. It was only my first night; it had to get better. Then, I saw a rat, comparable to those Chicago super rats, run across the floor. That thing needed a leash.

It was time to head back.

III

All purchase orders passed through a government trade corp. (We had two layers—a Hong Kong agent and the government.). The corporation decided where to place the orders. They picked friendly factories or ones operated by relatives. The trading company had enormous control over the export business but played a minor role in developing products and handling problems. They didn't need to help. They got paid either way, and we had nowhere else to go. The personnel working for the government made out like bandits. Not only did they give orders to friends and relatives, building up future *guanxi* and profits, but they also became the first choice to partner up with once companies could work directly. I knew trade corp. staff who got very wealthy even before the Chinese economy skyrocketed in the 2000s. The right place at the right time could be very lucrative in modern China.

In the morning, I walked down to the lobby and told them I needed transportation. Putian lacked yellow cabs. People with a car picked up randoms for a fee. The hotel said it would take thirty minutes and cost 50 RMB ($6), but I eagerly desired to check out the factories and didn't want to wait. Instead, I strolled out to take a motorcycle taxi.

As soon as I reached the hotel's gate, guys on motorbikes darted out from every direction. It felt like a scene from *The Warriors*. I was used to the weather from my days in Taiwan, but I never enjoyed the humidity; some people dealt with it better than others. The bike dudes handled it well with the wool ski masks they sported instead of helmets, as if the wool had extraordinary protective qualities. They didn't mind the hundred-degree weather and wore three-piece suits with sweaters. I assumed the suit made them feel as if they did something more substantial than shuttling individuals on their bikes. It seemed out of place—like guys in suits working with picks on the road. Motorcycle taxi drivers did not need formalwear, but the presentation helped sell their services. The suit guys looked more presentable than the crusty dudes with the pleather motorcycle jackets.

Before bargaining, I crossed the street to the mom-and-pop shop to get info. I surprised them when I spoke Mandarin, but Pop said,

"Of course, he can speak. How do you think he found the disco?"

"How did you know I was there?"

"We saw you in the streetlight. There aren't any foreigners here."

"Yeah, I guess so."

Rule #18: Be careful. Someone is always watching.

I purchased a few cases of beer, water, and coke and asked them to send the drinks to the hotel. They only sold dry goods, so I wanted little beyond beverages, pistachios, and 555 cigarettes (no Camels in China, but lots of Russian Marlboros and fake British 555). Everything looked inexpensive after starving in Hong Kong.

After negotiating with the bikers, I hit my target of 3 RMB for a one-way ride (40¢). It seemed inconsequential to spend a lot of time bargaining over a few RuMBas (RMB), but they would take advantage of me if I didn't. Individuals who did not fight for every "fen" or penny were considered a mark. I negotiated several times a day and adhered to **Rule #3**, checking for forgeries. Paper money in a small town would often be dilapidated. Torn bills repaired with crude tape were rejected as much as counterfeits. I received a handful before I grew accustomed to inspecting every RuMBa—it was tiresome.

If given a lousy bill, I needed to hand it back ASAP and be prepared for the "that's not mine" argument. If I got stuck, I camouflaged it within the other bills and hoped to slip it to someone else. I didn't enjoy doing it, but it was the law of the land.

I hopped on the bike, and we headed towards the trade office. The motorcycle guy gave me a sketchy hard hat, similar to something a kid might wear during Halloween. I doubted it would protect my head in a crash, but at least it complied with the regulations.

I also didn't relish thinking about all the people who wore the hat before me. Therefore, I held it over my head, similar to a halo, with one hand on my hat and the other holding onto the bike. Rather than wrap my arms around the waist of the driver, I gripped the back rail. The motorcycle guy had difficulty balancing my weight, and I felt the front bounce when we hit bumps. If something went wrong, I figured I would jump off to avoid a crash—be quick and avoid falling into oncoming traffic.

The driver had just gotten the hang of it when we arrived at the trade corp. in five minutes flat (one km). Downtown Putian had about six major streets. It wasn't too hard to get around when flying on a motorcycle.

I entered the office and asked for the boss. Nobody recognized me. Perhaps we really did look alike. The owner didn't expect me so soon or thought I would remain in the hotel until someone picked me up. Had the place been an international chain, I might have been tempted, but The Heavenly Concubine was not oozing with comfort.

Mr. Zhang assigned an account manager to take me to the factories. If I had a question or a complaint, Charlie Lu handled it. He expected this to be easy, but he had never met a foreigner like me. Most customers relied on the trade corp. for everything. This would not be the case with me. They even switched to Putian dialect when I walked in.

Charlie had access to the company car when a more important customer was not using it. Mostly, I rode motorcycles to the nearby factories. I traveled frequently to a workshop down a dusty, unpaved road near a mountain they'd chipped away to build new concrete boxes while destroying the undisturbed countryside. After riding a cycle on a dirt road for twenty minutes, I showed up at the factory sticky and dirty. But I took a bike because I wanted to show them nothing would stop me except the rain.

On the way to the first workshop, Charlie pointed out a cleared-out area. He said, "The government does public executions over there. Do you want to see?"

Wandering around an execution pit would not be wise. I was here to inspect shoes and not start an international conflict.

The name of the plant we visited sounded like *chao fan* (fried rice), so we nicknamed it the "Fried Rice" factory. It was located off what I called "Latrine Street." The Doors sang about "Love Street," and I frequently heard that song in my head when I waltzed down Latrine Street. This little road had an overwhelming amount of outhouses. They were single-use holes with crude, short brick walls just high enough to hide the person. Each family had a toilet in front of each hut—like a mailbox. Typically, there would be a neighborhood toilet in larger towns, but not here. From one end to the other, I passed by about fifteen of the smelliest latrines and dodged the large, black, potbellied pigs roaming through the neighborhood, feeding off the trash.

Fried Rice made various styles of black-and-white sandals called "Fisherman." Once the shoe was finished, they slipped in a footbed and packaged them for export. It was a simple process, but many things could go wrong.

Because of the high reject rate and the proximity, I traveled to Fried Rice every morning. The manager was unwilling to keep up the charade daily and ignored me after a few days. That was fine; I bypassed the office and headed to the warehouses. Then, I sat on the packing line and removed bad pairs before they boxed or bagged them. If I rejected too many, someone would call the boss. She would have to leave the comfort of her office and did not enjoy seeing me. We worked with more than a few female factory managers. I preferred them; they seemed better at follow-up and execution than many male counterparts. However, working with men had the advantage of bigger and better meals. There needed to be a harmony between execution and entertainment; both were important and moving the needle in either direction threw off the equilibrium.

Most factories expected I would go away after a week or a month.

"Why would a foreigner stay in China for so long?"

I never left and kept coming back with different agents. That happened often; an agent brought me to a "new factory," and I ended up at a place I had been before but now with a different name. I returned to Fried Rice through six separate agents during a ten-year period.

We both never seemed to go away.

IV

Finally, after ignoring my presence for a week, the government trade corp. manager welcomed me to the city. He invited me to the top restaurant in town, on the first floor of my hotel, where I ate breakfast, lunch, and dinner. I memorized the menu, which had little I wanted beyond Yangzhou fried rice (poorly made) and a stir-fried beef or pork. Any dish not local would not be authentic. They couldn't make *gong bao* chicken (no chili) but served plenty of seafood dishes.

The welcome dinner was my first time having snake. I saw the cages of serpents on my way to the toilet and wondered who ate that? The trade corp. manager enjoyed it and ordered one for the table. They brought out the live reptile for my inspection. As I talked away, the server said, "Mister," and I turned to find a viper in my face. He held the head, but it surprised me.

It also gave me something to think about when we finished it.

Sure, it was a low-calorie protein used in Chinese medicine for over two thousand years, and it arrived crispy, garlicky, and tasted like chicken. No, the meat was not the problem. I'd seen how they served snakes in Taiwan on Snake Alley (Taipei has a street specializing in edible reptiles.). The cooked snake came with a shot of blood and the raw gall bladder in a glass of *baijiu*. That concerned me. And as the guest, they offered me the shots. I read about a guy developing worms in his lungs after eating a raw gall bladder. I was adventurous but had to draw the line.

Most of the other dishes were seafood or intestine. Putian (PT) locals enjoyed boiled or steamed seafood with little flavor. They took these sea creatures, many resembling something extinct in the Western world, and dipped them in dark vinegar, nothing else. It was murder for someone who preferred spicy food.

Putian County had many famous dishes, such as jellyfish. It was crunchy and reminded me of cartilage, which I also tasted. If you fancy jellyfish, then you will love sliced pig ears.

Three others stood out: *mifen* (rice noodles), *men doufu*, and *tu sun dong*. Putian rice noodles were thin and stir-fried with dried shrimp, baby oysters, eggs, green onions, and other bits, while *men doufu* was a steamed egg and tofu dish with oysters, dried shrimp (they loved their seafood), black mushrooms, and chopped peanuts. After picking out some pieces, I grew to love them, but the last dish was too much.

Tu sun dong was sandworm jelly. They boiled the worms until they generated a collagen gel with the skins suspended inside. Next, they refrigerated the gel to firm it into gray jello. They served it sliced cold, like canned cranberry sauce, where you received a perfect disk of sandworm jelly. On some occasions, I thought I would give it a go, but I chickened out. They said it was the best worm jelly because they farm-raised the sandworms. They were very proud of it. Once, I ate dinner with individuals from two separate factories from different regions of Putian, and each swore their hood made the most flavorful jelly. Like NYC, where every neighborhood claims they have the best pizza. Imagine worm jelly slices on every corner!

At least the snake blood and gall bladder came with the *baijiu*.

The most entertaining part of the hotel was the grand karaoke hall on the ground floor. It turned into the only place drawing nightly crowds. I avoided it for the first couple of days because they only had large sofas, but as I sat alone, drinking beer, the reverberations shook me out of my room and downstairs to check it out. Bryon said to eat, drink, and meet people. It was time to go to work.

Inside the spacious rotunda, circular couches surrounded the dance floor. Every night, Taiwanese and Hong Kong shoe companies packed the joint. Each company claimed a section as its turf. Although our head offices fought tooth and nail to grab the same orders, the scene in China was friendly. The other companies heard I planned to stay long-term, but I wasn't Taiwanese or from

Hong Kong. I lacked the hometown connection, and no one wanted to approach me, thinking I was a problematic *gweilo* (Cantonese for foreigner, translation: ghost man. So, I was an old outsider in China, a big nose in Taiwan, and a ghost guy in Hong Kong. Lovely!). I had little in common with them and didn't want to blow $200 on fruit, beer, and flowers.

The karaoke employed a few professional performers, but you could order your own song and sing in front of the entire hall if you were that guy or a movie star. They hired dancers who wore big Vegas dresses or tight *qipaos* and entertained the mainly male customer base. Most bore numbers to credit them for table service and flowers, similar to Kaiping. I presumed they received some money, but not all.

It was a lot, too.

If a girl looked decent and sang okay, tables competed to show appreciation. They arranged bunches of flowers in five-foot-tall baskets. The staff rushed them out when someone raised their hand approving payment. Baskets ranged from 100 to 500 RMB ($60), depending on the size. It became customary for top girls to receive ten or more baskets for a song.

Imagine working in a hot, sweaty factory for eight hours a day, six days a week, and at the end of the month, you received 250 RMB while someone with the same level of education earned ten times that for singing a song.

Life was grand for some.

When the hostesses finished singing, they walked around, shaking hands with the dudes who bought the bouquets and sat on the sofa that spent the most. Everyone knew who each girl "belonged to." Other guys rarely bid the highest amount but paid their respects to the rival company that favored her. The same guys paid the same ridiculous amounts for fake flowers.

Then they returned home and did it again the next night.

With no friends, I took over the holding area for the girls, who waited for someone rich to favor them—the perfect arrangement. I couldn't afford to sit on a regular sofa (sofas had a $150 minimum), and

I would look lonely on an enormous couch alone. The best location was near the entrance with the flower girls. The ladies hung out for free, and I could easily access the exit.

What more could I ask for?

Most girls came from areas known for their spicy food, such as Hunan, Anhui, and Jiangxi Provinces. No one was local because society looked down on women smoking and drinking, especially with random men. It's better to work far from home and say you toiled in a high-paying factory on the coast.

If somebody could point me in the right direction towards spicy food, these ladies would be the ones. They told me about a joint down a small alley with the only scorching fare in town.

All the locals I spoke with had never heard about it. It was as if I had discovered Eden—a hole-in-the-wall with the spiciest food, packed daily with dancehall girls, and I seemed to be the only guy who knew about it. This place had four cramped tables, no menu, and nothing fancy. I would walk into the old-style kitchen, inspect what they stocked that day, and tell them to stir-fry everything with lots of chilies. They didn't consistently have meat, but I always found food to eat. Besides, my meals consisted of beer drinking to pass the time, and they had a special treat, Pabst Blue Ribbon! No idea why, but I took it as a sign. This was the type of restaurant that connoisseurs searched for. It instantly increased my credibility as someone different. Even though it was not a place where you would think to spot a movie star, it became my go-to for lunch until the city tore it down a year later. I cried when I found out and had to see the rubble.

All good things must come to an end.

Production started a month after I arrived. I spent my days checking out factories and inspecting materials. I barely had enough work to keep from dying of boredom.

Soon, I set into a routine of going to the factories in the morning and drinking by myself in the afternoon. I seldom saw anyone else drinking during the day. They were too busy working, and leisure time was a rare commodity for the hard-working.

Other than the spicy hole-in-the-wall place, I had a non-spicy hole-in-the-wall joint I frequented. They sold slightly cooled and frothy beer on tap (sometimes). Hole-in-the-wall #2 served dried sliced beef and fried rice. Except for the hotel, this was the only eatery that made these dishes. It also had small tables. Try enjoying a meal by yourself when sitting at a table for ten. Many places only had two or three tables inside individual rooms. That was great with nine friends but weird with just me. Locals only went out when they celebrated; hence, no small tables.

After lunch, I wandered the town, peeking into each storefront, ensuring I didn't miss any eating establishments that would have improved my choices. Drinking, strolling, and talking to myself became my favorite things to do. It took fifteen minutes to get from one end of town to the other.

I purchased stupid stuff when strolling with pockets full of cash, such as a tiger skin from a skin seller that roamed from town to town. It was probably the skin of a dog, and it reeked.

Then, I bought an *erhu*, a traditional Chinese instrument similar to a vertical violin with a snakeskin cover. My hotel hired a classical Chinese quartet to play at dinner. I asked the *erhu* player if he would teach me. He came to my suite and said he would instruct me if I taught him English. I tried once, but it was a more significant commitment than I wished to make. A month later, the hotel dropped the quartet, thus ending my *erhu* career.

Occasionally, when I walked the streets, I crossed paths with one of the two naked zombies sleepwalking. A naked woman strolled in one part and a naked guy in another. I wondered if they knew each other. They both had dreadlocks, looked as if they hadn't showered in years, and wandered in a daze. No one paid attention to them. In fact, people struggled to get a glimpse of me, but they didn't bat an eye when the walking dead drifted by.

I passed through downtown daily to visit factories and to change money. I carried HK Dollars, and Charlie showed me where to get the highest rate. Two ladies working out of a clothing shop exchanged cash for the town. They stood outside, loudly announcing, *"Gang bi bo eh,*

Gang bi bo eh," which I understood meant something like, "We want your H.K. and U.S. dollars," in PT dialect. They gave a much better rate than the hotel, but I needed to watch my back while checking for counterfeits.

The highest denomination in HK Dollars was a one-thousand-dollar bill; in China, it was a hundred-dollar bill. The women gave me a rate of 115 RMB for 100 HKD. If I exchanged ten thousand HKD ($1,280), I gave them ten thousand-dollar bills for one hundred and fifteen 100 RMB (or double if they only had 50 RMB). Since everything needed to be paid in cash, I required huge bankrolls of RuMBas, and they loved my business.

Once I stuffed my pockets with thick wads, I hopped onto a motorcycle and headed back to my room before getting robbed. There must have been folks hanging around, knowing that anyone who entered the store carried lots of bills.

In my hotel, I kept a large safe. This thing was impossible to lift. I purchased it for 300 RMB ($35). The cost of the steel had to be more than the price of the finished item. I didn't need to worry about someone stealing my ducats with the safe in my room.

Besides a cheap Atari knock-off, I splurged on a new Flying Pigeon bike. I had the bright idea of riding across the countryside on a heavy bicycle with no gears. It seemed healthy.

I got up one Saturday to start a journey to the next town, thirty minutes by car. I put on my headphones and hit the road. Once I left downtown, I realized how dumb it was to ride where monster trucks cruised faster than they should have. I ate dust and inhaled truck fumes. The buses were just as bad.

Locals were not accustomed to riding in moving vehicles, and their stomachs couldn't hold down the morning's meal. Almost every bus had individuals vomiting out the windows. They never looked because who biked on a road like this? Only dumbass fools like me.

If I managed to dodge the trucks and buses, I worried about the Mad Max machines. The more prominent the vehicle, the more they commanded the road. In the U.S., the pedestrian was king. When I returned from Asia, it took time to adjust to cars stopping for walkers. I waited for the signal to turn while my friends crossed the street. In China, it felt like Frogger with obstacles everywhere. Bicycles and pedestrians were no match.

V

Since I had a new position, no one could show me the ropes. I started from scratch. Half the factories were in difficult-to-reach areas; motorcycle taxis would not work. I searched for a driver, but finding individuals willing to do the rough, long-distance driving was troublesome. The front desk gave me the number of an older man who drove a Russian Lada. It looked like a giant marshmallow with its bulbous design, but it seemed safer because of the steel, similar to a tank. Mr. Zhan was a patient driver, the third most crucial quality behind safe and sober. He drove me to workshops in north Putian and Fuqing City, three hours away (now it takes thirty minutes). When Mr. Zhan was preoccupied, his niece took me. Little Chen, a fiery young girl, desired to know everything about life outside Putian. She taught me to swear in PT dialect in exchange for our conversations. We got stares because no one had seen a Chinese woman drive a foreigner. Many, especially in the countryside, assumed we slept together. I sat in the passenger seat to control the cassette deck and get the front seat excitement, like on a roller-coaster. The car had no seatbelts, which added an extra sense of living on the edge. I also made friends with the drivers. Good drivers were essential. They not only got me where I wanted to go, but they looked after me. I gave them tips and gifts for watching my back. In addition, I had them eat with us as long as they abstained from drinking.

I hired another tall, robust driver from Western China called Little Yu. It was strange to refer to him as "Little," but everybody did. I never understood what ritual you needed to pass to move from "Little" to "Old" before your surname. Some guys in their forties and fifties were still called "Little." That was not the case with me. I sure as hell didn't want to be referred to as "Little Thunder," and I felt sorry for the guys with the most common surname, Wang (King). People called them "Little Wang" for most of their lives, which sounded different from royalty in English.

Little Yu drove fast. He worked for a top hotel in Fuzhou, taking Hong Kong and Taiwanese to Putian and beyond. He didn't like foreigners. Perhaps that was because of his lack of English. I had to prove I was not the typical *laowai*. Little Yu enjoyed spicy food, so I introduced him to spicy hole-in-the-wall. He didn't expect I would frequent that type of place. Not only did the food taste excellent, but the joint also had four or five dancehall girls. I made him swear not to divulge my secret. He could only eat there with me or by himself.

When daily production started, our Hong Kong agent hired staff to check on the orders before I arrived. These guys worked all night if needed. They were real soldiers, but they neglected to catch everything. That was where I came in. I had an uncanny ability to recognize current and potential problems. But as an American who spoke and read Chinese, roaming freely, I was not always welcomed. Some treated me as a spy. I never forgot the individuals who attempted to isolate me, thinking I would crumble and go home. I lasted longer than most. However, it made work difficult as a one-man army.

Just as necessary, the agent staff kept the factories in line—a time-consuming affair. Even though few produced great products, they earned tons of cash. American companies knocked on their doors, hoping to place orders. No one was worried about social compliance or human rights. If you represented a customer with demands, getting someone to accept your business would be hard. It was just buying and selling, but first, you needed the factory to give you space. The agent staff needed to stay on top of the production timeline. That took presence.

I knew one of the agent QCs, Little Ma, from my Yangzhou adventure. Ma was a great help when the trade corp. and factories ignored me. Government workshops had it good and did not need to grovel. It reflected in their lack of attention. Their mood changed when business became difficult.

Little Ma was always ready to throw down and follow me around town, looking for places to eat and drink. I often treated all the QC staff as they lacked a budget, and I didn't have anyone else to eat with. We usually pregamed in my hotel room, sucking up the cases of Beck's beer I stocked before going out. The brewery was not far from my hotel, and the beer became widely available.

Sometimes, I would venture to the QC apartment. They lived in a newly built concrete shell on the other side of town, not quite finished. After seeing their digs, I felt privileged to have two rooms while five guys shared a bed.

The first time I checked out their place, I rode my bike. We drank a lot, and I regretted riding back. The road had a gradual slope, requiring extra energy. It seemed more challenging than usual, similar to riding in mud. As I passed by a storefront, a guy waved. I couldn't understand what he said, but it was an opportunity to stop. When I looked down, I noticed I had a flat.

In my drunken stupor, I figured the guy must be a repairman. I wheeled my cycle over, handed it to him, and said,

"Thanks. I'll come by tomorrow."

Then I wobbled home. The following day, I had a slow morning and decided to visit hole-in-the-wall #2 for lunch. I failed to see my bike in the rack behind the hotel. I thought someone had stolen it, and then I remembered.

"Oh, shit! I left it at the shop!"

So I went door to door until I found it, but they didn't have my bike. They were closed at midnight. A guy from next door came out saying,

"Hey, I have your bike."

"What?"

"You left it here, but I told you this isn't a bike shop. You said no problem."

He had the actual repairman fix the tire. I apologized and gave him 20 RMB.

Whenever I passed, he pointed me out and told my story.

A few weeks later, I handed over my cycle to my QC posse; no more riding.

VI

Almost a month into my stay, Little Ma introduced me to the boss of the factory across from my hotel. I became addicted to walking around workshops and jumped at the opportunity to inspect a new one. I wondered why he wanted to meet, even though I didn't have purchase orders.

Little Ma said, "When he heard a young American was living in Putian, he had to see you."

"Can he drink?"

"Yeah, he can drink."

That sounded fantastic, and he had a car. I needed a friend with wheels. We met at a restaurant, and Zhang Bo ran late. By the time he arrived, we had finished. I didn't want to eat there, but we had to stay in one location while playing pager tag. Naturally, I got ticked off when he showed up late, but I would get over it if he took me to a place with cold beer.

Zhang Bo was the same age as Little Ma and me. He wore his hair slicked back in a pompadour and strutted with his arms out with a key chain and a pager on his belt. He was shorter, but the hair gave him extra height. Zhang Bo talked in a deep, booming voice, making him sound bigger. People paid attention when he threw an order.

I forced him to down a handful of *ganbeis* for being late. Then we hopped into his truck and headed down the lane into a crowd, checking out what street vendors sold. I now regretted getting into the vehicle after we could have reached the club quicker on foot. I wanted to get to the venue as quickly as possible.

Zhang Bo was a supreme Alpha male and had no problem driving around town, either drunk or sober. He honked his horn and crept through the mob, banging people with his side mirrors. No one complained because he looked like a guy you did not mess with.

We planned to hit a nightclub, I noticed in the alley. Being in town for a few weeks, I walked down every street searching for entertainment or a hidden KFC. Unfortunately, I arrived five years too early.

The club had cold brew, but they played the same lame Euro disco and love songs. Zhang Bo told me his neighbor owned a karaoke. He said I could play my music as loud as I wanted there. Why didn't he mention that earlier? Jin Li Lai was a tiny joint with a rectangular dance floor the size of my hotel room. As soon as I saw it empty, I needed CDs.

"Take my truck. It's a short drive."

I had enough drinks to agree. Usually, I would have avoided the liability because of the darting and weaving pedestrians and bikers, but I made an exception for the music.

Zhang Bo drove a Toyota pickup with a loose clutch. I was rusty but figured it out and cruised at a slow ten miles an hour. After I parked, I ran through the lobby, up to my room, grabbed a couple of CD books, ran out, jumped into the truck, and took off. I never knew if someone would suddenly cross in front of me, so I had to be ready to break. It was stressful.

I made it back and prepared to blow the roof off the building.

With no patrons in the club, I introduced my friends to "The End" and "Break on Through" at volumes that echoed down the street. I couldn't imagine what the locals thought when they strolled by. I also played Led Zeppelin, Bauhaus, Black Sabbath, The Cure, and the Reservoir Dogs Soundtrack.

My posse didn't mind. They enjoyed watching to see what I would do next. This felt like my hotel, except the place was louder, darker, and had a strong whiff of black death mold.

I set up a chair and a table for my drinks in the middle of the floor. We ordered a few cases of big Beck's bottles and snacks. I liked pistachios and found them on every snack tray, from the train station to the karaoke bars. Most of my drinking companions preferred sunflower seeds, which led to piles of shells on the floor. A good amount of the pistachios said they hailed from California. The packaging also had the American flag printed on it. It was my patriotic duty to buy a bag. I helped with the trade imbalance.

With complete control of the tunes, we stayed until they closed. Afterward, we walked to the nearest lighted intersection for BBQ chicken legs. Restaurants appeared when the streetlights came on, and "The Man" took the night off. Sometimes, I saw the police eating and drinking at these illegal night markets. That was the contradiction of China.

These places produced any stir-fry or stew using the raw items on display. None of the objects looked appetizing. If I couldn't tell if it came from the inside of a land animal or the bottom of the ocean, I had to pass. Most of my evenings ended at the chicken stand because I had little to look forward to in the morning.

The hotel provided food on a first-come, first-served basis. That didn't mean it was a buffet. They made three orders of steamed buns and no more when finished. I found little I wanted even when I was on time. Braised beef tripe and rubbery chicken feet did not make my delicious breakfast list.

I woke early one morning and walked the streets looking for foods such as *shao bing you tiao* (a freshly baked flaky sesame bread with a fried dough stick folded inside—my daily Taiwan breakfast) or even a Beijing-style egg sandwich (*jian bing*). I only discovered a few places with plain congee or hot soy milk. People didn't eat outside.

As time passed, privately owned restaurants spread, and my choices grew. One of the most exciting venues to open was called Golden Mouse. Every character looked like a stoned Mickey Mouse. It became the number one location to be seen, a dim sum joint selling dumplings, balls, and congee. It also coincided with a return to wild animal eateries. This was a natural evolution of the dining scene. Locals already sold dog stew. Adding a few obscure animals to the menu didn't look strange.

Zhang Bo also jumped on the wild animal bandwagon and brought me to a spot near the supposed execution grounds. We hung a left at Fried Rice and drove down a dirt trail in the dark for about ten minutes until we arrived at a reservoir. He pulled off the road at a small shack, floating on pontoons. And yes, they'd decorated it with Christmas lights. Zhang Bo guided the way, strutting over the rickety gangplank while giving orders in PT dialect.

We waltzed straight into the kitchen to inspect the meats. They cooked boar, deer, rabbit, and others. I needed to learn more protein vocabulary besides pork, chicken, and beef. The owner pulled frozen carcasses from the freezer, telling us what each was. They would stew everything with lots of chilies. That's all she had to say—chili, dodgy meat, beer, and, to seal the deal, they had *baijiu*. Now we were talking. Nowhere else I knew in Putian served *baijiu*. For the devil's juice, they asked,

"Low-level alcohol or high?"

"High, of course. We're professionals."

We passed through the wooden shack to the other side, with a view of the reservoir. It must have been wonderful during the day. Now, it was pitch-black. It was a secluded place, and only a particular type (rich, government, or gangsta) ate here. Unfortunately, some diners were unaware of environmental conservation and tossed the empties into the water. I had to look the other way, as there were too many battles to fight—gotta let some go.

VII

I dug the everyday adventure of my Putian life, but my thirty days were up. I had two options to get to Hong Kong—fly from Fuzhou or Xiamen. As bad as the ride to Fuzhou was, the road to Xiamen took twice as long. The rugged terrain damaged the cars when they rode over sharp rocks and deep holes. If it rained, add a couple of hours and be prepared to push the car out of the mud. And when we moved, we couldn't make up time because of the bikes, pigs, and Mad Max machines. Hitting any of the three would be disastrous. It was awful witnessing all the accidents, but people never learned. In addition, they imperiled our lives.

I heard a theory that pedestrians **DID NOT** want to look left when moving into oncoming traffic. If you glanced left, there was a decent chance you would catch the driver's eye. You should stop if you see him coming. If you didn't look, it was his fault. No one discussed how much time you would spend in the hospital. But hey, who cares as long as you were right?

Locals told me the CCP never built infrastructure because they didn't want to assist in an invasion. I also heard that the density of mountains prohibited building coastal roads. Both reasons made sense. Shortly before I arrived, they started constructing a road connecting cities from north to south. They developed the road straight through houses along the way. It resembled Berlin after WWII, with individuals living in half-dismantled buildings as if it was normal. Anytime the government planned to do something, you prayed they spared your house. They gave new meaning to "not in my backyard."

Little Yu drove me to the Hot Spring in Fuzhou the day before my flight. When I stayed the first time, I never had an opportunity to check out the neighborhood. On this occasion, I spied a KFC. I had not eaten Western cuisine in a month.

At the end of our long car ride, I checked in, dropped off my stuff, and hurried down the ramp to the main street. KFC was a fifteen-minute journey. I planned to take the food back and enjoy my meal while watching TV. Local television showed promos, revolutionary movies, and Go lessons (similar to chess). One cable channel played American TV shows, such as *Manimal* and *MacGyver.* I became addicted to two soaps: *Santa Barbara* and *The Bold and The Beautiful.* Sometimes, you learn new things about yourself.

The Hot Spring had CNN unless they reported a negative story about China. Ironically, the only method to receive news in Putian (no CNN) was through the Taiwan English radio station and the VOA signals I picked up on a shortwave. I now understood my Beijing friend Wang Yi's joy when he listened to VOA four years ago.

On my way to KFC, I dodged many motorbikes riding on the sidewalk. They whizzed by in both directions. Sometimes, they warned me by constantly beeping their horns.

"Beep. Beep. Please let me pass. Beep. Beep. Beeeeeep!"

Cars did the same. Soon, everybody became numb to the sound, and it no longer had the effect they hoped for. Then they honked more. I never appreciated someone on a bike telling me to move. When it happened, I refused. The person found another path around, but sometimes, they bumped me with the tire or the mirror. If they turned and saw a foreigner, they'd take off.

Finally, after jumping over roadblocks and avoiding disgruntled moped riders, I arrived at my fast food Mecca and stood in the sea. Similar to my experience in Beijing, customers jammed into the entrance with no distinct lines. Gone were the days of the foreigner register (FEC). I had the choice to let the flow push me forward or widen my stance and create a line.

Not only did I need to stand my ground, but I required a little luck. There was a fifty-fifty chance the person ordering would turn towards me with their tray, thus blocking the cash register and allowing the customer behind to swoop in.

Even fast food had a Sun Tzu- *Art of War* to it.

After picking up my chicken, I had to Heisman my way to keep it warm. My last KFC dinner occurred in Beijing, and the urge for original recipe was strong. The meal had to be perfect.

On the way, guys outside the hotel promoted female services. The later it got, the further away they appeared. They spoke little English. Instead, they said something like "Ride the airplane" or "Beat the hole" in Mandarin, which seemed like a reasonable advertising technique. Some would say "Girl" or "Chinese girl" and poke a finger through an "okay" sign they made with their other hand.

They didn't stop there. I received phone calls from girls in the middle of the night asking if I wanted to have coffee. They thought all foreigners loved the drink—maybe at 6 a.m. but not at 1 a.m. Besides, I drank tea.

Other times, people knocked on my door late at night. Usually, it would be a drunk guy.

Rule #19: "Never get off the boat."

In situations like these, I referred to a scene in *Apocalypse Now*, where a guy got off the ship, ran into a tiger, hurried back, and said, "Never get off the boat." I encountered many situations where I should not exit the boat. Answering my door at midnight with a drunk dude outside was one of those instances.

A few times, the front desk handed people a key to my room. The safety latch was the only thing that stopped them. At first, I thought someone had attempted to break in, but they gave me keys to other people's rooms. Most likely, it had to do with registration incompetence.

With my feast finished, I tried to sleep to the sounds of the lobby opera singer. I never drank on these monthly visits to Fuzhou. I poured so much alcohol down my throat in Putian that I needed a drying out.

Once in Hong Kong, I felt compelled to eat and drink during the entire trip, which lasted two days. This was my shore leave. After that, I returned to the war for another thirty. My monthly trips saved my sanity. I stocked up on everything Putian lacked, taking in a few movies, eating something other than Chinese, picking up durables, and replenishing my wallet. It was a much-needed break.

VIII

I landed in Hong Kong later than expected. The PLA controlled the sky, and they didn't mind making the one or two international flights wait. We circled above the islands for an hour. I learned to get used to it and showed up whenever I did.

Once we touched down, I took the airport bus to the KCR rail station and rode the train to the company flat in Sheung Shui District near the Chinese border. It added another hour and a half to an already long journey. I arrived at 9 p.m.

The inside latch on the door to the apartment barred my entry. I double-checked, but I had the right place. Then I heard Bryon's voice. He opened the door and stood in his underwear, asking,

"What are you doing here?"

Apparently, he hadn't seen my fax announcing my arrival.

"I thought you changed your plans. I have a guest."

"Where do I go?"

"Hold on." He came back and gave me HKD 2,000 ($250).

"Go stay at the Royal Pacific."

I accepted the cash and grabbed a cab to Tsimshatsui (TST District).

Walking into a luxury hotel felt like I had finally made it. I slept on a bunk just four months ago in the cheapest place. Now, I was staying in a lavish room with a view of the harbor. I appreciated the short-term comfort.

Before returning to the mainland, I stocked up on canned soup. It would be swell to have a bowl of minestrone while catching up on *Santa Barbara*. I became so hooked that I turned down lunches depending on the cliffhanger.

Both sides of the border checked the bag with the twenty cans of soup and asked, "Why?" I said I had eating restrictions similar to Jewish people. That worked. I called it the incredibly high-salt diet.

Upon arrival, airport personnel insisted on inspecting everyone's luggage tags. I couldn't remember someone checking my tag in the U.S., but I worked with Chinese rules. I ripped the tags off my suitcase and attached the claim receipt. Then, I handed it over as I navigated through. Occasionally, ambitious staff yelled or grabbed my bag, but they released me when they realized I'd given them both tags. It also worked well when traveling with a group. I matched up all the tags and gave them the stack. By the time they reviewed them, we had already left. It was a minor victory on my terms.

If I carried too much baggage, customs would inspect it. I usually had one rollaboard carry-on. That made it easy to speed past the staff, who appeared to stop foreigners for fun. Fujian Province seemed more sensitive than other places like Shanghai or Beijing. Customs flipped through my books and magazines, looking for controversial things. They must have been searching for naked pictures because they let me go with my readers by Henry Miller and Charles Bukowski.

Sometimes, they cracked down on electronics and confiscated anything undeclared. We had to bring electronics in from outside because Chinese products were outdated, bulky, and expensive. The easiest way to supply a mainland office was to carry everything from Hong Kong. I did this after I tried to purchase a fax machine. Fax machines were new technology. The only place to buy in Putian was the post office. The government wanted control. That meant lots of paperwork, and I needed a local person to guarantee on my behalf. They could prosecute that individual if I did something subversive and left. Faxes were a scary item for governments that liked to monitor all information. Before cell phones, they were the best method of communication. The cheapest machine in Putian was $500. I acquired one in Hong Kong for a third of the cost.

IX

Upon my return to Putian, a professor at the local university contacted me to chat with the students. Others asked me to teach or do business once word got around that I was in town. Individuals approached me when I walked the streets or while I ate, desiring to make friends. I appreciated the attention, but I felt like an exotic animal, and everyone stopped and pointed me out as soon as they saw me.

"Run! The foreign devil is coming."

It reminded me of the Godzilla movies. I was in no danger, but everybody wanted something.

When the teacher from the college approached, I expected it would be ten or fifteen pupils—a casual talk. Hell, I used to wing it for two hours every night in Taiwan. This should be easy.

She met me at the gate and guided me through a maze of buildings until we stopped at a lecture hall. I strolled in and saw row after row of students and more standing at the top of the stadium seating. There were a hundred and fifty undergraduates—NOT what I expected. I had done zero preparation, and now I had a lot of eyes focused on me.

First, I started with my background and requested them to write some questions to give me material to work with. They were slow to ask; some wrote in Chinese, perhaps to test my language ability. They asked,

"Why did you come to China?"

"What is the difference between China and the U.S.?"

"Do you like Chinese girls?"

"Are you married?"

"Why is the U.S. dollar green?"

This lasted for an hour until the session ended. I thought I handled the situation well, but the university never contacted me again.

I also gave a talk at an elementary school. That was easier. As soon as I walked in, everybody laughed. A class of giggling grade-schoolers was less pressure than a hall full of college undergrads. At least with the youngsters, I was the most intelligent person, but probably not for long. Anytime I said something, the kids laughed. I turned into Mr. Bean. I endured ten minutes of this before I left.

After those experiences, I was done with classroom speaking.

Being the only fluent English speaker in town, I had people wanting to practice. My biggest stalker was the one I couldn't shake—the hotel manager. He knew when I returned. For two weeks, the phone rang when I entered my room. After sitting most of the day in hot weather on the production lines, practicing English was the last thing I wanted to do. I kept telling him, "Maybe tomorrow." He didn't seem to get the hint, or perhaps he did. One day, he called to see if I would meet downstairs. I gave him the standard response. This time, he countered,

"Two girls also want to practice."

"I'll be down in two minutes."

He finally figured out a way to get my attention.

We met in the lobby and chatted over tea. I talked about my funny experiences. One girl asked direct questions about America, such as:

"Why do Americans like violence?"

"If America is the richest country, why are there poor people?"

This line of questioning surprised me because I was there to speak English and meet girls, not to defend my country's policies. None had visited the U.S., so I recommended they travel there before making an opinion. However, the girl who asked the tough questions piqued my interest. She was inquisitive, and I liked that.

I wanted to know her better and make my case for America.

I tried to keep busy, but time passed slowly—almost at a standstill. And just when I was tired of the routine, my life changed when the first bowling alley opened. Bowling became huge in the early '90s, and every city I traveled to had an alley.

Putian's first grew popular, but they used shoddy materials. Not long after, a larger place opened with international equipment and twenty lanes (land was cheap). They also installed karaoke rooms in case we felt the urge to sing after. This alley offered prizes for scores above two hundred, including a brand-new scooter for a perfect game. That seemed unattainable until I watched a guy hit eleven strikes. The building blacked out just as he prepared for the last strike. When the power returned, they reset the scores. They said he needed a complete game, or they would give him a cigarette lighter as a consolation. Everyone, including the workers, saw he had eleven strikes. Only fifteen people were in the joint, and everybody betted against him. Naturally, the bowler and the rest of his party argued with the staff.

I finished my game but stayed to enjoy the argument. Since we lacked decent TV, watching a fight was entertaining. If I headed someplace and passed by a heated disagreement, I would stop and join the masses. Often, somebody next to me would offer a cigarette. They didn't care that I was a foreigner. We were all spectators.

Rarely did locals throw a punch. They shouted, "I'll beat you to death!" or banged tables and chairs, moved their arms a lot, and loved to shake their fingers in your face. That would cause someone to hit you in America, but no punches here. Arguments resembled ping-pong matches as each side attempted to crush the other. It didn't matter if you were right or wrong. If you were skilled, you could be incorrect but still persuade bystanders to side with you and shout at the victim on your behalf. It took a pro, but not impossible.

I sided with the guy and told him he was right.

"Even the *laowai* saw I had eleven strikes!"

Once he called me a *laowai*, he lost my support, but he must have had someone get relatives because his crowd grew. The police showed up, and I left. I think he won the disagreement as the scooter disappeared.

Soon after the bowling alley, they built a go-cart track. I didn't understand the connection, but other cities had the same bowling/go-carting revolution. We continued to drink while riding go-carts around. Drinking and driving did not have the same stigma in China. Few drivers got stopped, even though most of the cars had to be driven by somebody who had imbibed. What else would people do with only nightclubs and karaoke open?

The next development was a public swimming pool. When living in hot weather, nothing looked more refreshing than a blue pool. Every week, I watched them build it and anxiously awaited the opening. I wanted to ensure I made it to the pool while still clean. I wasn't confident they would use the proper amount of chlorine.

When the time arrived, I grabbed some cheap hotel towels and a six-pack. I had visions of sitting in the water, drinking a cold one. No matter how splendid the pool was, they would not have drinks but wouldn't care if I brought my own.

I tried it on a Saturday morning, and no one was there. How could it be? Wasn't everyone as excited as me? It was hot as hell, and I expected a line. That's okay. I had it all to myself.

Then, the situation improved. After chilling for a half-hour, a few dancehall girls arrived. They surprised me as Chinese women avoided the sun like Nosferatu. They wanted the pasty white Goth look. Sunscreen wasn't available in town, or maybe in all of China, and I prepared to burn. Perhaps the gals hadn't thought it through, for they left shortly after arriving.

And as I predicted, the water looked less blue after a week. I bought sunscreen on my next trip to Hong Kong but never returned to use it.

Twice, my posse and I visited the port, a half-hour away. We rented a wooden skiff and crossed the ocean channel to Mei Zhou Island. We ate fresh seafood and swam on the empty beaches. I enjoyed the limitless opportunities (relatively speaking). As long as you had the means, there was a way. Most people lacked the right connections or money. They worked extended hours for small salaries. They had little cash to blow on renting boats and pool parties.

If I woke up with a clear schedule, I wondered, "What kind of good trouble can I get into today?" or "Where should I spend an afternoon eating and drinking?" Why not? I passed the time, waiting for something to happen.

I fished in the U.S. and looked for an opportunity in Putian. Zhang Bo said he could get us into the reservoir area.

"Fishing is illegal, but I know a guy."

If Zhang Bo said it was not a problem, I didn't worry. I once saw him punch a motorcycle taxi that came too close. He didn't jab the guy; he knocked the headlight out and swore in PT dialect. Then, the motorcycle taxis all retreated. When I witnessed that, I knew he was a valuable person to have on my side.

He had everything under control and secured the fishing rods and bait. I expected the standard rod and reel similar to what I used, but he had Chinese poles. These rods were a foot long but extended to twenty feet, like a super Pocket Fisherman. It wasn't the type of fishing I looked forward to, but it was better than nothing.

Once baited, I dipped the short line in and waited. No bites. I guessed it might be the pig liver bait. It attracted small fish, but not the gigantic monster I had waited for. The reservoir was large and deep. There had to be enormous carp lurking around. If I had snagged one, it would have snapped my bamboo pole into pieces.

The following year, I brought my rod and reel from home with salmon eggs and florescent stink baits. I planned to show my posse how to fish by casting far from shore. But I still received no hits while they pulled in panfish. I gave up and blamed it on my bait. Local fish didn't dig Western food.

While I bowled and fished to fame, Bryon tried to hire more Americans and laid off two guys. One dude stayed in his room and never visited the factories. Bryon made an excuse to get the employee to leave for a few hours. Then, housekeeping let him into the room (Bryon paid the bill) to pack the guy's stuff. Bryon had it waiting in the lobby for when he returned. It was a cruel way to exit a company. I felt secure about my position because I always visited the factories, and it would be harder to come to Putian to pull a stunt like that.

Living in Putian for a period, I realized how easy it was to lose myself with the separation from the rest of the world and the vast amount of alcohol. Some foreigners in China fell deep into the bottle and couldn't find their way out. Others went super local and shed their foreignness. I did a little of both, but I kept a harmony. If I could no longer balance between my Chinese life and my American one, it was time to depart.

Bryon asked me to fly to Qingdao to help interview guys for the manager's job and inspect production. He hired an assistant manager named Paul, who narrowed down the group and would pass off any candidates he found suitable for the China test. I met Paul during his interview in Hong Kong when I came in on my previous visa run. Bryon said, "Here is one of our front line workers. He was an Olympic qualifier in Greco-Roman wrestling (I was a state qualifier when I was fourteen—Bryon liked to stretch the truth). Now he is the movie star of a place called Putian. If you land the job, you will travel there someday."

Paul got the position, and as an eager recruit, he phoned me while I ate my lunchtime soup to discuss my Qingdao arrangements. Not knowing anything about my situation, he asked,

"Can I get you something that will help improve your life?"

"You can start by sending me a hamburger. That would make things great, but I also need the purchase orders, a computer, a printer, etc."

"Well, I can't do anything about the hamburger, but let's see what we can do about the other things when you arrive in Qingdao."

CHAPTER EIGHT

QINGDAO: BEER CAPITAL

The official purpose of my trip to Qingdao was to meet applicants for the manager's position and to watch over production. But my real motive was to find the Tsingtao beer I drank at home. Where I grew up, if you were under twenty-one, you had the best chance of being served at bowling alleys and Chinese restaurants. They ignored the age limit, but Chinese restaurants served better-tasting brews, including Tsingtao. I assumed I would see this famous beer in every restaurant. Instead, I found everything but Tsingtao.

How did China produce a great-tasting brew? The Germans claimed Qingdao (Tsingtao) as a colony from the 1800s until 1916, and they built their own brewery to appease their tastebuds. When they left, the Japanese took control then the Chinese Nationalist Government. After they retreated to Taiwan, the CCP produced the beer. They sold it overseas to reap hard currency while they peddled a weak concoction domestically. If any place stocked the *Deutschland* version, it would be Qingdao, and I was on a quest.

There were no direct flights between two medium-sized cities, such as Fuzhou and Qingdao. What should have been a two-hour journey took most of the day. That was on top of the seven-hour car ride from Putian and a night's stay in Fuzhou. It was a hell of a journey for a beer run.

I arrived and took a taxi to the Dynasty Hotel—the location of our office. It made sense to locate our company in a hotel when getting approval for international phone and fax lines was challenging.

The two best hotels had a monopoly on decent accommodations. They knew it and priced the rooms at $200 a night (compared to $80 for my Fuzhou hotel). I could get something luxurious for that price in Hong Kong.

When I walked into the lobby, I realized I had made a mistake by not calling ahead. The Dynasty had run out of rooms, so I checked in at the Hai Tian, a better and more expensive option. Actually, I preferred to reside there, or I would go stir-crazy if I lived in the same place as the office. Similar to what happens in Vegas, you stay in the hotel.

Also, like Vegas, I didn't plan on things being so expensive. I neglected to bring the stacks of RuMBas necessary for a two-week stay. My cash stash would only last for a week. Luckily, the hotel accepted credit cards. Very few places in the entire country accepted international credit cards.

By the time I reached Qingdao, Paul had narrowed the applicants down to two guys. He reviewed their backgrounds while I prepared to give them the hardcore China interview involving a factory dinner and enough drinking to see if they fell apart. We didn't want to set someone loose without ensuring they wouldn't embarrass the rest of us.

Besides the foreign manager who needed a replacement, we had two office staff and two inspectors. The most critical guy quit with the foreign manager. That left an office assistant (dating the employee who walked), a QC (he resigned), and a QC who gave a false name. That guy ended up being the brother of the dude who had left! No one discussed this secret web of relationships that became clear only after Paul and I arrived. We placed orders for millions of pairs here with a skeleton crew. While we searched for workers, we ran things.

Our company used a fax system, updated from a telex. Within the thirty pages we received daily were new orders, sample details, customer-specific packaging instructions, shipping date requests, problems, customer chargebacks, L/C info, payment details, and anything else they wanted to write. All points needed to be answered before the U.S. started work at 8 a.m. NYC time. If the factory declined to respond, we ensured they answered. Every day was a race against the clock.

As the enforcers, we had to be on call twenty-four hours to receive complaints and questions from salesmen. Even if they realized we couldn't help, it felt good to yell at somebody, and they knew we understood every word. It was therapy for them but not enjoyable for us. To be reachable, I carried my first mobile phone. The Big Black Mariah, an analog Motorola hand-held, was a significant step up from my Putian pager. China did not have digital service yet, so we made do with the massive transmitter devices. It looked like a car phone from the '80s, a significant piece of technology, demanding a frightening price ($3,000).

Like fax machines, the post office controlled the mobile phone business. They also offered the phone service at a blistering rate, but cheaper than the hotel.

One benefit of this marvel of electronics was EVERYONE KNEW YOU HAD A BIG-ASS PHONE! Macho guys whipped them out and slammed them on the table, standing erect to announce their arrival. It was a status symbol in a country that had just started paying attention to that sort of thing. You couldn't hide this phone. It was a black brick with a hand strap. Many players carried them and the lumps of RuMBas they dished out in a leather man bag the size of a toiletry. I didn't go that route. Instead, I destroyed a couple of pairs of pants by trying to squeeze the brick in my back pocket and many wallets by stuffing wads of RuMBas in them. With the Black Mariah, I moved from a nobody to a somebody. People respected the brick, but it came with the baggage of being on call. On the positive side, China had weak telephone service. If the call came from an international source, it would rarely connect.

"The subscriber you are dialing is not in service. Please dial again."

Even when not in use, it was busy. I'm sure people gave up after listening to the recording more than they desired; I did after calling the factory a few times and hearing the message.

As soon as we received the fax, we divided it by category. We had to gather the urgent answers with enough time to clarify anything before the factory staff left. Then, we typed them up on a DOS computer that often crashed, printed out thirty pages of answers, faxed them, and resent them when the unstable phone line cut off. We waited for the fax report every night to see if we had sent it successfully or needed to start all over. We didn't leave the office most nights until 8 or 9 p.m., much later than the Export Dept. staff.

The single phone line for ten employees was part of the headache. If I got through, the export staff said they would call back. That's when we decided to head there and wait until they answered. It was an excellent opportunity to introduce ourselves. Paul stayed in the city for a week, and no one had bothered to welcome him. They didn't sound hospitable.

The plant was a large state-owned enterprise with over ten production lines. Inside, it felt like stepping back in time with the large character slogans and pictures of the boss hanging on the walls. They specialized in basic white action-leather shoes. Once they worked out the sweet spot for steady production, they could mass produce millions superbly for as long as necessary. Make a single change, and everything fell apart until they held meetings to discuss. It was a side effect of government control: Nobody made a move until told. By then, it was too late. Individuals only did as per their job description and never moved outside the box. Although the state jobs paid less and controlled every aspect of your life, people craved them for their iron rice bowl benefit. Privately run operations were more agile and paid better but lacked job security. If you wished to work for an independent enterprise, you had to ask your designated work unit (*danwei*) for approval. If you left without consent, you lost control of your personal file with your information. Later on, you needed that file, and you had to return to your *danwei*, begging for it—not a suitable position for bargaining.

Paul and I entered the factory grounds, and the three-story pink Buddha surprised me. It stuck out as truly out of place with the gray, rectangular buildings. The Buddha had red nipples that lit up on special occasions. Something seemed wrong about that. The boss liked animals and built a mini zoo between the walkway from the workshop to the company restaurant. I thought we were choosing proteins to eat, like passing through a grocery store.

It was not the case—a good thing since only monkeys were available. The Buddha, the monkeys, and the boss rode around in a black town car. It felt odd but peculiar seemed at home in China.

We located the Export Department and pressed them for the info. As we prepared to head back, they said the Export Manager wished to see us. It was about time. Export Managers held tremendous power in large government factories because they pulled in dollars. We waited, and she took her time. An hour later, Manager Wen arrived to inform us they planned to move our production to a new workshop on an island an hour away. We waited for this? She assured us the quality would remain the same because the line managers were also moving—a forced commute. We were opposed to any changes mid-stream and reluctant to give up the stability of the main factory.

"If something goes wrong, we will move back."

She said that, but we understood we had nowhere to go. As always, we remained at their mercy.

Manager Wen invited us to dinner to celebrate the arrangement. Finally, we would have a full-on feast to create good *guanxi*. Bryon told me about the over-the-top meals he had in Qingdao with enormous platters of giant sea creatures, and, although I looked forward to the spectacle, it would not be the food I preferred.

Before the feast, we had to fax out the answers. Manager Wen lent us a company driver and an account manager named Edward to expedite the process. He was a lanky dude who did the work nobody else wanted—such as waiting for two Westerners. While we worked on the replies, he remained in the lobby. Then, it took forty-five minutes to reach the factory.

When we showed up, the restaurant was dead. The factory owned the place, and the staff turned up when someone told them to.

We found a few workers sleeping in the back. Edward said, "I'm with the Export Dept. and Manager Wen arranged a dinner."

The cooks replied no one had informed them. They needed confirmation from someone with authority. Edward did not want to call and said, "Manager Wen will arrive soon, and she can straighten it out."

I reminded him it would take time to prepare. Either he calls, or I will.

I walked out to have a smoke. When I returned, the workers had opened a private dining room and turned on the lights and A/C. The VIP room sounded nice, but it barely had enough space to fit the round table for ten. We sat in the chairs opposite the door out of respect, but they were also the most challenging to get out from. The room had that damp, moldy odor. It would have been more striking if not for the *baijiu* scent. Like Beijing, they drank the hard hootch.

The server said, "The Export Manager will arrive shortly," and closed the door.

We sat for ten minutes and nothing, not even a little tea. I sensed massive disrespect, worse than what I received in Putian from the government factories. I asked Paul,

"What the hell did you do to piss her off?"

"Nothing. The manager is a hard person to deal with. That's why we have jobs."

I wandered outside looking for a waitress but struck out. I told Edward to call again. It was eight o'clock, and we were starving. Edward had eaten while he waited. He was more intelligent than he acted.

"She said she will be here soon."

"Did she say *ma shang* (immediately)?"

"Yes."

"Isn't that what she replied an hour ago?"

"Yes."

We discussed giving up, but Edward begged us to stay. He agreed she should have done better with the arrangements, but he would be yelled at if we left. We stuck it out a little longer since he took my complaining for an hour. Twenty minutes later, she showed up and assumed we would start without her. Why not tell the cooks?

She arrived with her assistant.

"It's my pleasure to meet you. My name is Swallow."

Wait a minute, did she say 'Swallow?'

"Swallow, like the bird, swallow."

Oh, that swallow. I thought I'd heard every English name as a teacher.

I glanced around the table and knew this would not be the rocking feast I had hoped for. There would be no *baijiu* to accompany the stench. Even worse, they didn't have Tsingtao beer, not even the watery one.

Just like the shoes, we were at their mercy.

The Export Manager told the restaurant staff to start, and I requested a menu.

"No menu. It's a set meal."

With a growing stable of products and retail outlets, they had to ensure the different departments didn't throw outlandish meals, so they prearranged the selection. Depending on the customer's status, they could raise the menu's level: grouper and prawns for the top clients and river carp and snails for the lower ones. Judging by the food, we fell somewhere in between. I asked the cook to make something spicy, but it didn't turn out well.

The evening was a bust. There wasn't any drinking. I nursed a hangover from the night before and didn't want to waste liver cells on this lot. Everyone needed a day off.

I had no plans to eat with Manager Wen again, nor did she ask. Months later, she got demoted to the African office. She must have pissed off someone a level above. Swallow became the new manager. With the additional responsibility came a name change. She transformed into Lisa. That was easier to say with a straight face.

‖

Qingdao lacked recreational activities. Mt. Lao (Lao Shan) was the leading draw. I hiked it once but didn't wish to do it often. The city had stunning German villas; however, they were not accessible. I discovered an aquarium with glass so dirty I suspected the tanks remained empty. The beach appeared to be the choice option despite the brown seawater. On a Saturday, I walked across the street and tried it.

I arrived at 11 a.m. and had never seen so many individuals on a slice of sand. In the U.S., we kept a distance from the next person, but not in China. They squeezed enough people to cover the beach except for a single area that charged 50 RMB ($7) to rent oversized umbrellas. If you put down the RuMBas, you had use of a vacant part of the waterfront. No one wanted to pay, which made it a brilliant investment.

People in the free section pointed at me as I took my place on the sand.

"Look at that rich *laowai*. I told you foreigners have lots of money!"

They also yelled at the umbrella rental attendants.

"Why do you treat foreigners better than Chinese? This is China."

I often heard that when I boarded flights with priority. I paid extra for the front-of-the-line service. People at the beach had the option to pay. Nobody was refusing them.

I brushed it off, put my headphones on, and slept in the sun. When I woke, I noticed nobody had taken the offer to rent space, but a family was squatting under my umbrella. I only fell asleep for an hour.

"*Ni Hao*," I said to a woman eating sunflower seeds.

"You speak Chinese so well."

"*Na li, na li* (a modest way to say 'no'). Why are you lying under my umbrella?"

The woman beside her, also with a pile of seed shells, said,

"He speaks Chinese well."

"I studied at Peking University."

"Oh, do you know Big Mountain, the Canadian?"

"Yes, he was there. Can you explain why you are sitting under my shade?"

"You weren't using it."

She got me. The umbrella attendants seemed preoccupied to notice a family taking over my real estate. Lucky for them, I was tired of the beach. I packed up and gave them the shade, but the attendants wouldn't return my 200 RMB deposit unless I returned it. As a result, the clan needed to join the crowded masses again.

After sending the fax every evening, we hit the streets searching for nightlife. There weren't any bars outside the hotels, and hotel lounges were sad affairs with businessmen who didn't speak Chinese, seeking somebody to talk to. I wanted a venue to hang with locals and get shots of whiskey to ease my withdrawal symptoms. Some place had to have hard liquor for a reasonable price.

We hopped into taxis and asked them to take us someplace fun but ended up with mixed results. One driver sent us to a children's park with coin-operated animal rides similar to what I would find outside a grocery store. Another time, a taxi dropped us off at a bar on top of a mountain. They played loud music with no customers. We entered, sat on a gigantic sofa, and viewed the menu card (**Rule#7**). Most items were not available, including cold beer. This was Qingdao, the Beer Capital of China! Locals loved their ale so much that they sold bags of it on the street. Guys set up kegs, and you chose your bag size; they filled it up, tied it, and handed it over with a straw for a few RMB. If they sold draft beer in a bag, I should be able to drink chilled brews in a dark, cavernous karaoke on a hill. Our cab had left long ago, forcing us to walk down in the dark to find another venue.

Rule #20: Only let your ride leave once you are sure you no longer need it.

Eventually, a cab took us to a joint called the Spaceship Bar. It looked promising, with Western tunes blasting through the velvet curtain. We paid a 50 RMB cover and took a chance. It was the most bustling spot we had discovered so far. The DJ looked American Indian and spoke Mandarin with an accent. I guessed he was from the Philippines.

We parked at a high chair table and requested a pitcher and shots. Before they arrived, a short, stocky guy with curly hair waltzed over with a jug and introduced himself as Allen from Canada. He had a strong Canadian accent mixed with a bit of Popeye. Allen wore a Hawaiian print that matched his shirt with his shorts. It appeared he had on Garanimals (kid's clothes with animals on the tags to match the patterns), so that's what I nicknamed him. Plus, Allen was a handful when drunk reminding me of the muppet Animal. He designed golf courses in Asia and the Middle East. China was the newest market and very profitable.

Garanimal invited the DJ over. Dee Lo was the first foreigner working in a bar that I met. It surprised me that he could get the proper paperwork for a work visa, but he said he was legit. He drank with us before returning to playing music. At the top of the hour, he put on Beethoven's Fifth, and a spaceship slid down a track over the dance floor. Then, an explosion of sound, light, and smoke ensued, after which he reverted to the same repetitive techno popular all over the mainland. Disco, Disco, Disco. Everyone started dancing. It was an obligation. On future visits, I got him to play my music, and I stood behind the turntables to tell him which song to pick. I required better tunes to sit in a bar for a few hours.

Since they were local, I inquired about other drinking establishments. Dee Lo claimed the Spaceship Bar was the only one. Garanimal alluded to a few places by the airport, drawing a late-night crowd. The airport? Why not? China had exciting and exotic things around the corner. I never knew what to expect, and I thrived off that feeling.

We grabbed a few beers and rode a taxi to check it out. With no traffic at 1 a.m., we arrived in a half-hour. I did not expect to uncover a half dozen restaurants in the middle of nowhere. Although we found ourselves at what appeared to be an oasis of roadhouses, it didn't seem dangerous.

Garanimal led the way into a restaurant, and the manager welcomed him like they were good friends. Despite his height disadvantage, he carried a brick and had a strut. Anyone with a brick must be respected.

The restaurant wasn't what I would call a "bar," but they served cold beer. Guys played cards and drank while we ate and tried to figure out how they played. We saw no women until the manager asked if we planned to head upstairs.

"What's upstairs?"

"Go see."

Yeah, I suspected there had to be something besides cards that drew all these dudes.

I was still shocked that they could do this business in socialist China. It must've started after I left Beida, and it seemed to be picking up steam.

I thought back to the ticket taker on the bus in 1990 who flirted with me, and now women were laying out everything. Prostitution would spread to every corner, and it became hard to find a place that didn't have working ladies.

One peek at the crack-den-like atmosphere of the second floor, and we headed back to town. No thanks.

After three weeks in Qingdao and a short trip out of town to Confucius' birthplace in Qufu, I itched to return to Putian. I had one applicant to interview who Paul felt was the right guy, but I didn't have a good factory nearby to drink with to test him. We hired him anyway. Everything seemed normal, but we had to let him go. We instructed him to arrive at the office to read the daily fax. Our office assistant would open the room and print it out; all he needed to do was show up. I arrived around 9:30.

When I walked in, I asked, "Where's the foreigner?"

"He's in the shower."

I couldn't believe it. HE TOOK A SHOWER IN THE OFFICE ON HIS FIRST DAY! He stayed in the same hotel and could have showered in his room. I knocked on the door, and he said, "I'll be right out."

He walked out wearing just a towel and said, "I waited for the fax, so I took a shower."

We let him go on that day.

With no candidates to interview, I returned to Putian. Paul ran the shop until he found a proper candidate. And I discovered the real Tsingtao beer in my hotel lobby. It was the only location with it, making Hai Tian my home whenever I visited the city until something better opened.

CHAPTER NINE

FUAN: BAGELS AND PBR

I made the long trek to Putian from Qingdao after a quick dip into Hong Kong to restart my visa clock. When I walked into the lobby of The Heavenly Concubine after being away for three weeks, the lone worker at the front desk asked me,

"Why are you here?"

"Why am I here? Don't you remember me? I am the foreign devil, ruler of the second floor, Mr. Thunder!" (It was my "Damn it! I'm Gumby." moment.)

"Mr. Thunder, I know who you are, but the government shut off the water for ten days or more."

I hopped up the stairs to confirm she was right. That left me with no choice. I grabbed some money and clothes and drove back to Fuzhou. I planned to visit a workshop in Fuan, a small town with a population of 600,000, located a hundred miles north of Fuzhou. Even the agent determined the place was too challenging to reach. They placed the order through a local trading company without investigating. I think they chose isolated factories to discourage customers from visiting. They never expected someone like me.

I hired Little Yu, and the two of us left early from Fuzhou to get a jump on the jams. We took a narrow, winding, two-lane path through the mountains. Most of the drive lacked a safety barrier. We might have gone over if too close to the edge. The fog was so dense that we could barely see the brake lights of the car ahead. None of this bothered the chain-smoking lorry drivers, who had no problem blindly passing a slower Mad Max machine while hurtling around a bend at high speeds. It turned my beltless passenger seat into a nerve-wracking experience; even I had to sit in the rear, not that it would have made a difference. Either way, I would have flown through the windshield.

A trip of this distance should take three hours. With the road being rebuilt, the mountains dynamited, and the houses chopped in half, it took between seven and twelve hours. My record was nineteen nonstop from Putian to Fuan. Nineteen hours for a 160-mile trip! That allowed me to learn more curse words.

The beginning of the journey was quite pleasant. The scenery resembled an excursion through Sequoia in some places and a war zone in others. Once we progressed up the hill, we ran into the start of the construction and the convoy. The local police stopped traffic in one direction for a few hours to let the traffic flow from the other. Also, each village controlled the section through their area. They stopped us at one town, and we were halted further down the line. Sometimes, we got lucky and tacked on to the tail end of the convoy as we cruised through the stop point. Other times, they closed it down right as we reached the front.

When we hit our first delay, we settled in and hoped for the best. We knew we had to wait long if vendors came from the villages to hawk goods. Elderly men and women hustled down the mountain footpath with a pole on their shoulders, balancing two straw baskets filled with products. It looked as if they carried a giant scale. I tried it once, and the bamboo pole left a mark. I wasn't cut out for the hawking business. These entrepreneurs wore thatched rain ponchos, topped off with a farmer's flat straw hat. I bought one as a student but left it when I realized how stupid I looked with it. For these scarecrows brought to life, the hats became an indispensable part of their attire and would appear odd if they put on anything else, such as those that sported a plastic bag. It worked but was missing the cool factor. Only certain individuals could carry off the bag on head look.

Most of the time, the goods lacked appeal, such as warm cans of mixed congee or marinated eggs and tofu. But sometimes, I found a surprise, like Pabst Blue Ribbon (PBR). Yes, they sold warm PBR and bagels in the mountains. They weren't authentic, but they looked like them. That was enough for someone who rarely saw bread without a paste or processed meat oozing from it. However, the bagels were so hard that they could crack your teeth. I doused them in PBR and imagined the taste of cream cheese and chives for the perfect improvised breakfast.

During the first stop point, I passed the time by mingling with the villagers, but the novelty of being a movie star quickly wore off. I dreaded these stops, especially when hungover. I wanted to finish the work and return to my Hot Spring room. Instead, I got stuck in a jam, far from comfort. When it rained, the roads turned into rivers of mud, and the backup worsened.

To make up time, Little Yu sped down the side until we got caught by the police. I used the foreigner card when they stopped us. On some occasions, I was the no-nothing *laowai*. Other times, I played the fluent China-savvy traveler. Both worked in the right situation.

If we drove towards Fuzhou, Little Yu would tell the police, "The *laowai* has a flight to catch."

If we headed towards Fuan, he would say, "The *laowai* is an investor, and he must get back to catch a flight."

It always revolved around "my flight." It didn't matter if I flew to the U.S. or in China. Few people had flown. It still had a sense of stature. Something of that importance must not be missed. They understood and respected that. The flight excuse worked well until more individuals started flying. Then, the response from the police was, "Flights are late all the time. It will wait for you, or you can take another."

It was good while it lasted.

A few times, "The Man" commandeered my car and told Little Yu to drive. It was an innocent hostage situation, and the po-po exited at some point. They probably thought I couldn't speak Mandarin, not that they planned to ask for permission. Local district police were king-like. They did as they pleased. I didn't complain because they took us in the direction we wanted to go. With the cop, we made it through the checkpoints. Plus, they handed out a few cigarettes—a benefit.

I laughed off these situations until I reached my limit—the final straw. It didn't have to be a big thing to set me off. Sometimes, it was a minor issue, like someone cutting in line for the hundredth time or not having hot water for my shower. Other times, it was the right moment for a blowup. Every foreigner had an internal "bad China day clock," which ticked away in the background. Anytime a good thing happened, the hands moved away from a blowup. Red tape? Turn the hands forward. Five-hour traffic jam? Turn the hands forward. Drunk or hungover? You might have multiple eruptions. The inner clock varied for each person, and the longer you stayed, the less things irritated you. I experienced many foreigner outbursts at hotel registration desks and flight check-in counters. I would glance over, smirk, and then continue with my business. It wasn't my time.

My blowups occurred as sarcasm. I never resorted to breaking things, screaming, or violence. That stuff would end up in expulsion or a week in jail—not good for somebody building a career. All I wanted was a small "victory" to get where I needed to go.

I wasn't looking to change China.

One of my memorable "triumphs" happened en route to Fuan. We moved slowly behind the other vehicles when Little Yu swerved to miss a giant pothole. A cop directing the stoppage motioned us off the road. Little Yu usually talked his way out of trouble with a fifty spot. But he returned, pulled over to a waiting area, and said,

"The cop is holding us for five hours because we crossed onto the new road."

That was unacceptable. I took matters into my own hands (**Rule #9**) and got out to approach the police. Local law enforcement would need to save face and not look as if they kowtowed to a foreigner. Maybe he would let us leave if I attempted the poor, pathetic routine in broken Mandarin. Well, he didn't go for it. He waved me off, turned his back, and walked away. I felt my clock hands winding forward until the alarm went off, and it was loud. I scurried to get in front of him without taking a slide and said (I became fluent),

"Fine, if I have to stay here for five hours, I will follow you everywhere you go. If you go home, I will go home with you; if you go eat, I will go eat with you; and if you go to the bathroom, I will accompany you."

Then I followed behind, so close that I was in his face when he turned around. He could have made my life worse, but it was indeed the last straw. Fortunately, instead of jail, the guy tired of me after twenty minutes and let us go. I irritated him after five, but that would be too short.

My "bad China day clock" reset again.

We reached Fuan at 4 p.m. The town was tiny compared to Fuzhou. The surrounding mountains prevented urban sprawl. Similar to Putian, there were a few main roads. The address the agent gave turned out to be a factory-owned restaurant. I got out, hiked up a flight, and asked the staff,

"Where's the shoe factory?"

"Who are you?"

"I am Mr. Thunder."

A girl picked up the phone and called the plant.

"There is a *laowai* here."

"No need to have someone come over. All we need is the address. We can find it."

Sitting for nine hours made me antsy. Plus, it started to turn dark. I wanted to catch the workers making production before they paused for dinner. No one would make a move until somebody from the factory arrived. Ten minutes later, the manager walked in to greet me. Evidently, it was close—a welcome surprise. Mr. Wu was a tall, thin guy with a long face. He introduced himself and an assistant manager, but before any more small talk, I told him, "We can continue with the introductions later. We need to go right now."

Little Yu followed the manager's car up a winding, narrow road. They built the street out of cobblestones, slippery when wet. The bald tires on our car struggled to gain traction. There were traditional shops, similar to those in Putian, on a slant along both sides of the steep path. It was a major artery into town from the mountain villages, with wet market sellers and shoppers taking any available space. Everyone seemed immune to Little Yu's constant horn honking. They didn't wish to part the sea, allowing our car through. I wondered how the overstuffed trucks got in.

When we reached the factory compound, I headed to the production line. I didn't care to waste time and wanted to check the product as soon as possible. Fuan had the same gray haze the other cities had; even during the day, it wasn't that bright out. The workshop had barn ceilings with tiny lightbulbs dangling from the high beams. They illuminated a yellowish glow, which did little for visibility. I hurried through the inspection before I ran out of light.

They made ladies' casual shoes called palladiums. They stitched the uppers, attached the rubber outsoles, and cooked them in ovens. "Clang, Clang, Clang!" The sweet music of the shoe lasts, hitting the metal bin walls, announcing that I had landed at a vulcanized factory— my favorite. I enjoyed watching the entire shoe-making process on a single production line, from start to finish. The shoes came out of the oven like loaves of baked bread with a cooked rubber smell.

They staged the tour, and I couldn't find anything wrong. If the inspection was problem-free, we would have a wonderful evening of eating and drinking. If things did not go well, we still would have a great evening, but it was uncomfortable after telling the manager to rework thousands of pairs, pay for overtime, and wastage. Sometimes, a rework required air freight charges that gobbled up any profit. It was unfortunate, but they produced the product. Just because a company accepted an order didn't mean they knew how to construct it.

"Lock it down and then ask questions" was their *modus operandi.*

I ended my tour at the warehouse, where I pulled a few cases for the inspection. The quantity of boxes depended on the size and breakdown of the order. I instructed them to lay out each pair without touching them up. They could do all the touch-ups on the production line, but the shoes should be store-ready once packed. It came down to the math; the number of defects against the inspection size determined if the lot shipped. It was subjective, but we lacked a better system.

Once I selected the cases, I initialed them. I had already run into a situation where somebody had switched them on me. After that, I signed each box. I never checked to see if someone had faked my signature. If they would go that far, there wasn't any way to stop them. No matter what, they would sneak the inferior product in.

The factory took the shoes out of the boxes. They appeared spotless, with straight stitching. But when I pressed the heel counter, it shattered. It should have been stiff but flexible without breaking. All the pairs had the same problem. Then I noticed the bottoms came off with little effort. The technician had made the wrong glue mix. It was their job to resolve. I knew the shoes would be a hundred percent rejected. It was terrible news for the factory and the evening. The current shipment was only 1,200 pairs, but they had produced the entire order (12,000).

Mr. Wu had used his money, not the investment group's cash. He asked if we could work something out. I tried to find a solution, but these shoes contained major defects and were unsellable. He thought because they **looked good**, they should be acceptable. If I refrained from pressing on the counter, everything would be fine. "Could I disregard this?" He proposed we ship and worry about the claim later, thinking it would be less than the cost of remaking.

"Sorry, I can't. What if it was you? Would you purchase a pair?"

He had to try. "It doesn't hurt to try" was a way of living in the PRC. Everyone did it without a second thought, and if you didn't, you were the fool.

Mr. Wu said he needed to call his investors. He told me to go to the restaurant with his driver. He would have Little Yu wait for the perfect sales samples I needed to take back. They would join us later. Normally, I wouldn't leave the security of my driver, but I let my guard down. Since breakfast at 6 a.m., all I had to eat were beer bagels. My hunger clouded my thinking.

I grabbed two pairs of defective shoes for safety's sake to show why I had rejected the order. Then I got into the factory Jinbei bread van (I assumed locals called it a bread van for its rectangular shape) and put myself in the hands of the company driver. The problem would cost Mr.

Wu at least $20,000. It was a considerable amount, and they could have someone threaten me for less.

The driver was in his forties and a serious cat. His left eye barely opened, and he squinted in a pirate way with a growl. His face looked leathery and sullen, and he was missing a few teeth. I figured this guy would only require a few seconds to kick my ass. He was tough as nails. I called him Igor. Nobody referred to Igor as "Little." He also didn't seem to be *"Lao"* or old. That title belonged to Mr. Wu. I think an unwritten rule said each group should only have one *"Lao"* person. It didn't matter how many "Littles" there were. Like my friend Zhang Bo, Igor fell into the group referred to by their full name. That settled problematic title issues and gave him respect—a win-win situation.

To my relief, we arrived at the restaurant without incident. Igor turned out to be an all-right dude. He had an opinion on things such as the one-child policy. He tried for his third kid, hoping for a male heir.

"Didn't anyone stop you or issue a fine?"

He said the Birth Control Dept. officials walked up the path to his home, and he told them, "You try to stop me from having a son."

If Igor had answered the door, I would have also walked back down the mountain. This guy did not fool around, and I needed individuals like him for protection.

I followed Igor into the restaurant. They had a few patrons now and a platoon of servers standing at attention. They prepared to serve if only customers came in. Like Putian, locals did not eat out.

The hostess directed me to the private room, a closet with none of the frills of VIP rooms of the future, like karaoke, a restroom, or a disco ball. This one barely fit the standard Chinese table for ten. Why did every place make the rooms too small? Naturally, they guided me to the seat opposite the door, but I took a pass. If I drank lots of beer, I would need multiple trips to the W.C. I did not want to get stuck on the other side, having to squeeze through. I would have rather sat in the main hall, but the hostess said an investor from Hong Kong would dine with me. He gave instructions to put me in the VIP room—forced preferential treatment.

After all the trouble of getting to this factory, I hoped for an over-the-top meal. If the Hong Kong investor planned to join, it should be a quality evening. I waited for five minutes alone in the room until a waitress with a red vest entered and served me a cup of pond water (tea with leaves). It was too hot to pick up. Besides that, the leaves floated on top; I sipped the tea and spat out the leaves that got through without losing the liquid. Most people skipped it altogether; too much trouble. Once I mastered the leave filtering part, I moved to the advanced level of drinking the fluid at scalding temperatures and being able to hold a flimsy, transparent plastic cup. Squeeze too hard, and hot tea splashed all over my hand and lap—not a good place when wearing khakis before a room full of people.

As I waited, it hit me: I had stashed 20,000 RMB in my bag. It was too much cash to stash in my wallet, and I didn't enjoy walking around with two bulges in my pockets. It would be better not to draw attention to the situation and hope for the best.

There was no telling when the investor would arrive. It depended on the roads. When I asked the hostess, she said, "He will be here immediately," which meant another hour.

I was at ease when Little Yu showed up with my bag and the cash. Not long after, the investor arrived. He introduced himself as Jackie and said they would replace the shoes and air freight if necessary. Great! Later, Mr. Wu told me the investors forced him to pay. That sucked.

Jackie said he heard Americans could drink a lot. He wished to test that theory, but it would not be fair for him. He recognized that and called two production managers to join his team. Mr. Wu would meet us at the karaoke (down the hall) after leaving the factory. He was trying to save his investment.

Meanwhile, we rushed through the meal to let the servers leave. It was past ten, and they closed at nine. We finished more than a case and a small portion of food. I felt bloated with the beer sloshing in my stomach. When we transitioned to singing, the other guys slipped out. They returned to work. It was just Jackie, Little Yu, and me until Mr. Wu and another worker snuck in. Mr. Wu abstained from drinking, but he was a thigh slapper (mine)—that superseded all other relationships. I wasn't sure when the thigh slap should occur, but it followed a *ganbei* or something funny I had said. He only toasted me with tea.

Rule #21: Don't *ganbei* with someone drinking a lesser drink.

If somebody wanted to *ganbei,* they should drink the same poison I drank. Otherwise, I had individuals toasting me with Sprite while I drank *baijiu.* If they didn't want to, it was better to "cheers." It sounded like a silly regulation, but people toasted me at every meal. Even though I tried, I couldn't out-drink everybody. Mr. Wu was one of the select that I relaxed my rule because I respected him despite his inability to drink.

I didn't get excited about singing for a couple of guys, but even the hostess from the restaurant sang. She hit the window-shattering, high-pitched notes on folk songs like *"Qian Fu De Ai"* while I sang the deeper male parts. Mr. Wu sang classics such as *"Chang Jiang Zhi Ge"* and "Moscow Nights." Jackie sang H.K. songs like *"Xie Xie Ni De Ai"* and *"Zhu Fu."* I sang "Nine Hundred and Ninety-Nine Roses" and studied the classics from Mr. Wu. They wanted me to sing an English song, but they only owned a single English laser disc. I chose "Blue Bayou" by Roy Orbison. No one complained about my high notes, but they were being kind. I promised to do another English ditty. The only other tune I knew was "Billie Jean" by Michael Jackson. I butchered it.

Thank God smartphones were a decade away.

The karaoke remained open as long as I stayed, but the other guys faded, so we called it a night at 1 a.m. I planned to head for Fuzhou at six in the morning and needed sleep before the car ride, as did Little Yu. It was a decent night of *guanxi*-building.

They took me to the hotel, the only building with lights on. I wanted to crash, but I'd consumed so much beer; it had filled my stomach, and I starved. The hotel served meals during set periods; the last ended at 8 p.m. However, there was always Chinese takeout down the street. Even in small towns, at least one or two dudes operated makeshift restaurants.

I walked down the desolate main road until I discovered a pocket of late-night stalls. I bought some stir-fried noodles and vegetables, then inhaled them in my room while laying out my clothes for my 5 a.m. wake-up call. No matter how late or how drunk I was, I packed my stuff, ready to go in case I left in a rush, like when sleeping through the wake-up call. I didn't want to search for things when hungover, not thinking straight, and in a hurry.

Once I had everything ready for a quick exit at sunrise, I passed out. About an hour later, I abruptly sat up to prevent choking on my regurgitation. Nothing felt worse than waking up by projecting the entire contents of your belly all over yourself. I was in an intoxicated haze but found my bearings and ran to the toilet to get the final bit in the proper place. It was not a good idea to be eating street stir-fry before going to bed on a gut full of PBR.

When the heaves stopped, I caught my breath and searched for the light switch to survey the damage. I took off the sheets, dragged them to the bathroom, dumped them into the tub, and tried to wash them. Everything looked stained and reeked. The weak hotel soap helped little. I needed to do something with the sheets, or I wouldn't be able to take a shower to wake up. I walked to the window and leaned out to see what was below. All I saw was pure darkness, a black hole.

"Why not throw everything out the window? No one will notice, right? They'll blend in."

This was the madness of a drunk at 3 a.m. I wanted to sleep, so I dragged the pile over and threw the sheets without falling out. I solved the problem. Out of sight, out of mind. I closed the windows and slept on the second bed. Fortunately, I had a double.

As soon as I fell asleep, my wake-up call jolted me awake. Gradually, I recalled the events from a couple of hours ago, which seemed dreamlike. I looked at the bare mattress beside me and realized it was no dream. Then I glanced out the window, and there, all spread out, were my vomit-stained sheets and towels. The space below was a construction site. Perhaps it was too early to notice.

I got my shit together and went downstairs to check out. The poor girl who had the early shift handed me my bill, and I had an unrecognizable expense. She said in a casual tone,

"That is for the sheets you threw out the window this morning."

I thought it was eerie she knew I did it, but then I recalled that no other foreigners stayed in this town (**Rule #18**).

Ordinarily, I complained about the foreigner's price for five minutes, but this time, I quietly accepted my extra charge of $10 and got into the car. We had a rough day ahead.

Before leaving the city, I saw a cart peddling Fuan bagels. It would be the best thing to settle my stomach acids. After expelling the meager contents of my belly, I didn't relish starting a long ride without getting something in me. The bagel would expand like an airbag to give me a full feeling until I arrived at Fuzhou.

That would have to do.

The vendor deep-fried a batter mix to slide in between a sliced bagel. Bagel sandwiches! They looked fantastic and the closest thing to an Egg McMuffin in these parts; I had to obtain one. I also wanted to look at the knife he used to cut those stones. Maybe his bagels came fresh out of the oven. That would be nice. The fact that he dipped a ladle into a bucket of dodgy batter should have been a warning. Once again, I broke my rules about hygiene—a mistake. I took a bite and found out the bagels were just as rock hard, and the batter contained baby oysters. The thought of squishy baby oysters on a hungover stomach made me sick. It wasn't the breakfast I had hoped for. I tossed it, and we started our journey.

A few hours into the trip, I got cold sweats, stomach pains, and general discomfort. Every pothole we hit felt excruciating. What could I do? I wasn't ready to use a mountain outhouse. My squatting skills were amateur. I had to stand my ground and will myself to "hold it" for six hours. It was amazing how my mind tricked my body into doing things when I faced the option of using a smelly hole with no toilet paper! How do I manage that? Would I lose the battle?

Well, I survived. I checked in and hurried to my room. Once my mind knew I had gotten closer to my destination, the urgency became more intense.

Do not eat the breakfast sandwich.

A week later, I returned to check the production. When I picked a few cases, I discovered they neglected to match the size labels with the correct shoes. It made me think this place had never produced for export anywhere. We had a store audit scheduled. The last thing I wanted was for a customer to observe them repacking shoes; it was a worrying sign for anyone, not to mention someone who traveled eight hours by car. I moved two of our employees to stay full-time while I worked with the management to set up a quality system.

Our local staff enjoyed being stationed at Fuan; it reminded them of home, and everything was 1980s-cheap, but not for me. Months after announcing the end of the dual price system, the hotel still charged me double the rack rate. The official news had not trickled down, and local authorities did not care. I was the only visitor affected. I had some pretty heated arguments with the front desk when I left at 6 a.m., and they charged me extra for a room with no hot water. Nothing like a tired, hungover foreigner to be your first checkout.

The program our agent placed was so high profile that Bryon and our boss from the U.S. accompanied the client. Sometimes, when you tell somebody how lengthy a ride will be, they don't understand until they have to endure it. I could do nothing about the roads, but I tried to soften the blow by providing comfort from home. We had to avoid having an angry customer coming in hot to do an audit, so I called Paul and explained the meal situation. He planned to travel with me ahead of the visit. I wrote a shopping list of things to bring from Hong Kong to create a Western dinner option. We also stocked the rooms with bottles of Coke, Evian, chocolates, gigantic bags of M&M's, cigarettes, and brand-name toiletries. The factory bought new sheets and embroidered "Welcome to Our Factory" with their names on the pillowcases. Hopefully, these amenities would distract from the rugged roads, rock-hard beds, and spotty shower service.

I returned to the plant to ensure they solved the issues. Next, I headed to the restaurant to make the food. I didn't know if the customer ate Chinese or had dietary restrictions. We provided a second option, just in case. I made tuna sandwiches and salad.

While preparing the food, I caught myself in the mirror, making sandwiches, wearing a suit and tie. I was overdressed, but then I thought of the motorcycle taxi drivers. It made sense in a Chinese way. The restaurant staff enjoyed the spectacle. They looked at the spread and wondered what was so great about Western food. Little did they realize their kids would grow up on such classics as the Big Mac and Filet-o-Fish.

The group left H.K. early in the morning, passed up lunch, and drove straight to Fuan. By the time they completed the drive, they would be hungry and irritable. I finished by 6:30 and waited. I didn't want them to arrive and catch me stuffing my face. It was after 9 p.m. when they did show up. We skipped dinner altogether, so much for the imported food. I waited for the customer to hit the roof about the journey. This was what set off "bad China day clocks." But all he talked about were the hawkers selling PBRs and bagels. The absurdity helped people deal sometimes.

The client said he slept well and didn't notice the stiff bed. Also, the hot water worked, and he found something for breakfast. Besides the longer-than-expected car ride, everything went smoothly. When we arrived for the inspection, he was in good spirits, and the evaluation finished quickly. We prepared a feast, but he took off to Fuzhou. I hung around with Paul to eat and drink before leaving for the sanctity of the Hot Spring. It was a relief when an important trip ended, and we returned to our never-ending struggles.

After starting the key order, I traveled to Fuan twice to ensure they solved their previous problems. I stopped using Little Yu's car because his price was too high, and he became reckless. He searched for ways to trim the trip by speeding and honking his horn. His aggressiveness scared pedestrians. Sometimes, they jumped out of the way. He installed a military siren hidden in the floor, giving off a distinct sound when he tapped it. It was loud and echoed. Questions would need to be answered if the PLA heard a civilian using the horn. Eventually, the police caught him, but he got off with a fine. He reinstalled it after the coast was clear.

Then, he used a fake government toll pass. The tolls were part of the amount I paid him, and every toll became a hassle when they doubted the authenticity. We got through until an attendant called his bluff, and Little Yu had to pay. The fee was only 10 RMB, but every bit counted.

On my last trip with him, we sped through a town halfway to Fuan when we got into an accident. The streets had railings separating the cars and bikes like Fuzhou. We drove in one direction while a woman on a scooter came from the opposite, on the wrong side. She crossed in front of our car. Little Yu swerved, but the bike hit our vehicle. The woman slammed into the windshield and broke her neck. I rode shotgun without a seat belt and hit the other side of the windshield with my head. Thank God, I was unscathed beyond a mark while looking pathetic with a blown-up pillow around my neck.

Little Yu jumped out, picked up the body, put her in a three-wheeled cart, and took her to the hospital. He left me and my QC with his car blocking the main street as residents came out to discuss the accident. This appeared to be a dangerous situation. If the villagers saw a foreigner, they would think they would get money and possibly beat me up as retribution. This was no joke. When this happened, peasants flipped out. They looked for a way to release their anger.

I crawled into the back, snuck out with my coat on my head, and didn't stop until a small tea shop owner whispered to me to come over. It was my best option. The guy said I should stay hidden because the people would beat me up. He reconfirmed my fears. I didn't feel like getting beaten up, so I drank tea until my local QC found me and said,

"Don't go out."

"How did you get away?"

"They knew I was not the driver, but it would be different for you."

We called Mr. Wu, and he said,

"Don't go outside. They may beat you."

I assumed they really would beat me, but Igor came to my rescue. He drove us to the safety of the factory. I inspected the goods with shaking hands and a possible mild concussion—nothing that cold PBR wouldn't fix. Little Yu showed up to drive me to Fuzhou. He thought he might not get paid. I gave him double to help with the lump sum he would have to give to the woman's family.

On the way, the police stopped us because of the shattered windshield. I sat in the back this time. After this incident, I ALWAYS wore a seat belt when available.

A few weeks later, I heard the woman died, and Little Yu paid a small fine since it wasn't his fault, and he had *guanxi*. Life on the road was tragic.

I visited Fuan several more times and developed my singing skills while they attempted to make good shoes. Neither of us was successful.

The following season, our agent moved all orders out of Fuan, and I never met Mr. Wu or Igor again. I encountered the same situation repeatedly; an agent placed orders, I spent time improving the factory and making friends, then the agent moved the orders, and I never worked with the old factory again. Unless they could keep up with the increasing demands of our customers and found ways to lower prices, factories fell by the wayside.

CHAPTER TEN

PUTIAN: RAGING BULL

I last stepped foot in my Putian hotel a few weeks ago and didn't know what to expect, but seeing the lights on was a relief. Following **Rule #20**, I told the driver to wait. The staff ignored me when I walked in. If they were still out of water, they would have mentioned it. A mildew smell hit me as I continued upstairs to the second floor. The windows in the hallway were open wide. I proceeded further down the hall towards my suite, and the carpet appeared squishy. When I opened my door, my living room floor was soaked. Water seeped through my shoes and socks with every step. I turned on the light, and my CDs, purchased in the U.S. at full price, were out of the cases and mildewing. Some of my clothes and books were destroyed. It was a disaster.

I marched down to the front desk.

"Mr. Thunder, what is the problem?"

"My room."

"Is there something wrong?"

"Yes, there is water."

"Yes, the water is on."

"I'm aware of that. What happened to my room?"

"When the water came back on, your sink flooded."

"Who will pay for my stuff?"

"You need to talk to the manager."

The match-making/English student manager moved on. They sold the hotel to someone, but it was unclear to whom. That left me out of luck. As I returned to my room, she told me I needed to pay for the nights away. Really? I kept a room for four months despite the lack of services. It was time to move to the second-best hotel in town.

Most people only knew of The Heavenly Concubine or guesthouses without a private bathroom. I found a place in the old town called the XH Guest House. It was a government-run establishment with a few buildings surrounding an open square.

Zhang Bo drove me to check the rooms and negotiate the price. He had a friend managing the sauna and assured me he would get the lowest rate. The XH was a two-star. What the place lacked in character and basic facilities was compensated with size. I no longer governed the entire second floor, but they gave me a king with a lounge at the rate of $12 a night.

Old trade shops lined both sides of the cobblestone lane. They looked as if they'd done business in these stands for a few hundred years—it was picturesque, like Lijiang.

At night, the only light in the alley emanated from the hair salon outside the hotel gate. Their glow shone pinkish red. If customers filled the joint, they slid the planks in, thus killing the beams. I didn't worry about my security; Putian seemed safe. But I got concerned about getting hit by nasty water when people tossed it out their windows and doors. You could walk down a quiet alley, thinking how cool it was to live in such a historic area, and Bam! You got doused with wastewater. Don't ask what type.

I moved my things over in trips and kept rooms in both hotels for a few days. When the time came, I strolled downstairs and advised the front desk I would only pay for the days I slept in the hotel. The place fell apart during the mysterious ownership period; I was lucky to have them clean every few days while they charged me a fifteen percent service fee daily. "What service?" They locked the Chinese restaurant and closed all the stores and the karaoke hall. Then they shut down the elevator, so I left my massive safe in the middle of the stairs. It was too much trouble.

The Concubine and the XH had similarities. Both had dreadfully hard beds, starched razor-sharp sheets, and late-night karaoke. The XH sounded louder, with the music echoing off the courtyard buildings. At

The Heavenly Concubine, I had a view of the pond. The windows at my new residence possessed a blue stick-on window tint, peeling in places. When mixed with the gray winter skies, it gave the room a depressing disposition.

I had no English TV, which was the best way to wean me off daytime soaps: go cold turkey. On my next trip from Hong Kong, I brought a VCR up and a few VHS movies I purchased from Blockbuster (it shut shortly after). I fit three films in my carry-on bag. What three movies would you choose if you got stuck on an island for thirty days? I picked *Ben Hur* for the length, *The Blues Brothers* because of my home, and *Raging Bull* since I never tired of it. I ran the movies on constant rotation while I ate my canned soup.

The hotel rarely provided hot water in the morning or night. Every time I returned, I checked for it. If it was on, I took a hot shower. My posse knew about my obsession and waited. I'm sure they thought I was a freak, but I felt the same about some of their habits.

II

Since Putian lacked everything Western, I celebrated U.S. holidays elsewhere. For Thanksgiving, I dined at Dan Ryan's Chicago Restaurant in Hong Kong. Unlike Taipei, I had the funds to afford it. Every year, they threw a meal packed with Yanks and friends of Yanks. Reservations were required, or no turkey. Dan Ryan's also became the venue for Monday morning live viewings of the Super Bowl—nothing like eating sausage and eggs while enjoying the big game.

For Christmas, I made my long-overdue return to Beijing. I wanted to get back to where it all began, and I couldn't wait to see Han's expression. Unfortunately, I lost contact with Wang Yi. It was challenging to keep in touch without phone numbers or email addresses.

After I arrived, I traveled downtown by bus and discovered a small tourist hotel between the Qianmen and Hepingmen subway stops. This was my favorite area, with dozens of old alleys (*hutongs*) dating to the Qing and Ming Dynasties and some of the oldest shops. The location was close to Tiananmen Square and the first KFC. The line was shorter now. I checked into the hotel, dropped off my bag, and headed towards the neighborhood near Beida, my college playground. I recognized little, but I identified the correct lane. My anticipation grew as I exited the taxi and crossed the street. Few foreigners traveled to China, and fewer returned. Not only had I come back, but I'd secured a job.

Walking down the alley, I realized I had passed the place. I turned and looked again. Sure enough, I located the right spot, but the restaurant had disappeared; the entire building was gone. I stood there trying to figure out what to do.

I saw a karaoke bar and entered, thinking he had started a new business. It was a dark room with tables and chairs around the dance floor, similar to every nightclub. I asked about The Hutong. The girls didn't know, but a guy said,

"Two years ago, the government tore that restaurant down."

"Did the owner open another place?"

"No."

It made me sad to lose another friend. I had nowhere to go, so I remained at the karaoke and downed a few. I finally located a venue with Christmas lights in season and a full-sized, blown-up Santa on stage. However, the customers sang and drank like any other evening. The more beers I finished, the more I itched to order a song. Sometimes, the urge to croon crept up on me. I liked the attention.

As I sang, I held the microphone in my left hand and wrapped my other arm around Santa with a cigarette. I singed a hole in him and watched him deflate. That was my signal to leave.

For three days, I revisited The Forbidden City, the Temple of Heaven, The Great Wall (my third time), Mao's Mausoleum (no line), and the Rainbow Market.

At night, I wandered the *shuan yang rou* alley near Qianmen. Nearly every joint served lamb hotpot, with brass pots and coal. This, to me, was Beijing, hanging out in an ancient neighborhood in the cold, eating my favorite dish with bottles of Yanjing Beer. I felt the Beijing magic that had brought me here. But that China was disappearing. In a year or two, it would be harder to locate. I intended to enjoy it before then.

I strolled up and down to find the best spot. Restaurants tried to entice me in, but with no hotpot or lamb in Putian, I had to get it right.

Eventually, I picked a place and ate plate after plate of frozen lamb shavings, cabbage, tofu, and glass noodles. I put away three *jin* (Chinese pound, almost equivalent to an American pound) of lamb at less than $1.50 a *jin*, five large bottles of beer, and a bottle of *Erguotou baijiu*. My feast lasted over three hours. It was indeed an epic case of overindulgence.

The toilet was a public outhouse down a maze of alleys. Every hour, I put on my coat and walked out to relieve myself before returning to eat more. Soon, I no longer required my jacket with all the *baijiu* and lamb in my belly. I paraded around in zero-degree weather as if it was a sunny day. People in the alley looked at me in disbelief. I felt amazing. Maybe they'd laced the hotpot (some places spiked it with opiates), but I think it was the perfect Beijing day.

On the last evening, I visited my teacher's father. I phoned him out of the blue. When Lao Zhu heard my voice (and old Chinese name), he said in a thick Beijing accent, "Luo Landi, my daughter taught you perfect Beijing dialect. What happened? You sound like a Southerner."

As he said that, I realized how lazy my tongue had become, and I needed to step up the accent. He had remarried, so the giant hotpot and *baijiu* feasts were out of the question. Instead, he took me to a duck restaurant, the better move after I'd devoured half a sheep the night before.

I spent a jam-packed few days and was sad to depart.

At least I lived closer.

III

When I returned from Beijing, I telephoned the girl I met when the hotel manager squeezed an English lesson out of me. Her name was Debbie. She worked for one of the development enterprises. Putian expanded and modernized like never in history. New roads and street blocks had risen from the dirt where nothing stood before. The real estate market boomed.

I called her, and Debbie said she would meet me but wanted to invite her girlfriend. She told me to wait at the entrance to the university. From there, she directed me to her classmate's apartment on campus. As we walked towards their flat, I mentioned I guest lectured at the school.

"And don't be surprised if students recognize me." (Nobody did)

We entered her friend's apartment, and she introduced me. Her friend's father taught painting and pulled out his best artwork. He assumed I would buy one. I explained I lacked a home to hang them in but would purchase a painting if I did. This wasn't a date. She'd brought me to an art sale! Debbie said to meet at noon, so I expected we would eat. It turned out to be a dumpling party, and everyone (Debbie, her friend, her parents, and I) took part in the wrapping. Although I was pleased to eat something I enjoyed, it appeared to be a setup with the wrong girl. I finished my dumplings and met with my QC posse to drink and bowl.

After this meeting, I laid low until Debbie phoned me. "She must be interested," I thought. But when I saw her friend, I realized she still played matchmaker. How do I let down the friend while keeping a relationship with Debbie?

I decided to meet her at my guesthouse and explained the situation. She was surprised. "I assumed you liked my friend, and she likes you. It will devastate her."

These girls grew up in stricter backgrounds than my wild youth, but the closest we came in contact was our chopsticks touching the same plate. I accepted that a relationship would be serious, but I wasn't aware I was in one.

Before I organized how to break up with someone in Mandarin that I wasn't seeing, her girlfriend showed up. In the softest of terms, I explained I did not like her romantically, but we could continue to have meals. It didn't take long before the girl burst into tears and ran out with Debbie chasing after her. I sat at the table, stunned and embarrassed.

Locals noticed when a Chinese girl ran away from a foreigner, crying. And no better place than the lobby of my guesthouse.

"That did not go well. I should have offered to buy a painting first."

During the next few months, I arranged a few meals with Debbie. We had a hard time finding places to go, and at every location, EVERYONE stared, pointed, and talked about us.

"Look at that *laowai* with the Chinese girl."

"Maybe she is his tour guide."

"Perhaps she isn't?"

"Wait, he speaks Chinese."

After dealing with this unabashed behavior from day one, I became numb to it, even if I didn't appreciate it. Debbie had no idea what it felt like to date a movie star.

We had a more challenging time locating a place for after dinner. We tried the movies, but I couldn't stand everyone talking (I mean *really talking*). They also dubbed the films into Mandarin. Try watching *The Godfather* in Chinese; it's an entirely different film.

I considered heading to the WH Disco, but the last time I went there, they charged a cover and had a book with pictures of grade school girls that would sit with us. Where did they hide them? I never saw that service when I drank there on my first day. It now appeared too seedy to take a date.

Instead, I talked Debbie into checking out a KTV (a karaoke with individual rooms). After we entered, I heard a slight "bang, bang, bang."

"There's a rat in the ceiling," I said.

The ceiling had a hole as wide as a softball but no fan. Not long after the "bang, bang," the sucker fell and landed in the middle of the room. I grabbed a broom but couldn't find him, so we left with the staff pushing me to pay.

"The fruit plate is cut. Someone needs to pay for it."

I didn't order the fruit. It came with the 200 RMB minimum charge.

"Ask the rat to pay."

I argued for fun, but spectators gathered, so I gave the KTV 50 RMB to settle the problem before the crowd got too big.

Debbie had a classmate working for a famous athletic shoe factory. They transferred an American technician over to live in the plant. Her friend asked me to talk with him so he wouldn't go insane because he couldn't speak Mandarin. I welcomed the opportunity to swap China stories and drink with a fellow Yank, especially one living in Putian. I figured he would be thankful to have a Mandarin-speaking friend from home.

We met at a run-down disco in the back of a shopping building. The club had more people than the WHD but was only twenty percent full.

The other American, Chuck, was twice my age. Before he worked in the shoe business, he was a Marine. He seemed cool, and we drank more than a few *ganbeis*. I brought my CDs and had the DJ play a compilation of '70s disco as we overran the dance floor. Finally, I had a compatriot to drink with when I needed an escape for a minute. But as the night progressed, I noticed him working on Debbie. He said, "Don't date young Americans. They will switch girls. Besides, most prefer ladies from the Philippines."

Debbie didn't tell me until days later, but I had received a bad vibe. He called her at her job to ask her to meet—dumb move. If I couldn't speak Chinese and lived in Putian, I would have done everything to keep a friendship with a dude who spoke fluently. She informed me, and I never hung out with him again and stuck to my posse.

They were loyal. I trusted them with my life.

I dated Debbie for six months when she said she wanted to visit a mountain in Sichuan to study a meditation like *Qi Gong*. Excuse me? Was she going to travel 2,000 km by bus and train to a mountain to be reprogrammed by a spiritual leader? By herself? She told her family she would be back in a few weeks. When I heard this, I figured I would never see her again.

How does a person who has never traveled move to a place she knows nothing about? It was rough traveling, and many things could go wrong.

A week later, her sister called to say they had lost contact and were worried. I offered to fly to Chengdu to check it out. I had been looking for an excuse to visit Sichuan to have *mapo doufu* from the source.

Hell yeah, I'll go.

Debbie's parents didn't trust me to see it through, so they sent her sister with me. I would have given up the search after a few dead-ends. Plus, a single foreigner wandering around in the mountains was not wise. I might enter a secure zone and get arrested for spying. It was smart for her to come along.

We flew into Chengdu, rode a minibus to Dujiangyan, and used that as our base as we hiked up the mountain. When we reached the studying base camp, I was on edge. People meditated and prayed everywhere. Each room had a picture of the leader (*Shi Fu*) and a few three-story ones outside. I waited for someone to offer us Kool-Aid and robes.

We wandered for a full day, asking people if they had seen her. One guy thought he did, but he was guessing. It got dark, so we were forced to head back. The following day, her sister phoned home to update them and discovered that Debbie had returned. She had arrived at the worship school and felt that the place was extreme. That was good news because I didn't want to go back. They engaged in some strange activities on that mountain.

Since the search was called off, we made the best of the situation and traveled to Leshan to see the 233-foot sitting Buddha carved out of the mountain during the Tang Dynasty between 713 and 803 AD. It was a wonderful visit, and it set the stage for trips through Chengdu, for excursions to Tibet, and a nature park called Jiuzhaigou.

IV

I asked Debbie's friend to find me a flat. I was required to keep a hotel room for the bathroom and stable electricity, but I could cook and hang things on the walls of an apartment. She looked for three months before finding a place. It took a while because of the low supply. Multiple generations lived in a single house. People also did not want to rent to a foreigner. I needed somebody to vouch for me, but why? The accommodation was a two-bedroom concrete shell with no furniture or flooring. The bathroom had a sink and a shower pipe over the squatter.

Imagine the multitasking possibilities with a setup like that.

The flat was in a community of families, a street over from Taiwan Street (named after the Taiwanese companies operating there). The first floor of my building had a shop owned by my landlord. They kept a close eye on me because they didn't know what to expect.

I paid $50 a month for rent and bought lots of beer. They delivered it to the fourth floor, but I had to go down to order it.

To furnish, I picked up a fake leather sofa and a single, hard bed for $40. Next, I purchased a TV, a refrigerator, a propane stove, and the biggest fan. For the walls, I decorated them with the only pictures in the town bookstore without cuddly animals, little children, or fruit; I bought posters of Mao, Lenin, Engels, and Marx to accompany my Budweiser banner.

It was a mix of C&C—Communism and Capitalism.

The entire community's power would blackout during the boiling months (most of the year). I had never noticed it before since the hotels had generators. Now, I experienced problems with things I took for granted.

When the electricity turned off, my apartment became a sweatbox; no lights, fan, TV, or music, just crickets and heat. My body dripped with sweat from picking up my beer. I thought the landlord cut the power to force me out when I played my tunes too loud, but the electricity in the entire neighborhood was off. The government declared production limits during the summer because of a lack of electricity. This put pressure on workers to compensate for lost time, causing quality problems. That gave me job security. I tried to remember that.

In front of my building was a small public area with bushes and a pair of children's rocking horses resembling hungover Donald and Mickey. This "park," the size of a suburban cul-de-sac, was the sole green space. I never saw kids playing, but I figured out why.

I passed through one night when I noticed the bushes rattling in the moonlight. When I approached, a gigantic, black potbellied pig marched out. It scared the shit out of me.

Next time, I would be prepared.

Once I secured the basic needs, I rushed to cook. The first dish I planned to make was *gong bao* chicken.

Most stores sold dry goods. Locals bought their food at the large wet market near the money exchangers. But I could barely walk past because of the odor. They brought the market indoors to clear up the streets. I doubt they considered the stench would be so foul.

I wanted to buy chicken breast meat, but they only sold live chickens. What the hell would I do with a live bird? One guy offered me chicken legs, so I took that. Except for chili, everything was available. I planned to cook for my QC posse. They had never eaten Sichuan and wouldn't know the difference.

Two of my posse came over, and we drank while I introduced them to more Western music. A few beers later, they asked about the food. I explained that I hadn't considered all the items I required. Whenever I turned around, I had to buy knives or gas for the stove. Each purchase took a lot of effort.

It seemed too much hassle.

I handed them the uncooked chicken and other ingredients. My kitchen closed before it opened. And in China, giving someone raw meat didn't seem that strange. On one occasion, a factory gifted me two bags of live crabs. There were twenty in each wet straw sack. After I arrived at the hotel, the doorman loaded the bags on the luggage cart with my suitcase. I drew a few stares as the crabs made bubbling noises. They had serious value. Although I didn't eat them and hated dragging things around, I wouldn't leave them on the street. I appreciated the presents, but it never occurred to individuals that giving two dozen apples or two bags of crabs was a challenge to carry.

CHAPTER ELEVEN

SHANGHAI: EXILED

In May 1995, Bryon gave me the opportunity I was aiming for. I flew to Hong Kong for my shore leave and ran into him on his way out. He asked me to grab a bite while catching up. We had a Hardee's downstairs that served as our makeshift meeting room. It was less crowded than McDonald's.

Over a much-needed injection of fast food, I talked about life on the front line. Bryon told me the Shanghai manager planned to join our customer. It was a typical move for people in our line when stores took their business direct. Bryon said hiring someone without dropping a load on a headhunter would be difficult.

"What about me? Did you think I want to stay in Putian for the rest of my life?"

"I thought you liked it there. Would you like to relocate to Shanghai?"

Despite the quirks and inconveniences, I did enjoy Putian and had great friends, but I was tired of "roughing it." I aspired to get back to the big city. My life was a 90:10 mix of Chinese to American, and I wished to adjust that balance to 70:30. I reminded him I hand-carried canned soup and rode around town on the back of hooded biker taxis. So . . .

"Yeah, I'm ready to move. I can pack my bags today. That's how prepared I am."

I wanted to lock down the position before somebody slipped in. Who wouldn't want to live in Shanghai?

"It will be harder to find someone to take your position. I would choose Putian because you get a better China experience, and you are the movie star."

"I've been a movie star for nine months and am ready to become a regular person."

In Shanghai, I would attract attention but less—I'd be a TV actor instead of a major box office draw.

"How about I manage both areas? I'm traveling every day as it is."

"All right, book a flight and meet Skip to learn about the factories."

Just like that, my life got more comfortable. I might even make friends that speak English. If I hadn't run into him, he would have placed an ad. Once again, a fast food restaurant played a significant role in my career. I saw a pattern.

When I returned to Putian, I moved from the hotel to my apartment. I couldn't believe I was leaving the drab confines of the guesthouse for the city.

My QC posse helped me move using Zhang Bo's truck. Later, we had a going-away bash, even though I would return every week for six months. Since I arranged to leave, I gave up my honorary title of Mayor. I would miss being a big fish in a small pond, but I needed arts, activities, and English TV. It was time for a change.

Then, I broke the news to Debbie. I told her I would be back, but she had an offer for a merchandising job in Shanghai and moved there independently. She lived in the company dorm in Pudong, a newly developed area on the other side of the Huangpu River. If it weren't for her living there, I would not have known it existed. The side of the river with the action was Puxi. Meanwhile, I checked into The Sheraton Huating, on the edge of the Xujiahui District, one of the few five-star hotels in the entire city. Tragically, my budget only allowed me to reside at the three-star guesthouse connected to the five-star building. For a three-star, it was a respectable place and better than my previous digs.

Next door at the Sheraton, they had a full breakfast buffet—an omelet station, unlimited coffee, juices on tap, bread, and cheese. It felt decadent after the meager offerings in the towns I'd stayed at. They also had a Western deli with sandwiches, pasta, and pizza—comfort food.

After nine months in Putian, I was transported to another world.

I had a restricted expense account, so the Western meal was a splurge. I would've eaten here more if not for the prices ($8 for a glass of iced tea, $30 for the breakfast buffet) and a fifteen percent service charge. Things seemed more expensive when I paid cash instead of tucking it somewhere between laundry and business center charges. Eventually, I got over the prices but never accepted the service charge. Except for the five-star hotels and a few places, no one charged a fee, nor was leaving a tip customary. When no longer accustomed to paying taxes or gratuities, it became hard to fork up the extra cash on top of the exorbitant fees for the food and drinks. Generally, I received the same poor service from the places that didn't charge the fee. Excellent service was in short supply. It seemed to be a side effect of the socialist system—if everything belonged to the government, why bother to provide exemplary service?

I remember going to stores in Beijing as a student. They kept everything behind a counter. If I wished to look at a toothbrush, I had to get the attention of a sales attendant. The staff stood in the corner near the hot water thermos, talking to each other, drinking tea, and ignoring me until I waited long enough. The clerk would speak to me as if she was doing me a favor, and I better not waste her time. Rejection and fear were powerful sales tactics. I never wanted to piss these women off like the 'Soup Nazi' on *Seinfeld*; they abused me, but I took it to buy a brush for my teeth.

That kind of service was extreme and fading, replaced with a newer, kinder model society.

II

My hotel was close to Hongqiao Airport, the busiest domestic airfield in China. It was the sole airport in Shanghai until they erected modern ones in the 2000s. The international part had a couple of departures daily to Hong Kong and Seoul. As the People's Republic opened, other flights were added, and more individuals accompanied me on the plane. It was no longer empty in the back, and I had to fight for overhead space, forcing me to relocate to the front. I missed the days when people feared flying or couldn't afford it.

When I flew every week, I booked the first flight between 7:30 and 8 a.m. If I left for the airport before 7:15, I would be there in ten minutes. Check-in ended fifteen minutes before departure (with no luggage), and I cut it close. If I missed my flight, I would take the next one or buy a ticket to another city and pocket my old one. It didn't matter if I booked China Eastern, China Southern, Shenzhen, or Xiamen Airlines; all Chinese airline tickets were interchangeable. I flew first class to give me the most benefits, such as no fee for unlimited changes, available seats, a special check-in counter, access to the lounge with a decent bathroom, and guaranteed overhead compartment space. First class tickets cost slightly more than the foreigner economy price. The extra benefits made it worth it.

Typically, it was smooth sailing on an empty Hongqiao Road until I reached the departure level ramp. The government did not keep up with the growing number of cars, and they built a narrow road feeding into the airport. They fenced off a third for the vacant taxi line, picking up arriving passengers and adding to the mess. It turned into a logistical nightmare, with empty taxis going from the right to the left and all other vehicles moving in the opposite direction. I would miss my flight if I didn't arrive before this heap.

Best to leave before 7:15.

As I started traveling more than once a week, I arrived earlier to avoid the heavy traffic and to eat the Western breakfast meal (two eggs, toast, and tea), particularly if I knew my lunch would be liquid. About five years after moving to Shanghai, someone heard my prayers: a McDonald's opened outside international, and it served breakfast! I was proud to shock my coworkers with it. They appreciated it almost as much as I did. In fact, the first time I surprised a coworker from the U.S., his "bad China day clock" went off. We ordered but had to wait for the food. My U.S. compatriot slammed the counter as it approached our takeoff time, saying nothing. This guy was a mellow dude, but he lost it.

And I thought I needed an Egg McMuffin badly.

Once I arrived at departures, I quick-stepped my way to the first class counter. I only brought carry-on luggage, so it took a minute to receive my ticket.

Check-in was the stress-free part. The security control turned out to be the hassle. The airport used the same painstaking interrogation process they applied when flying was a privilege. Now, ten times as many people traveled by plane. Frequently, a sea of passengers, just like at KFC, jammed into the secure zone with no lines. If the stragglers got stuck, they caused flight delays. Soon, more travelers flew first class, and they opened a special security check-in window, which helped me avoid the wait, but it also meant more individuals utilized the first-class ticket counter.

I still moved from curbside to the flight gate in fifteen minutes, so I couldn't complain.

I knew all the ins and outs of the airports. The best toilet in Hongqiao was in the international departures building. Nobody used it (**Rule #13**). Occasionally, I knew how things should run better than the staff, and I explained what they needed to do. It didn't bother me to expedite the process as it decreased my waiting time.

When I returned to Shanghai, the arrival hall was a pain. The pilot parked the plane far from the gate, and we rode a bus to the building. It took ten minutes or more for the bus to drive over. It wasn't a big airport; I figured the drivers sat in a room, smoking cigarettes and drinking tea, until they felt ready. There was nothing to do but remain in the scorching sun until they showed up.

Often, people became angry and walked. If I didn't have checked-in bags, I would go along. I waited when I had luggage because the baggage truck was slower. The baggage handlers required more time to get up.

Inside the arrival hall and past the luggage tag check was a neutral zone, like Switzerland. Nobody bothered you for about two hundred feet as you walked up the ramp to the main hall. Individuals crammed inside the waiting area, hoping to receive relatives or scared-looking foreigners. A metal barrier held back the crowd, and a security guard ensured no one entered the safe zone. Most airports had a similar setup. While in the secure section, it was wise to size up the crowd. I looked for a weak link before breaking through to the other side. Sometimes, I had a hotel car pick me up when I traveled with a customer. This diffused the situation. The hotel guy would grab my bag and push through while I followed behind in his cut path. He would lead us to a clean, comfortable, air-conditioned luxury sedan. Since I flew weekly, it was too expensive to hire hotel transportation, which cost ten times the actual taxi fee.

All that convenience came at a price.

As soon as you crossed into the crowd, you were fair game.

"Hello, my friend."

"Taxi!"

"Where are you going?"

"No line. Follow me."

There were a few guys like this on the way to the taxi line. Most of these "black taxis" parked far away and charged a flat fee of 50 or 100 RMB, many times the regular rate. These dudes often attempted to block my way. I pushed through and ran over their feet with my rollaboard if they declined to move. That sufficed, but sometimes, a guy might follow me and continue to offer his services. I would ignore him standing next to me, talking to the side of my face, until he spotted another foreigner to latch on to.

Although a minor annoyance, it added to the hassle of the trip, especially if I came back from a hard-drinking tour. The wait for a taxi would be thirty minutes to an hour in sweaty weather. It was the same bottleneck that held up the cabs arriving. I hated waiting in the sticky summer heat (worse when it rained) while several characters surrounding me smoked away the stress of flying. But I figured out a shortcut. The international arrival hall had a separate taxi line, only a two-minute walk from domestic. Most foreign arrivals were tour groups, so the taxi line had no wait. Even better, the security guard waved taxis from domestic when individuals waited in line at international. Each car that got through was precious, and everybody eyeballed it as it pulled up, thinking they would escape, only to watch the car drive past. I didn't want to be obvious; otherwise, others would follow. Instead, I walked through the buildings and came out of the international exit. I saw the guards turn away others who walked over from domestic. Nobody troubled me—another win.

The quality of the taxis was irrelevant; The fact that I got into a cab was important. Most drivers became upset when I told them my destination because the fare ran about $4. They waited, on average, for two hours. Starting and stopping the vehicles in the brutal summer heat shortened the lives of those cars. Some drivers only turned on the vehicle if the taxi in front moved a certain distance, but then they risked rogue drivers cutting in, causing an argument and further delaying the line. Other drivers put the car in neutral and pushed it. They tried to save gas and build Herculean calves. I could do nothing about the wait, but I ordinarily gave the driver extra if he didn't complain my ear off.

The airport was hassle enough, but I only had to go there twice a week. I visited my bank three or four times to withdraw cash to pay for everything. My U.S. bank set up an office on the ground floor of a historic hotel on the Bund, the waterfront area where foreign banks and trade companies built their Neoclassical branches over a hundred years ago. Following Liberation in 1949, the buildings turned into CCP offices and were used as housing. They eventually fell into disrepair but have been rehabilitated into chic restaurants, designer shops, and hotels. It seems someone destined them for commerce in one form or another.

Through the ATM, I pulled cash from my Hong Kong account. I no longer needed to bring H.K. dollars and exchange them for RuMBas at the bank or on the black market. In Putian, everyone knew the money-changing ladies; they were part of the town. In The Hai (Shanghai), the mongers stood outside the Bank of China Building. They changed money right in front of the bank! If you had a lot to exchange, they would fill in transfer forms for you. First, they transferred RMB into your account, and then you moved U.S. dollars into theirs. The currency guys never looked tough, but others would have stopped you if you tried to run out without doing the return transfer. They probably had *guanxi* with the bank security, considering they flaunted their services on the steps. It was too risky to change money this way, and I didn't want to jeopardize myself when a security guard or a bank worker blackmailed me with cameras omnipresent.

The downside of the ATM was the daily limit and the distance. Every trip cost $10 one way by taxi and took an hour in traffic. When I first arrived, Shanghai had a single-ring road around downtown, a two-lane, elevated "expressway" that was jammed. A couple of years later, the government built another elevated highway cutting through the city's heart. Then, it took a half-hour during the day and ten minutes at night to reach the ATM. Traffic in Shanghai was a nightmare. Whenever I hit the town in the evening, I stopped by the Bund to fill up my wallet, even if I had to travel from one side of the city to the other. It was worth it to bypass the daytime traffic.

III

When not traveling, I worked with a factory on the edge of town in Minhang District, forty minutes south of my hotel. The distance was ten kilometers, a short but stressful journey, with everybody fighting for space.

On the way back, we squeezed together with black, smoke-belching buses and cement trucks delivering the massive volume of concrete required to build the buildings. The vehicles out-inched each other and honked as if everyone possessed a nervous tick. Sometimes, when stuck going nowhere, I reminisced about my Peking U days and the emptiness of the streets. That was only five years ago. The cities had moved from bicycles to cars in a short amount of time. Many of the taxis in Shanghai were small hatchbacks called Xia li. They were cheaper than the more spacious VW Santanas but lacked quality. Often, the vehicles had broken arms to roll the windows down and faulty air conditioning, allowing me to sit in a hot box or take my chances with the black clouds of exhaust generated by the monster trucks.

After returning from the factory daily, I took a shower to wash the filth off.

One afternoon, as I sat in the passenger seat of a Xia li, staring ahead in a sleepy summer daze, watching the mess of cars in front of us, I heard a loud "pop." The manufacturer had not treated the windshield properly. With the chill on the inside combined with the heat from the sun, it had shattered into a thousand fragments. I shook the glass off and stepped out without standing on the pieces in my shoes. My hotel was near, so I left while the driver chased me, demanding I pay him the 25 RMB ($3) fee. I kept walking, and he gave up.

Most companies bought cars and hired a driver. I didn't have that option and struggled to find a ride. It was competitive. The area near the workshop was more challenging, and I had to walk a kilometer to catch a cab. The government pushed factories out further to help with the pollution, but the additional vehicles erased any benefit. As bad as the air was in The Hai, I never blew black snot as I did in Beijing in the winter. That level must have been beyond measure. Perhaps, like smoking, the damage repaired itself after twelve years of abstinence.

The same agent (Louis) we utilized in the south owned the Shanghai plant. It was located down a small country road across from a farm and was constructed five years prior, but it looked as if it had been around since the '50s. The color gray had that effect. Walls surrounded the compound, and it had a gate controlled by guards.

After I arrived, the gate broke, and they decided a rope was a suitable substitute—an early sign the factory had a *"chabuduo"* (close enough) attitude. The guards sat in their shack and released the rope or pulled it back. They didn't need to stand up. Wasn't the point to prevent someone from driving in? Perhaps it was a strong twine.

They split production among four rows of lengthy warehouse buildings. Inside, I discovered a wide range of odors, such as melted rubber, the stench of EVA (Ethylene-vinyl acetate) foam burning, and the aroma of chemicals and glues that took you higher if you remained too long. Another scent that tortured my nostrils was the stink of urine. I smelt the toilets from across the plant, about half the length of a soccer pitch. The toxic fumes from burning polyester didn't seem so bad.

Outside the gate, we had the smelly Huangpu tributary. The city attempted to clean it, but obstacles, like factories and farms dumping, stood in their way. In 2013, newspapers reported that the government discovered over 6,000 dead pigs in the creek. Farmers disposed of the pigs because the city passed a law banning the sale of meat from animals that died of certain illnesses, and burying or cremating was costly. I can only imagine what people had discarded before they found the pigs. The gray water sure did stink.

The swampiness of the creek also drew flies and mosquitos, which attacked me once I stepped into the compound. They were a sign we should not be placing orders. Instead of paying attention and leaving, we bought bug zappers and stayed.

In the center of the compound was a grassy field. They heaped cloth scraps at one end and used the rest for soccer matches. They needed to keep the fabric wastage for a period to show customs before they torched it. In compensation, they received a tax benefit. It made sense, but there had to be a better way to store the leftover pieces and save a prime lot of real estate. This field begged for a gray, four-story concrete production building to be erected, and they built one two years later.

We stationed a local QC (Eric) at this factory. Every day, he played soccer and would eat and drink with the managers. They developed a brotherhood-like friendship. If you considered somebody your "brother," you would do anything to help him. I assumed supporting a brother could include not recording flaws on the inspection reports or letting shipments go. I uncovered a high rate of defects and questioned if Eric might be looking the other way. It was a dilemma for our staff. They needed to develop relationships with key people and stand firm. I reminded them that competent management would reduce the flaws. The factory should apologize for not doing the job right. We trusted them with our business. We also helped them avoid chargebacks, produce more orders, and earn significant profits by calling out the issues and pushing them to improve. Most factories appreciated this, but others saw us as pests. The ones who listened outlasted those who resisted.

Eric didn't seem to be corrupt. He needed direction and a manager to support him. I enjoyed going to the workshops and finding the inferior product, the needles in the haystacks. How many could I find before lunch or in a single day? I became skilled at it as if I possessed intuition. I always picked the lot or machine that produced defects. Either I had a gift, or there were more problems than I thought.

After identifying the defects, I had to ensure those poorly produced shoes were not in the shipments. To do that, I built up my relations with the managers. If I had *guanxi*, they cooperated. For me, that involved endless nights of banquets followed by karaoke. Excessive boozing was essential. I wasn't sure if people appreciated me more for my Mandarin skills or my drinking ability. I worked hard to improve both. Without my high tolerance, I would not have functioned after three-hour feasts. We decided on a lot of issues over meals and created friendships. You couldn't get that level of camaraderie without drinking.

Occasionally, I did the treating, but more likely, they treated me. It would be better if the factories settled the checks. I lacked the open expense account those guys had. Money wasn't a concern. If I picked up the bill, I would not order bowls of 300 RMB shark's fin soup ($50 per person for chicken broth with shredded fin), abalone the size of my fist, or bird's nest made from hardened swiftlet (a bird found in Southeastern Asia) saliva. If someone else paid, I would try almost anything. As time dragged on, I noticed an escalation in the quality of the feasts as China's economy took off. The food turned more delicate, and the alcohol got better. I enjoyed taking part in the transformation.

Before arriving in Shanghai, I thought I was decent at cultivating relations, but Eric became a *guanxi* master. That skill was worth more than his salary. He could build a relationship with anyone or smooth over any disagreement. Eric threw humor in and twisted his characters to make a joke or used a Chinese idiom to further a point. It helped to lighten the mood.

I knew his *guanxi* talents would be helpful, so I didn't fault him for anything that happened before I showed up. I would wait and see after I explained what procedures he needed to follow before evaluating his performance.

At first, the factory welcomed my arrival. There would finally be a foreigner who spoke Mandarin. I would be the point person to explain why we had shipment delays. However, I knew how things worked, and the days of letting unacceptable merchandise ship ended.

The initial excitement turned into animosity as I jeopardized the daily soccer games. I encountered significant troubles and urged them to halt production. They tried to talk it out with Eric, but now he answered to a higher authority. I discovered so many issues; it concerned me they might dump me in a field. I read about foreigners being locked up or held for ransom and watched my back.

The ownership structure of the Shanghai operation was similar to Dongguan: The trade corp. ran the business, and factory management handled manufacturing. In theory, they should have been flexible. In reality, they blamed each other. They shared a two-story office building. Louis gave our company a room on the ground floor, but we had no AC and kept the windows open. All day, I listened to the machines clanking and steel lasts banging while getting bitten by mosquitoes. At least our guys had a place to write up their reports.

Louis and I had crossed paths a few times since I worked at his place in Dongguan a year ago. He was a China success story. When the stock market opened in 1990, he made huge coin but always loved trade, so he built a factory. Louis was a skillful salesman and assured customers he could do anything. Regrettably, he had problems with follow-through, and the staff didn't tell him the truth. I got along with him until I called out too many mistakes. They imported almost all the materials, and replacements had to be air-freighted. They also flew the finished goods. These costs were more than the price they sold the shoes for.

Once, I sat in on a chargeback meeting between Louis and our company. The charges were substantial (in the hundreds of thousands) and the factory's fault, but he wished to negotiate. We started in the lobby lounge of the newly opened Westin in Gubei and moved to the coffee shop for breakfast. After service ended, we returned to the lounge until lunch, then back to the restaurant, and we stayed until dinner finished at 9 p.m., a thirteen-hour negotiation. I drank about $150 worth of iced tea and never stepped outside. Louis argued that the material suppliers shipped late from Taiwan; they made production fall behind. He tried everything to lower the charge and got the costs deducted from future business, which meant we needed to give him more orders. I moved to Shanghai around this time, which showed me what I would be dealing with.

The entire experience should have been a wake-up call, but problems persisted. Louis' solution was to hire family members. Your family could make matters worse. I worked with another trading company that hired a relative to purchase the materials. He skimmed on quantity and charged more. That factory accepted the situation as the cost of doing business, but the quality was not what we ordered. Louis' relatives told him they had everything under control while hiding the truth. It took a few years to claim the money. By that time, he had earned more chargebacks.

Even though his factory made poor quality, his trade corp. had more orders than they could produce. These were the golden days of manufacturing, and factories turned away business. But not Louis— he took every order and worried about the details later. Sometimes, he accepted requests for styles he had never produced: He bought the machines and did trial and error. It was costly.

Generally, it took workers a few weeks to reach maximum speed. Any problem would cause a domino effect. Then, line managers pushed the staff to work longer. The workers became tired and sloppy, causing delays. Once again, they pressured the employees. It was a downward spiral. Louis' Shanghai factory struggled to keep up, so he built a new plant to handle the overflow and requested my input.

"Sure, let's go look."

Louis drove the same American-made minivan he moved up from Dongguan. It was nice to see an old friend.

The complex was in a separate suburb (Jia Ding), about an hour north. It took two hours with truck traffic, but we made it through. This workshop had an actual gate, an upgrade from the other place. It was a massive, rectangular, three-story, white, vacant building surrounded by farmland. He set up a machine for trial production and had some stitchers show me their skill level.

"Not very good, but it will improve," he said.

We walked around the empty concrete structure, and Louis explained how he planned to fill the space.

"It will be better for me to return after everything is completed."

I didn't want to waste time improving something we might not use.

After the tour, he said it was too late to drive back. Some of his staff arranged to eat at a place near us. He suggested we go there. It was a celebration of the new location. I assumed they had set up the bash, and the tour was an excuse to get me out there. If I had known it took two hours on a Friday night, I would have passed.

We reached the restaurant at 5 p.m. It was a two-story, standalone building. I followed Louis up the stairs to see if his staff had arrived. We were early, and the cooks rested in the backroom. The only room with lights on had some employees playing mahjong. They drove the factory van. The rest rode the bus.

That day, I took an early flight and missed breakfast and lunch. Now, I felt hungry and looked forward to a feast. I talked a server into bringing salted peanuts with beer. While watching the guys play the tiles, I glanced around to see what I had to contend with. There were two large tables set for twenty people, which I could handle.

An hour later, they moved me to the next room. It surprised me to walk out and see the hallway lit up. At one end was a medium-sized banquet hall with six large round tables and a dance floor on the other. I thought it would be a handful of people. It was a party for both the trade corp. and production managers.

Now that my potential exposure to an attack had increased, I revised my drinking plan. Some guys wished to drink with me for fun, but the trade corp. dudes sought to get me drunk. I welcomed the challenge, but I had to be smart about it with sixty people.

Louis directed me to a small room with a VIP table. As the customer, they showed me to the innermost seat, trapped on the inside with the boss. I would get drawn in whenever an employee drank with him. Louis backed out after a few drinks and found a replacement.

I showed that I could handle whatever they threw at me.

It was 6:30, and all we had were cold dishes (**Rule #1**), beer, and tea. The restaurant had a small kitchen and struggled with a dinner of this size. The food arrived, one dish at a time, allowing us to drink more. Each table had opened beer and soda bottles, and people drank when the first dish came out.

Louis asked me to say a few words of encouragement to his staff while we waited. I enjoyed watching the shock on people's faces when they saw a foreigner speak Mandarin. The workers assumed the managers spoke English with me. When I communicated in Chinese, I heard a collective gasp, laughter, and finally, applause (the movie star).

"We will help you identify the issues earlier and develop off-season styles," I said.

Louis' workshop made seasonal products. He had production from August to May. The workers hoped to have orders to make during the summer, or else they had to find employment outside.

When Louis spoke, he gave thanks to companies like ours. Without us, there would be no business. He thanked the staff, and then we did a group *ganbei*. These kinds of dinners turned into joyous affairs. No one held hard feelings when the alcohol flowed.

Next, Louis got dragged into individual table drinking. Once he stopped, I became the focus. I drank a few glasses but returned to my seat when I saw food heading in that direction. The last thing I wanted was the leftovers after the dish completed a full spin on the lazy Susan.

I asked the restaurant hostess to bring the meat and vegetable dishes first, but no luck. I felt bloated after downing beer on an empty stomach. If I didn't cut back, I would end up in Shanghai, starving. It happened many times.

If I planned to get a meaningful amount of morsels, then I needed to switch to *baijiu*. I would have preferred something in between, like red wine, but they didn't serve that at a countryside eatery. Most places had beer, yellow wine (sweet and smokey), and *baijiu*. I asked them to order a bottle, and they jumped to it. The factory manager also drank the devil's juice. We got a few shots in before my food turned up.

I requested fried rice, and they brought a lame version with egg and frozen vegetables, like what they served on airplanes. I skipped the meal when flying, but now I required a solid base to soak up the alcohol.

With food in my stomach, a line of employees showed up. They wanted to toast Louis and me. I didn't mind a few glasses, but I drank with everyone at my table while I downed shots with the workers. Louis sipped his beer now that he was "drunk," but I was going strong with the power that *baiji*u gave me.

However, I noticed some toasting me didn't drink the entire glass. It was fun when I outdrank everybody, but not when they faked it. What was the point of toasting? Unless you agree beforehand, consume the whole thing.

To even things out, I required that anybody who wanted another shot had to drink *baijiu* (**Rule #21**). That ended that.

I endured rapid shots before hunting for the toilet. When I found the darkly lit room, I did not expect water on the floor. The tiles were glass-like, increasing the level of slipperiness. My foot slipped as soon as I stepped on them, and I ended up flat on my back. A few people lifted me to my feet. Except for damp clothes, I was fine.

A restaurant guy said the sink pipe broke, but he didn't seem reassuring. I was upset that they thought I fell because I drank too much. Someone should have told me about the water.

I checked out the disco when dinner ended, but nobody consumed alcohol—a clear sign I should leave. The restaurant owned a few laser discs but no Western tunes. I asked the driver to retrieve my luggage with my CDs, but I wasn't prepared for a dance party. Even when I played music, everyone stayed on the perimeter. I seemed to be the only one enjoying myself.

"Why am I wasting my time out here when I can hang out at Malone's (an American-style bar downtown)? How do I return to the city?"

The bus would leave in an hour. I asked for a taxi, but it had to come from Shanghai. That took twice as long. Instead, Louis arranged for his driver to send me in the van.

I never returned to that restaurant or the factory. Louis had trouble finding workers, and after a few months, he never mentioned it again.

IV

The principal orders at the Shanghai factory were the same style Louis produced down south: aqua socks. They had a massive problem making white soles. Often, the upper material bled. They blamed the fabric for not being rinsed enough, so the heat from the injection activated the color runoff. I didn't know if that was true, but they had trouble fixing it.

One new style that caused headaches was a kid's suede work boot. I never thought a little shoe would produce so much trouble and add to my banishment. No one seemed to know what color a work boot should be, and they had no experience using suede. I expected something beige/tan. These boots turned out to be orange, and the leather pieces didn't match. We gave them a test order. By the time I arrived to inspect it, they had finished, and I rejected the entire lot. Louis attempted to squeeze me by saying he would not start production until I traveled to the leather dyeing workshop to confirm the color. The suede factory also made moccasins for us. It was a dirty operation, and I wondered if they would ever make the right hue.

I jumped at the challenge. Instead of taking the train for five hours to Nanjing, I took a plane for thirty minutes. The flight left at 7 a.m. and returned at 8:30 p.m. Upon arriving, I arranged to take a car for four hours to Yangzhou, check out the skins, grab samples, drive back to Nanjing, visit another workshop close to the airport, fly to The Hai at 8:30, and be in bed by 9:30.

Of course, it didn't work out this way.

When I arrived at the suede manufacturer, I found several shades of orange. They didn't notice the difference between what we showed them and what they had made. I took three swatches to see if the salesman wanted to use them. Then, I returned to Nanjing to visit the other factory.

I turned up at dinnertime and did a quick walk-through, pointing out problems before we sat for a banquet. This was a huge *baijiu* drinking place. We drank plenty. I became concerned about the time, but they said,

"Relax. The driver is fast and knows a back road."

All I had to do was board the plane and take a taxi to my hotel. No sweat. I continued drinking and relied on the driver to give me one hell of a ride.

And he did. He got me there five minutes before check-in closed. I felt alive and reeked of booze. I rushed to get my boarding pass and encountered an angry mob fighting with the airport staff in front of the counter. They had canceled the flight. The airline planned to take us to a hotel to room with a partner.

It didn't bother me that the flight got canceled, but I wouldn't shack up with a rando, nor did I want to wait until they sorted everything. The material samples needed to be in the mail by morning. With this in mind, I left the airport and took a cab to the train depot.

I reached the terminal at 10 p.m. There was a slow train at midnight, arriving at 7 a.m., but there weren't any tickets. I walked around the waiting hall, looking for a solution. The only staff on duty were the PLA. Since I stank of *baijiu,* I tried the pathetic lost foreign businessman routine. I spoke slowly in English and told them I needed to reach Shanghai but didn't know what to do. They let me through without a ticket and advised me which platform to wait on.

That was perfect. When the train showed up, I boarded like the boys in green instructed. Passengers packed the cabins, but I found a space between the cars and sat on the floor. It was a long, loud, and dirty night.

The train stopped at every single station all the way to Shanghai. I didn't sleep but arrived as scheduled, hungover with a severe headache.

That happens when you try to rattle the hootch out of your body on the floor of a moving train for seven hours. It felt like I had been through a life-altering experience and lived to tell. As I headed towards the exit, I realized I had never bought a ticket.

Nobody had asked me to.

Now, I needed a permit to get through the gate. I passed through these exits many times. The best option was to get in the middle of the scrum, ride the crowd, and push through before the ticket taker grabbed me. I would have purchased a ticket, but buying one now would have caused more hassle.

Once through, I headed to my hotel, showered, and mailed the swatches.

The customer chose two shades, but the factory couldn't match the color in production. The order got canceled, and they kept the shoes, hoping they would sell them to someone else.

It was a lot of trouble for something we never shipped.

A year later, they sold them. By then, the metal on the shoes had rusted, and outsoles peeled off.

It was a fiasco from the start. I had hoped Louis learned his lesson and never produced another order outside his expertise, but he did.

We supported Louis' summer season by giving him a large order of animal slippers, like bears, dogs, and dinosaurs. They were challenging to stitch. His Shanghai factory lacked the skills to make this product, so he outsourced it to a workshop in Anhui, two provinces west. To get there, I took a fast train to Nanjing and traveled over that big Nanjing Bridge, making the journey lengthier than it should have been. The automobile traffic I encountered erased any benefit I received from the modern train system.

I arrived at the slipper factory and realized they could not make the amount we needed by the date promised. The workshop was one step up from farm level and required much work. Despite the requirements we threw at them, they insisted they would finish on time. It sounded sketchy. I informed our staff what to follow up on and said I would return in a week.

Before we left for my hotel in Nanjing, we ate at a single-table restaurant. It was a hole-in-the-wall: They literally hammered through the concrete to add the kitchen. The cook told us what he had, and he cooked it. Surprisingly, they had a keg of beer. At least we would have cold brew on a summer day. But the ale showed up flat and foamy. I shouldn't have gotten my hopes up. It was like going into a bathroom and seeing a soap dispenser; your first feeling was, "Great, I can FINALLY wash my dirty-ass hands. What a wonderful thing!"

Then you discovered it was out of soap.

The warm beer was the first sign that this wouldn't be a satisfying lunch. Next came the food. The problem with many small restaurants was that they rarely cooked straightforward stir-fried meat and vegetable dishes. They used some other part of the animal. I found little I desired besides rice, vegetables, and beer.

With all the drinking, I made a trip to the restroom across from our room. It resembled a janitor's closet with a deeply stained porcelain bowl and no seat. I reminded myself never to eat spicy hotpot the day before coming here. There was not a suitable toilet in a fifty-mile range. Things turned more peculiar when I peered down and saw a fish in the bowl. A live fish, two inches long! I entered through the hole in the wall into the kitchen and said,

"There's a fish in the toilet. What should I do?"

The cook came over and flushed it. Problem solved.

I returned to the table and told my American coworker, but he didn't believe me.

"Wait a while. The fish might come back."

Then, they brought an edible dish: a plate of fried pork chops with black pepper. After eating one, I realized the flecks of pepper were deep-fried ants. I said nothing until my coworker asked me.

"You're crazy. Those are just flecks of pepper."

He looked at the pork chop closer and noticed the pepper had tiny legs.

"Ok. You got me. Those are legs."

We returned to the beer. I predicted lots of piss stops on the way to Nanjing.

Once we arrived, we checked in, and I took my compatriot to a recently opened Western restaurant called The Black Cat. They were the first place serving pizza and decent draft (**Rule #16**). Long before the explosion of fast food, the only escape from local cuisine was through entrepreneurs with a taste for Western food. Anytime someone opened a new venue, I tried it.

Everything at the slipper factory fell behind, and I spent more time there than I wanted. I knew they outsourced and tried to catch them in the act. But I relied on their car to drive me. I hoped if I visited often, they would tell me the truth. I had three local QCs stationed here. They informed me they moved the product at night. I changed my schedule, hired a hotel driver, and arrived to witness a couple of Mad Max machines pulling into the compound, hauling mounds of burlap bags. Each tractor carried stacks fifteen to twenty feet high. They tied ropes around everything, and somehow, it stayed together, but they smashed the slippers.

By this time, I had exhausted the manager. He gave up and told me everything—a bona fide case of 'be careful what you ask for.' I did not know how bad things REALLY were. He said there were not one or two but **eight outsourced factories**, each an hour away down a different dusty farm road. I attempted to visit all but only made it to six. The last two required a Mad Max machine to reach.

I walked into a workshop in the middle of nowhere and found twenty stitchers. I asked for the manager, and a worker opened the door to the field and called him. Evidently, he wore two hats. It would have been better for him to watch our production.

These outsourced factories never dealt with foreigners. They rarely knew the customer. They were "the help." You can imagine the shock of having a car pull up with a Chinese-speaking *laowai*. Most mistook me for a hairy mainlander with a big nose or a Uighur from Xinjiang. They felt no need to hide anything, including chickens wandering around with naked children chasing them.

With these farmhouses making only a single size or the left slipper, the product arriving in the gray burlap bags did not match up. Some animals had gigantic heads because that factory overstuffed them, or they were shrunk by another. It was a catastrophe. The slippers needed to be fixed in Shanghai by hand, nearly all 250,000 pairs! Later, the orders moved to another place; Louis and the factory shared air-freight costs.

I never returned after we finished and didn't miss the ant-specked pork chops.

VI

One more problem style was starting later that year—another suede boot. This time, it was a massive order for several customers. Every pair had severe flaws, and I rejected all lots. They reworked everything, but the leather quality was so bad that there would be nothing to ship if they disposed of all the trouble shoes. Instead, they repackaged the product, but I rejected them again, sometimes three or four times. After each time, the factory attempted to lower the bar and push through shoes that we all agreed were defective. Louis got frustrated. It would have been better to cancel and produce them somewhere else. He wanted to ship and gamble but couldn't do that without a "passed" inspection report. With no other options, he tried something radical:

HE BANISHED ME.

When I arrived one day, the guards refused to drop the rope. I got out and walked up to the gate.

"Why won't you let my car in?"

"Are you Mr. Thunder, the foreign customer?"

I drank with these guys at the office banquets.

"Yes, of course. You know who I am."

"Our boss said you are barred."

I thought it was a joke, but I noticed some trade corp. personnel looking out their windows and snickering. The day before, I ran into Louis, and he said nothing. He didn't show up. Instead, he let me arrive and disrespected me. He showed his staff he had the power to kick the foreigner out. Louis planned to use his *guanxi* with our U.S. office to go around me. All anyone had to do was open a case to see the problems.

"Can I tell my staff?"

"They can stay. Only you are not allowed."

"If you bar one, we all need to leave. Can I remove things that belong to us and drop off stuff?"

"You can drop off, but you can't take anything."

The guards escorted me in, accompanying me on each side like a criminal.

I said to my guys, "They have banned me. We need to leave."

They gathered their stuff. I couldn't grab things, but no one cared if I asked my people to take it for me. Meanwhile, I dropped off my brand-new bug zapper, and we stepped out. I made the guards lower the rope as a minor concession. It almost felt like a victory. I would be free of this abomination. Louis thought he would have me removed and continue the business. He didn't know I would take our staff.

I called him for a few days, but he turned his phone off. He barred me but lacked the balls to face me. This guy treated me as a close friend for two years. We often ate dinner together, and he invited me to all the company functions. His abrupt change in behavior caught me off-guard. Unfortunately, it was a pattern that repeated with other agents and even some employees. Loyalty and excellent character were rare. I would work with him again because of the cash he owed, but I didn't know how I would step back into his factory after my experience. Instead, I prepared to quit my company. Louis owed too much; they couldn't walk away from him, but if they tried to override me, they would take away my power. With a name like Mr. Thunder, I had to be strong. My only option would be to go somewhere else. But then I reminded myself that I had done nothing wrong. If I left, the problems would continue. I wasn't ready to exit just yet.

Louis shipped the shoes but required a signed inspection report to get paid. He called on Eric. I assumed he would do this and arranged for him to inspect in another province. The only person with signature authority was me. Louis changed his tune when he realized he had created a mess. Every day he delayed cost him more money, but shipping without an inspection report meant no payment until the goods sold out after six months or more. He complained to my head office, but his excuse for barring me was ridiculous. What company did not want the product as ordered?

Louis phoned me to meet at a restaurant a week later. He apologized and told me he received bad information from his staff (relatives). We needed to patch this up, but I could never forget him banning me. He also tried to hire Eric, but he refused to go despite increased pay and shares in the factory. Now, he threw Eric under the bus, suggesting he had conspired against me. I knew individuals around me wanted to see me removed. It went with the job.

I accepted Louis' apology and agreed to allow my guys to inspect production on one condition: He had to come down to the gate, welcome me in, and apologize in front of his staff. Louis didn't enjoy that part, but I told him I would not budge. I still remembered two of his people laughing at me from the office building.

He needed to do this.

The next day, I arrived, and they dropped the rope. I paid the driver and let him leave.

"Mr. Thunder, you can enter."

"Call the boss to welcome me."

"Is that necessary?"

"Yes."

A guard ran off to get Louis, who showed up.

"Tell them you made a mistake and should not have exiled me. I should be free to go wherever I please."

Then, we walked into the office. Louis told the staff he was incorrect and should never have rejected me. They caused the problems and needed to work harder. It ended as quickly as it took everybody to get to the conference room. At least I felt better.

As I predicted, the troubles did not stop. One day at lunch, we received a call telling us there was no need to return; the material warehouse burned to the ground. A faulty wire on a makeshift water heater had sparked the flames. When an imported fire truck appeared, they forgot to fill it with water. The countryside had no hydrants, so they sat and watched it burn. The factory lost everything and needed to reorder and air-freight material from Taiwan.

While they sorted out their troubles, I spent more time on the road.

CHAPTER TWELVE

HUAIYIN: BULL PEANUTS

Besides stopovers in Fujian, I made trips to Wuxi, Suzhou, Changzhou, Yancheng, or wherever an agent placed an order. The need for lower prices inspired this busy schedule, and I would have traveled daily if I didn't need a break from the drinking. But it became impractical to manage all this business by myself. I needed to hire more inspectors. I looked for people who spoke and wrote adequate English, possessed a fair knowledge of footwear, and were willing to relocate to a far-off city to work independently under harsh conditions. Few in Shanghai wanted this job. It was easier to recruit from small towns or factories. Experienced employees jumped between companies or got poached. It happened to us too, but most staff stayed for ten years or longer. That was a lifetime in new China. Foreign managers were just as tough to hire and keep. Most demanded high salaries and benefits without being qualified. They assumed that being willing to live in China was enough. We searched for months before finding someone acceptable. Meanwhile, I put out "fires" and became a fixer.

On one occasion, I was called to settle a problem in Lianyungang, Jiangsu Province. We purchased low-end casual shoes called gathered vamps, and the difference of three cents per pair won or lost an order. It was cutthroat, and factories cut corners to get the lowest price. I initially gave this workshop a pass because I had my hands full. Later, we received complaints from the customer and told the factory to hold shipments for an inspection. The American guy hired for our Qingdao Office took a trip to inspect the shoes. When he arrived, they ganged up on him with *ganbeis*. He even drank *baijiu* for the first time. After the meal, they toured the workshop, and halfway through, he threw up on the manager's shoes and the factory floor. It was a mistake not to give him my China interview. I had an obligation to set the record straight after that loss of face, so I flew there in the cold of winter and showed them how this foreigner held his own.

Ultimately, we canceled the order of two million pairs because the quality was poor. I squandered my liver cells on nothing but pride.

Besides holding down anchor on the company drinking team, I also set up best quality practices. Whenever we worked with a factory, I evaluated and gave them a list of things to correct. Most customers lacked a compliance program, and not all factories appreciated my efforts. I pressured the Hong Kong agent to fix the issues. After all, they picked the factories. Agents had use because they sourced the latest materials, financed the orders, and arranged for shipping. Government-run workshops had yet to learn how to find superior quality components, nor did they have the ambition to do so. Somebody needed to do that for them.

Eventually, prices and competition provoked the factories to improve their service, but during the '90s, we needed agents.

One of the biggest I worked with in Fujian built a factory in Changzhou, Jiangsu, two and a half hours from Shanghai by train. We had the opportunity to get it right from the beginning and helped them implement quality and compliance standards. I visited weekly to check the progress and stationed Eric here during setup.

Regrettably, the agent courted our customers and took over those accounts. We put so much time into the venture, but it was par for the course. Like with Louis, little loyalty existed even among "friends." The worst part was that we returned to inspect other orders and watched the styles we worked on going down the line but not through us.

Another agent we did a tremendous amount of business with sustained an entire factory with our production. We placed so many orders that the factory gave the agent three offices for product development and order placing. Later, I spotted shoes we did, but the labels had our competitor's name. The samples sat on the table before me while I drank that fantastic Iron Buddha tea.

"What's this?"

"I don't know where that came from," said the manager.

When I approached the agent, she told me she couldn't stop the factory. We accounted for ninety percent of the orders. With that ratio, I didn't believe her. It was proof they worked against us. I always showed up unannounced to keep them on their toes. Every time I visited, I walked straight to the production lines to catch them making the competitor's stuff. After calling them out, they rented the workshop next door to produce the copy orders, and I knocked on the gate to see if they would let me in, but the guard wouldn't do it.

A few weeks later, they got tired of sneaking around and sledgehammered a hole in the concrete walls between the factories to move materials. I asked them about it, and they told me they planned to repair the wall, but they never got around to it. I often ate dinner with the managers, and we got along well, but they were in a difficult position because our agent placed the orders. They just wanted to do business and not rock the boat.

Fortunately, not all factories were so deceiving. Some were semi-candid. When I came across a workshop that was easy to work with, I supported them. One such factory was in Huaiyin, northern Jiangsu Province, commonly referred to as the "Subei" territory. It was near the birthplace of Zhou Enlai, a prominent figure in Chinese politics who helped the Communist Party rise to power. For me, it became the place where I learned how to drink *baijiu*.

Evidently, I had been doing it incorrectly.

One of our agents placed orders, and I tackled the challenge of finding and visiting the factory. That was my favorite part of the job. I relished traveling to unfamiliar places, and Huaiyin was far out in the hinterland. The journey started with a five-hour train ride to Nanjing. Then, we crossed that confounded bridge and rode in a car for four hours. The round trip took three days. I embarked on this excursion every other month in the summer until orders dropped off.

Huaiyin didn't get a mention in Lonely Planet, so I had no idea what to expect. I arrived in Nanjing in the afternoon, and a manager named Mr. Gu picked me up. Once we crossed the bridge, we passed through a piece of Anhui Province. It cut time off the journey, but that stretch had a string of restaurants serving as brothels. It was twenty minutes of love shacks, low on the sanitary scale for food and favors. My hosts said these places served truck drivers getting a quickie. The girls stood outside with ghoulish-looking faces painted white, waving at every vehicle. They put massive stones on the road to stop the traffic, thus increasing their chances of catching your eye. If the rocks didn't slow you down, the potholes did. I sat in a minivan going down this road two years later and hit a pothole that shattered the side window. We bought duct tape to keep it in place.

Those were severe craters.

It became clear we would not reach Huaiyin in time for dinner. Instead, they searched for a roadside joint. The driver needed a rest, too. He had driven from early morning, going over that Nanjing Bridge four times the same day, and it had worn him down. I prepared myself for heavy drinking after I noticed multiple advertisements for *baijiu*. It appeared that Northern Jiangsu Province had a fancy for it. This was an unexpected development, but I would have to wait until the second day because nobody in the car drank the hard stuff. They said the women managers were the drinkers. Interesting.

Shortly after we passed 'hooker avenue,' we stopped at a restaurant that looked decent enough even though no one ate there. The driver patronized the place. He drove back and forth between Nanjing and Huaiyin several times a week and dined here. I trusted his judgment.

The menu was a sheet of paper. It listed parts of animals and how they would cook them. Many eateries in the countryside didn't have formal menus; they displayed the goods or wrote them on a chalkboard. I attempted to find something resembling chicken or beef. The menu had the "beef" character, but I didn't recognize the following symbol. Sometimes, restaurants wrote dish names poetically to seem unique.

Not wanting them to know I didn't understand, I asked if they cooked any beef dishes. The cook said they made *"niu bian."*

Niu meant 'cow,' but what part of the cow was *"bian?"* My teachers had neglected to teach that.

"Is that beef?"

"Yes, it's a type of beef."

This would be a quick dinner, not the big meal of the trip. I kept it simple: a beef dish, a vegetable, and rice. Mr. Gu ordered a few more items. I impressed them by selecting *"niu bian."* They said it was the most popular dish in the Huaiyin area.

"Hell, if that's the case, perhaps it will be tasty!"

The plates started coming, but nothing resembled a stir-fried beef dish. Mr. Gu tried to get me to eat the other foods, but I avoided the cold plates (**Rule #1**). A normal-looking soup arrived with gigantic pieces of calamari. They put a sizeable chunk into my bowl. I picked up a piece and took a bite. The texture was chewy, not for me, so I discreetly hid the squid on the outside of my bowl. I inquired about my beef dish. They said everything was on the table, so I had to guess,

"Where's the beef?"

Mr. Gu pointed to a soup. Perhaps there was beef at the bottom. I took the ladle and dredged it but found more squid.

"There's no beef. They must have forgotten to add some."

"There's plenty."

I thought they were playing a joke on me.

"All I see is squid."

"That's not squid. It's *niu bian.*"

"*Bian.*" There's that word again. Finally, I asked, "What does *bian* mean?"

"It's a type of beef, a part of the male cow or bull."

Oh shit, now I understood. It was the frank or the beans. When I looked at the "squid," I realized I had a bowl of bull penis soup. The pieces were white and circular, and I visualized the cook chopping the uncooked member with a cleaver. I made a joke saying I couldn't eat anymore because I'm heterosexual, but they didn't get it. All they saw was I chewed a sizeable chunk; therefore, I must have enjoyed bull cock. And just like that, they forever tied me to it. On each occasion I ate with this factory, they ordered bull penis because I liked it, of course.

Over the years, I had bull penis presented to me in many forms, using China's long culinary history. They served it stewed, stir-fried, and braised. I even had "whole bull soup," which consisted of the bits we never eat in America (ear, nose, tail, hoof, penis, and other things) mixed in a milky broth. Yum!

I encountered an identical incident with another factory and sea cucumber. Sea cucumber is a rubbery slug, resembling something you might see in a sex shop. I ate it because of the price. And so I got acquainted with sea cucumber. It came in a single serving, not family style. They served me a small plate with a six-inch braised slug with brown sauce, and the servers waited for me to finish before taking away the dish. There was nowhere to hide that sucker. I can honestly say I miss many things from China, but not sea cucumber or bull penis.

We reached Huaiyin around 9 p.m. after a nine-hour journey. The streets looked desolate, with only a few lights. Mr. Gu confirmed they had little nightlife. But, he said they installed a karaoke on the roof of the workshop, where they celebrated parties. That was something to look forward to.

They drove us to a garden-style hotel with several three-to-four-story buildings. They couldn't make the structures too high with no elevators—going up eight flights with luggage would be a bitch. Despite the lack of amenities, I enjoyed these older, socialist inns. They gave me an idea of life before China opened up. Back in the day, this was luxury.

No one was standing at the front desk when we arrived. Mr. Gu made some noise to rattle someone out of bed. The colder it got, the earlier people stayed in, and few business travelers ventured this far. An attendant showed up and checked me into a room in a renovated building at the rear of the complex. The factory guys drove me there and set me up before leaving. I didn't see anyone staying there, not even an attendant. Even Eric stayed in another building. That happened frequently: The factories booked me into the "better building," which seemed more hassle. My room was on the first floor, and when I opened the curtains in the morning, I had a view of a wall with hot water pipes. I felt disorientated as I walked through a maze of gray buildings.

I entered the main building and wandered the long, dark hallways past many rooms with padlocks until I discovered the meeting hall, where they laid out a buffet of cold food and congee, plain and corn style! The dishes resembled leftovers from last night's dinner. There were a lot of items I wouldn't consider mouth-watering breakfast foods, such as sliced river eel and coagulated pig's blood (red tofu). Still, I needed to find something to create a solid base to soak up the booze I would pour down my throat at lunch. In this situation, I tried to consume as many carbohydrates as possible. Toast, steamed buns, or rice worked well, but the hotel breakfast was not cooperating; I needed to be more creative. When I asked the staff if they planned to bring out more food, they said no and that I should arrive earlier. It was only 8:30 a.m.! Breakfast should last until ten. I wondered what other guests thought, but judging by the number of dirty plates, everyone seemed to be aware to get here early. Most of the diners stayed outside the guesthouse. They were military and government officials who enjoyed the freedom to do as they pleased.

With no carbs, I reconsidered some foods I passed on the buffet. They had cold fried dough sticks called "*you tiao,*" which I dipped in the rice congee with soy sauce. That became my daily breakfast in Huaiyin, along with tea and smokes. They served fried eggs, but they cooked them long ago and now were cold, rubbery, and swimming in oil. The thought of them mixed with the other dishes induced a series of dry heaves. I would have prepared my own eggs if they allowed me. Some hotels did—or didn't stop me. I got so good at it I took orders from my coworkers.

Mr. Gu picked me up and drove me to a medium-sized plant fifteen minutes away. Huaiyin wasn't a huge city, but the county spread wide like Putian. We weren't exactly in the middle of nowhere, but it surprised me that the agent had found this place. Similar to most locations outside the capital, they rarely met Westerners and never encountered Chinese-speaking ones.

This would be the first time they worked with an American company. They did business with an Italian firm and understood what the Italians would accept. But, they had difficulty communicating because the Chinese couldn't speak English or Italian, and the Italians didn't speak Chinese. Even though I didn't know Italian, the managers asked if I wouldn't mind eating together to translate. They had been dying to ask them things. I wondered how they did business. Naturally, I did not argue against lunch with two twenty-something Italian girls. I rarely met other foreigners on the road, not to mention ladies, so I anticipated meeting them, but I first needed to inspect the factory.

At the very least, I wanted to ensure the workshop didn't employ underage workers. We produced slippers here, and it was reassuring the managers took it upon themselves to be clean and efficient. Their products didn't use many chemicals, making approval easier. Workers came from the villages and lived at home, so I didn't have to check the dorms. The employees either worked in the fields or the workshop and sometimes both. In Qingdao, so many laborers originated from the countryside that they had a seasonal harvest holiday and returned home to help. When doing business in China, it was essential to know these things to prepare for a drop in production.

I finished walking around and stopped in the warehouse to pick cases for inspection. They opened the cartons, and I noticed the shoeboxes were different shades of the same color. They left the boxes in the sun, and the colors faded depending on how much sunlight they received. The factory managers couldn't understand why I wouldn't accept their packaging.

"They're not smashed, and the customer doesn't buy the product for the box."

They didn't get the importance of branding and pantones. I reasoned they only needed to replace a couple of hundred boxes. They would have shipped the entire lot if I hadn't made the journey. Then, the slippers would need to be repacked in the U.S.—very costly. For that, they were thankful. However, after further inspection, I noticed they paid no attention to the price ticket and used whichever packet of tickets they opened; every pair was "White X-Large." The agent didn't write the Chinese translation on the order sheet, thinking the Huaiyin factory should be accustomed to dealing in English like the coastal factories. Everything had to be redone.

Besides the packing, the product looked good. They still stocked enough correct boxes to finish the test order, and they asked me to remain another day to inspect the packaged goods. That was a fantastic opportunity to explore the city. It had taken me so long to get here; I might as well stay, cultivate *guanxi*, and see the town.

We wrapped things up in the warehouse and let the workers start repackaging to identify the sizes and colors they needed to manufacture. The test order would be air-freighted if they didn't have enough to fill the size run. With the high cost, I assumed they would finish in twenty-four hours.

We returned to the conference room and met their Italian customers. The ladies attempted to communicate with the factory, and it sounded painfully slow. They finished, and we walked downstairs to the restaurant. The factory informed me the food outside was dirty, so we should dine at their place. I wondered why nobody else told me about the contaminated food. Also, I never recalled seeing a clean factory cafeteria. That was not the type of place I would pick, but I agreed because I anticipated having lunch with two Italian ladies. We could have eaten on the production line for all I cared.

The dining room was in front, so we walked outside the gate. It consisted of a ten-person round table and two smaller ones. The kitchen was minuscule, but the cook prepared quite a range. I never had to order; he kept bringing dishes until someone said no more. I sat next to the designers to translate. Somehow, these women survived and were doing business despite the language barrier, which was impressive.

On my other side sat the three factory managers. There were more ladies at the table than men. Generally, it would be a low-key meal with more women, but not in Huaiyin. They drank more than the men. As the feast started, they asked if I could drink *baijiu*.

"Sure, I can put away a bottle or two, but I also need cold beer."

This surprised them for two reasons.

1. No one admits they can drink a lot, or the others will make you consume more.

2. You shouldn't mix drinks. "You'll get drunk faster."

Maybe that was true, but it added to the legend of my drinking skills. Plus, I needed a chaser for the first couple, and beer worked best. Locals used other chasers, such as hot soy milk or corn juice. Never had corn juice? Picture a more liquid version of cream of corn, and you have corn juice. One manager used hot cola as a chaser. I couldn't imagine drinking any of those drinks with or without *baijiu*. They seemed like something I endured during hell week in my fraternity.

I set them up for the drinking contest that would begin shortly. I also clarified that if they aimed to get me drunk, don't try. It would be better if we drank at our own pace.

But I underestimated the drinking abilities of the managers; they drank hard. Madams Wang and Zhang were both in their late fifties and had lived through some rough times, similar to the guys I worked with back home. Don't let their sweet and kind exterior fool you. They had to be tough to rise to the top. Right away, they introduced me to a local custom, where if someone asked you to *ganbei* and they clinked glasses, you needed to drink four shots with that person. You didn't have to drink them all at once. It was between you and the other individual, but you owed four shots. I did two shots at once to make it easier to count because I engaged in multiple toasts simultaneously during each meal as they tested my tolerance. Everyone wanted to drink with me. When I finished one challenge, someone else clinked my glass. It never ended.

And so I kept drinking, and the food kept coming. Besides my "favorite" penis dish, we had river eel, lamb, crabs, and fish. I saw the cook killing the eels on the street, and it was a bloody mess. After cooking, they looked like a plate of stir-fried garter snakes. The crabs had little meat but required too much effort. I had no idea how to eat them and ate the wrong parts, like the lungs. Now, I knew I did not enjoy hairy crabs (*da zha xie*), but everybody ordered them wherever I traveled in these parts. We mostly ate stews with the same delicious brown, spicy sauce. They served large disks of hard, naan-like bread to dip into the stew. They called the dish "*xiaoyu guotie*" (little fish potstickers). It was one of my favorite dishes, but I only ate the sauce and the naan. They used little jumping fish called "*tiao tiao yu*," about four inches long, and cooked them whole. Eating them required skill to separate the bones and organs and spit them into a pile. This dish went well with booze.

The Italians told me they lived in Nanjing and came to Huaiyin during development season.

"Then you must have had Huaiyin's most famous dish."

"What dish?"

"Bull penis."

The woman sitting beside me had a slightly better knowledge of English, but she didn't understand.

"Bull . . . peanuts?"

"No, bull penis."

"Peanuts?"

"Umm, penis, not peanuts."

"Peanuts?"

"No. peeee . . . nis."

"Peanuts?"

We went back and forth while the other woman smiled. I didn't get anywhere and took a different approach.

"It's a part of the male cow, not the female."

I tapped my index figure on the table for added effect. Suddenly, the quiet woman turned bright red. She got it and explained it in Italian. Then her coworker turned red and said, "NO, no, no . . . never."

I pointed to a bowl on the lazy Susan and said, "You just ate it."

They didn't know what they had eaten, and nobody could explain.

After that, they asked what every dish was. I did the same for American and European coworkers. Usually, I ordered dishes for weaker stomachs, like sweet and sour pork. But the further we traveled from the major cities, the harder it became to find nosh for weaker tastes.

On one trip, I accompanied a few first-time visitors to a factory in rural Sichuan. Not many Westerners visited this area, so it was a massive deal for us to stop and eat lunch. The local CCP leaders came out to welcome us and get their drink on.

The government clamped down on lunchtime drinking, but they relaxed the rule for officials if a foreigner or a dignitary was present. Our group of four foreign devils set off a glaring green light for a three-hour *baijiu* bender. Maybe they lit up a "Bat Signal," advising all the chiefs they could booze up. It was an unexpected gift that one visitor (me) liked *baijiu*.

Since I traveled with the uninitiated, I ensured things did not get out of hand, but the restaurant gave me little to work with. They specialized in everything lamb. Every plate turned out to be a separate organ. A female coworker sitting next to me passed on everything once I told her what it contained. But then they brought out a white soup, which looked like wild mushroom, not uncommon in a rural place. They had long stems with a small mushroom cap. I said it was okay to eat and handed her a bowl. When I took the spoon to pour myself one, I realized they weren't mushrooms. It was a hot bowl of sheep penises.

Luckily, I stopped her from eating it. Otherwise, I would have never heard the end of it. That was a lot of penises in a single bowl. Ouch!

We enjoyed a lengthy lunch, and the Italians drove back to Nanjing while I stuck around. They invited me over for home-cooked Italian food, but we never worked it out. Now, I had time to kill in a town with little happening.

Beside the factory was a PLA training school, and the soldiers shot hoops. It was an excellent way to pass the time. I strolled over and walked through the gates to see if they wouldn't mind me jumping in. Why wouldn't they want an out-of-shape foreigner who drank rocket fuel for the past three hours to join?

The fact that I had not shot hoops since grade school didn't matter. I felt invincible on a sunny afternoon in a small town.

They passed me the ball, and I lasted for a few shots until I came to my senses.

Everyone thought I would be good coming from Chicago, home of Michael Jordan, but I missed every shot, not even close—all air balls. As I chased the ball, I was out of breath, and the alcohol gushed through my veins. Then, I got the *baijiu* burps.

I needed a respectful way out of this situation while the factory staff observed from the second-floor windows. They watched to make sure the PLA didn't lock me up. That would have caused problems with our dinner plans. I told the soldiers I had to leave and made my exit. They were relieved and locked the gate after me.

When I returned to the factory, I asked if there was anything else to do. They mentioned the Zhou Enlai Museum, a half-hour away. As tempting as that sounded, my inebriated mind looked for something more entertaining, with a few cold beers to help me survive the afternoon and on to dinner.

"Does Huaiyin have a zoo?"

I learned that most of the towns had zoos. It seemed like a requirement to own a few poorly treated animals locked in concrete cages. The zoos also operated a handful of beat-up amusement park rides like bumper cars and go-carts. I never knew what to expect, but it was an acceptable way to waste time if there were no temples or scenic spots.

Huaiyin had a zoo, and I requested the factory to drop me off there. They thought it was odd, but they played along. All the managers helped with the rework; they were probably pleased to be free of me.

The Huaiyin Zoo had a few rides from the '50s (or so they looked) and a decent collection of random animals—a camel, a bear, dogs, and snakes. They should have contacted the Kaiping Hotel to borrow and save some exhibits from the dinner table. At the zoo, I encountered an AIDS exhibit with graphic pictures of people with full-blown AIDS.

Locals never seemed shy about posting raw photos as long as they drew a black line across the eyes.

The AIDS exhibit dampened my drunken, sunny afternoon, and I headed back to the hotel to prepare for dinner.

The driver picked me up at 6 p.m. to review the progress of the rework. Then, we returned to the dining room and continued where we had left off. This time, their Japanese customer joined. They ran a joint venture with a Japanese company, and they sent a technician to live inside the factory. And I thought my life was rough. He spoke no Mandarin but had a translator. I tried to remember something from my Japanese classes, but considering the switch in my brain had been stuck on Mandarin for the past few years, it almost refused to speak anything else. Hell, I now had difficulty speaking English correctly without better Chinese words popping up in my brain first. All I managed to say was: "I studied Japanese in college," and "American cars are #1."

Everyone laughed at the last line, so I continued to throw it out when we drank. Seeing the Japanese customer following the four-shot rule made me feel better. I thought they did it to get me lit.

We had an epic feast that ended when the managers talked us into moving upstairs to the karaoke. It was a large hall with about fifty seats arranged on the dance floor for workers. They used an old-school setup similar to Fuan. Since they rarely used the room, it took a while for the AC to remove the musty aroma.

While they bought drinks, I examined the sound system. As expected, they lacked English laser discs. I brought my CDs, but my road music was not karaoke-friendly. Try singing along to Bjork or Talking Heads. I sang horribly, but my version of The Doors' "Break on Through" was better. It didn't matter what music I played. As long as I had fun, they relaxed. The managers drank past their limits and couldn't believe I kept going like a tornado that turned everything upside-down in my wake. It was best to take cover until it ended.

They moved the chairs aside when Chinese songs came on, and everyone, including the managers, ballroom danced. I resisted, but they pulled me out, and I dusted off my three-step/four-step skills from Putian with the managers and the Japanese customer. It felt weird dancing with another dude, but I got over it.

When I took a break, I walked out onto the rooftop and looked across the low-lying city while testing my digital phone. I finally had the paperwork (I needed a Shanghai company to sponsor me) and money (10,000 RMB, $1,200) to buy my first Ericsson 332. It's impossible to forget when you get your first digital device, bringing you one step closer to *Star Trek* space-age technology. Also, the last four digits of my randomly assigned number sounded like, "I want alcohol, but I don't have it." What a coincidence.

Although it wasn't a brick, my pockets were pleased. Like a kid with a new toy, I tested the phone service everywhere I traveled—a "Can you hear me now?" situation. It felt good talking to friends and family from the U.S. to bring me down to earth. That was the greatest gift of the cell phone. Before, I drifted, untethered to the outside world, living in an alcoholic bubble. After I owned a phone, I reconnected. However, my conversations were incoherent because the situation was unfathomable, and I drank too much. I'm sure it wasn't fun to receive a call from someone talking about eels and penis soup at 9 a.m. U.S. time.

As it got later, workers slipped out until only a handful remained, and I had exhausted my playlist. They sent me back for a few hours of sleep before picking me up the following day. We had a shortened lunch but equally heavy on the sauce. Then they drove me to Nanjing with a case of *baijiu* but no bull penis.

On future trips, it was the same routine: factory, hotel, factory, karaoke, then back to the hotel. When I had time to kill, they took me sightseeing.

Despite the hardship of traveling to Huaiyin, I was glad I made the effort. They were great people to work with, and I returned when I could.

Because of the hard-drinking ladies, this factory became the ideal place to interview potential expat managers. I learned from the guy losing his lunch that it was necessary to see how they dealt with the business meal before getting hired. If they could handle themselves in this scenario, they should be able to deal with anything. I advised prospects not to push it or keep up with me, especially at lunch. Inexperienced *baijiu* drinkers habitually had their food revisit them. Nothing was more shameful than vomiting in a squat toilet or in public. Vomit would splash on your pant legs in the squatter, and you might stink like the puke you just regurgitated. That was better than throwing up at the table or in the car, as one guy did. Thankfully, he threw up outside the window, but it sprayed along the side. I warned him before we drank that if he spewed, he would have to clean it up, and he did.

You should also identify what foods caused you to spend time in the toilet. Huaiyin factory had a miserable restroom. It was a single trough separated by three-foot-high walls. You squatted and watched the shit from the person in front, floating underneath. If there was any confusion about whom it belonged to, just stand up and look down. In addition, they overlooked installing a door. As people made smells and noises, office workers passed by. Occasionally, you might pass as someone finished their business and stood up to buckle their pants. It was too much information.

It was wise to avoid anything that prolonged your trip to the bathroom and to carry toilet paper or newspaper would have to suffice.

We worked with the Huaiyin factory for a year when Bryon called to say he planned to leave our company to join a customer. He said one final time, "Remember, YOU ARE THE MOVIE STAR."

When he resigned in Shenzhen, he showed up with two ladies, one on each arm. He went out in style but returned a few months later to visit Huaiyin.

While planning the trip, I informed the ladies he would drink the devil's juice if they locked him into four shots each. But he wasn't a *baijiu* drinker, and it was best to stick with what you knew. *Baijiu* could be a disaster for some. Bryon found out the hard way.

He ended up sitting on the floor in the squat toilet, puking his guts out in the dark. We drove slowly to the hotel because he had his head outside the sliding minivan door, leaving a trail of vomit. I wouldn't call it a glorious return, and he never came back. He had troubles with his new job, and the China trip seemed like an excuse to get him out of the office.

I ran into Bryon two years later on the Hong Kong subway. He said he sold used cars to China—that fit. I never saw him again, but I thanked him for opening the door for more than my foot.

Our partnership with the factory continued for three years. The plant turned private when a manager bought the other two out. Then, they set up their own workshops, and the talented laborers were divided. Our agent accused the main factory of skimming on materials when the agent's relative was the culprit. But it was a done deal; they moved the orders to one of the sub-factories for a lower price. Just when my dancing skills improved, the rooftop karaoke parties ended. Damn.

We got along well with the new place because we knew everyone. Mr. Gu was the only manager who couldn't drink. His face turned into disgust every time he took a sip. Since he had a problem with booze, he brought me to the corrugated carton-making factory far down a country road that went on forever. I noticed many fish hatcheries on the way and wondered if the box boss had *guanxi* to take me fishing. We discussed it over *baijiu*, and he said no problem.

I got excited about doing legitimate fishing, but the morning we arranged to go, it rained. I worried the box boss might cancel, but he said, "No problem." We stopped by the local dry goods store to inquire about rain boots. They didn't have large sizes, so they cut open the toes, and I wore my shoes on the inside. It worked. Without them, I would have slipped.

Once I had wellies, we drove to the rural area and met with the box factory owner. He took us another thirty minutes into the wet farmland until we arrived at a couple of rectangular ponds with a narrow walkway around each. Fishing at a hatchery would be easy. We only needed to dip our line in the water, and the fish jumped on the hook. It ended up being more complex than I thought. First, it still rained, hard at times. I wore a heavy rubber poncho that stank like an oily tire. Despite my wellies, I almost slid into the pond a few times until the manager grabbed me.

He also baited my hook while I held the fifteen-foot bamboo pole. I slipped with the rod in my hand and hooked his fingers twice. It had to be painful, but he never complained.

The fish pond contained humongous carp, five pounds each. We caught thirty monsters in total. What would we do with them? Even though they offered, I did not want to drag a mesh bag of carp back to Shanghai. They planned to cook some for lunch and dinner.

"I forgot to point out I don't prefer to eat fish, but I enjoy catching them. In America, we practice catch and release."

"Why would you do that?"

"Because I'd rather eat a steak."

It was not a problem. They didn't have steak, but they brought out a bowl of crawdads they had cooked in a fishing shack. My hands were filthy and funky from fish slime and the pig liver bait. I would not peel crayfish and put their meat in my mouth without washing with soap, so I waited until we returned to the village.

The restaurant was a classic countryside joint that resembled someone's home, and the country dudes hit the bottle heavily; I mean, really hard. We strolled in, and a few tables were engaged in fierce *baijiu ganbei'ing*. They made a big uproar with shouts and brags. I wanted to join their fun. Nothing felt better than these joyous afternoons spent drinking immeasurable amounts of the devil's juice without a care in the world. They seemed dream-like until I glared at those cold eggs in the morning. The best remedy was to start again at lunch and commit to a two or three-day bender.

The cook used the fish to make my favorite dish, *xiaoyu guotie* (same sauce, larger fish) and gave us the naan bread, including a crispy cornmeal version, similar to a wok-sized tortilla chip. They cut the carp into big steaks. One piece was more than enough. Meanwhile, they bombarded me with *baijiu* shots, four at a time, of course. When the factory people reached their limit, they told the server to drink with me.

It was a requirement in these parts.

We enjoyed a never-ending lunch that carried on to dinner. They wanted me to stay to croon next door. It was ample space, but I passed.

Singing in the large room with five guys passed out would be depressing. I didn't need to sing that badly.

I couldn't get into my usual hotel because of a government meeting, so I had to stay at a one-star at the bus station. The rate was 50 RMB, and they wouldn't trust me with the key. I told the attendant I would return late, but he said someone would be at the desk all night. Because my room door looked thin, I brought my bags to the new karaoke in town with Mr. Gu.

Later, I returned all liquored up, and the front desk had nobody on duty. I headed up to the room and tried to push the door open. It wasn't my brightest idea, but I had been drinking for ten hours. Next, I kicked the door, and my foot broke through. I didn't know my own strength. Finally, Mr. Gu showed up with the key ring and opened it for me. I forgot about the damage and didn't notice it as I left, still hazy. When I attempted to check out, they charged me 50 RMB for the room and 100 RMB for the door.

"What door?"

"You came back last night and put two holes in your door."

Really? They also said someone broke several thermoses sitting outside the doors on my floor. Now, it was coming back to me. I knocked over the water bottles as I strolled down the hall while waiting for somebody to open my door. I had no idea they would break. And when I saw my door, I confirmed the existence of two holes. Oops. I paid my bill and left. Something had to give after a night like that.

Every year I visited Huaiyin, the roads and trains improved. I could now leave and make it to the airport in time for a flight, and I didn't have to hang around chasing animals at the zoo. When they paved the streets, the traffic moved faster. Most of the time, I sat in the front (with my seat belt on now), trying to sleep off the booze. Sometimes, I might hang my arm outside the car while I dozed.

Rule #22: Never hang my arm outside a car window. Never.

Once, I had my arm outside and brought it in while I slept. Twenty minutes later, I woke up to our car swerving wide left and a large truck tire rubbing against the side. I was in shock and needed to shake the marbles out of my head. While our driver passed the truck, it swerved to miss a pothole and slammed into our vehicle. If I had kept my arm out, it would have been gone. This truth, combined with the liquor in my system, made me angry. My "bad China day clock" exploded. I joined the arguing and finger-pointing, which shocked everyone. Eric reminded me I had a flight to catch. Mr. Gu walked up to every car that passed to see if they were headed towards Nanjing. He found someone willing to carry an inebriated *laowai*. I think Mr. Gu gave them some money.

I was happy to be back on the road with my arm intact.

That incident was one of my last trips to Huaiyin.

I returned after a few years to visit the workshop across the street. Between negotiations, I walked over to see if anyone I knew still worked at the slipper factory. Unfortunately, the manager was retired, and my Japanese friend had left. I felt sad knowing I would never return.

At least I had a last look, but my bull penis days were behind me.

CHAPTER THIRTEEN

SUQIAN: GRADUATION

One of my inspectors contacted me to warn about a situation at a workshop in Suqian. The factory acknowledged they produced inferior products but completed thirty-six thousand pairs and continued. They threatened our QC to accept the order or else. It was shocking and impressive that they dared to do this. When we encountered a problem of this sort, I would reject if necessary. I had to be alert every time I entered a scene like this.

The order was a basic white cotton shoe. How badly could they mess it up? I requested our QC to send me samples. He said he kept them in his room, but the factory owners forced their way in and grabbed them. He feared for his life and prepared to escape, but I told him to stay until I arrived.

First, I had to figure out where Suqian was and how to get there. The location was three hundred miles west of Shanghai, in Northern Jiangsu Province—*baijiu* county. I discovered a regional airport but couldn't find flights. No travel agents I questioned knew when planes flew there. Our employee took a five-hour train from Shanghai to Nanjing, then rode buses for an additional seven. I had to find a better way.

Luckily, Eric uncovered a fast train passing through Xuzhou. After riding the rail for six hours, I had to take a car for two. It still beat taking a sleeper bus.

The crisp air hit my nostrils when I exited the Xuzhou train station. Coming from Chicago, Shanghai never seemed cold enough. I welcomed the frigid temperature and wore a light jacket to show I was fearless. I aimed to arrive incognito and told our QC to meet me with a taxi at the station, so it shocked me when I saw him with the manager. Our guy said he had no choice. Then, he boarded a train to his hometown. It raised the stakes.

The factory manager took me to check in at my request. I preferred that part be completed instead of registering when I came back liquored up. He accompanied me to my room and showed me where to find breakfast. Next, I searched for the hotel bar. I wanted to avoid getting jacked up and dropped off at 10 p.m. with nowhere to go. I required a venue to come down from the *baijiu* high. The bar was behind the times but had a cassette player. I always carried mixtapes for car rides.

With the hotel sorted, we headed to the workshop to assess the damage. Similar to past occurrences, they employed varying hues of white. The manager argued it was also our fault since our staff did not stop production, but I possessed the inspection reports. They said to stop. The factory refused to sign.

The manager feared the owners, who worked in the mining business. He needed us to release the shipment for his sake. I offered to mail a case to the U.S. to see if someone would take them. That wasn't a guarantee, but I wanted to give them hope.

We continued to exhaust all avenues of discussion until dinnertime. This was the moment I had prepared my liver for. Where would they take me for this Battle Royale? The workshop was on the edge of town with nothing around besides other factories. When we exited the office, it was dark, and the temperature had dropped. Everything turned to ice, which is a serious situation when wobbly from drinking massive amounts.

We walked out of the compound, crossed the road, and into the complex on the opposite side. They directed me to a small room with the white laboratory lights I disliked. It resembled a terrorist interrogation cell rather than a place to eat with bare concrete walls. There were two tables, one with nothing on it and the other with ten bottles of one of my favorite *baijiu* brands. They had no idea I drank vast amounts, but I knew they did, considering the area manufactured *baijiu*. If I wanted a contest, this was it.

Perhaps the generous collection of the clear nectar from the gods was on display to scare me. That was fine, but I required some beer to chase.

"It's too cold for beer. The bottles will burst when left out at this temperature," remarked the old lady wearing a dirty apron, four or five sweaters, and the white sleeve protectors of a worker. The situation looked ugly.

There were just three of us: two managers and myself. The trading company QC disappeared. That's alright; he wasn't helpful. This wouldn't be much of a contest with two guys. I over-prepared, but it seemed extravagant for a business short on cash to have ten bottles.

"Is somebody else showing up?"

"The owners from the mine will be here soon."

Fantastic! We would have a contest, after all. Four guys (a fifth arrived later) paraded in wearing the standard "*laoban*" uniform complete with long, leather, oxblood red overcoats with big, bushy fur collars, like foxes wrapped around their necks. They also carried man bags for their bricks. I felt inadequate with my tiny Ericsson and thin windbreaker.

The shoe factory manager introduced us while we sat on stools around the wooden table. I chose a spot against the wall, facing the door to see what came next; no surprises. They provided no heat, and everybody except me wore their jacket. They all said I was strong not to need a coat. That was their first warning.

We began the meal with a few *ganbeis* while waiting for dishes to arrive. Each owner drank with me for reasons such as "The first time we met" or "I spoke Chinese well." In rapid-fire, I drank shot after shot while craving a plate of stir-fried something with rice to come busting in to give me a breather. Because I took an early train, I missed breakfast and lunch. My stomach required a base. I asked for beer, thinking someone may have forgotten they had a few bottles hiding in the corner, but no such luck. The same was true for bottled water.

The first dish was a soup. Not needing more liquid, I passed and continued to drink. Then, another soup showed up, and another.

"Aren't there any stir-fried dishes?"

They said the kitchen was somewhere else, and the food would be cold by the time they brought it over. Why didn't we eat closer? Or did they make the meal in the canteen? They also ran out of rice. How convenient! They wanted to hurt me. It was time to play offense. When we started, I said I didn't want to consume an abundant amount because it would wind me up.

"We shouldn't start unless you want to go to the end of the evening."

I gave them my Hulk warning (Don't make me angry; you wouldn't like me when I'm angry), and I made good on my notification. One by one, they slipped out and didn't return. We finished the *baijiu*, and now I was twisted, ready for what came next, but the competition ran away.

Only the factory manager remained, and he sent me back. Everyone else bailed. He had one of those acceptable excuses that allowed him to avoid *ganbeis*, but he wasn't the target. They tried to break me to get me to accept the shoes and gave it their best shot.

I made the manager help me close the bar. He watched my drink as I walked up to the stage to fast-forward my cassettes until I found the tunes I desired. The music helped distract me from my hunger. The restaurant closed around 8 p.m., and nothing was available outside in the freezing weather. So I called it a night. The manager returned home, and I passed out. With no food, I needn't worry about throwing up. That would happen in the morning as I retched stomach acids, lovely yellow toxins deep from within my tortured bowels, like a sign of surrender.

After what seemed a short time, I heard a deafening alarm. I woke up in such an intoxicated trance that I assumed it was part of my dream. Then somebody banged on my door and yelled,

"Fire! Everyone needs to leave."

It sounded urgent, and I smelled something burning, so I attempted to get up but was off balance. When I found my legs, it pleased me to see that I had left the cork out of the thermos to cool the water. Before I rushed out, I chugged a glass. The fire didn't appear catastrophic, and

I presumed it would be over quickly, so I wore a T-shirt, a windbreaker, and boxers. I couldn't find my shoes and wore the hotel slippers. They weren't actually footwear but two pieces of paper-thin material (EVA) interlocked with a thin bottom. I tip-toed on the ice and snow to prevent my slippers from falling apart while the freezing air slapped me in the face. This was not the wake-up call I wanted.

While we waited for the fire truck, I noticed little smoke. There was no apparent damage to the building, and after a half-hour, they allowed us back in, just in time. My stomach acids bubbled up, irritated by the rusty-tasting water I drank, and I knew in about five minutes, my body would expel the yellow liquid. I'm not sure if I was angrier because they forced me out of bed for this fire drill, stood in the cold with no pants on, or because I remembered the predicament I faced. In all three situations, life sucked.

The workers salvaged some pairs that looked acceptable under the poor lighting of the warehouse and wanted me to inspect them. I planned to look, grab a case of the terrible stuff, survive lunch, and move on to the following factory. Considering how long it took to reach this area, I arranged to stop by Huaiyin and swing by the suede workshop in Yangzhou (also a *baijiu* drinking place). I neglected to consider the toll three massive days of heavy *baijiu* boozing would take on my body. This would be an arduous trip, more demanding than most.

They removed the shoes from the plastic bags and separated them into piles of white. It looked hopeless. Try looking at shades of white for a couple of hours. Again, I offered to send a case, but they resisted and hoped I would release the order in good faith. There was no way I would let the shipments go.

We negotiated until lunch. I faced a hard cut-off time to reach Huaiyin before the workers quit for dinner. The Suqian factory could only do so much damage in two hours.

At lunchtime, we returned to the scene of the crime. When I sat down on the same stool, I felt *déjà vu*. I glanced across, and there was a new table of *baijiu*. No worries, if I was slightly drunk, the miners would be worse. But they never showed! A few minutes after we arrived, four different bosses came in and said the guys from yesterday needed to join a meeting. Great, four new players and no assistance.

This time, word had spread that I operated on a higher level. I impressed everybody with my tolerance. The manager shared that I continued at the nightclub, which gained me more respect. The story got back to The Hai when the trade company QC returned. Soon, my ability to imbibe preceded me whenever I visited a workshop.

If I learned to drink *baijiu* in Huaiyin, I graduated in Suqian.

They talked me into staying for three hours. We finished our last *ganbei* and walked to the car waiting to take me to Huaiyin, seventy-five miles away. It was a bright day, and the snow had melted. I sat in the back and pulled out my magazines and CD player. Even though I knew I would pass out, I wanted everyone to think I would read as if nothing was wrong.

Everything was set, including the case of shoes they released, and before I left, they gave me a wrapped gift. I said thanks and put it on the seat next to me. The car sped off, and I fell asleep. An hour later, we got stuck in traffic because of construction. It wasn't too bad, meaning not five hours, but one or two. The driver said we would arrive at 6 p.m. The Huaiyin factory told me to head to a place in town.

At lunch, I was flying. Now I slurred my words and felt like shit. I focused on sobering up when I looked over and saw the gift. I vaguely remembered someone handing it to me. It was a music box with a twirling ballerina. I would have never expected it. The peculiarity of the gift fit right in with my stay in Suqian.

We reached the boundary of Huaiyin, and the Suqian driver handed me off. I collected my belongings and slipped into the other car while he popped the trunk and moved my luggage. Once in, we took off. The factory managers waited in the restaurant. I told them to start, but they wouldn't. The driver passed every car and honked his horn during the entire drive. It resembled what a police escort would be if we chased ourselves. We arrived in record time, and he grabbed my stuff from the trunk. The Suqian factory threw in the bottles left over from lunch. That was not something I wanted.

The Huaiyin factory upgraded from the canteen to a glitzy food palace. Business thrived, and China as a whole modernized. New restaurants, hotels, highways, and airports sprang up in each city. Life improved. Initially, there was an expansion of KFCs, followed by the trendy Chinese joints serving salmon and lobster *sashimi* in the country's far corners. It was an excellent time to be traveling, with places opening often. We dined in a private room on the second floor, and I followed the driver up the stairs. He carried my bags, and I balanced against the wall and held onto the hand railing. Although the venue was new, the red carpet on the stairs and hallway had become stained. The entire place reeked of *baijiu* and smoke. The odor hit me the moment I walked in. My legs began to give out, and I was unsure how long I could continue. At least at this stop, Eric would support me, but I needed to avoid the four-shot rule.

The driver directed me past several private rooms filled with smoke and red-faced guys forcing each other to drink more. I did my best to walk in while the managers and other staff sat without food. They waited for me to order.

The menu was an enormous publication of glossy pictures of animals and parts not on my list. It measured two feet in length and one and a half feet in width and weighed about ten pounds. There was no way they would misplace this menu. I stood up and laid the book flat. To make things more challenging, I had a severe case of the shakes— so bad that I avoided lifting my teacup because the tea splashed out. It worsened when I stood. I flipped through ten pages of bird's nest soup, shark's fin, abalone, and sea cucumber before finding some essential stir-fried meat dishes such as *gong bao* chicken and Yangzhou fried rice. I most definitely required some rice.

The factory ordered other dishes. Naturally, they chose a bull penis soup for me, but I had other problems: I discovered I could no longer hold chopsticks. This never happened before. My fingers refused to grip them, so I used a spoon. I drank more to overcome this rough period, but it failed to work. Then I got up to shake my legs. I used to brag that I was a "Weeble Wobble" and said, "Weebles wobble, but they don't fall down." This was a real-life example.

I sat back down, and they hit me with more shots. I told them about Suqian, but it sounded as if it was an old story, not one that happened five hours ago. This factory wanted some *baijiu* drinking, too. I didn't think it was possible to get any drunker, but they wanted to test my limits. Halfway through, I faded and barely kept my eyes open. I told them I had to crash, and soon. When I walked around, I paid the bill to help speed up the exiting process. That trick caused more trouble since they would not allow me to pay. They would have lost face. I insisted but didn't have the energy to hold up my end of the charade.

They dropped me off and made sure I got into the room. I said goodbye, shut the door, and passed out in my clothes. It was 8 p.m. The driver would pick me up in thirteen hours. That gave me twelve glorious hours of uninterrupted sleep!

I woke up at midnight to grab some water but had no idea where I was. Most three-star hotels used the same furniture, and I confused them. Tragically, I forgot to uncork the thermos; all I had to drink was boiled water. While I tried to sip it to quench my thirst, I recalled the events from the past two days.

All in all, I did well: I never fell down. I was just sloppy, which was okay, considering the bathtub of *baijiu* I chugged. I looked at the clock, and I had six more hours. The alcohol began to wear off, but I would suffer from the shakes for days. I sipped as much scalding water as possible, hoping to be fine in a few.

My alarm rang at eight, but my body refused to rise now that I had ceased to have booze surging through my veins, only a trickle. It was my third day without a solid meal, and I perceived there wouldn't be much waiting at the hotel breakfast buffet. There would be no chance I could stomach one of those cold-fried eggs. My morning meal would have to be cups of tea and cigarettes. But before then, I needed to move. I reset the snooze a few times, after which I dragged myself into the shower.

Then, I grabbed my things and walked towards the main building to check out. I always attempted to be on point to show that the previous night was no big deal. As the years took their toll, I gave up being on time and focused on arriving around the scheduled pickup. It grew harder to get my shit together, but I forced myself to move to make it back home a day sooner instead of lying in a hotel bed nursing a hangover.

My visit to Huaiyin was to maintain the *guanxi*, so I had little to do. But I walked the production lines no matter how quick the stop was. I wanted to see what other companies produced, and I kept moving to make the time pass faster. For lunch, I set a goal of two hours to limit my consumption. Fortunately, my Italian and Japanese friends were away, and two managers traveled. That turned it into a low-key meal with just a few bottles of beer. What a relief because I needed a rest before dinner.

We had trouble with the production in Yangzhou, so I added a visit before returning to The Hai, a three-hour side excursion. It was the smallest workshop I dealt with, making handmade moccasins. They supplied the leather, dipped the skins, dried them, cut them, and stitched them. All of this manufacturing occurred inside a few single-story farm buildings. The site looked locked in time, with weathered socialist posters in each room. They even had a CCP meeting office, like in the Cultural Revolution.

During my first encounter, we had lunch together and downed a lot of beer. When I needed to use the toilet, they pointed me towards a series of stone holes with the shit and piss ending up in the field below, an actual "poop shoot." As I stood there, peeing into the hole, I saw a giant black pig scavenging for something to eat. After returning to the table, I swore off pork for a few months. We finished all the brews, but the closest mom-and-pop shop was towards Yangzhou. I decided not to wait for them to go on a beer run, so I took a raincheck. The factory was further embarrassed when I revealed I drank the devil's juice, but they were out. It was a rare opportunity to consume rocket fuel with a *laowai*, and they came up short. They wanted me to arrange a return visit to drink the good stuff. I didn't intend to show up *baijiu*-soaked, but I had to represent.

The Huaiyin driver wasn't familiar with the Yangzhou countryside, and it took some trial and error before finding the place. We pulled into the compound before sundown. This gave me time to finish everything and be on my way. But first, I clarified what we accepted and what we rejected. They agreed and planned to remove the inferior product. Thankfully, the negotiation went quickly.

Sonny, our manager at this factory, was new but could handle his liquor. He answered our ad and received an offer to replace me in Putian. Before leaving the company, Bryon had hired another manager to take my position, but that dude lasted three months. He had difficulty with Mandarin, was slow at resolving issues, and had a Chinese name that sounded like "foreskin." This guy was an ex-Marine and a black belt. Bryon preferred a macho persona as a deterrent (that's why I was an Olympic-level wrestler in his mind).

Sonny became a more robust replacement. When he interviewed with Paul in Hong Kong, he heard about some of my stories to show what it took to do the job. Sonny said he had heard about my drinking skills, but we never met. He studied at Peking University the semester after I returned to the U.S., and my escapades got passed down to the next class. That someone I had never met found out about me and even remembered those stories when hearing my name referenced during a job interview in Hong Kong five years later was quite remarkable.

Paul arranged for me to meet Sonny in Hong Kong for an interview, so I flew in, put on a suit, and took the subway to Dan Ryan's in Admiralty. I didn't know what he looked like, but he said he wore a sports coat without a tie. I saw a guy sitting alone with a beer and smoking a cigarette. He seemed to fit the bill. It was a casual way to be waiting to start an interview, but he knew a few stories about me.

We enjoyed a long evening with a copious amount of booze (my China test) and hired him after. He endured basic training, then shipped off to Yangzhou to learn the ropes before the fall production started. Sonny was a dependable guy and a strong drinker. I knew I could rely on him to carry the burden. I neared my limit, and another few might put me over. It was early, and I wanted to avoid walking with rubber legs. I had to protect my cup.

The cook prepared dinner while we discussed the quality issues. I noticed a couple of chickens roaming in the courtyard, and I figured we would eat them when I saw the chef come out with a large cleaver.

When the food was ready, we walked over to the round table in the next room. I warned Sonny I needed him to pick up most of the *ganbeis*. It was the only point in my career I surrendered and asked for a life preserver. He deflected the factory people when they toasted me. I drank, but not what I would have. During the meal, I bit my tongue while I chewed because I was sloppy. It gushed blood and wouldn't stop. Then the cook brought in two bowls of soup—one with stewed baby birds and a softshell turtle in the other. As the guests of honor, they put the head and tail of the turtle in a bowl, and the shell in another, then offered them to us. We decided who got what. Sonny ended up with the head while I struggled to swallow the turtle shell. I recalled chewing on the rubbery parts with the oval-shaped shell in my mouth while nodding to show that it tasted delicious. Since I responded with approval, I got called in to drink more. The *baijiu* stung every time it rolled over the gashes in my tongue. I hoped it sterilized the cuts, but it didn't get me sober.

It got dark, so we called it a night. Once on the road, I needed water. We located a mom-and-pop, and Sonny stepped out to buy the beverages because he was in better shape. He came back with a pair of flashlights but no water.

"They didn't have bottled water, but we may need these flashlights."

It felt like a *Fear and Loathing in Las Vegas* moment as if he would say to me, "As your lawyer, I advise you to take these flashlights and this peyote."

It sounded reasonable, but it didn't satisfy my thirst. We found another shop further down. This time, I got out with my flashlight. They stocked water in flimsy plastic bottles, which appeared tampered with. Instead, I chose a warm can of Coke—anything but alcohol. I gulped it so fast it took a while for the cola burn to catch up.

We made it to the hotel, and I swore off drinking (again) until the next trip.

Ultimately, we canceled the orders in Suqian and Yangzhou.

I never returned to Suqian, but Yangzhou constantly called me back.

CHAPTER FOURTEEN

QINGDAO: LEGEND

After I endured the onslaught of nine guys and remained standing, it seemed no meal would ever reach such levels of alcoholic exuberance, but factories continued to test me.

Six months after the Suqian incident, Qingdao required my services. Since the Export Department relocated our business to a plant that manufactured for local consumption, our defect rate increased. The production lines should be separate for domestic and export. If you worked on an export line, you did not make domestic. We would have passed on a place that ONLY produced for the Chinese market, but we assumed the Qingdao factory could get things under control. That did not happen.

I received a phone call from our QC advising that the factory declined to halt production despite a problem. They also refused to allow our inspector to send me specimens. They made no threats, just a lot of unsatisfactory shoes. I was unsure if we would accept the shipments without samples. Someone needed to grab a few.

Since our American manager traveled, I flew there to investigate. I took a two-hour flight from Shanghai, rode in a taxi for an hour and a half to the ferry, sat on the barge for just as long, and then drove fifteen minutes to the factory. It was a lengthy journey for what I thought would be a short meeting. I wished to show our sincerity by meeting them face to face. They knew how long it took to go from A to B in China. They wanted to negotiate.

When I arrived, I met Edward from the Export Dept., who accompanied me to the manufacturing lines. After I inspected the packaged product, the plant manager planned to meet to hear whether we would accept it. Sometimes, we asked them to remove the defective shoes and short-ship. Other times, we bought the order at a discount. In most cases, there was nothing wrong besides cosmetic defects, meaning they didn't affect the performance. You might choose a different pair if on the shelf next to a defect-free one, but they wouldn't hurt anyone. Here, they used contrasting shades for the eyelets the shoelaces went through. All the various whites (I didn't anticipate that white would be so problematic) got mixed, giving each shoe a combination of red, yellow, and blue-white eyelets. That may seem inconsequential, but it would surprise you how stringent the retail stores are. It took a hell of an effort to ship perfect shoes selling for $9.99. There was no way I could accept, so I grabbed a few pairs and told them I would mail them. It was bad enough I poked around, but sending samples to the U.S. would not please their boss, not to mention the 135,000 defective pairs that nobody had told him about.

They wished to deal with it quietly.

We returned to the conference room and discussed with the Export Dept., the plant, and the line managers. I sat on one side with two of our staff while the factory and Export Department took the other. A picture of the big boss hung on the wall, watching the proceedings closely. It was intimidating, but the facts remained. We all agreed there was a problem, but they kept producing. I would help them salvage, but they put themselves in this situation. Discarding 10,000 pairs was easier to hide than 135,000. They intended to show off the success of the move and kept the monthly production numbers high. The factory and export management had a significant stake. I understood and allowed them the courtesy of hearing what they wanted to say all four hours! They examined the problem and gave numerous explanations. Sure, what they argued contributed, and they needed to fix the issues, but we had shipments to fill now.

They told me I would need special clearance to remove shoes, even though I always grabbed them for reference. I refused to leave without samples because it took so long to get here. We were in a standoff when we moved to dinner.

It was 6 p.m., and the final ferry departed soon. I needed to check in, so it would be a late meal if we headed towards the city. No need—they set up supper in the canteen. They said they would drive me back. It would be about an hour. Then I realized I wasn't on an island. The ferry took us across the bay. That made a world of difference. I no longer felt stranded. To ensure the car wouldn't drive off, I had the driver park outside the canteen to keep my eye on it. They put my luggage in the trunk, but I held on to the samples to avoid contamination of the evidence.

I entered the dining room with a bag of shoes and noticed a table stacked with a dozen bottles of *baijiu* on the left and one with even more bottles of beer on the right. They prepared for war. I didn't expect this as it was not a heavy-drinking establishment, but I would put them away if they were brazen enough to challenge me.

I chose my seat opposite the door and put the shoes under my chair. The probability of the big boss showing up was low, but I looked forward to meeting him at some point. With his pictures and praises in every room (including the dining room), I almost knew him.

When I met him on my next trip, under better conditions, he appeared to be a man with simple tastes, almost rural and overlooked the pictures, but he gave the sense that he enjoyed being "the man." I mean, they built a museum about this dude. He was ballin' on a much higher comrade level.

Rule #23: Always close off one side with a friendly and be clear on strategy before the meal.

Yes, plan a strategy. I usually had at least one coworker to cover my flank, but not at this dinner. On my right was the factory manager. The Export Department leader boxed me in on my left. She abstained from drinking (a choice she got away with due to rank), so that wasn't the problem. Instead, she talked about how hard they tried; this dispute wasn't their fault. She continued to say that the shoes weren't defective, as if she attempted to brainwash me. I thought only I practiced Jedi mind tricks.

I looked around to size up the competition as we waited. There was Edward, a production manager, some export staff, and two unfamiliar dudes. Lisa said they came from another department. They had nothing to do with my visit, so I neglected to pay attention. I stared straight at the two tables of sauce. Then I glanced at the people at the table again.

"Who's gonna drink all this alcohol?"

Apparently, it would be the unfamiliar guys and me. Everybody else toasted lightly. The staff had to be at the office early and were careful not to overextend. I never had the chance to give toasts. I only received them.

Once the dinner commenced, the two no-name cats conjured up reasons to *ganbei*.

"Let's *ganbei* because this is our first meal together."

"Let's *ganbei* because you speak Chinese well."

"Let's *ganbei* because your job is hard."

"Let's *ganbei* because you are a friend of Qingdao."

To make matters worse, they brought nothing for me to eat. It was country stuff such as beets and yams (the big bosses' favorites), chunks of tubers, or seafood such as cockroach shrimp (mantis shrimp) and razor clams. Qingdao turned into a place I counted on to introduce me to something I never knew existed.

I asked for peanuts, and they brought the wet kind, so I passed, but the factory manager dug them. Throughout the night, he would talk to the person to his right while spitting the shells to his left, where I sat. Great, now I had a pile in front of me.

As the dinner proceeded, I checked on the shoes. With all the talking Lisa did, I figured they might prevent me from leaving with them. They would find an opportunity to snag them when I was distracted by the booze brothers. Every time I used the toilet, a closet-sized space twenty feet from where we ate, I took the samples. When I opened the door, either Lisa or Edward waited for me.

"The shoes are acceptable, right?"

"We can drink as much as you want, but I won't change my opinion."

"Let's go back and continue."

They used *baijiu* as a method of torture but didn't understand how futile that would be. The more they pushed me, the more I stood my ground. I wanted to make Lisa drink but couldn't fend off the two guys.

The dinner finished after three hours. It ended when the kitchen closed, and the driver complained about the drive. I remembered proudly walking, unassisted, with the bag in my hand. It was a victory, a *Rocky* moment. I commemorated it by jabbing Edward in the stomach as I exited. They tried to take me down but failed. I got into the car and turned on my autopilot.

I woke up the following day at 7 a.m. Blackouts are a curious thing. They erase pieces of your memory selectively. At best, you hoped they eliminated the sloppy parts, but sometimes they wiped out the whole evening. I had no idea what time I arrived, nor did I remember the check-in process. Luckily, I set the alarm to visit the factory before heading to the airport at noon. I wanted to show them I was stronger than they imagined: a true Weeble Wobble. My youth shielded me from feeling horrible in the morning, mostly thirsty and buzzed. On heavy days, I remembered the Sinatra quote:

"I feel sorry for people who don't drink because when they wake up in the morning, that is the best they are going to feel all day."

Plus, waking up in China inebriated gave me that sense that anything could happen, another day of kicks. It was only a matter of motivation and money.

By the time lunch rolled around, I would be ready to get back into the game. But that was five hours from now. I could have had a leisurely breakfast (a full Western buffet) and made my way to the airport, but I opted for the tough guy route. The best thing to do was jump up as soon as the alarm rang before I changed my mind.

I packed my bag and prepared to check out, but couldn't find the shoes. Did the driver take them? I used DPS, but he didn't know that. In autopilot mode, I functioned normally (well...), so people were unaware that my brain did not fully work. It was doubtful that he had snatched them from me, and I wouldn't have gotten out of the car without them. So what happened? Did someone sneak into my room while I slept, or did I leave them in the elevator? I fought so hard; I had to find them.

After tearing the room apart, I discovered them under my pillow. In my drunken stupor, that looked like the safest place. My autopilot performed well.

On the way to the workshop, our QC told me the factory had hired two professional drinkers to take me down. That professional drinkers existed seemed both scary and beautiful. Imagine getting paid to eat and drink. And then it occurred to me . . . it sounded similar to my job. It boosted my ego to think they would pay someone to take me on. They chose not to attempt it on their own. Mad respect, son! But it also meant they really thought they would change my mind.

I arrived dragging my Rollaboard in the hot weather. Edward looked as if someone had beaten him up. He had his head on his desk and said his stomach hurt because of the jabs I laid on him. I vaguely remembered and guessed I hit him harder than I realized. It was the Hulk-like strength that came from an evening of jet fuel. I asked how the two pros were. He said they both had gone to the emergency room to receive IV drips. I sent the professionals to the hospital? How much did we drink last night? I knew it was a lot, but not A LOT.

We accepted discounted shoes and continued working with them. I assumed the big boss had heard about the problems; not soon after, they changed managers and moved staff around. Poor Edward got shipped off to the African sales office to join Manager Wen. He faxed me a picture of his unhappy face before he left.

After this trip, the legend of Mr. Thunder and my tolerance became well known. Meanwhile, the export manager placed our business further out to their satellite workshops in Shandong Linyi, Henan Zhengzhou, and Hubei Wuhan. They relocated inland for lower prices, but we had quality issues, and it was costly to have employees inspect at these locations, so they never lasted. However, in each place, the story of the night I put the professional drinkers in the hospital preceded my arrival. Like Houdini, they all tested me. But, as time passed, the business changed, and we refrained from using these factories at the end of the '90s.

In the 2000s, we placed orders for ladies' casual footwear in a city two hours north in Shandong Yantai. The town sat on the coast, and, like Qingdao, they specialized in seafood, especially trepang. They took me to a restaurant that served it in multiple ways. It was impossible to avoid. The stuff didn't excite my taste buds, but it was more manageable to eat than bull penis if you paid no attention to its appearance.

Yantai restaurants serve many kinds of seafood and other creatures. They displayed the live critters in a supermarket room, and a server followed you to write what you selected. Even if someone else ordered, I took a gander to see what grub or life forms were ready to eat. China may have had a long history of consuming exotic things, but only in the '90s did these items return. Rising incomes made this overindulgence possible.

Along with the extravagant food came the pricey *baijiu*. Every place reeked of it. In one restaurant, they had a sick but genius facility. They placed full-sized garbage cans beside the urinals to puke in. Vomit buckets solved the problem of drunks clogging the sinks, which happened ALL THE TIME! What a brilliant idea but a disgusting way to handle excessive *baijiu* boozing.

I bragged about it when I returned to the table.

"Gotta check out the vomit buckets!"

My eating companions lacked the same sense of awe that I had.

Wine was the beverage of choice in Yantai. They established the local Chang Yu winery in 1892. The wine tasted rough at first, but after a few years, they came out with better strains, and it reminded me less of my teenage hooch, Richard's Wild Irish Rose. It was a pleasant change to have a vino paired with my rubbery sea slug. This factory had heard stories about my high tolerance but had no interest in engaging me in a drinking contest.

In between dealing with the problems, I would go out with my old friend Garanimal. The DJ Lido worked at a giant disco/karaoke across the street from my hotel. Few hung out at the club, but he played my music like Fat Boy Slim, The Prodigy, and even Screamin' Jay Hawkins, whatever tunes I had purchased from Tower Records in H.K. After Lido finished for the evening, we dined on a late-night snack of grilled chicken legs before I walked back. Garanimal opened his own restaurant with the buckets of cash he earned. It had a "Western" theme, with cowboy burgers and fries, but locals weren't ready to try something unfamiliar, and the foreign population was non-existent. He closed it after two years.

I ran into him in the airport on a trip with a customer in 2002. He still worked on the golf courses, had gotten married, and stopped boozing. He always imbibed to the point of no control, but now his wife had a leash on him. That was the last time I saw him.

After traveling to the city for a decade, I never visited the beer festival. It was less popular in the '90s. I joined an All-China Hash run here in 2008, and we ended at the beer garden. Compared to my visit to Oktoberfest in Munich, I left unimpressed, but the locals enjoyed it.

Over the years, I visited three or more times a year. Every time a new hotel popped up, I tried it. In 1997, the Shangrila opened, and that changed my world. Now, going to Qingdao was like a vacation. The rooms were amazing; the breakfast had everything, and the bar rocked. They placed cameras in the pub to enable you to view the action from your room to entice people to come down. It also became a way for hookers to sell their services, probably not what the hotel had in mind.

I stayed at the Shangrila until my final trip in 2013. I was a loyal customer, and they rewarded me with a framed picture of myself at the Shangrila.

CHAPTER FIFTEEN

TAIWAN: WE ARE ALL FRIENDS HERE

While solving issues in other areas, I still dealt with a fire back home: a bleeding material problem. The predicament festered for several seasons, costing the factory hundreds of thousands of dollars. At that rate, I would have expected Louis to be up in arms, yet we continued to have the same trouble. I recommended he send somebody to visit the suppliers in Taiwan, but Mainland Chinese couldn't go without undergoing a strenuous application process. The island was forbidden fruit, so it fell upon my shoulders to take the trip to let the manufacturers know the severity of the defect, show them samples, and push them to fix it. There had to be a solution.

Since our production in Putian suffered from the same headache, I invited my coworker Sonny. One American customer at your doorstep was irritating, but two would show that we meant business. Plus, I required a boozing buddy to accompany me to my favorite haunts.

Sonny was the guy.

Over two years had passed since I had last set foot on the island, and I was a little apprehensive. On the one hand, many places reminded me of good times and that sense of adventure as I steered my path through the unknown and created something out of nothing in a foreign land. However, I also remembered the tough times, not knowing whether I would survive, and the loneliness induced by living overseas. Life in the U.S. moved forward while I had experiences that were hard to relate to and share without people losing interest because of no commonality. After a while, I stopped telling stories. It was the same with gifts. On my first trip, I bought presents for everyone. By the third, my relatives got less excited about receiving a souvenir, and I was tired of buying trinkets now available in Chinatowns.

When I lacked clarity about my chances for success, I felt a hole in my soul—an emptiness that would consume me if I didn't keep it in check. Two years later, that emptiness had vanished, and I returned as a made man. No longer did I have to be concerned about taxi or cover charges. I could order anything off the top shelf and eat at any restaurant. That was liberating, but I needed to keep an eye out for suspicious BMWs.

There were no direct flights from Shanghai or anywhere in China. Instead, I flew two and a half hours south to Hong Kong, disembarked, and took off to Taipei on a separate flight north. We planned to make an early departure the following day to Taichung, in the middle of the island. It would be pointless to book a high-end hotel for a few hours of rest and a shower. Even though I had an expense account, I avoided wasting money. Once you got used to living cheaply, it was difficult to change.

Since we would finish our bar-hopping tour at the Combat Zone, that would be the best location to hunt for a place to stay. It never occurred to me that the small hotels charged by the hour. Of course, they did. They were in between the girlie bars. People didn't stay here for the breakfast buffet.

We searched the alleys and uncovered a guesthouse that appeared to be a proper hotel with no heart-shaped neon lights in the windows. They only had a double with a wall separating the beds. That sounded strange, and we wanted to see.

They segregated the beds with a mini-wall that blocked half. Why did they need a wall? Did individuals practice voyeurism? Was it a foot fetish den? The room had mirrors on the ceiling and walls, and the TV channels were porn. Once again, we found ourselves at a love hotel. Perhaps two guys without luggage, searching for a place to crash, might have given the wrong impression.

"Screw this. Let's go high-end. We already wasted time."

I wanted to start the bar-hopping, so we jumped into a taxi to the Howard Plaza, a legitimate hotel with a single mirror and not on the ceiling. On my way to English class, I passed the Howard but could never afford to eat there. It was first on my list and close to a few clubs.

There wasn't time for food after we sorted the rooms. I arranged for an agenda to visit multiple bars in rapid succession. It was excessive, but we were hungry for a pub crawl. From Fuxing Road to the Combat Zone and then down to the Taida clubs, where I introduced Sonny to the 7-11 microwave popcorn and hot dog feast. I no longer relied on the convenience store stop for my meals and booze but slamming a few while sitting on the mopeds and taking in street life was enjoyable.

Because of my *baijiu* training, my tolerance fell off the charts. I now needed whiskey, whereas I would have gotten buzzed off beer two years ago. That wasn't the only difference. Much of the life I remembered had vanished. Everyone I knew had disappeared. It seemed as if I had never been here. As I moved around the mainland, that became a reoccurring sentiment. Cities were no longer recognizable; drinking pals came and went; places dematerialized. I was the only constant, but I changed, too.

We booked a 7:30 a.m. flight and needed to leave the hotel by 6:15. It was 3 a.m., and we were in the club. I headed back while Sonny enjoyed the vibe and chatted up a young lady. Few places in China played live music, and he took advantage of the opportunity. I said,

"Let's meet in the lobby at six. No matter what, I'm leaving for the airport at 6:15. We have a job to do."

I hoped that the warning would prevent him from showing up late.

Back at the hotel, I rested for two hours before showering and leaving. There was no way to remove my smoke and alcohol stink. I smoked a cancer-causing number of cigs; the smell was ingrained in my fingers, and no soap would eliminate it—no matter how many times I washed. I counted on Sonny smelling worse.

At six, I ventured down to the front desk and booked a taxi. Sonny was MIA. I paid my bill and entered the cafe to grab a bite of toast to soak up the liquor. At 6:20, he still didn't show. My cell wouldn't work, but his did. I called his number from the business center, which was on voice mail. I thought something had happened, but I would deal with that later. Perhaps he would turn up at the airport. I told the guys to enjoy themselves to release the stress of day-to-day life on the road, but ALWAYS, ALWAYS, BE ON TIME and get the job done. NO JOB = NO FUN. Plus, I got jealous. He probably hooked up with the girl and passed out at her place. I would have respected that more than passing out alone and not answering the phone.

I waited until 6:25 before leaving. While I sat in the departure hall, glancing at my watch, I saw Sonny run in five minutes before the flight departed. He came back to the hotel after I left. He never used the room. Sonny appeared to be functioning well but required a shower. My smelly cigarette fingers didn't seem so terrible.

Luckily for him, our flight got canceled because of a lack of passengers. That explained why he checked in so close to departure. The shuttle was a thirty-minute ride on a prop plane, but most rode the bus. That left us waiting for enough individuals to fill the aircraft. Our rescheduled time had us landing right before lunch. The factory folks waited on the other end. We didn't know anybody, but we would be identifiable, being the only big noses.

We arrived and rushed to the factory. As the driver sped down the road, Mr. Chen, the owner, introduced his company. Meanwhile, I kept the window down to prevent everybody from getting inebriated off my fumes. Sonny reeked, but not as severely, or I couldn't smell him over my intoxicating aroma. We turned up at the workshop just as they shut down the threading machines, and Mr. Chen said the words I dreaded.

"Let's go to lunch."

And so we returned to the car and drove to a roadside seafood place. They directed us to a private room while Mr. Chen ordered. We didn't need to stress about the quality as my experiences at countryside restaurants in Taiwan had been problem-free. Taiwanese joints paid an almost Japanese level of attention to preparation and presentation. I knew I would enjoy the cooking. It was classic Taiwanese, virtually impossible to find in China. Once Mr. Chen exited, we agreed (**Rule #23**) to take it easy. Not only did we need to walk through this plant, we had one more to visit. We had no work to do, and we weren't technicians or the customer; that would be the Shanghai factory. We were an indirect client complaining about something we never ordered or paid for and had little leverage.

A few minutes later, a server brought in about ten big, brown bottles of my old friend, Taiwan Beer. Sonny and I acknowledged we could handle that amount. But then Mr. Chen entered with an unopened bottle of Remy Martin.

"Do you guys drink XO?"

When he said the letters "X" and "O," I had a flashback to when I drank with Apache and the gangsters. Good times.

"Well, maybe a few glasses, but we still have another plant to tour, so we need to limit the lunchtime drinking," I said.

Regardless of how often I repeated it, it never worked that way.

We hit it off with Mr. Chen. As he put it, we were so "Chinese-like." He had never met foreigners who spoke Mandarin, some Taiwanese, and Putianese. We talked about politics and life on the mainland. It felt great to be eating Taiwanese food and drinking Taiwanese beer. I could have remained there all day, but we only spent three hours. We polished off the XO and a dozen beers. Sonny and I drank the beer to avoid consuming more than a bottle of XO. The restaurant boss helped finish it by inviting us to *ganbei* every time she walked in.

After a big night out, boozing at lunch seemed right.

"Should we open another bottle?" asked Mr. Chen while the server had entered the room with one.

It was easy to say yes. I wasn't drunk and felt I had the power to conquer anything, but we had the other factory to tour. I preferred not to show up looking lit.

"Which factory are you going to?" I told him, and he said, "Don't worry. We are all friends here. That boss is a huge drinker. He's probably drinking right now."

Mr. Chen called him and told the second boss we drank.

He said, "Take your time and drink as much as you want. Don't worry about showing up late."

The fun would have continued, but we had to check the production lines. Mr. Chen seemed alright, but we had problems that required fixing.

He called his driver and walked out to pay the bill. Looking at the empty bottles, I noticed Sonny fading.

He said, "I just can't drink like I used to."

"Dude, we just finished a bottle of XO and a dozen brown bottles for lunch right after an all-nighter. How much did you used to drink?"

We circled back to the factory and took a tour. Long machines with hundreds of spindles spinning in unison filled the building. It was fascinating to watch the threads pulled across twenty feet, producing a complete sheet of fabric. I walked with Mr. Chen and asked him questions as we toured. I stood close to hear him, but I didn't have to be concerned about my stench since we were all friends here, and we all stank.

Sonny strolled alone, but I saw him from the corner of my eye, and he wobbled like a drunk. I feared he would fall into a machine and get twisted. Luckily, that didn't happen, but I caught him falling to the ground. First, he leaned over, then a little more, until he crumbled. I asked Mr. Chen a question to divert his attention while I motioned for Sonny to GET UP.

After the tour, I told the boss we needed to get moving. We would arrive at the second factory in time to turn around and return to the city. Although the owner requested drinking time with us, we never planned dinner with him. Sonny would not survive another session. There would be no pub crawling tonight.

The plant was closed when we showed up, but there wasn't much to see. It was just machinery. We talked with the owner over tea while I showed him problem samples. He asked if we enjoyed lunch. The second factory boss said Mr. Chen drank a lot.

"That's what he said about you."

He laughed and told his staff to grab two boxes of fruit and gifted them to us. They didn't grow these, but his family grew other fruits, such as kumquats and dragon eyes. He made moonshine from them and said it was more potent than *gaoliang* (*baijiu*), which registered it at seventy percent alcohol.

"It's excellent. You have to try it."

I did my best to escape it, but he had someone fetching a bottle. I downed a glass, and it was the genuine stuff, sweet but strong like turpentine. We would have polished off a bottle had we stayed. The boss offered to give me one, but it was clear with no label. Even though it was five years before 9/11, I assumed they would not allow me to carry that on the plane, so I declined.

We got into the taxi with the cases of Taiwanese pineapple custard apples and headed towards the city. It took two hours. Mr. Chen booked rooms for us in a swag place. I looked forward to at least five hours of rest. Sonny passed out and slept the whole way. The sleep did him well, but we voted for no alcohol that evening. Instead, we found a Friday's restaurant and enjoyed American comfort food. I faded halfway through, paid the bill, and crashed.

The following day, I caught my flight to Hong Kong and then back to The Hai. Sonny avoided dealing with the fruit, but I refused to throw it away. To transport it, I purchased a giant suitcase and put them in. When I picked up the bag in Shanghai, everything seemed okay. Not until I opened the suitcase did I find that the weight of the fruit had crushed itself. I shouldn't have removed the Styrofoam egg crate packaging in my attempt to squeeze in too many. I salvaged a few but trashed the rest. It was quite an adventure that went along with that fruit, and it was tasty now that I had sobered up.

Somehow, the factories fixed the problems, and we looked like heroes even though our livers had done all the work.

Never underestimate the power of *guanxi* building.

CHAPTER SIXTEEN

SHANGHAI: THINGS ARE LOOKING UP

When exiled from the Shanghai factory, I instructed my guys to rent an apartment to function as our operations center. We kept the clubhouse, but we needed a place to go if they expelled me again. Plus, our company had a growing business with other factories. We didn't want Louis to know.

As this happened before the building explosion in The Hai, there were few affordable options. My staff searched for months before finding a flat in a government housing project three miles from the workshop. The residents were local, and my frequent visits caused a stir.

"What's the *laowai* doing here?"

"Look at the *laowai*!"

The movie star image was hard to shake.

Outside the block-long housing complex was a narrow, one-way lane with a ragtag collection of noodle joints, KTV booths, and market stalls. At the far end was an unofficial bus stop. Travelers found their way here despite no signs or apparent schedule: You had to remain until your coach turned up. Once on, don't vacate your seat, or they might take off without you.

On my way to work, I used this road and caught them loading and unloading. Every day, individuals arrived from the countryside with their candy-striped bags, looking to strike it rich and going back with packages for the villages. I assumed the buses traveled to the surrounding provinces until I noticed the destination said Putian! What were the odds?

I thought it was a different Putian, so I walked over to hear if anyone spoke the dialect. Sure enough, they used the same PT twang I had learned.

I asked the driver if he'd come from Putian, in Putian dialect. His face looked as if he'd felt a minor earthquake. A foreigner in Shanghai, speaking Putian *hua*? The guy turned speechless. The other Putianese on the bus tripped out, too. After throwing down a few phrases, I hurried away before they realized I had nothing more to say besides curse words.

The bus stop was a fantastic find. Now, I had a convenient method to send packages. I threw my stacks of VCDS (an earlier form of DVDs), English books, magazines, clothes, and anything I was tired of into a box and dropped it off. They tied them to the roof for 80 RMB ($10) and drove them to a fly-by-night station in Putian County, five hundred miles south. It turned into an excellent way to lighten my load.

Once the boxes arrived, I informed my QC posse to retrieve them and do whatever they saw fit. I pictured them gathering during box opening time to see what treasures I'd rid myself of.

My girlfriend said someone could become wealthy by following me and collecting the things I'd abandoned. I stayed in a hotel and had no space. If I discarded items, the cleaning staff would be the beneficiaries. It was better to give them to an acquaintance. But the situation turned weird when I noticed individuals wearing my old shirts. I often bought clothes in bulk during my U.S. trips. If I throw out an item, I had another identical to it. That suited me well until my clothes filtered into society. I had to find another outlet for my hand-me-downs after seeing an employee wear something I was wearing.

Apart from the unforeseen direct delivery service, a small Sichuan joint between the noodle stands became an even more extraordinary discovery. I neglected to notice this place until the characters "Si" and "Chuan" caught my eye one day while I rode past in a taxi. Living in a city soaked in vinegar and sweet sauces, I craved that same Sichuan (Chuan) flavor from my Beida days. I expected it to be easier to find. That's why this spot was so special.

This gem sat empty when I uncovered it as if they had waited for me. Local Shanghainese avoided the slop houses on this street not because the food was dirty (or perhaps it was); all the eating establishments on the road resembled what you would expect at a bus stop.

After I moved here, I never saw plates of red chilies in any dining establishments. The massive quantity (outnumbering the meat by tenfold) intimidated diners. Only a handful of venues with authentic Chuan operated in The Hai. I had to crawl through traffic for an hour to reach one, then wait to get seated. With a city populace of eleven million (1996), more than enough spicy junkies like me wanted to eat mouth-numbing morsels. Here, I'd found a restaurant with no wait. The dishes cost a third of the downtown places and tasted better. I had to travel to the edge of town to get here, and I wouldn't have been here if we didn't do business down the road. But it would have been worth it to embark on the journey.

The restaurant was owned and operated by a husband (Li Laoban) and wife (Laoban Niang). Mr. Li was missing a few front teeth and had a haircut similar to Moe Howard from The Three Stooges. He greeted everyone with his funny personality, which got further animated when he drank. Laoban Niang was the straight one.

A year ago, they had arrived on a bus, seeking to establish a trading company. Their venture had failed, so they tried the culinary business. Why not? They both possessed cooking skills and ran it by themselves. It seemed the most suitable alternative, but they should have considered that Shanghainese were not ready for spicy cuisine.

Then I showed up.

It was the size of a single-car garage with space for a solo kitchen, cashier, and a couple of tables but no toilet. If I had to go, I had the choice of walking across the road and using the bushes or waltzing through the kitchen, out the rear door, and down the alley about a hundred meters to the public restroom. At the public lavatory, they had two prices: ten cents to use the pee trough and fifty for the squat hole—that price included two square sheets of toilet paper, like cocktail napkins constructed out of crepe, non-absorbent. I never used the squatter, but I imagined I might want more paper if I did. With no soap, you better get it right the first time.

I tried the long-distance option for a while because I figured someone would notice a foreigner urinating in the bushes.

However, I never carried coins; my smallest bill was 20 RMB. The guardian refused to let me pass for free, even at ten cents.

"My name is Mr. Thunder. I don't have coins, nor do I wish to carry them. Instead, I will purchase all the future trips for my friends and me. If they say my name, don't charge them, okay?"

She refused but took it because she lacked change.

I returned and told Eric, "If you go to the W.C., just tell the guard you're my friend."

They were the magic words that opened the fragrant doors of the pee palace. And it seemed to work; I never paid after that. But despite the royal treatment, I, too, gave in to the proximity of the bushes. I also did it to avoid seeing the kitchen. As long as they made the food right, I didn't need to examine the conditions. Eating here violated **Rule #5**, but I was desperate for good Sichuan.

The husband/wife duo churned out classics such as:

"*la zi ji*" (chicken buried in a mound of dried chilies), "*suan tai la rou*" (fried garlic stems with Chinese bacon), "*yu xiang rou si*" (shredded pork with garlic fish sauce), "*shui zhu niu rou*" (spicy boiled beef), "*gong bao ji ding*" (kung pao chicken), "*pao jiao rou si*" (shredded pork with special chilies), etc.

Their *la zi ji* was crispy on the outside and juicy on the inside. They used Sichuan peppercorns called "*huajiao*," which burned and numbed my mouth. Excellent stuff. Laoban Niang made a better, so I requested that she cook. As she toiled away, Mr. Li would stroll over with a bottle of the devil's juice and shot glasses. Sichuan was another province famous for *baijiu*. He said he avoided starting too early or would drink through dinner. I knew the feeling. Li Laoban was always ready to throw down when we walked in. Laoban Niang was less enthusiastic and told him to take over the cooking to stop him.

Later, Li Laoban built a bunk with a sliding door above the cash register. He crawled up to pass out in the afternoon. Often, when I showed up for lunch, he would sleep in the cubbyhole. While Laoban Niang cooked, I would knock on the door to see if he was in. If so, he would slide open the panel, stick his head out with his hair sticking up, and say something funny before closing it. A few minutes later, he would climb down and drink. Laoban Niang would put up with it for a while before she nagged him.

This was a great venue to spend a few hours, and I needed places like this to fill up my time. To ensure I found something special, I tried a copycat joint a few doors down, and they confirmed my conclusion: Li Laoban's kitchen produced fantastic dishes equal to none. They would earn good money if they expanded and moved downtown, but it stayed a closet-sized restaurant with customers peeing in the bushes. There were tens of thousands of eateries similar to them. They cooked outstanding dishes but lacked the ducats or *guanxi* to rise to the big league. Sometimes, they didn't want to. It satisfied them to prepare savory fare that people came back for.

Li's place became the most popular establishment with everybody in our circle at the plant once I introduced them to it. Maybe seeing a foreigner dining here helped make it acceptable. The business grew so that they looked for a bigger location and found a space three times the size, a short walk away. The best thing about the unit was the functioning air conditioner. Their AC in the old spot had broken down, and feeding on spicy cuisine in the summer turned a person into a puddle of sweat. The new AC was an enormous tower that cooled the entire room and was a terrific enhancement.

We had less pressure to give up our table with more seats for others. We could hang out for hours, eating and drinking dozens of twenty-ounce bottles of Reeb or Suntory beer, multiple flasks of *Erguotou,* and more than a single serving of my favorite dishes while playing the drinking games I learned as a student. Often, other tables asked me to *ganbei.* It was easy to spend an afternoon here when caught up in a situation like this, and the bill would come to 150

RuMBas ($18)! They had excellent nosh for an affordable price, and word spread; soon, more diners filled it. Now, we had to call ahead to save "Mr. Thunder's table" in front of the AC. Sometimes, I heard grumblings about the *laowai* getting the best seat, but when I ordered, their attitude changed.

I was no tourist.

I never ate at Li Laoban's at night unless we worked late. There were other eateries and hair wash/foot massage places on the same street. It got rowdy with dudes carrying their drunk buddies out of the restaurants or into the massage parlors.

Once, an argument broke out on the street when I ate a late dinner with the factory. Two dudes argued while a woman struggled to pull one away. I loved a good spat and stood up to watch. They kept yelling and pointing their fingers at each other. What was the point?

I helped them reach the next level by chanting, "*Da! Da!*" (Fight! Fight!). They glanced over, then continued. I lost interest and returned to my chair. As I sat down, the guys charged in. They no longer fought and joined the same side.

"Who yelled *Da! Da!?*"

"I did," but I think they knew that.

They rushed over and focused their anger on me, accusing me of getting involved in their affair.

"You disturbed my dinner. You should fight somewhere else and not make so much noise."

That did not improve the situation. They resorted to pointing their fingers in my face across from the table, raising my anger level. My "bad China day clock" was ready to spring.

"Stop pointing your finger in my face. I don't dance like you guys."

I had the upper hand with Eric, four factory workers, and their Bolivian manager on my side. One guy tried reaching for my neck, almost flipping the table. Li Laoban saw a lot of destruction if a fight broke out. He kicked them out by promising to call the police. Only a few plates were broken; it could have been worse. Li Laoban poured shots, and we continued.

In 1998, we moved orders to the suburbs of The Hai, and I had an opportunity to spend more time here. Shanghai boomed, and new venues opened. The quality level and selection of dining choices improved with each addition. Even though I felt the Chuan was the best, the luxuries of hand soap, ice cubes, and cold drinks lured me away from the down and dirty. I patronized both worlds until a last visit to the Chuan sealed its fate for me.

I met my guys on a Monday before I traveled to catch up. After an extended stay away, I received a hero's welcome when I dropped by. People expected that, as a foreigner, I would disappear at any moment, but I kept showing up for so long that it was strange when I didn't appear. When I returned, Li Laoban was nowhere to be seen.

"A while back, he got drunk, fell, and chipped his (only) front tooth. After that, Laoban Niang forbade him from drinking *baijiu*," a server from his hometown said.

He avoided his place, or his customers would entice him. However, the Li family had other things that required him to sober up. They earned enough money to buy multiple apartments and another Chuan outlet. Laoban Niang needed him to deal with the renters and other issues. They hired more relatives to do the grunt work. Not seeing Mr. Li was a downer, but I anticipated the Chuan.

We sat at my table and ordered our standards. The last time I visited, I smelled a faint chemical odor. On this occasion, it was stronger. It appeared to be bug killer, but I had hoped that was not the case. When I dug into a dish, it had the same chemical seasoning. Then, I noticed a few cockroaches on the other tables. The server brought out a can of roach killer, and that's when I knew my gut was right (**Rule #12**). Whether imagined or real, everything had the flavoring of Raid. The final straw was when a couple crept up my pant legs. I endured for old times' sake but had to draw the line.

They opened a new place closer to Louis' workshop a year later, but we barely worked with him by then. I took a trip to see the venue, which was bigger than the last place. I showed up, and no one recognized me, so I asked for Laoban Niang. They called her.

"Tell her Mr. Thunder is here and needs the best *la zi* ji in Shanghai."

She lived nearby and came to cook. It was a rare occasion since she no longer did that kind of work. They purchased property in the area at a low price because nobody expected The Hai to grow this far. When the city absorbed the outlying suburbs, they made a fortune. I reminisced about Li Laoban poking his head out of the cubbyhole back in the day, and now he was sending his kids to an international school.

They became a China success story.

II

I lived in the same 250-square-foot hotel room for a year, like a caged animal or a raging bull. I needed to search for an apartment. The rental market had opened, and the government had less oversight of people living in private residences. They could no longer keep track of the growing foreigner population.

Initially, I considered service flats. They had satellite TV, a swimming pool, maid service, a restaurant, etc., but my $2K monthly housing budget put me $2,000 short of that level. Yeah, Shanghai was not as cheap as Putian. Living a baller expat life would be expensive. I lowered my expectations.

I focused on finding a place on the west side, near the airport and the factory. In addition, I required a home with a tolerable combination of watchable TV or at least CNN, a kitchen larger than a shoebox, an oven, a sit-down toilet, a washer and a dryer, air conditioning, and a grocery store or fast food joint nearby. I looked for comfort rather than historical relevance. For most of the week, I lived on the frontier. When in The Hai, I desired convenience.

Since Shanghai had a limited supply of flats, any agent would do as long as they met my demands. I wanted to start, so I gave my list of wants to a random broker and waited.

A few days later, I received a call from a woman asking me to meet outside a department store in a target neighborhood, the Xujiahui District, a sizable shopping hub. Most grocery stores operated in the basements of department stores. With three leading ones at this intersection, it gave me more choices. If one lacked what I required, the second might have. Grocery shopping for Western food was hit-or-miss. If I desired to cook something exotic, such as tacos, only one supermarket sporadically stocked frozen tortillas. If out, I had to proceed with Plan B.

"No tacos tonight; how about Chinese!"

The location of the meeting point was ideal. The agent led the way past the department stores and kept going. We walked thirty minutes to a side street. Construction caused us to navigate over wooden planks to prevent from stepping in the mud. With all this hassle, I was reluctant to look. They said the property owner expected us and would be upset if we didn't walk in.

The building was a four-story concrete piece of hell with no elevator. Right away, I knew I would pass. It was a miserable collection of boxes with no windows. The landlord had strung Christmas lights along the ceiling to compensate for the lack of lighting. It resembled a roadside karaoke. The place had almost nothing on my list besides the sit-down toilet. It even lacked an international phone line. I hadn't asked for it because I thought that was understood. Now, I realized I had chosen the wrong realtor.

I ran for the exit once the owner said there was no international line. Outside, I told the agent I needed something, NOT like what they just showed me.

"But that apartment is within your budget and near the grocery store."

A thirty-minute hike was not close. They told me they had another place to show back at the main intersection.

"Why didn't you take me there first?"

"The flat we just showed you seemed closer to what you required."

Sure, I should have told them I wanted windows, but it was not a good selling technique to waste my time.

The second residence had higher-grade furnishings and, more importantly, windows! They installed an international phone line, and the building was a few doors down from a KFC. Despite my love for the Colonial, I wouldn't pay over $2K for a flat with no satellite TV.

The agents had another listing. They guaranteed it would be better than the first two. The problem was the location on the other side of the elevated ring road. The nearest market was a taxi ride away. I hesitated but caved after hearing the "landlord is waiting for us" speech.

I got in a taxi and sat in the front while they squeezed in the back. It took half an hour to snake through the streets (less than three km). Yi Shan Road was the home decoration street for much of the city. For about a mile, decorating and remodeling companies did a thriving business on both sides. Guys on bikes with wagons blocked the path as they stopped to load up the decoration materials required for the flats. It was a narrow lane, and all the wagon bikes transformed traffic into a snarling, entangled mess of honking metallic beasts.

What a great introduction to what life would be like here.

We finally broke through this interwoven jam, crossed underneath the Zhongshan elevated road, and rode straight into another bottleneck. This time, it was a hospital. A melting pot of parked bicycles, food carts, and people from the countryside begging for cash to pay for treatment blocked part of the street. Cars dropping off sick patients clogged the rest.

Once past this, we turned down a newly constructed lane leading to a group of residential buildings and a commercial complex. They had cleared the area of the low-lying shacks and alleys to make way for the high-rises. It was a dead-end with a couple of DVD (VCD) stores and barbershops. On the corner was a three-star hotel named after a heavenly goose. I hoped they operated a travel agent, a decent Chinese restaurant, or a convenience store with bottles of foreign alcohol.

As we drove up to the complex, I noticed the mall was empty. The agent said stores would soon move in, including a supermarket. That sounded fantastic.

We parked when we ran out of road. The landscaping needed to be finished, even though the apartments had been completed two years earlier. We walked over the wooden planks again, but I got better at it.

Naturally, this burden turned me off, and I got stuck with the taxi fare. But I had gone this far; I might as well see it through.

The flat was on the fifth floor, which I preferred; it was high enough to avoid some noise from the street and low enough to escape by the stairs. We rang the doorbell, and it made that bird chirping sound—something that needed to be changed. As the owner opened the door, the bright yellowish lights of the living room lit up the outside corridor. It appeared every gray structure had the same situation: dark hallways contrasting with the flood of light and air-conditioned air coming from the apartments. It felt comforting to return to be dazzled by this brightness as soon as the door opened—like a golden oasis.

The landlord was a woman in her early thirties. She told me a few stories: she was married, getting an MBA, starting her own business, and investing in the stock market. None of it sounded right. She had money and expensive taste but needed help selecting decor. This explained the super-soft, lime green, fine Italian leather sofa set mixed with a large, deep red mahogany dining table and high-back chairs. Tackiness aside, the apartment was equipped with everything: A/C in every room, a washer AND dryer jammed in the closet-sized bathroom, cable TV, a cookout balcony, and AN OVEN! The owner asked for $1,800 a month, but she would reduce the amount to $1,600 if she took out the mahogany table. Even with the discount, the flat seemed pricey. I could get something better, but I would need to go for another ride with the realtors. The thought of doing that pushed me to rent this unit and look again in a year. I signed the lease and received the keys.

It felt satisfying to evacuate the hotel and live an ordinary life.

But my golden oasis came with problems that appeared after I moved in. The biggest turned out to be the electric wiring. The system was too weak to operate the heavy energy-devouring electric appliances filling each apartment. This thirty-story building was built in 1994, and the power grid couldn't handle more than a single AC unit. Sure, I had a clothes dryer, but I couldn't run it at the same time as the washing machine or AC—dry clothes but a sweaty body.

To make the situation worse, the flat lacked a fuse box. If I blew one, I didn't have the luxury of walking over to a gray box and flipping a black switch to the left. They locked it in a closet. I had to visit the guard's room and ask him to contact a worker. The repairman would wrap some thick copper wire around an exposed switch. The infrastructure looked ancient and was a hassle, so I tried not to trip those fuses. It was worse to break one at night during the winter. When that happened, I piled on the blankets and hoped I wouldn't freeze while waiting for somebody to call the maintenance guy.

I also found out the TV reception was not stable. On a windy day, I lost my signal. I called the landlord, who sent a worker to check the connection. He went up to the roof and made adjustments but said I would continue to have problems because the receiver needed a more substantial base. I thought the dish belonged to the building and they sold the TV services. That wasn't the case. My landlord paid somebody to install a two-meter (6.5 feet) satellite on the roof. He then dropped a wire down the side (26 floors) to my balcony and into my apartment. Other people liked the idea. Some spliced my cable and hooked up their TVs. The guy who installed it secured the massive dish with a few screws. If a strong wind blew, I would lose the signal and have to call someone.

I lived here for a year before the building management complained. First, they knocked on my door, and I directed them to the landlord. Later, the guard at the entrance reminded me to remove it each time I passed. Shanghai Government put pressure on buildings to dismantle dishes. Only certain approved places and star-rated hotels could own them. My two-meter dish was too big to go unnoticed.

The building supervisors weren't the only ones knocking. I also had the tax people looking for rental tax. A foreigner living outside the hotel must be renting because buying was not an option. Being the only *laowai* in the neighborhood made me a target. The tax collectors came every month and attempted to get me to cough up. I wasn't sure what they based it on. They knocked at lunchtime when I returned from work, enjoying my meal and, if my TV worked, watching *Late Night with David Letterman* or the *Today Show*. I picked up U.S. programs from the Armed Forces Network in Seoul, which was better than the hotel.

At first, when the tax assessors arrived, I spoke English, and the conversation quickly ended. However, the more they bothered me, the more frustrated I became, especially during "The Daily Top Ten." After a year of this, I got so discouraged I dropped the inarticulate foreigner act and broke into fluent Chinese. I told my landlord to deal with the problem, or I would move.

She said, "Don't answer the door."

It was genius and so simple. "Don't answer the door." What would they do, knock it down? It wasn't my door. The next time they came, I froze, trying not to make a sound while hitting the mute button on the TV. They knocked again, and I waited silently, sitting five feet from the door. After a few minutes, they left. "Don't answer the door!" I found it a helpful tactic in many situations, like **Rule #19**. The people knew you were inside, but what could they do? I ultimately needed to leave, but the taxman never chased me down.

The dead-end road leading to the complex turned into another drawback. It transformed into "Watermelon Street" during the summer. One day, a handful of trucks overloaded with the green gourds showed up, and they stayed until the season ended. They slept on tarps and played cards while selling the melons. The stench of produce rotting in the summer heat became intolerable. Every time I passed, I held my breath.

Then, The Heavenly Goose Hotel had nothing of use. They set up the restaurant to receive domestic tourist groups and didn't stock foreign alcohol. I walked in once and never again.

A new district west of me called Gubei had individuals opening restaurants and shops. I never knew what I would come across, but if I saw something desirable, I bought it before someone else did.

Because each excursion took time, I got obsessed with filling my refrigerator whenever I went out. I multitasked. Just finished drinking and near a great grocery store? Better do my shopping. Near a KFC? Take some home, so I don't need to journey out the next day.

Many nights after finishing a big evening, I did my best not to wobble as I strolled through a brightly lit market or waited for take-out.

My favorite location to buy groceries was the Westin Hotel (now a Sheraton) in Hongqiao District. They stocked a first-class collection of raw U.S. and Australian steaks, prawns, chicken, cold cuts, pâtés, cheeses, desserts, wines, and fresh-baked bread. Meanwhile, department store supermarkets were a hassle with a poor selection. Not only did I need to navigate the crowds, but I did it while hauling sacks of groceries. Then I fought for a taxi. When I carried bags for twenty or thirty minutes, I bought only the necessary items. At the Westin, I didn't have that trouble, and a line of empty cars was waiting. I stocked up on as much as my wallet would tolerate.

I booked all of my customers and coworkers at the hotel when they visited The Hai so that I could do my grocery shopping. Executives and business travelers arrived in suits with their luggage while I exited with bags of steaks, shrimp, and loaves of bread.

Besides an excellent grocery store, my neighborhood lacked a watering hole. I later realized I didn't need one: I dined with my QCs or abstained from the sauce after returning from the front lines. With my staff, we ate at the Chuan, followed by bowling. There were four alleys near the workshop. We switched venues as each set of lanes outdid the last. Our favorite was an enormous warehouse with a go-cart track. We showed up with factory guys in various states of drunkenness, occupied a few lanes, and all the cold beer while I plugged in the jukebox and blasted the Jackson Five and Spice Girls. I couldn't play my CDs, so I was constrained. We bowled several rounds and drank more before ending the afternoon with go-carting. Nothing seemed strange about drunken grown men chasing each other like children.

I rarely wandered downtown to drink. Nightlife in Shanghai in the early '90s was limited to the hotels, but things changed fast. A three-story Canadian American restaurant/pub called Malone's became the top choice for Yanks. They served decent Western food and stocked a full bar. On the main floor, they installed a barber chair for shots. Most nights, patrons and even the Marines guarding the consulate took turns getting liquor poured into their mouths while sitting in the chair. It was a slice of America in the middle of The Hai.

Long Bar, Shanghai Sally's, and Churchill's were some bars I hit up. The Long Bar had a lingerie show that gave them a leg up on the competition, drawing crowds of Western dudes. My staff and the factory preferred discos, such as the Galaxy Hotel. They introduced me to a massive joint on the north end of the Bund called New York, New York—a great location close to one of the only Sichuan hotpot restaurants (Chuan Mei Zi). Occasionally, we ate Chuan and drank *baijiu*, followed by a few rounds at NYNY. The disco filled up on weekends, with bystanders hanging around outside. The last time we stopped by, I saw guys breakdancing. Naturally, I showed them how it was done, but my glory days were behind me. I didn't embarrass myself, but it was time to hang up the back spinning. Perhaps I needed Tevas.

When we left the disco, we drove through the thicket of ravers, and somebody hit our car with a bottle. Everyone got out and argued with the dudes. I grew restless and told them to forget about it. Then, someone pushed me from behind. I couldn't react because the police dispersed the crowd. My guys lifted me and drove away. They said they knew who had shoved me. I was more interested in starting the drive to my home. They wouldn't get out and pummel him, would they? That was precisely what they did. We drove around the deserted streets of the Bund until they found him. They all jumped out and whipped his ass. It ended quickly, but I felt terrible for the guy. I didn't request the beating but thanked them.

Due to that disaster of an evening, I never returned to NYNY and wondered if they'd thrashed the right dude.

DD's was another place I discovered by accident when asking a driver to take me to someplace with music and drinking. He drove me down a dark alley near the Holiday Inn Hotel and stopped at a door with a stocky guy, who I assumed handled the riff-raff. The club looked unlike anything I had seen in China. It was a modern, fabulous bar/ lounge. Everything differed from the loud and tacky discos, and it was closer to my flat. The problem was they refused to allow in my factory crew. I think they wanted a fashionable crowd.

I did a lot of walking around town, looking for places to eat and drink. In between the decorating shops at the far end of my street, I discovered a Xinjiang restaurant. They had a large fake tree "growing" in the center of the venue, giving it a Rainforest Cafe atmosphere, nothing like the deserts of Western China, but it didn't matter. The juicy lamb skewers they brought to the table by the dozen and stout beer drew customers. Uighur performers entertained diners while getting people up to dance, which was not something that locals enjoyed. This joint was so good I returned after moving away.

III

The situation got better after Louis welcomed me back. They treated us with respect and installed an A/C unit in the clubhouse. Since things had improved, I suggested we have a soccer match between the factory and the staff from my company. Five of my American coworkers planned to visit for a meeting. It would be the perfect time. Louis liked the idea.

He said, "How about the loser pay for dinner?"

With twenty people, the price would be four hundred bucks at a decent place. For sure, we would lose. None of us Yanks understood how to play beyond kicking the ball into the goal. Only our three local employees possessed knowledge about the game. We would get killed.

I evened out the situation by saying,

"We'll do one game of soccer and one game of American football, tackle."

We would win the football. Plus, with tackle, I could exercise revenge on some individuals who ridiculed me when I got barred. Louis said it was unfair because they lacked an understanding of American football.

"We have never played soccer, nor do we stay up all night watching the European League."

"All right. Let's do it. "

It was rare for more than two of my coworkers to be in the same place. Everyone remained in their own territory except for me. I traveled to all the provinces to check things out. Also, communication was troublesome and costly: email usage had a slow start, and cell phone coverage was irregular. Catching someone at their hotel was the only way. Because of these hindrances, we met in one location to trade notes once a year. We referred to these gatherings as "The Quickening" since they involved plenty of heavy expat drinking and exploring.

This meeting was no different. Three American coworkers arrived from smaller cities and wanted to revel in what the big city provided. I planned to keep things low-key the evening before to increase our chances, so I invited everybody to my apartment for a barbecue. We bought imported beer and steaks from the Westin. None of the other guys had anything like this. It was an enormous deal. I also impressed everyone with my oven and made them jealous when I said a restaurant now delivered pizza. What??? That was too much. After a rough business trip, pizza sent to your home would be a luxury.

With guests coming over, I used my 7 X 5 miniature balcony. Normally, I cooked on an indoor grill when I treated my QC staff, but this time, I found a hibachi, charcoal, and lighter fluid at the grocery store. I put in the briquettes and threw a match; then, "poof," a cloud of black smoke engulfed every apartment above me for fifteen floors. I rushed to extinguish the fire before receiving a knock on my door and switched to the electric grill, but I needed to turn off the AC before tripping the fuse.

I finished cooking the steaks but noticed the air seemed smoky. Most of us smoked, but it appeared worse than that. Soon, someone rang my doorbell and pounded on my door. I couldn't hide from this one. The music was too loud. When I opened it, I faced the police. Oops. They said a neighbor had complained about a smoke smell. I told them we cooked earlier, so the smoke should disappear. When I looked back, I saw it was smoky as hell. I closed the door and ensured I had put out the coals. And then I recalled one guy had bought a frozen apple pie, which baked in my oven. The pie turned black as night. Sure, I had an oven, but I forgot how to use it.

We drank for a couple of hours, but they wanted to explore, and I was eager with the liquor in me. So, we hit it hard for a few more at Malone's and got hungry again. I informed them about a late-night Tex-Mex place that had opened. They served tacos and nachos, two words we rarely used. Few people knew about the joint, so we took it over and ordered everything on the menu, followed by tequila—another rarity. The low-key evening I had hoped for never panned out.

While we waited on the empty street for taxis, a coworker showed off his kung fu moves (he was the guy who threw up on the factory floor). He stood in front of the door and said, "Check this out." He lunged forward, punched through a small diamond-shaped window, and badly cut his hand. I assumed he felt nothing because he didn't react. We told him to wash up in the toilet, but he wiped his blood all over the walls and mirror. He was too drunk. Paul, Eric, and I took him to get stitched up. I didn't mind going to the emergency room at 3 a.m. What bothered me was losing a player. He turned out okay but couldn't take part in the game.

When it was time for the main event, we arrived looking for victory. Rain soaked the field with big puddles of mud. It was an excellent pitch for tackle, but we played soccer first. They won 7-0. The loss would have been more considerable if not for our local staff. The workers relished in the spectacle. Now, it was our turn. We gave them a primary tutelage about football; then, it was kick-off time. The game only lasted twenty minutes, with a score of 42-0. Two factory guys needed to go to the infirmary for minor injuries. Louis missed the match. He called before the start, saying he had flown back and would meet us at the restaurant. I wanted him to play to receive a few tackles.

We all met after and enjoyed a typical eating and drinking festival.

The factory guys never wanted to play football again.

CHAPTER SEVENTEEN

PUTIAN: THE WEDDING

After more than a year in The Hai, my relationship with Debbie had reached a crossroads. She lived a miserable life in dark and underdeveloped Pudong while I traveled and only saw her twice a week.

I offered to let her stay in my flat when on the road to give her extra comfort, but she opposed it. We had to complete the deal or split. From her side, it was the natural progression of the relationship. Otherwise, why did we date? She didn't pressure me; it was time. She came from a different way of looking at things, but I wasn't thinking about marriage when we met. I had too many uncertainties.

Matrimony in China became an agreement between families rather than a love story. Indeed, we loved each other, but that would not be enough: There needed to be a discussion between the households about wealth, social status, and whether you own a flat. Even today, parents sit in the park in Shanghai and advertise the attributes of their unmarried children, trying to hook a better than spouse. I lacked wealth and an apartment, but my social status as a foreigner helped, and I had potential—lots of potential. However, being a foreigner meant I could be a flight risk. At any moment, I might leave, thus causing immense problems for her. She wouldn't be able to rebuild her life in a small town because locals would view her as damaged.

By this point, I remained in China for almost three years and traveled extensively. I had no intention of leaving. As a further backup, my friend Zhang Bo assisted with the marriage negotiations. He replaced my parents, who would do this sort of thing. Zhang Bo owned a factory and drove his own car. He was a local and would plead in Putian dialect on my behalf. That helped placate my future in-laws (**Rule #14**).

We drove to her neighborhood in an older part of town and parked at the closest point possible without wedging the car between the lane walls. Everyone used motorbikes or three-wheeled tricycles to whiz through the narrow walkways. If you ignored the rubble in the lots torn down, the neighborhood looked picturesque. Her house was also scheduled to be demolished, and they fought against it while pushing for more compensation. The amount offered was less than the market value, which quickly increased. When going against the might of the government, it was hard to win. Houses similar to theirs got decimated as modernization picked up speed. Soon, their dwelling would bite the dust, too.

Zhang Bo and I walked down the winding lane to the door of her house, a traditional Putian dwelling in her family for over a century, a genuine treasure. The entire hood resembled a Zhang Yimou film, with large wooden doors and sliding wooden locks. They were beautiful but flammable. The new houses built in place of these ancient works of art were poured concrete boxes. They removed the flavor from the area.

We knocked, and her father answered. He and his wife worked as schoolteachers and had paid a price during the Cultural Revolution in the '60s and early '70s when their students denounced and paraded teachers out in the street. The schools closed during that period, turning the country upside down. It became a horrible decade for many. Her parents survived and continued teaching.

How do you return to normal when your students publicly criticize you?

He welcomed us into their courtyard while his wife waited in the living room. A few smaller rooms connected to the lounge, and the sleeping quarters were on the second floor.

We sat and exchanged small talk while drinking tea and smoking cigarettes. Since I dropped by whenever I visited, I got along with her parents, but I felt unhappy when I found out I needed to "pay" for the honor of marrying Debbie. Not only that, but people advised me about the scale, which increased depending on wealth and status. An average local would be required to compensate less than a factory owner.

Because I was a foreigner, my charge would be higher. How high? Nobody knew. Everyone assumed it had to be greater when I removed a local girl—making her one less available, further throwing off the boy-to-girl ratio. There had to be some penalty for that. I threw the question out to my QC posse for group analysis. They came up with between 30,000 and 50,000 RMB ($4K–7K in 1996 dollars). I thought 10,000 ($1,500) would be a suitable amount on top of the wedding banquet, which would cost me about 20,000. On the high end, I looked at paying $10,000 unless we negotiated a deal. At twenty-six years of age, that was a lot.

I had just finished paying off my college loans and saved up cash. Now, I needed to spend it on getting married. Still, I got off easy compared to the 2000s, when prices and wedding services jumped astronomically. In 1996, all I could think about was why I had to pay to get married. I shamed Debbie about it. Wasn't she concerned I would "own" her? Perhaps she knew in the end, she would control me.

I figured I brought a lot to the table, considering I was an American who traveled freely, had color TV my entire life, grew up with a KFC down the street, and learned to drive a car when I turned fifteen. Shouldn't I be the catch and the one paid? My posse reassured me that approach would not work. Instead, Zhang Bo did all the talking while I observed. As a factory owner, he didn't sweat 30,000 RuMBas. I explained that not all foreigners were wealthy like on *MacGyver*. Some just started out.

I understood bits of the conversation, but not enough. My posse waited in town to eat dinner, giving us a limited negotiation time. I only visited a couple of days every few months now and made the most of it by dining with multiple factories and building *guanxi*. Once we left, we had a fifteen-minute walk and a thirty-minute drive. The restaurant stopped serving at nine. If we didn't return before then, supper would have to be night market grub.

How long would it take to agree to a number? I thought we would be in and out within a half-hour. I didn't consider how long the niceties took. They could spend an hour talking about superficial things until bringing up the reason we were here.

Finally, we came to a deal where I would pay for the redecoration of their house, like putting tile on the floor and installing a new TV and a bathroom. For this, I would give them 30,000 RMB. Even though the total surpassed what I preferred, and they would tear down the home a year later, I felt less like I had bought a wife. Instead, I helped her family spruce up the place, which sounded better. Semantics.

We started the official application for the marriage license, and I prepared for trouble. My wife's household registration was in Putian. China tied individuals to the city they were born in to prevent the movement of the masses. It had worked for decades. All your documents (birth, marriage, passport, etc.) must be processed at home. This gave cadres in the towns enormous power. Our situation was not so straightforward. We had to apply in the provincial capital, Fuzhou. Not many Chinese in Fujian married foreigners, and we had difficulty. Everywhere we went, people wondered why we wanted to get hitched. Sometimes, they didn't know how to handle it.

"How do we put his English name on a Chinese form?"

"What to do since he doesn't have a Chinese ID?"

We faced one obstacle after another, then made corrections and redid the forms. No mistakes allowed! It took quite a few trips to complete the process.

Then, I endured a physical. They did blood tests, including the all-important HIV, and an inspection of my privates. I had to produce urine and drop a deuce on demand in a stinky toilet, which turned out to be an arduous task. I read about foreigners having to give sperm samples to show they had good reproductive capabilities. How would I have provided that specimen in one of those toilets?

After I submitted the samples, we waited. The longer they took, the more I suspected something had gone wrong. Did I have HIV? The test was nerve-wracking, especially when I knew they would expel me from the country if I came up positive. The hospital utilized a new procedure, which required a few hours compared to the two-week tests I had taken in Taiwan. I worried they would make an error.

Three hours later, the results came back, and the police didn't escort me out. I already had a flight to catch and dragged my luggage as if I were planning an escape.

I listened to the doctor go over my health report with Debbie, and a Fuzhou aunt called in to give us local cred. "His genitals look normal (thanks for sharing that with everyone, doc), but there's an excess of protein in his urine." I was aware of this from my previous illnesses. The doctor said he could not approve me. Debbie and her relative prepared for pushback and had a red envelope to grease things. I objected, but it was the way in China. They knew and got ready. I never realized doctors were on the take. When does the skimming stop?

Since I was out of my element, I jumped into a taxi and headed to the airport.

I assumed we were done with the application, but we required one more document. They demanded proof of my single status. I had never heard of such a thing. Either I was married or not. Who would know? The best I could do was head to the records office in Chicago and ask for a document. They looked at me like I was insane. I explained I was getting hitched in China, and the civil servant asked,

"China? Is that a mail-order bride?"

"Not exactly,"

"The best we can do is give you a letter stating we didn't find a record of you being married in Cook County."

That would have to do, so I handed that to the U.S. Consulate in Shanghai to translate and guarantee. The result was a lot of work for a meaningless paper.

Once we had our documents in order, we walked into the small Marriage Registration Office. Two women sat across from each other; one reviewed and approved, while the other stamped. We needed to bypass the first woman, the gatekeeper and breaker of hearts. For other couples, it was easy. They had approval from their work units. We did not, and our application was rejected.

The clerk said we missed something and criticized us for not preparing everything. A crowd of other couples leaned over Debbie to listen in. They heard more than I did. She worried I would worsen things and wanted me to stand near the door. From a distance, I could tell the administrator was complaining. A few minutes later, Debbie emerged, and the swarm engulfed her space. I asked,

"What do we have to do now?"

"The woman wants a gold ring."

"Excuse me? Did she tell you or use sign language?"

"She didn't ask for a ring but made strange complaints while rubbing her finger as if it missed something." She impressed me. That was some serious Sherlock Holmes kind of insight.

"If all it's going to take is a ring, by all means, let's buy that precious."

I needed to buy one for Debbie, and here I was, buying a ring for the marriage office clerk! We had to rush; the office closed soon.

We hightailed it to the closest department store. The ring cost $300. For safety's sake, we purchased a carton of Zhonghua cigarettes—the preferred brand for patriotic folks. You could never go wrong with a stick of cigs as a "gift."

Debbie thought the clerk would refuse the presents if a foreigner stood in the room. I agreed and waited outside. Although I decided to pay for them, I didn't enjoy it. With my dissatisfaction, I might say something sarcastic that would blow the deal. We weren't sure a ring and a slab of smokes would do it. The best thing would be for me to lie low. Ten minutes later, she came out with the stamped documents and the marriage license.

That was December 31, 1996, New Year's Eve, and I was sober.

It was time to plan the ceremony. Considering I would foot the bill, I wanted a say. Up to that point, I had attended two weddings in my life. At my first in Taiwan, they invited over two hundred guests. The bride and groom changed clothes three times and hired a professional emcee.

I didn't want that kind of ceremony. Besides, I only had enough friends to fill two tables (twenty people). I said, "To make it even, let's invite enough to fill five tables (the number four sounded like death—not a good number). With a smaller gathering, we can have quality food and drink."

My wife shot this idea down. Relatives from all over Fujian and past coworkers needed to be invited. The list grew. My modest number of tables expanded to eighteen, and that was after they reduced it!

As the number increased, my planned dinner menu dwindled. I assumed that if I married, I would do it up with expensive liquor and delicious Chinese cuisine. With most restaurants specializing in steamed sea creatures, I couldn't have gone high-end even if I wanted to. It would be seafood on top of seafood. Some items, such as sandworm jelly, cockroach (mantis) shrimp, and baby octopus, had to be on the menu. That was okay, but we didn't require them for the foreigner table. I gave up the idea of ribeyes and lobster and made it simple by requesting *gong bao* chicken and fried rice. My wife and her parents decided on the rest. They knew what auspicious foods were required. The guests would be upset if we only served the chicken and fried rice.

Besides the food, we needed to find a hall. The best time for the event was February 1997, the Chinese New Year's (CNY) holiday. Most places closed, and staff returned home. There was one available venue, but they would separate the party into individual rooms, and what they charged made it a non-option. Plan B was to have an indoor/outdoor wedding at Debbie's home. I liked Plan B, as it reduced the cost. We would hire local cooks and restaurant staff. To accommodate the invitees, they put tables everywhere: in the living room, the courtyard, the lane outside, and in a torn-down house across the alley. There was no telling if this would work.

My mother arrived in Shanghai to travel with me to the wedding. Without one parent coming, the balance would have been disturbed, and negative karma could have affected the marriage. It was her first trip to China, and she suffered from culture shock. But before we traveled south, I had to visit a factory in Tianjin (two hours from Beijing) and figured it would be an excellent opportunity for her to see Tiananmen and The Forbidden City.

"How will I talk to people if I get lost?"

"You won't lose your way. It's a vast square. Everyone knows it."

"When are you going to be back?"

"Three p.m. It's a quick trip to check a factory."

My coworker, Sonny, who now worked in Qingdao and would oversee these orders, traveled with me. Kung Fu Johnny, who put his hand through the window, had moved back to the U.S., and we hired another dude to cover Sonny's position in Putian. That guy didn't take to small-town life and lived in Quanzhou, a city down the coast. It became easier to travel as they completed the roads.

By the time we reached the agent's office, it was lunchtime. The Taiwanese owner talked about his company and products. There wasn't much to see, so it became a *guanxi* visit. Before lunch, he opened up a cabinet full of high-end alcohol.

"What do you guys prefer to drink?"

We looked at each other, and I said,

"The Johnny Walker will be fine, but bring that bottle of Absolut, just in case."

He also brought a bottle of XO. He said he had nothing to do and was pleased we came. We needed to hit the road by one p.m. to make it back by three. I should have said my mother waited and I would have to take a rain check, but when I saw something besides *baijiu*, I couldn't resist.

During lunch, we polished off the whiskey and various amounts of the others, including some *baijiu*, after I said I fancied it. We left at three—when we should have been in Beijing. To speed things up, we grabbed a taxi but hit traffic. My brain was thinking about 1990 Beijing, not 1997, which had significant traffic issues. We returned around 6 p.m. I had arranged a dinner with Lao Zhu at his home, good ol' lamb hotpot, but we ran late. We hurried to our rooms, and I grabbed my mother, jumped back into a cab, and drove straight into another jam. The city transformed in just the two years since my previous visit. I no longer recognized the roads that snaked through downtown. Underneath the modern streets were the old lanes if they hadn't destroyed them. I directed the driver by memory.

We arrived an hour late. Sonny and I were sloppy, and the *baijiu* at the meal added to the mayhem. Sonny dropped his chopsticks a dozen times. At one point, my mother cried as we spoke Mandarin. She also got lost looking for Tiananmen and the hotel. Culture shock hit her hard.

I never apologized to Lao Zhu for our behavior that evening. I tried to squeeze too much into a day and forgot we were hanging with civilians. Lao Zhu was a great friend I lost contact with because I rarely traveled to Beijing, but I was lucky to spend time with him. I will treasure that. He enriched my life in China.

The next day, we took a trip to The Great Wall (you can't fly to Beijing without it), then returned to The Hai and flew to Fujian. My mother went with me to do the cultural ceremony. This comprised my wife and me bowing three times to the parents and handing over gold chains. A monk was on hand to officiate and bong a brass bowl. I presented a ring and received gold ones to wear. I put them on to humor them and removed them after the ceremony: Gold jewelry didn't suit me. We bowed a few more times, which completed the formal part. The city gov. had banned fireworks as they were a hazard. Instead, we played a cassette of firecrackers. Pop, Pop, Pop. Then came some *erhu* music and opera singing. The whole thing was over in an hour.

The cook set up shop in the crumbling house across the alley. Large beams protruded through the collapsed wooden roof. It appeared unstable, but nobody minded. He had giant fire pits with huge woks. His assistants chopped and prepped the ingredients. Meanwhile, the white, puffy chickens (called silkie) ran wild in the courtyard. This was the countryside; they ate fresh chicken, prepared on the spot, never frozen. They used the black chickens in medicinal soups, and it tasted just like, well . . . chicken. It only looked shocking because of the skin. In the afternoon, the chef came to chop the necks off those birds and pluck the white plume. Some guests pitched in with the plucking. If you had a knack for it, why not? I was useless and saw nothing edible.

"What happened to my dishes?"

They fell off the list. I paid for everything, and nothing enticed me. Because of my hangover and the requirement to stay put, I missed breakfast and lunch. I had purchased a bottle of Old El Paso pickled jalapeño peppers from Hong Kong to add Mexican flair to the dishes, so I snacked on those. The jalapeños reminded me of nachos. That would be as close as I would get to Mexican food on that day. I advised my coworkers to eat before they arrived.

"You won't enjoy any of the dishes. And please bring me a shitty sandwich, if available."

I knew The Heavenly Concubine (now open under new ownership) lacked a Western restaurant, but they had the white bread sandwiches served on airplanes. I needed something.

All day, I waited on a dehydrated and empty stomach. My body cried out for a beer while I sat admiring the refurbished living room. The workers did a decent job, and the W.C. was a welcome addition. Most found it easier to pee across the lane, but you should be careful when it is dark. Debbie and her parents refused to serve me liquor until the meal. They told me I would drink a lot at dinnertime and wouldn't last. They had never seen me at a factory meal.

It was Chinese tradition to gift a red envelope with cash instead of a present. Imagine, out of two hundred guests; you might receive ten heaters and twenty woks. How many woks does a family need? Cash made sense. These red envelopes provided an incentive to make the dinner pay for itself. But it shouldn't be considered a "loss" because they would count on you delivering the same when they invited you to their wedding. People expected you to give more if you had a higher status or a close relationship with the couple. At most weddings, you handed in the envelope as you entered and signed a big red book, writing your name and the amount you had given (for all to see) for two reasons:

1. The bride and groom knew how much you valued the friendship.
2. The bride and groom knew how much you paid so they could reciprocate.

The best friend would be the last to sign in to ensure they gave the most significant amount. At the first wedding I attended in Taiwan, I gifted

$20 (500 TWD). In Shanghai, people told me giving 100 RMB ($12) was customary. In Putian, the friend amount should be thirty ($4). That wouldn't cover the food. If that amount set them back, I didn't want their money that badly. But I never got the chance to refuse. No one approached me with a red envelope. Somebody had received them. I focused on collecting the gifts from my coworkers, and they came through.

Many guests were unfamiliar with foreigners and had never seen one up close. They weren't sure I could speak Mandarin, so they had no problem talking about me while I stood before them. It took a while for them to get comfortable. By then, the van showed up with my coworkers, an array of *laowai*.

They brought the only thing available for me to eat—a smidgen of canned tuna and dodgy mayo smashed between two triangular slices of white bread. No thanks. My friends also carried the other item I asked for: booze. Almost everyone flew in from Hong Kong, purchasing large bottles at duty-free: Jameson, Smirnoff, Jack Daniels, and Cuervo. They filed in from the dark alley with a hand gripping the neck of a bottle of booze. It seemed strange to the relatives. Why would you show up at a wedding with hootch? I explained we had special dietary requirements.

We all sat together, breaking tradition; the bride and groom should be with the parents, but I wanted to enjoy the festivities. It was a splendid opportunity to laugh and get drunk. This was "The Quickening." It would be better for her parents to join the relatives while the expat table lifted the party to a new level. Before the dinner started, I swapped my tea for Jameson.

Let the games begin.

The table was small, and the alcohol commanded the entire real estate. We sat on stools, and it wasn't long before people fell off. My other group of invitees comprised my QC posse, Zhang Bo, and a few factory owners, including the trade corp. manager from when I first arrived. He provided a minibus to shuttle everyone. That was a good thing, with all the drinking.

The guests drank soda and beer. They weren't a big boozing crowd. One of my wife's uncles sitting beside us wanted to play—a big mistake. He wobbled over with a bottle and did a shot of *baijiu*, then one of tequila, and repeated with somebody else. It was not a healthy mixture for a person who only imbibed *baijiu*. Later, that same uncle wandered out to whiz, tripped over a brick, and fell. He chipped off a front tooth (a reoccurring issue for drunks). Someone dumped him on a three-wheel bike to send him home.

It was dangerous to drink with us.

Towards the end of the meal, we had to go to every table to thank and *ganbei*. The best man and best friend of the bride assisted with the drinking. I didn't have a best man, but a coworker followed along, not because he helped with the *ganbei-ing* but to hit on my wife's classmate. I looked forward to the challenge of eighteen shots. My in-laws prepared a special pitcher of watered-down *baijiu*. It was clear, and you couldn't tell the difference. Once I tasted it, I swapped it for tequila. With the bash in full effect and too many individuals to *ganbei* with, I only completed ten tables before my in-laws switched the booze out again.

Debbie did the small talk at each table. I kept hearing people say something about having a baby soon, but the expression they said sounded like, "Hope you have a foreign ghost."

Perhaps the rapid tequila shots worked their way to my brain, so I focused. There it was again. Now, I got upset and told my wife to stop them. She explained it was an expression that meant baby in this context. It still sounded offensive. This was similar to "*nei ge*"—a place phrase locals used when looking for the right word but identical to a derogatory term for individuals of color.

I had an African-American colleague visit. He asked me to instruct people to stop using the term, which would be equivalent to asking someone to cease using "um" or "whatchamacallit." That was infringing too much, and he never returned.

After dinner, we converted the room into a disco. I hooked up a CD player and played music. The relatives stood in the courtyard smoking and talking while watching the foreigners dance. It turned into an epic night, but we had to cut it at eleven because of the neighbors. The rest of the hood tried to sleep. They asked us to turn it down, but old habits were hard to break.

I stayed over at my wife's house. Her parents wanted me to remain the entire time, but I preferred my previous digs. As a consolation, I agreed to sleep over one evening, but they forgot to prepare me for living in a traditional home. It felt similar to sleeping outside. The cold seeped through the cracks between the wood, and there were no heaters. When the temperature dropped, you piled on blankets. Try going to sleep with ten pounds of comforters.

The following morning, I headed to the hotel and got filled in on the events that had taken place on the ride back. When the driver cruised down the main road, a motorbike swerved in front, and the minivan knocked them down. The driver jumped out to yell at the bikers for damaging the car. Sonny checked on the folks on the ground. Once he determined they needed help, he ran into the darkness to find a house with a phone. In return for his quick thinking, the people on the motorbike blamed him. He must have been driving, or he wouldn't have run away. I told him to tell the trade corp. to handle it. They had the *guanxi* to fix this, and it was their van.

For whatever reason, Sonny helped to pay the hospital bills. That seemed like an admission of guilt, opening him up to bigger legal problems. Locals sometimes ran in front of cars to receive money. Imagine if you got hit, and it was a van full of foreigners. Always follow **Rule #19** unless an angry mob surrounds you, like in Fuan.

They continued to harass him to get more cash. I left him to deal with it.

||

We flew to Shanghai after the wedding. It never occurred to me to take a honeymoon. I didn't think local couples did that, and my mother remained with us. Also, Debbie had a Chinese passport, making it difficult to leave. Traveling in China was rugged. I knew because I did it every week. With no options, I returned to work.

Later in the year, we arranged a trip to the Silk Road, which could have been a honeymoon, except I invited my boss, Paul. We got along well off the clock, but we never seemed to be off the clock. Our personal lives became intertwined with our professional ones. The other Americans had an identical situation. We dealt with similar hardships, which brought us closer together. I also invited him because I wanted extra security. It could be dangerous in the desert.

We flew 2,500 miles from Shanghai to Urumchi, Xinjiang, then took a minibus to Turpan, two hours away. From there, we hired a car to visit the ruins of the cities of Gaochang and Jiaohe, the Bezeklik grottos, and the Fire Mountains. Gaochang and Jiaohe were built in the first century B.C. and were key cities on the Silk Road. They attracted multiple ethnicities and religions until their destruction in the 13th century by the Mongolian-ruled Yuan Dynasty. Marco Polo traveled the same route and would have stopped at these oases if still standing. The sites rivaled marvels in other parts of the world but were too difficult to reach.

After a day of mind-blowing sightseeing, we returned to Turpan for oversized plates of lamb ($3 for a roasted leg) and chicken. On the way, I blasted my desert mixtape with songs like "Dust in the Wind" and "Carry on Wayward Son." I felt like a trailblazer to be the first person in history to play certain music while I traversed the country.

Two days later, we headed to Hami and towards Dunhuang for the Mogao Caves. Then, we embarked on a seven-hour excursion through the Gobi Desert to Jiuquan to see where The Great Wall ended. We selected a coach that mostly traveled during the daytime. When the driver turned over the engine, it struggled. I should have followed **Rule #12** and gotten off.

The ride was uneventful, but the scenery looked stunning. We stopped at a shop halfway through. Besides the stand, there was nothing but darkness in all directions. Debbie got off with the other woman (only two). I was exhausted and closed my eyes. When we started moving, my wife wasn't on. I glanced around while rushing to the front, shouting for the driver to stop.

"A person is missing."

He put on the brakes and opened the door.

"Don't let them leave!" I said to Paul as I jumped off and ran in the direction of the light. As I reached the store, I found Debbie walking towards me.

"What were you doing? Everyone finished and returned."

"All the people stood in the same place, so I wandered further to get away."

"You should have monitored the bus, or you might have been stuck here."

We boarded and continued down the road. An hour later, the engine broke down. It had been miles since we saw another vehicle. Who would be dumb enough to travel at night? We were an hour from our destination, but walking didn't seem wise. All we could do was freeze and wait for the next bus to arrive in four hours. At the bazaar, I bought a thick, woven carpet I regretted after carrying it, but now it proved to be a choice selection; we used it to keep warm.

Hours later, I noticed a light. It was the next bus. The drivers calculated that not everybody would fit. They let the women get on, and my wife said for the other passengers to hear,

"Can you let the *laowai* on first?"

Even in remote Xinjiang, this request did not go over well.

"What do you mean, let the foreigners get on first?"

She looked out for us at the wrong time—it almost started a riot. I told her to get on. Paul and I waited outside, ensuring our backpacks got loaded while the others boarded. He said, "We won't fit."

I looked him in his eyes and said, "I guarantee they will not depart without us. Trust me."

And we squeezed on. I stood beside the driver, holding on to the post to prevent from flying through the windshield. It was a "bare-knuckled" escape, and I had a fantastic view of the sunrise.

The desert trip wasn't the only hiccup. We had misfortune on the ride to Lanzhou—the end of our 1,500-mile Silk Road journey. We took the rail for this leg, and I secured an upgrade to soft sleepers. Not long after we moved, a military dude came into our cabin, sat beside Paul, and put his gun on the bed. Guns were rare. Since he carried one, he was someone. Considering he had major *guanxi*, we ignored him while he made calls. He left after a half-hour, saying nothing. I was thankful he didn't start trouble with Debbie for hanging with foreigners. People had opinions about that.

Because it was a day trip, we put our bags on the upper bunks, and when I grabbed my backpack, my passport slipped out with my wife's ID card tucked inside the cover. Once again, I had a weird feeling.

I was unaware I had lost it until we arrived at the hotel. I searched my bag and broke into a sweat, fearing I should have checked the bunk.

"Damn it! Why didn't I follow **Rule #12**?"

When Paul filled in his registration form, I told her.

"I think my passport fell out on the train."

"That's okay. We can use my ID to check in."

"That's the thing. Your card was inside, so it's gone, too."

She wasn't pleased but moved into action. Debbie took my cell and searched for someone at the local station to telephone the train on its way to Xian, 350 miles away, and have somebody search "the *laowai* cabin." I presumed it would be a lost cause.

"Who will turn in an American passport and the unexpected prize of a Chinese ID?"

Luckily, I had kept our red marriage booklet in a different place, and we used that for registration. We went up to the room and waited. The following day, we planned to stop by the Labrang Tibetan Monastery (built in 1709), but currently, I had no interest in temples.

After a tense hour, we got a call. They found it.

"Did you find an ID card too?"

"What card? No card, just a passport."

That was not good news.

"They probably didn't check in the cover," I said.

Someone riding the train would transfer my passport to another person traveling in the opposite direction. Then, someone on that train would pass the book to a person at the Lanzhou Station. There were a lot of handoffs, and I wouldn't relax until I had it in my possession.

Before we rushed over, my wife wrote a letter of praise for the manager. I would have given him money, but she said he would prefer recognition—that made sense. We hurried over and entered the office. As usual, she told me to stand back.

"You might make him angry."

"It's mine, so there should be no reason to grovel. I hope that won't happen."

She approached the guy's desk. He was one of "those guys" who had the power. When he unlocked a black safe, I saw a multitude of passports. He grabbed a navy book and checked it against the marriage license.

"Thank you. I'll take my book now," I thought from the corner. But no, he had to scrutinize it.

"This is an important document. Why would you be so irresponsible?"

Hasn't he ever lost something? I wanted to jump in, but I remembered what my wife said. She apologized and agreed that we were careless, and then she pulled out the letter saying how he had saved this foreigner from a critical situation. He relaxed after that and handed it over.

He warned us to be careful. After that experience, I became obsessed with knowing where my passport was.

It was a great vacation/honeymoon, but it pleased me to return to The Hai.

III

The next time I returned to Putian, people referred to me as the town's son-in-law (*nu xu*). When I visited new factories, it surprised me they had heard about my wedding. It seemed that the news of the ex-honorary mayor getting hitched spread wide.

As a *nu xu*, I should return during CNY. I wanted to experience a proper holiday with all the customs, but I realized it wasn't much different from my life here.

Although I enjoyed immersing myself in Chinese tradition, I needed a hot shower and a warm room, so I stayed in a hotel. CNY developed into a dangerous predicament. Everyone wished to imbibe with me, but I only had one liver. With most companies closed, every day turned into a non-stop drinking opportunity that I had to run for cover now that Putian served hard alcohol. I escaped before I became pickled.

During one CNY, I stayed at a new hotel. The city had caught the modernization bug, and it blossomed. My jaw dropped when I noticed a drive-through McDonald's. I thought nothing would surpass the launch of the first KFC.

I checked in and met my wife for dinner at the hotel cafe. She stayed at home until I arrived. When we returned to my room, the door was locked with the latch. I assumed it had caught when I closed it. But through the opening, I saw the lights and TV were on and heard somebody taking a shower and blow drying their hair. I had a serious Goldilocks situation on my hands.

"Someone's been sleeping in my bed and using my shower!"

I called the attendant, and he explained two girls told him their friend booked the room and asked him to open the door. He let them in without confirming with the front desk. It turned out their friend had a room a few doors down. I kept them until the manager showed up so I could count the 20,000 RuMBas stashed in my suitcase. They'd taken nothing, but my bathroom was a mess. The manager gave me a free buffet ticket for my trouble and promised never to send girls again. Fortunately, my wife remained with me the entire time. Otherwise, I would have had more explaining to do if she had walked in without me and found two lassies soaping up. She would have thought I was the "friend."

My visits were now rare as my responsibilities continued to change. One trip back with a U.S. coworker in the middle of 1999 coincided with a factory celebration honoring our company. They earned so much cash they thanked us. While I watched them get richer and show it off with Benzes, BMWs, and jewelry, I got jealous. It was difficult to listen to managers wearing flip-flops brag about Rolex and Patek Philippe watches they had purchased or the apartments they'd bought in Macau. It seemed unfair, but these guys worked the system using *guanxi* and borrowed loads of RuMBas. They had a good gig until the orders dried up and factories went bankrupt or changed trades. One workshop in the shoe business for two decades built a plant to produce computer motherboards. How does someone make that jump? With lots of money from the banks and available land, it didn't matter if the business succeeded. This same owner built an expansive estate on a mountain overlooking the workshop. He even constructed a *baijiu* vault for aged rocket fuel.

You don't see that on MTV Cribs.

The night before the celebration, I met up with three American coworkers. We traveled with separate customers but ended up at the same workshop in Quanzhou. That meant "The Quickening" would occur.

The business we worked with specialized in entertaining, and they liked to party hard. First was the lobster *sashimi* and shark's fin meal, followed by pitcher after pitcher of red wine and coke. As soon as we kicked one, another showed up. The typical routine lasted for hours, followed by karaoke and drinking games until 1 a.m.

After that, we drank and bowled at the entertainment center until three.

When "The Quickening" occurred, we pushed each other to go further.

The next day, I headed to Putian with my U.S. coworker. We finished working and stopped by my old digs, The Heavenly Concubine, for lunch with the factory. The Chinese restaurant reopened, and it looked the same. I had flashbacks of when I dined alone five years ago, and the factories ignored me. Now, they sought me out to keep the relationship or start one. I wouldn't have thought it was possible.

On days like this, I could not replenish my fluids fast enough and searched for a stir-fried anything with some rice to soothe my empty stomach. I only planned to consume a big bottle of beer for the required *ganbeis*. If I drank past a few glasses, I would slide down a dangerous path. Once the meal began, I saw my other American coworkers walking in with a different factory. It was a small world indeed. Everyone knew each other, so we joined tables. My one-bottle limit expanded to several.

We ended lunch after two dozen bottles. *Baijiu* was off-limits because of the banquet in a few hours. I had nothing on my schedule except purchasing a flight ticket and picking up samples. Both seemed easy, but the workers needed more time to finish the shoes. That made me late for dinner. The party factory asked us to be there by 5:30, and they called my staff to inquire about my whereabouts. I instructed them to start without me. We'd just finished lunch, and I attempted to process that beer.

They blew off ten minutes of real firecrackers when I arrived. The ban was no longer in effect, or they greased the police. Table after table of workers sat in the courtyard and parking lot, expecting to eat. It appeared to be about three hundred people. Have you ever had three hundred starved laborers waiting for you? It wasn't pleasant, but nobody would complain. The owner said a few words, and they lit off more fireworks. They gave me the honor of lighting the fuse, but I declined to lose my fingers. When we regained our hearing and cleared the toxic smoke from our lungs, the dishes flew out of the temporary kitchen. The workers may have been waiting, but the cooks didn't. Within fifteen minutes, they stacked the table with plates of things I would not eat. There was no time to stop them. After the dinner started, the staff lined up to *ganbei*. It had the potential to be a dangerous situation. That and the lack of enticing morsels turned it into a shorter party for me. The owner also wanted to escape and took us to a karaoke.

It turned into another "Quickening."

The following year, a separate group of factories celebrated us. This time, it would be five of them and three tables each or 150 people. They all wished to have a drink with my American coworker and me. We were hit hard with competitive *ganbei-ing*, and I got slammed even harder because of my well-known skills and son-in-law status. The drink of choice was my old pal, Chivas. Putian had swag. Most individuals still sipped beer, but the expanding nightclub/disco scene sold Chivas with green tea. I saw it everywhere, which was a great thing, despite some being fake. The tea hid the taste and kept me up all evening.

We booked rooms in the same hotel as the banquet. The outside of the place resembled a giant mosque. It wasn't clear what design the architect wanted. Nobody had explained to me beforehand about the round beds. Why would they make a circular bed? I made the best of it but rolled off twice during the night because I was disoriented. It was easy to lose your way when you traveled nearly daily for years and drank too much. I often woke up in the dark, and it took me a few minutes to figure out what city I was in. The same thing happened when I returned home.

That was my final multiple-workshop gala. They became a problem for my health. I was fortunate to have so many people wanting to eat and drink with me, but these meals had no limit. Everyone was more than happy to keep supplying me with sauce, and I never said "when." I needed to avoid the dinners whenever I could.

In the 2000s, our product lines changed again. When I stopped by Fujian, I lived in Quanzhou and Xiamen. The hotels, food, drink, entertainment, and travel improved almost overnight. It became less of a hardship posting. For me, the significant change came when KFC delivered to the karaoke. I would no longer starve. Some of my QC posse ran their own businesses. They didn't need me to pick up the check. Knowing that I'd helped them along the way was a good feeling.

Zhang Bo was not as fortunate. He closed his factory and then the next one. The glory days ended, and companies adapted or died. Every occasion I returned, we ate at the wild animal restaurants and drank *baijiu*. We always tried to find that same down-to-earth feeling, but China had changed. Putian bustled now with hundreds of eateries—no more holes-in-the-wall. There was no way to turn back time.

I will always have fond memories of my days here.

CHAPTER EIGHTEEN

ZHEJIANG: DEER DONG

With the continuous need for lower prices, I traveled south to Ningbo, Wenzhou, Shaoxing, Zhuji, and Hangzhou in Zhejiang province.

In Ningbo, our agent placed orders in a town called Cixi. I assumed the factory would be crap, so I dispatched a QC to investigate. He sent word that they produced poor quality and fell behind schedule. It rained hard like it did during the summer, and production got damp. I knew I needed to plan a trip.

I rode a train to Ningbo, and we drove an hour to Cixi. The factory made plush animal slippers, similar to many workshops in the area. If they were behind, they would work late nights in poor lighting and make mistakes. It was certain. But even with overtime, they needed help. The manager said they had subcontracted part of the order.

"But don't worry. The factory is near. We do it all the time."

The distance was the least of my concerns.

The sub-factory was next door, but we crossed a creek by walking over a plank bridge with boards as bouncy as a trampoline. It poured outside, but I took a slow and steady approach. There was no better incentive than the dark gray water below. I wished they had built the planks wider and sturdier.

The factory was a barn with high ceilings supported by wooden beams. They had two dozen stitching machines, but the workers sat on the ground in circles, stitching parts of the animal bodies. It was not the best of environments, yet the white plush slippers looked clean.

Once the rain stopped, it turned humid. We retreated to the comfort of the air-conditioned office to inspect the product. I had sweated through my shirt and had white stains on my navy polo. A return to the refrigerated office was the correct call.

The factory opened the cases and laid out thirty-six pairs of finished animal slippers. Almost all possessed defects, such as dirt stains and open stitching. They were behind schedule, and now they needed to redo everything. They called neighboring factories to find help but would have to pay a premium.

I sat with the workers, opening cases and removing problem slippers. My efforts had limited effect, but I encouraged them to stay focused. Also, the boss brought in big fans because of my presence. They helped but blew the polyester stuffing around, which attached to my sweaty skin. Despite this, I stuck it out for five hours.

They picked through the product and found enough to fulfill the shipment. Meanwhile, I hand-carried pairs for a sales meeting in Arkansas. It was quicker and safer for me to fly for eighteen hours to deliver the samples than to rely on the slow China Express mail. I stayed a few days and jumped back on the plane to The Hai. That was door-to-door service.

A few weeks later, I returned with a U.S. coworker. He wanted to visit and agreed with my prognosis. There was a reason for the low price. To get out of this mess, I pulled staff from other areas to monitor things while I pushed the agent to provide around-the-clock inspectors.

We planned to inspect the following day and stayed over. I didn't feel pressured to have dinner with the factory and looked forward to a solid night's sleep. But after I entered my room, I received a call from the front desk. They asked if I could talk to the manager. Even though I was exhausted, my curiosity pulled me downstairs.

The dude was a young guy who gave up communicating with me in English after he heard me speak Mandarin. He noticed I came in with another Westerner and wondered if we might be interested in modeling for the hotel brochure.

"It depends on where you want to take pictures."

The elevator had advertisements for the sauna, with two hairy Western blokes sitting together with towels around their waists. If he had something like that in mind, I would pass. Someone might recognize me—the movie star.

Instead of getting sweaty next to my coworker, the manager wanted us to play tennis. That didn't sound too bad, except I had only brought black brogues. I packed running gear on too many trips, only to keep it buried in my suitcase, so I left it at home. Plus, exercising while hungover was not recommended or desired.

"No problem; we can find shoes for you." This sounded interesting.

"Let me check with my friend."

I returned to my room and called him.

"Hey, the hotel wants to photograph us playing tennis. Are you game?"

"I didn't bring exercise gear."

"They said they have shoes and pants are fine. We gotta go check this out."

There was a standard court in the rear of the hotel, unoccupied and locked. The manager had to find the man with the key. Meanwhile, the health club gave us ladies' size 8, white canvas CVOs (circular vamp oxfords), just like the millions we shipped to the U.S. Once again, they cut open the shoes, and my toes stuck out as if I wore slides. They worked but made running difficult.

While we waited, the staff offered cold Tsingtao beers. They knew what would keep us around. Forty-five minutes later, the custodian returned with the key, but the wrong one. He tried different ones on his massive ring. Why would they expect anyone to wait an hour to open the gate? We stayed because it was comedy, and they supplied beer.

After many attempts, the man with the key gave up and went away. It looked as if we wouldn't play after all, but wait . . . he came back with a bolt cutter to cut the lock off. It must have been locked for a long time. I walked onto the court with my floppy footwear and put my beer down, but the manager said,

"Hold on to it and drink while you play."

That seemed unusual, but I recalled seeing previous brochures, and then it made sense. They wanted the perception of the good life, not reality. Besides, they brought more brews.

Due to not picking up a racket for two decades, my game was rusty. I tripped over my open-toe shoes a few times, but nothing disastrous, and little beer spilled. The manager required a bird's eye view picture, so someone searched for the man with the key to the storage room with the ladder. We continued to drink and practice.

When we finished, he gave us free laps on the go-cart track. They fed us ale for two hours, but if they didn't mind, neither did I. Besides, I felt good about the carting scene since I earned my stripes on the demanding tracks of PT and The Hai.

It was a shame the factory wasn't better. Because of the problems, we moved to another place. I never saw if we were front and center in the elevator or the brochure. It was an entertaining experience, anyway.

||

Between 1996 and 1999, I traveled to Wenzhou to collaborate on several projects. It was a manufacturing hotspot, especially for shoes. The first project I worked on got dropped before production. My second program was with an American agent, a change of pace from working with Hong Kong, Taiwanese, and mainland companies. Finally, I would work with somebody who understood and agreed when we had a problem, and we didn't have to drink over it unless we wanted to. What I learned was it made no difference where the agent came from. They all had the "us against them" philosophy.

My office provided a contact number for the company's owner. He was in America when I phoned, asking for the factory details, and persuaded me to delay my trip until he arrived. It would only be an initial visit, but I waited. If I couldn't see the plant, it would be a waste.

The following week, I flew to Wenzhou and looked for the other foreigner. Monty was older, balding with a sprinkle of gray, and dressed as if he'd stepped out of Brooklyn with a tailored, black, three-piece suit.

Pulling off that look in the heat and when traveling to factories was hard. He apologized for how he had talked to me over the phone because he wasn't used to dealing with knowledgeable foreigners. Like me, he was a gatekeeper of information, and his power came from his awareness of how things worked. Most lacked an understanding of manufacturing and life in the Middle Kingdom. They relied on individuals like us to interpret. What do you do when you cross paths with someone who knows things better than you? Perhaps he tried to figure that out when he met me.

Monty hustled in the shoe business on the U.S. side. His venture as an agent was in its infancy. Many individuals tried to make the leap using their contacts but crashed and burned after blowing loads of cash. He knew salesmen in our U.S. office and drummed up orders. His operation consisted of himself, a Chinese woman he hired from another trading company, and an employee he borrowed from the Qingdao factory we worked with.

He attempted to manufacture wooden slides similar to Dr. Scholl's and found a factory that took three hours to reach. When we got there, I realized we could not use the place. It resembled a cheap wood shop. There was sawdust everywhere, and a match would send it up in flames. No one cared. Guys in the woodshed had lit cigs dangling from their mouths as they walked around. I didn't know where to start. No thanks.

In the city, Monty made up for the trouble by producing a bottle of Johnny Walker at dinner. This was a welcome surprise. During this period, most restaurants still did not carry Western alcohol, but Wenzhou was rich and had things smaller towns lacked. I told him I enjoyed drinking whiskey and rarely drank it outside Shanghai or Hong Kong. He was just as happy to have someone to drink Scotch with.

We polished off the bottle over an intriguing conversation from footwear to architecture. I knew someday that my work on the Frank Lloyd Wright exhibit at the Museum of Science and Industry would be helpful. After the meal, we looked for entertainment. Wenzhou only operated karaoke and discos. He was not that guy, so I suggested bowling. Monty didn't bowl, but I convinced him it would be a suitable place to carry on drinking. He agreed, secured another bottle, and off we went. This was my first occasion bowling with a bottle of whiskey. By the fifth frame, I surrendered. Monty never bowled. He asked how I would wake up at six for my 7:30 flight. Until that point, I had only missed one.

"No matter what, I get up. I have to. It's part of my work hard, play harder MO."

"I don't think you're going to make it."

He sent me to the hotel, and I set my alarm for 5:30, a few hours away. When the alarm rang, I hit the snooze for a half-hour before rising. Sure, I felt hungover, and the easiest thing to do would be to go back to bed, but I wanted to catch the flight. I gave it a good attempt; I showered, shaved, and had everything ready to leave by 6:30. Then I did the worst thing possible: I laid down for ten minutes, which turned into a half-hour. Just before seven, I woke up. I still had a shot, as the airport was fifteen minutes away or ten with the right driver. To arrive on time, I needed to summon all of my strength to rush out in a minute, but my body said, "Let this one go."

On the desk laid a tray with eggs and toast. I forgot I had filled out the room service breakfast card. The attendant came in when I was passed out. How could I have slept through that? My passport, wallet, and cash sat in the open.

Mr. Thunder was slippin'.

Around 9 a.m., I rang Monty, but he slept. When his staff informed him I remained, he called to laugh.

"It was the whiskey and bowling. I never had an issue with *baijiu*."

He told me to come over to his office. They installed a huge AC unit and a DSL internet connection better than the hotel. That evening, we had dinner, but just beer and lots of water. No way would I miss two flights in a row. We enjoyed a wonderful time, but the business with Monty did not pan out.

The following year, I returned to work with a factory direct. They drank a *baijiu* called "*Jiugui Jiu*," translated as "Liquor for the Alcoholic." It tasted the same, but I loved the name, and it came in a bottle similar to a crumpled paper bag. I consumed so much at dinner that they gave me a case. I never partook in *baijiu* at home, so my wife gifted it. Later, the factory turned me on to the poor man's sangria with cheap jugs of California wine that showed up around this time mixed with coke, lemons, and ice. I introduced this cocktail to the factories in Fujian, and anywhere else we could get the large bottles of vino. My Western counterparts found it easier to drink, and it didn't reek like *baijiu* but left a colorful mess if regurgitated.

A year later, we left Wenzhou and ventured to the next city.

III

In 1998, I worked with a factory near Hangzhou. After visiting other workshops in the area for years, I was familiar with the terrain and looked forward to staying at the Shangri-La West Lake Hotel. It was the premier high-end resort in Hangzhou when it opened in 1984. The location could not have been envied more by the other hotel groups. Besides the view, they had a fantastic spread for breakfast with fresh juices, an egg station, croissants, muffins, cereals, etc. Compare that with the dismal food in the discount places, and then you understand why staying here was a treat. The Shangri-La turned into a beacon of luxury for weary travelers. Relaxing on the terrace, having a quiet meal overlooking the mystical lake, I felt my soul healing until I had to get back into the car.

The new workshop was in a city called Zhuji. It wasn't on my map, and I knew nothing about it. Our staff discovered the place and said it had solid management and competitive prices. We gave them a test order, and I planned a visit.

Eric found a new train line that stopped in Zhuji after three hours. That was the fastest option. At the Shanghai station, I entered through the VIP entrance to sidestep the pushing and shoving. I always wondered why they built such small entryways. All those passengers had to pass through. Avoid the main entrance at all costs. If you stood too close, you might get sucked into the wave. Cover your wallet and privates and go with the flow when squeezed tight with a hundred other sweaty bodies. Inside, you still had to squeeze through another turnstile. If I had luggage, I felt relieved when I reached the train.

But I had nobody to contend with at the soft seat VIP entrance. The lounge provided pleather sofas for seating and sold refrigerated Coca-Cola and Evian. Cold drinks showed up in more places but were still rare. They also had three-in-one hot coffee mix, a treat on frosty mornings. It was relaxing to rest on a gigantic cushy chair, smoking a cigarette and drinking an ice-cold Coke while waiting. On the other side, the hard-seat waiting rooms packed passengers in with few places to sit, no cold drinks, and plenty of boiling water.

Due to how crowded the trains were, I tried to outmaneuver the system by purchasing three seats: one for me, one for Eric, and an extra to have space for my stuff.

Once we started moving, more travelers appeared. I attempted to keep my extra seat, but it was a losing proposition. A guy argued when I said I paid for the space and would sell it to him for face value. When the conductor came by, he ordered me to give it up. My instinct was to fight, but I remained cool and saved the anger for the next time someone cut in line or told me how fat I'd become—they said they meant it in a good way.

As usual, an attendant pushed a hot drink cart through each coach, and the people standing in the aisle hovered over the individuals sitting. I was used to this after my previous experiences, but it was uncomfortable. Despite this squeezing, the woman across from me bought a flimsy cup of hot soy milk. When the attendant handed it over, the train jerked, causing a domino effect, and someone bumped her. She dumped the cup right in my lap. A bullseye! My khakis looked as if I sprang a leak, not to mention it burned. She pulled out a pocket-sized packet of tissues and replied, "Sorry." You would think such an event would set off my "bad China day clock," but I didn't get mad. I was concerned about arriving with what appeared to be a pee stain.

The factory boss, Mr. Wu, waited with his roomy Japanese sedan. He looked thirty-ish and had a sarcastic nature. Sarcasm rarely worked, so it surprised me when he used it, knowing people wouldn't "get it." Why waste time playing around unless life bored him?

Mr. Wu had risen through the ranks as many did; his father bought a government workshop, and he expanded the business. He was the public relations guy, handling the customers and officials, while his wife managed the shop. He had the dinners and late nights while she toiled in the plant. It appeared she got the raw end.

They earned serious money from companies like ours. But when you were up, grifters came for handouts. On almost every visit, I saw government cars showing up. The officials smelled the cash and wanted to share.

Once, Mr. Wu picked me up before stopping at the bank. I sat in the front of his China-produced Buick while he went in. He returned with two bundles of 100 RMB bills, not bricks, but bundles of bricks the size of phone books. He flung them into the back seat.

"What's that for?"

"I need to pay some guys."

Maybe he had lost a bet. I left it at that.

The train arrived at 10:45 a.m., close to lunch but not quite. He wanted to stay downtown and eat at the hotel, as he was uncertain how I would react to eating at his factory.

"Do you play mahjong?"

"Sure."

"Do you enjoy mahjong?"

"I'm game, but we don't have enough people."

"I have a place, and I can call friends. We can stay there and then go to lunch."

"Alright."

The mahjong parlor was on the second floor of a storefront. We entered a dark, narrow set of stairs, and Mr. Wu called for the "*fuwuyuan*," or service staff. A young girl wearing a restaurant uniform, looking as if she had just woken up, came out to see what we wanted. Mr. Wu joked and flirted with her while he told her we needed a mahjong room. She escorted us through several hallways until she stopped at a door, opened it, flicked on the light, and turned on the A/C. It had my favorite odor of mold and smoke. There was a TV for karaoke, leather sofas, and a mahjong table; not high-class like the metropolises, but ballin' for the area. Mr. Wu ordered beer and snacks while we waited. He was curious about America and otherworldly things. He planned to visit Vegas for a footwear convention and had questions. We talked for a while, but the staff never showed up with the mahjong tiles.

"They're taking a long time with the tiles."

"Did you want to play mahjong?"

"Not really,"

"Isn't this a great place to drink beer? I wanted to know if you enjoyed mahjong."

We finished a few, then headed to the best lodging in town, a three-star slice of heaven. After a hearty meal with a few more beers, we started on the road to the factory, thirty minutes away. It was longer if the construction did not favor us. Sometimes, when delayed, I got out and persuaded the cop to unblock our direction. This impressed Mr. Wu when we were stuck in a jam, and I said, "I'll handle it," exited the car, strolled to the front, and offered to untangle the bottleneck (**Rule #9**). The shock of encountering a foreigner speaking Mandarin in a rural area probably caused them to comply, and my Jedi mind tricks helped.

They had a large, red welcome banner out for me when we arrived. Mr. Wu's wife waited with the other managers and our QC. We did the obligatory tea ceremony and toured the office building.

Next, we did a complete walk-through of the workshop. I inspected the goods with Mr. Wu's wife while he attended to the government guests. Everything looked correct, except they had misspelled English letters on the screen print. They needed to open the stitching, remove the canvas on the outsole, flip it over, and print a new logo. They did that to save costs, an expensive disaster averted, and an uncomfortable topic solved before dinner. Once the production managers worked out a plan, they arranged for rework. Smaller factories had little flexibility for correcting mistakes while producing current orders. It was a juggling act that put more pressure on workers. While Mrs. Wu talked with the line managers, I approached Mr. Wu's office to tell him.

"You're right. We should not have made this mistake. We will improve. Tell me more bad things."

He was writing a self-criticism.

To commemorate our business partnership, He handed me a gift. We produced reindeer plush slippers, and he presented me with a dried deer penis, a foot long, in a glass box.

"Thanks, but I'm clueless about what to do with this."

"Put it in a large bottle of your favorite *baijiu* and drink a shot daily." Deer penis alcohol? Pecker liquor? I couldn't imagine having friends over and saying, "Hey guys, try my aged deer penis hootch. It will boost your strength!"

I assumed you could also chew on it like jerky. If I had to partake, I preferred the alcohol version. It was a clever gift, but I had no intention of nibbling on deer dong. It would end up on my shelf with the others. Trust me; I received more than a few. I wondered why individuals gave me dried penises. Were they telling me something? Whenever someone gave a shriveled-up animal member, they would say, "It's good for man." So why give it to me? Did I not look virile? I'm Mr. Thunder!

I accepted the phallus, and Mr. Wu asked me to wait in his apartment. They built their living quarters in the plant to make managing production and entertaining customers easier. They woke up, rolled out of bed, and walked the lines. Their accommodation had a spacious living room taking over the second floor. I relaxed on the couch, watching Chinese cartoons with his young son. Then we sat down at the round table for ten to eat.

They said the food outside was dirty, so they hired a maid and a chef from the top hotel (the one we just ate lunch at). Their hot water dish sanitizer reassured me about their commitment. Most restaurants didn't have that level of hygiene. They also shrink-wrapped the dishes to prevent dust from getting on them and gave everyone a protected bowl, plate, and teacup set. If they were this clean at home, they should be able to produce spotless slippers.

The chef brought plates one after the other. He cooked meat dishes and kept bringing them until told to stop. There must have been over twenty, all served family-style on enormous platters for the five of us. We had to keep up before the plates were stacked. If I liked something, I had to say so, or they would take it away to make room. Mr. Wu drank beer, but his wife drank *baijiu* with me. With fewer *ganbeis*, I ate my fill, and they had food I enjoyed.

The meals lasted for three hours, after which Mr. Wu would drive to the hotel at high speed. None of my staff would sit shotgun, but I loved the acceleration, especially at night.

To further enjoy the ride, I would fill the five CD-changer with The Doors, Led Zeppelin, AC/DC and blast it as we rode through the darkness in the countryside. There was a two-lane stretch of road with trees lining both sides for fifteen kilometers. They painted the bottoms white, which now made sense when the headlights shined on them; they acted as guardrails. We had the windows down to spread the music as we sped past. What a ride.

I checked in, thinking we had finished for the night, and said I wished to visit the factory in the morning before I left for the airport.

"When do you want to be picked up?"

"9:30,"

"Okay, I'll wait here on the sofa while you wash up."

That was perfect. I got juiced up on *baijiu,* and the wind revitalized me. It was time for round two and a chance to use my DJ skills.

Mr. Wu said, "Let's wash our hair and then drop by my friend's club."

"Let's get our hair washed" was not a suggestion I would have mentioned to my U.S. friends. In China, nothing seemed strange about it. Most places did a thorough wash using two or three shampoos and conditioners. After they rinsed, you received a head, arm, and back massage. It was the right way to nurse a hangover or sober up.

The place in Zhuji took comfort to a higher level. They had me lay on a rubber-covered slab with a sink at one end. It was so relaxing; I fell asleep, only to be woken by my own snoring.

After an hour on the slab, I felt amazing and ready.

The club was in a concrete complex with a tall iron gate. Mr. Wu honked the horn, and an old man peered through a slot. He unlocked the gate to let us in. The place looked similar to a factory dormitory, with Christmas lights lining the stairs, and reminded me of my days with the gangsters. Mr. Wu told the staff to drink with me, and I drank with his friends. I had fun playing music. Nothing was more satisfying than a "Dazed and Confused" interlude between Andy Lau songs.

The next day, I struggled to remember how I ended up in my room. Mr. Wu drove me, but I couldn't visualize walking through the lobby. We closed down the nightclub after I called it a night. I always required one more for the road, which meant another bottle or bottles needed to be opened. Then we started again because I refused to leave half-empty bottles.

I noticed I had packed my bags and laid out my clothes. Thank you, DPS. Sometimes, I would go back and iron my things so I wouldn't have to do it in four or five hours and enjoy an extra half hour of uninterrupted sleep. It was a valuable habit to have.

My flight to Hong Kong from Hangzhou was in the afternoon. We had to move. I called Eric, who said Mr. Wu would take us. He kept a room at the hotel full-time, so he didn't have to register when he stayed.

We arrived at the workshop at 10:30, giving me an hour before the workers rested.

I checked all the workshops and production before returning to Mr. Wu's apartment for lunch, where the whole thing started again. At one p.m., I nudged him to call the driver. If we got stuck in traffic, I would be out of luck. "No problem. I'll drive you."

That comforted me since he drove fast, but we drank. I hoped he was sober enough.

Before we left, Mr. Wu requested me to walk the workshop one more time to put pressure on the workers. Then we hopped into his sedan and sped off to Hangzhou. He honked and passed cars on the shoulder. I had faith in him, but he cut it close. Check-in ended forty-five minutes before the flight departed. We pulled into the airport thirty minutes before takeoff.

"No problem. I know people. Don't worry."

I was anxious. He had pull, but this would be a big ask. He walked in and came out ten minutes later and said, "Sorry, they consider Hangzhou to Hong Kong, an international flight, and the airport cannot bend the rules, but they can book you on a plane to Shenzhen."

I had a ticket from a canceled trip, so I flew there. From Shenzhen, I needed to take a taxi for an hour, wait in line for an hour to cross the land border, and another hour and a half on the train/metro to get to my doorstep. All this traveling while pulling my luggage and a deer penis.

I felt miserable standing in a mob fifty feet deep at the Luowu land crossing with a massive headache while the *baijiu* fumes escaped my body. Sometimes, the line took two hours. Things improved once they opened more crossings, but I stopped going through Shenzhen by then.

The following year, we did more business with Mr. Wu, and I set up a trip for a customer. The visit coincided with the American bombing of the Chinese embassy in Belgrade in 1999, killing three Chinese journalists. According to the Chinese government, it was intentional because America has the most advanced weaponry. During this time, I lived near the consulate and watched protestors marching through the streets. The government gave the green light for rioters to pelt the U.S. consulate with stones and eggs. They bused in groups to attack and deface other American businesses and burned a section of the consulate in Sichuan. As an American, I kept a low profile. My wife told me I should tell everyone I was Canadian, but I lacked the accent.

Despite a warning, the customer insisted on making the trip. He told me to advise the factory not to hang a welcome banner. I informed Mr. Wu, but the message did not get through. He picked us up in a huge, white van with the factory name in oversized red letters splashed across both sides. The vehicle was spacious enough to seat twelve, but we only had three. It was not subtle.

When we arrived, I didn't see a red banner, but they had placed a smaller sign with our names outside welcoming the esteemed guests from America. The van entered the complex, where the staff lined up with a TV crew from a local station! I told Mr. Wu,

"Send the news crew away so we can exit the van."

Once they left, we took the tour and finished at Mr. Wu's office, where he presented the customer with a dried deer penis. They must have kept a stockpile or a dong processing center in the back. I received another because you can never have too many.

Mr. Wu wanted to throw a big celebration at the hotel, but I suggested eating at his home to be inconspicuous. He agreed, but he also arranged to have the hotel make a lot of entrees and side dishes—a second meal. Then he sent his driver to pick up the food. We had a massive amount of fare piling up. That's when a large wooden boat arrived with a five-pound *sashimi'd* lobster, still moving. It was a favorite, but it showed up too late. We already slipped into competitive drinking. It was an overindulgent feast, and everybody got lit. We needed to check in, so I directed the party downstairs, where Mr. Wu's sedan waited. They loaded our bags, and I put *The Best of Cream* in the CD player. It was going to be a fun ride with everyone sky-high.

Something happened I hadn't expected. When we prepared to leave, Mr. Wu asked the buyer if he wanted to drive. Before I said this was a terrible idea, he agreed and got into the driver's seat. Even with all the drinking, I realized nothing good would come of this, but it was China, where the rules were bent so hard that you felt you could get away with anything if you knew the right people.

The customer was a fast driver. As soon as we turned onto the empty country lane, he put the pedal to the metal. The sedan had pickup and floated like a boat. We cruised down the village road in the darkness, passing farmers on bikes while I blasted "Sunshine of Your Love," "White Room," and "I Feel Free." We forgot about being low-key.

When we reached the town, the car in front swerved to miss a pothole. We followed too closely and rear-ended the vehicle. Mr. Wu chased us in the van. Only the customer, Eric, and I sat in the car. I didn't know what to do, so I told him to keep driving while the other guy chased. Eric called Mr. Wu, and he said, "Pull over, don't get out. We'll deal with it."

We pulled over while Mr. Wu walked past to the other car. Then he waved at us to go to the hotel, where I got a look at the damage. Most of the passenger side was dented. Mr. Wu showed up and said they had settled everything.

"No problem. Are you ready to visit the nightclub?"

He might have been fine, but it had shaken us back to reality. It was a moment of clarity, followed by more haze. Mr. Wu was okay and didn't ask for compensation, but he probably added a penny or two to the price.

The next season, business trends changed again, and we no longer did the product Mr. Wu specialized in. He disappeared into the past like other good friends. I sure missed hanging with him. He was a stand-up dude who knew how to live life to the fullest, even when stuck in a smaller town.

CHAPTER NINETEEN

SHANGHAI: LOBSTER AND CHAMPAGNE

For three years, we endured taxman harassment, unreliable TV, and frequent power outages before searching for a flat with superior services. Shanghai had blossomed into a vibrant city, but having lived outside downtown and traveling, I didn't get the full experience. I wanted to join the party. This time, my wife managed the search and found a place closer to the heart and accessible to the airport. The apartment had three bedrooms, two baths, and a large kitchen.

It checked all the boxes, and we signed the lease.

A real estate company owned our building and a complex down the street. Every other month, I walked to their office with my stacks of cash for two months' rent bulging out of my pockets (30,000 RuMBas). I paid a woman at a cubicle, watched her check each bill, and then waited for the receipt. We never talked. I showed up; she counted, and I left.

She knew me.

Since the building was a higher grade, they had sanctioned satellite TV. I no longer worried about a gust of wind blowing my two-meter dish off the roof and crashing down on "Watermelon Street." Plus, English TV became less of a necessity, with the VCD wave turning into a DVD tsunami. Stores began to sprout up around town. They did great business if foreigners lived nearby. Most of us turned into junkies and consumed them in significant quantities. Everyone had a go-to shop they swore by (I liked Movie Time and the store across the street named Better Than Movie Time). The government targeted sellers during anti-piracy campaigns, but the vendors stayed one step ahead or had good *guanxi*. Some stocked a collection of actual CDs (classical, Kenny G, and Richard Clayderman) in the front and hid the latest music and movies in a secret room. (Jade Garden's fake watch and handbag sellers pulled the same maneuver.) A guy reading the newspaper at the entrance directed you to the back, where you would find a movable wall of shelves that concealed a room or a staircase. It became another way of doing business.

Then, vendors showed up at the bars with bags of movies. And when they did, everyone looked: You never knew what they might have. I would sit at the bar, having drinks, and a DVD hawker would appear out of thin air with the latest American films for the low cost of a buck fifty each. How was that for convenience and affordability? It turned into a guilty pleasure, an addiction; I realized I had many at home in plastic wrap, but I still flipped through them.

Besides satellite TV, another selling point was the outdoor pool. It looked like a suitable place to escape the city, except for the cars honking and the air quality. The water remained blue for two weeks, and then it turned greenish. I felt fortunate to dip in twice. The following year, they reopened, but never again was the pool sky blue. Also, families moved in, and they overran it. People swam laps while others tried to learn how to paddle with floatable armbands. I gave up.

So, the pool sucked, but we had a tennis court in the back, an excellent opportunity to improve my game. If only the people in the neighborhood hadn't booked it before me. There were no other courts in the area, which made ours popular. Bookings were on a first-come basis, and my neighbors beat me out.

I finally reached the service apartment level, and the services were shitty.

We had little in walking distance besides a hair salon and a convenience store. Shanghai sprawled, so no matter where I needed to go, taxis became the proper mode. I walked for twenty minutes to catch a cab at my previous flat. Rain or shine, it was a pain in the ass. The new building had cabs on my doorstep, but then I would be stuck in traffic as the car inched towards the intersection. I lived on a designated bicycle road (some streets prohibited cycles) with hundreds of bikes going straight while vehicles attempted to turn right—an impossible situation. It was wise to walk a block, but even catching a cab at a prominent intersection turned into a battle.

When locals got wealthier, they took the bus less and taxis more, ending my monetary advantage. I fended off others hailing cars while ensuring the driver didn't clip my knees. If it rained, whoever got in first won.

The best thing about getting a car from my intersection was the drive to the Bund and my ATM. If there was no jam, it took ten minutes on the elevated highway that snaked around the Neoclassical treasures of the waterfront and down a ramp merging with other traffic. It was the most exhilarating ride in The Hai.

A few years later, the government dismantled the ramp for aesthetics, safety, or a combination. Going to my ATM was no longer a joy.

II

A benefit of modernization was the increasing amount of items from the outside. China turned into a magnet, calling everyone and everything not tied down. It attracted loads of entrepreneurs who wanted to stake a claim. The country welcomed them, adding diversity to the 1.3 billion masses. Meanwhile, the PRC grew more metropolitan and international by the day. It was an exciting time to be part of the growth. I never expected it to modernize so quickly. I knew it would, but I didn't want to face what that meant—the end of the place I knew when I arrived as a student. Ten years prior, things never changed, and now Old China had begun to disappear.

Around this period, I traveled outside of Shanghai less and worked with factories in the surrounding suburbs, such as Qingpu, Songjiang, Nanhui, and Nantong. As a result, I explored The Hai and visited as many places as possible. I wandered the streets, similar to when I lived in Hong Kong.

A favorite eatery on the north side was a French cafe owned by a fifty-something Japanese dude. While riding in a taxi, the name *Champs-Élysées* caught my eye. But, I worried it would be a local attempt at Western cuisine because of the location between a moped repair shop and an industrial wholesaler, which is not where one would expect to find a French brasserie. I took a chance and stopped by. Inside, they jazzed the place up with pink wallpaper, gold and gaudy decorations, shiny railings, and bright lights, giving the tiny restaurant a yellow glow. The wait staff were mature Shanghainese women with big beehive hairdos, wearing embroidered qipaos. The boss sported a white tuxedo.

It felt like a David Lynch film.

The beehive ladies remained near your table, waiting for you to request something, while the boss waltzed around and asked if you enjoyed your meal. He aimed to ensure all patrons had a splendid time. No doubt the cooking tasted better than in the hotels, and the cost was cheaper. He would have expanded his base if he had changed the location and the menu to English and Chinese from French with Japanese. The beehive ladies broke the language barrier and translated for the locals while I attempted to recall something from the French summer school course I completed.

The restaurant was a significant discovery, but it shut down.

That was how things went—a new venue opening today and another closing tomorrow. When a place opened, I tried to dine there when everything was fresh. It might be gone if I waited, or they may have given up on serving their best.

Surprisingly, it wasn't the end for this Japanese entrepreneur. A year later, I uncovered a French cafe with the same name, closer to my apartment in a neighborhood populated by Japanese expats. I entered, and it was the same dude; he remembered me and gave me a tour. Now, it looked dark, modern, and sleek. He had a cigar lounge ten years too early—before cigars were a thing. The beehive ladies were gone, except for one who seemed tied to the boss.

He handed me a VIP card and welcomed me back. I wanted to return, but the increased price for smaller portions put me off.

Plus, every week, new restaurants entered the market. Unless it was exceptional, I never returned. When I attempted a second meal at the French joint, it was closed. Locals did not frequent Western restaurants enough, and the mobile expat crowd could not sustain many privately owned startups.

It was challenging for these early entrepreneurs.

Another of my favorites was a *teppanyaki* joint called Jurassic. They cooked on rectangular, flat grills in front of you, similar to Benihana. It was all-you-could-eat, the first I came across outside the hotels. I ordered meats, seafood, and others from the menu; they cooked it and brought more if desired. For a little extra, they served bottomless jugs of draft.

I took the factory guys and my staff here. Despite the lack of *baijiu*, they got hooked.

Chuan took a back seat to this dining trend.

We weren't the only ones that enjoyed this place. Word spread, and the wait grew. Even if I snagged a seat, it took too long to receive service. The hassle caused me to stop going.

Soon, other all-you-can-eat-and-drink Japanese restaurants opened. They had the same formula; you ordered anything off the menu until satisfied for one price. It was the greatest arrangement. We paid 150–200 RuMBas (about $20–30) a person for unlimited *teppanyaki* steak, seafood, *sashimi*, and dozens of others, plus all the *sake* and beer you demanded. It was impossible to figure out how they made money, especially when expats walked in and engaged in a three-hour feast. We joked they would ban us from our favorite joints since, as a group, we pushed things to the absolute limit, engorging ourselves and then taking the party to the next venue to do the same.

Similarly, I ate at an all-you-can-eat Spanish tapas place with a drinking buddy. The restaurant looked locally owned, run by someone who had been to Spain. They had a set lunch with a glass of wine for 100 RMB or endless tapas and Spanish wine for 150. The wiser choice was obvious. Before we started, I double-checked to see if they had made a mistake.

"We can order anything, as much as we want, and as much wine as we can drink, for 150 ($20) a person?"

"Yes."

The regular price for the wine ran 150 a bottle.

"Are you sure? We drink a lot, and we'll take our time."

"No problem. Stay as long as you wish."

She gave us an entire bottle, thinking that would satisfy us. We drank five and stayed for five hours. I would have remained longer if my wife hadn't called me. During the whole time, no one else came in. I paid the dinner price of 200 RMB ($27), but we got the better deal. That's what happened when expats showed up at an unlimited place because anything non-Chinese was pricey, and we were beasts.

That Spanish place closed two months later and transformed into a Thai restaurant.

If I didn't desire Japanese, I headed to the Brazilian barbecues (*churrascarias*) that popped up in the mid-'90s. Now, we could consume bountiful amounts of quality beef for 200 RMB (the price of a steak in the hotels). Brazilian BBQ became so popular that the restaurants multiplied, the price dropped, and the cuisine got more local. Others followed suit with Indian, Thai, German, Irish, Mexican, American, Korean, Vietnamese, French, and Italian, all having their own explosion of restaurants once one opened. This dining was new to the city. One day, we had Chinese and KFC, and then the selection expanded. I tried them all. My coworkers joked that I wouldn't always find the cheapest factory, but I could direct you to mouth-watering Indian or a taqueria. That may sound strange, but having another option from Chinese was energizing. Anytime I discovered a restaurant, I got excited.

The most significant contributor to my weight gain besides the business trips had to have been the *churrascarias*. Fresh cuts of large pieces of salted and garlicky beef, sausages, pork, lamb, chicken wings, perhaps a small salad, and rice washed down with pitcher after pitcher of draft or red wine. I ate bizarre and less-than-filling food (or just liquid) on the road. Whenever I had quality nosh, like at the BBQs, I overate. I felt rotund when I walked away from the table.

No tiny wafer-thin mint, thank you.

Japanese *teppanyaki* and Brazilian BBQ were the scenes of many excessive feasts. Still, if you really wanted to experience the over-the-top living, you had to go to brunch. In Chicago in the '80s, we went to brunch in the city; the Hilton on South Michigan was my favorite. They had grand ballrooms, art deco design, and a harp player to further the vibe. The Hilton supplied loads of shrimp and lobster on ice, caviar, a prime rib cart, etc. They served free-flowing champagne starting from noon, and I consumed a few glasses. Normally, I filled my Saturday nights with teenage trouble and whatever alcohol we scored. On Sunday, I craved that bubbly.

When I arrived in Shanghai, the five-star hotel next to me had one of the few brunches, but it was a dull affair with overcooked nosh sitting in catering pans for $30 a person. Around this time, five-star hotels celebrated Christmas and Easter. After spending the holiday in Beijing eating hotpot alone, I anticipated my first Christmas buffet. The day before, I toured factories and stayed in Nanjing at The Jinling. They had a Christmas Eve buffet, but locals booked it out. I was probably the only person who celebrated the holiday but couldn't get a seat. Instead, I headed to KFC and secured fried chicken to eat in my room. It was a letdown, but I had tickets to the Christmas gala in The Hai when I returned.

The Xmas parties were ballroom affairs, packed with folks who lacked an understanding of the meaning of the holiday beyond recognizing a fat white guy with a beard wearing a red suit. They served Chinese food, and I only received a glass of beer. A local band performed Mandarin pop and love songs instead of Christmas classics. Between song sets, the MCs entertained with jokes. I wasted $100 a person and stopped going.

Thankfully, the Easter celebration was a straightforward eating and drinking affair. I first tried the Hilton (old habits), which felt similar to what I would have found outside China.

Years later, I noticed more hotels offered brunches with champagne. Most weekends, I detoxed and ignored the call to get sloppy on a

Sunday. That changed when the Ritz Carlton opened in 1998. I woke up one Sunday and thought,

"There must be a fantastic brunch in a five-star hotel somewhere, right? It's 1998!"

I flipped through the Shanghai entertainment magazines to see what the city offered and chose the Ritz. Brunch was not in fashion, and half of the tables sat empty. Months later, more travelers showed up, and locals got hip to the scene. By then, the price had increased ($70 a person), and the wait extended to two weeks or more. It didn't matter. I had transformed into an addict and searched for ways to partake in the three-and-a-half-hour booze-filled extravaganzas.

Drinking on a Sunday was a great way to smooth out the night before. Then I had a decision to make: Do I have two glasses, stop, pick up a DVD, and sober up, or carry the party forward, delaying the sobering until Monday, the beginning of a business trip and more drinking?

I choose the latter.

Brunch turned into the ultimate excess. I traveled and lived on the mainland to the extent that I appreciated these overindulgences. I got excited about a can of soup two years ago.

Things were better.

As foreigners multiplied and China grew wealthier, the level of gluttony rose. Every restaurant, hotel, and entertainment establishment attempted to be more outlandish than the last: excess on top of excess. But in 1998, the Ritz was the place. Not only did they serve free-flowing Moet but also Maine lobster on the cold seafood bar. Maine lobsters!

I had lobster in Putian at a large trade company, "*Weiya*," end of the year dinner. The server put the crustacean on the lazy Susan and squirted mayonnaise all over it. I passed.

There was no mayo at the Ritz, just beautiful, bright red compatriots from Maine with meat white as snow, waiting to be removed and dipped into drawn butter. In addition, they laid out a proper salad bar with something besides Thousand Island dressing. Locals still avoided raw veggies, and finding a pleasing spread turned into a bigger deal than you might expect.

To get the first pick of the claws and tails, I arrived when the cafe opened at 11:30. When they replenished the trough, there would be a mad dash. I preferred to select mine before rush hour. Then, I sat back and consumed a bottle or two until it closed at three.

Even with the larger crowds, the Ritz had to stay ahead of the pack by offering delicacies, such as a *foie gras* station. I lined up and picked my piece of goose liver while the chef *flambéd* it with Cognac. It was so rich; I felt guilty but couldn't stop.

Damned if you do and damned if you don't.

Having gorged myself for most of the afternoon, I stumbled towards the taxi stand after grocery shopping at the finest supermarket in the same complex. Imagine how surprised I was to walk up to the line, and Luciano Pavarotti, the man himself wearing a Fedora and his trademarked scarf, exited a car and entered the Ritz. I watched him perform in Hong Kong and paid $300 to be twelve rows from the stage six months ago. Now, he stood right in front of me.

That was The Hai.

I spent countless afternoons at that brunch, but as time passed, my wife no longer saw the novelty of eating expensive meals and watching me continue the party. I resisted, protesting that other expats drank off a heavy Saturday night by getting into worse trouble than an afternoon of champagne. Case in point, we had lunch on a Sunday at a Mexican cantina. Two foreign dudes and a woman sat at a high top in the bar next to the dining area and were deep into the two-for-one margarita pitcher special. Halfway through our meal, I noticed the girl giving a guy a hand job at the table. She thought nobody saw them, but they entertained anyone who glanced in their direction. People did double takes to confirm a foreign woman was giving a dude a hand job in a Mexican restaurant on a sunny Sunday afternoon. Yep.

I overheard the manager, a foreigner, talking to the bartender, saying he refused to go over there. He gave them a few minutes to finish, but they kept going. The girl got tired and said it loud enough for us to hear. The manager sensed an opportunity and walked over, trying to keep a straight face when telling them hand jobs were prohibited. They were oblivious that everyone had shared the moment. The guy zipped up and entered the single male/female toilet. The girl followed. No one could use the restroom, so the manager kicked them out. Yes, there were many stupid activities to do, but I would never use this example. I didn't want Debbie to associate Sunday boozing with hand jobs in Mexican restaurants.

We agreed she would allow me to go on special occasions for many more years, long enough to make it to two of the newest additions, The Westin Bund (opened in 2002) and The Meriden (2006).

The Westin Bund became the hottest brunch in Shanghai for most of the 2000s. I had business associates who ensured they reached The Hai on Saturday to hit the banquet on Sunday. This was no regular feast. It transformed into a gala of Roman proportions. Nero himself would have been proud. The hotel's first floor showcased an indoor courtyard with tables between square pools of water. They looked glass-like, almost on the same level as the floor tiles. It was only a matter of time before someone stepped in, and they jumped out right away, too embarrassed to let anyone notice. A few trudged to the other side, numb from the booze, which flowed in bountiful amounts. Not only did they have champagne, but they would give you your own bottle if you asked. Why not? They provided an array of alcohol selections, including draft beer, a premium hard liquor bar, and a *caipirinha* station. Not enough? They also stocked a collection of wines and distributed cocktails, all part of the meal. The chefs cooked an impressive spread of international cuisines, but it was secondary to the liquor.

This was expat living at its finest.

To ensure parents could imbibe without fishing their kids out of the pools, they operated a kids' club to sign your ankle-biters in and pick them up in three hours. The hotel supplied hot dogs, cartoons, and cotton candy. They would be preoccupied for days.

The Meridian had a satisfying food lineup with free-flowing booze, now standard for great brunches. Like the Westin, they had a kiddie corner outside the eating area, and I could monitor my kids while getting shit-faced on champagne and vodka. If you showed up at brunch with a hangover, you drank more. But here, a few young ladies dressed in nurse outfits walked from table to table, giving "shots" for the pain. They resembled strippers, but nobody complained. The nurses used large syringes (no needle) filled with chicken soup, cocktails, or straight liquor. They squirted the liquid into paper cups or in your mouth. A couple of guys talked them into sitting on their laps while administering the cure.

It was a family brunch, but it seemed okay because things often looked amiss.

Sometimes, it was the old man on a bicycle with a refrigerator strapped to the back leaning to the opposite side to balance while he peddled or the young "nurse" squirting a cocktail into your mouth while you had lunch with your family and in-laws.

It seemed surreal but fine. It wasn't the type of thing you would do in your own country, but in China, you ignored it or accepted it as TIC (This Is China). And in China, things weren't supposed to be the same.

After three hours of champagne and French fare, I pushed through the revolving door into the crowded streets again. One minute, I sat in the lap of luxury, and the next, I strolled among the masses. I wondered if the initial wave of foreigners arriving more than a century ago experienced this emotion; inside the old clubs and hotels of the Bund, they had a grand time; outside, locals struggled.

The only times I crossed over the river to Pudong were to send Debbie to her dormitory and to visit factories. I never ventured there for kicks until the Jin Mao Tower(JMT) opened.

They started construction in 1994 and completed it five years later. Before the JMT, the Portman Ritz was the tallest building at 541 feet; the JM Tower blew that away at 1,380. The Grand Hyatt took the top thirty floors with a lobby on the fifty-fourth and a high-end buffet. I didn't head there for the food; I went for the wine.

As I spent more time in The Hai, my tastes improved with China's. Instead of going bowling after drinking beer and *baijiu* at the Chuan, I made the trek across town (an hour in traffic) to the Jin Mao to drink wine. I invited my guys because sitting in the cafe and consuming bottles by myself would look pathetic.

I downed chilled Sauvignon Blanc like water after slamming *baijiu*. This was an outstanding venue with an unparalleled view. We smoked and drank for three or four hours, stopping at my limit of four bottles. At nighttime, we carried on to another joint for dinner, or I would have to return home when my wife called.

I shared my wine club with her once, and she enjoyed the view but didn't appreciate the $300 I spent and the all-day drinking. It became difficult to turn off when I returned to civilian life. I had to feed the beast.

Later, I no longer invited her and hid my habit until it got restricted. No worries, the party continued somewhere else.

Shanghai opened like a flower, and the fun had just begun.

III

When I arrived in 1995, there were few activities besides nursing a hangover and doing it again. I didn't know anyone outside of my staff and my girlfriend. I needed to expand my social circle. That happened when I saw a post for the Shanghai Hash House Harriers on the bulletin board. I enjoyed running on the Hash in Hong Kong, so this looked promising. The group gathered on Sunday, downstairs from my hotel. All I had to do was board the bus.

They set an 8K in the countryside, followed by loads of beer and swimming to cool off. Shanghai developed and expanded, but most suburbs were farmland. Fifteen minutes outside of downtown was rural.

I expected to join every weekend until they asked me to step outside after dinner because of my cigarette habit; I wasn't welcome. Cigars were fine, but no tobacco sticks—pure prejudice! It showed me I didn't belong, so I gave up and took my drinking elsewhere.

Five years later, my wife came across an advertisement for the Hash. They celebrated their 500th run. Not knowing I had a history, she pushed me to join to prevent me from attending brunch.

"It will be good for you to exercise and meet other foreigners."

I lived in The Hai for five years, knowing nobody. I had no time to make regular friends when traveling, and foreigners I met rarely ventured beyond the hotel or the bar. The longer I stayed, the less I had in common with recent arrivals or the service apartment crowd. This was clear when I joined the American Chamber of Commerce. After a *baijiu* and an exotic food-filled trip, I would attend the chamber dinners. No one I talked to experienced similar situations. I was a product guy who didn't work for a Fortune 500 company—not a model networking target. Members focused on making connections that would spring them to the next level. When I handed out my name card and said what I did, most walked away to find someone who worked for GE or GM. But joining the chamber came with benefits. Through my membership, I ate breakfast with President Clinton and Madeleine Albright, shared a table with Sam Donaldson, drank happy hour cocktails with Al and Tipper Gore, and met Hillary Clinton, Michael Dell, Mayor Richard Daley, Kareem Abdul-Jabbar, and Moses Malone. In the U.S., I wouldn't have had those opportunities.

"Hash House Harriers? I know all about those guys. I'm not interested if they are the same people as five years ago. If they are like the Hash in Hong Kong, you do not want me to join."

She didn't believe me and wanted to check it out—a big mistake.

The management team (mismanagement) happened to be a fresh group. Only one person from before ran. She remembered me and asked why I had never returned. It was a single guy who complained.

I missed out on five years of running but not on five years of drinking.

This mob of about twenty-five foreigners and a dozen locals were fun-minded folks. Every Sunday at 3 p.m., we showed up at a location to run, followed by a circle lasting thirty minutes to over an hour. Each Hash had their own formalities. Some made a simple toast with a sip from your own can; others poured the drinks into common drinking vessels, pisspots, bedpans, or buckets.

If you received a down-down, you walked into the center to drink your penalty while the rest sang a quick song. It was only beer, and someone cleaned the pots beforehand, but it disturbed anyone passing by.

"Why would foreigners be drinking out of pisspots?"

"They really are crazy."

We tried to pick locations away from pedestrian traffic because gatherings in China turned into magnets for the police, especially during sensitive days. But sometimes, it was impossible to avoid the interest of the locals. If near a major street, people on motorbikes stopped to observe. There had to be something special happening whenever a crowd formed, and they remained to watch. Others craved our empties. If more than one collector showed up, they fought. But all was okay until a cranky neighbor rang the police to control the unruly *laowai*. On arrival, they sought out a local female to harass.

"Your foreign friends are causing a public disturbance, and they should disperse. They may not drink out of pisspots!"

They warned us, and we retreated to the restaurant. Other times, they attempted to arrest the women. Once, they called for backup and a police van. We had done nothing wrong. But sitting at the station answering questions was not how I planned to spend the evening. We entered the restaurant, grabbed our bags, and escaped out the backdoor. A few thought they could reason with the coppers, like an expat who just arrived and spoke a little Chinese, to each their own. While they talked away, I enjoyed cold beers on the bar street.

After the circle, we ate dinner at a cheap restaurant in groups of ten. If a table ran low on brews, they started a chorus of "*Mei you pijiu, Mei you pijiu* (no beer)," and ale would appear. It was the job of the Beer Master to ensure each table had plenty of 20oz bottles that we chilled in large garbage cans.

We sat at round tables and competed to see who could be the loudest. Regularly, someone started tapping the glass lazy Susan with the bottom of a beer bottle until everyone did it in unison.

"Boom, crack, boom, crack."

It made an ear-shattering sound when the entire table tapped the glass. It also pissed off the owners and any non-Hashers. Twice, I watched the lazy Susan shatter. Those joints did not welcome us back, but we had thousands of places willing to accept thirty hungry and thirsty individuals on a Sunday evening.

Things sometimes got out of hand, but most members were respectful. People needed to let off steam from whatever bothered them. When we gathered at two-thirty to stretch, we were civilized expats such as general managers of hotels, business leaders, teachers, and engineers, ready for a healthy (don't think about the air) jog through the streets. When we finished the meal, we transformed into a mob of crazed alcoholics, wondering where to go next. The choice was Jululu, the only place active on a Sunday.

Julu Street had about ten small pubs squeezed into a one-block area. Some were standard watering holes, while others employed gals to push drinks for tips. Inside, they were less obtrusive, but you had more than a few working girls tugging on your shirt as you sauntered from the corner to the bars. They aimed to get the first dig. With two dozen boozing punters like us, it became the perfect place to continue. For the pubs, we solved the problem of a slow night.

The group would splinter into individual bars of choice until reaching a final resting point at a joint called Nice Time, run by a guy named "Hot." It was a tiny place with only two staff, and I handed them music to play like Fatboy Slim's "The Rockafeller Skank" and House of Pain in between beers and shots of Jager. The crowd got smaller as folks disappeared to avoid a last shot. Time flew by while inside the dark pub until my wife dragged me out.

It was an excellent way to spend Sunday but a lousy start to Monday.

When Jululu lost its luster, we moved to Maoming Road in the center of town. The atmosphere on Maoming took debauchery to a higher level. There were bars/discos on both sides, and partygoers spilled out onto the pavement, drinking, dancing, and fighting. Beggars walked and crawled, wanting your RuMBas. Guys with monkeys hoped to receive your change. Children sold flowers to drunks. Prostitutes did business in the open. Meanwhile, the police strolled by, doing nothing.

Maoming was not the China you expected.

The undisciplined behavior increased with the injection of wealth and the importation of worldwide partygoers. Everybody had a plan to strike it rich by opening a business, a restaurant, or a bar. It seemed there was no end to the possibilities. It was only a matter of time before you made it, or so people thought. And they arrived in droves.

In the '90s, China longed for foreigners to come. Besides tour groups, only a select collection of general managers and CEOs made the journey. Adventurers were few. That changed in the 2000s. Now, it became hip to be in The Hai, and partygoers with no ties to the country linguistically or otherwise dropped everything and bought a ticket for the ride. Every time I wandered out at night, it amazed me how far individuals pushed the limit without regard for the culture. I was guilty of Americanizing my life with my love for music and the Colonial, but I remained respectful and appreciated where I lived. The recent arrivals came for the party. The government appeared okay with this as long as it stayed in one area. Eventually, the immorality and noise got to be too much and tarnished the image Shanghai wanted. They expunged the fun from Maoming while extinguishing the smaller bar streets. But until then, we added to the craziness.

I ran with the Hash for the next ten years. It was a splendid opportunity to hang with foreigners and to travel to places I would never have seen. Every week, someone volunteered to set a run from a different location. Even if I knew the area, I discovered something new. Some started the run from their place of work, like a runner who arranged events from the toilet factory he managed. A few worked for European consulates and held the Hash from the turn of the century villas they occupied. I'm sure their home countries would have objected. Others used their gated communities in Pudong, paid for by their companies. The best city trails guided us through the alleys of old Shanghai and the Bund. If you saw people running on Sunday reciting "On On," that was the Hash.

One of my favorite runs ended with a jump—a bungee jump. It was my second time; if others found the nerve, I had to do it, too. They were the same guys I jumped with in Taiwan. Unlike my first over a river, this one was from the rafters of the Shanghai Stadium. We took an elevator as far as possible and walked to the roof's edge. The worst part was the moment before when I glanced down and speculated if they connected the bungee correctly.

My wife objected and stayed home. She couldn't understand why foreigners wanted to get drunk and do dangerous things.

"We can't help ourselves."

As the Hash grew, it splintered into subgroups like mid-week runs, out-of-town runs, Saturday runs, male-only runs, female-only runs, and Pudong runs. I lost count. I joined the out-of-town Tai Ping Hash, the Saturday Drunken Dragon, the Pudong Full Moon, Sunday Hash, and the men's Hash called The DOGS.

The out-of-town runs were a superb opportunity to leave the city, but we had to pass through traffic. Sometimes, we spent five or six hours on the bus for a one-hour run. Also, a coach of individuals who drank all day stopped for piss breaks. When there was no toilet, the driver pulled over. They refused to stop if we reached Shanghai municipality as it was an elevated road with nowhere to whiz except on the barrier wall. You could get away with that in the '90s, but not later.

A group of foreigners coming back from an F1 event outside the city forced their driver to stop on the elevated road. Videos and pictures of them peeing in a line went viral. Locals got mad and fined them for defacing public property.

I grew tired of the antics of some on the Hashes. The Hai changed, too. It became more rigid, controlled, and anti-foreigner. Before, locals admired us; we were "rich" and preferred, but now we had turned into poor inferiors who came to seek a fortune and live parasitic lives off the fruits of locals. Chinese stopped looking at us as walking dollar signs but as a scourge that should be removed. The Middle Kingdom no longer had its door open to everyone, only those with something they needed. It was the end of an era.

IV

It was hard for people to relate to my experiences, and I recommended they visit. Friends discussed trips over drinks only for those plans never to materialize. It was easy to say you would go to China, but few did.

A group of mates visited during Chinese New Year, the worst time, considering most places were closed. That trip coincided with the Super Bowl, and they experienced how we enjoyed the game by showing up at a pub at 4:30 a.m. on a Monday for a prime seat. We downed Bloody Marys until our stomachs could handle something more potent, around the first quarter. After that, we threw back beers, Jager, and whiskey until noon or dinner. We watched it at Big Bamboo, a popular sports bar. Instead of the half-time show, they had scantily clad dancers on the tables. That became the highlight for my friends.

When someone came to visit, the amount of alcohol we poured down our throats shocked them. They surrendered while my expat friends and I kept going. We were pros.

One classmate from college talked about flying out.

"Dude, I'm coming out there."

"Sure, I'll take you on a tour, the finest you could ever have. You just need to get there."

I grew accustomed to weak promises and paid little attention until he called me out of the blue and said he had worked it out. He used frequent flier miles and had to circle the globe but ended up in Beijing.

"Great, I'll fly there and take you to a few cities. Then you can leave out of Shanghai. All I need is your arrival info, and I will wait for you outside of customs."

"Just in case, give me your address in Shanghai so I can find you if something happens."

"No need. It's too complicated. Make sure you're on the plane."

I planned on making him sweat. Nothing intimidated people more than arriving in China, seeing the sea outside the glass doors, and everything written in Chinese. I had a similar feeling when I showed up eight years earlier. Now, I replaced the shock with readiness to deal with the crowds.

On the day my friend Duane landed, I traveled to Beijing and checked in at the same three-star hotel in the Qianmen Hutong area. Then, I took a bus to the airport and waited. I watched him come out and be attacked by taxi pimps. I could sense his fear as he wandered, looking worried, until I tapped him on the shoulder.

He was glad to see me.

We dropped off his stuff, and even though he suffered from jet lag, I insisted we head out. Since my last trip, many things had changed, and I wished to reacquaint myself with the city. Sanlitun Bar Street was our starting point.

"Beijing is more restricted than Shanghai. I don't expect a wild nightlife, but we can check it out."

The street looked active, with some clubs overflowing. We selected a lively venue and ordered two bottles. There appeared to be a problem with the exhaust, causing noxious air from the kitchen to be blown inside. We escaped with the others and found a guy lying on the sidewalk with torn clothes and bleeding. A circle formed while three guys beat the shit out of him. They hit him with anything within reach, including an empty keg. "Bong," right on his head, and no one stopped it. It was entertainment for the crowd, a feeding frenzy. Duane watched with shock.

"Dude, Beijing is rough. People don't get the shit kicked out of them like this in Brooklyn."

I asked an officer if he would step in. He ignored me, so I returned to the fight. One of the guys approached me and reached for my bottle, but I turned. Duane was not fast enough. The dude snatched his and broke it on the bloody guy's head. Chinese beer bottles were weak and sometimes exploded when too warm or cold. But it had to hurt. I asked Duane,

"Why did you give him your bottle to hit that guy?"

"How did I know he would do that?"

"Well, you have to be ready for anything. This is the wild, wild West or East."

The bottle seemed too much for the po-po. They broke it up and booted the bloody dude down the street. They kicked him like a dog! It sucked for him.

We visited more bars, but the scene lacked the same vibe as The Hai, so we left.

For the next two days, we toured the famous sites. It was my sixth trip to The Wall and my countless trip to the palace. They never disappointed, except for being more crowded. Local tourism took off, and I missed the years when people stayed home.

Then, we flew to Xian to check out the Terra-cotta Warriors. It was my second visit, and I knew my way around. Inland cities did not change as fast as the coastal ones. It was possible to be familiar after being away for years. While in Xian, I introduced Duane to a favorite lamb dish, *yang rou pao mo*—the most famous dish in Xian besides lamb skewers. The restaurant gave a hard, circular bread, the circumference of a CD, and a large bowl. You tore the bread into tiny pieces, after which a server retrieved it and returned with lamb soup. Long ago, people ate *yang rou pao mo* before a journey through the desert. The hard bread acted like a sponge, filling their stomachs for days. Duane enjoyed it, but it backed him up. By the time he broke through the impasse, he got sick of me mentioning how travelers ate the dish before long trips through the desert.

But now he knew I told the truth.

Next, we headed to Chengdu, Sichuan, the Southwest part. A few months ago, a classmate from Beida tracked me down. He managed a factory in Leshan, two hours south of Chengdu, living the same movie star life I led. This was an opportunity to return to my spicy Mecca and catch up with him.

We checked into the Traffic Hotel, the low-end traveler's oasis I had stayed at, then hit the streets searching for kick-ass food. It was my fourth visit, and I had a spot to go for chili oil dumplings and *ma po dou fu*. I ate my fill (Duane sat on the bench), then we hopped into a taxi, and I said,

"Take us someplace fun."

The driver drove away from the city until the darkness swallowed us. Duane got concerned we were going be robbed and dumped.

"It's too much trouble to mess with foreigners. The worst that will happen is he'll charge a hefty meter fee. Let's see where he's going."

I also got concerned but refused to tell him. Not long after, I detected lights in the distance that appeared to be a karaoke; it turned out to be a massage parlor. The steam room sounded good after the hard traveling and drinking. It might also help Duane digest the *yang rou pao mo* that caused him discomfort. I had the driver wait (**Rule #20**) for a quick exit if necessary.

This place had facilities similar to the YMCA, with steam and dry saunas to sweat out the booze. Inside the shower room, an old man used knives to slice dead skin off your feet for 10 RMB. I got that done while Duane passed out on a massage table. Later, I woke him to return to the bar scene. He had plenty of time to sleep after the pub crawl. We must go, go, go. It was my anxious nature.

After sweating it out in the steam room, I took a quick shower before getting dressed. While I faced the wall, letting the water rain down on me, I caught Duane standing next to me. The room was lit, with no separation between the water pipes coming out of the wall. Besides us, a few old guys walked around naked. There was more privacy in prison.

I glanced over at Duane and noticed a guy behind him, aggressively soaping up his ass. Duane put his hands on the wall as if he was being frisked.

"Dude, what the hell are you doing?"

"I don't know, man. I thought it was part of the deal," he said in a high-pitched voice, like someone who got caught doing something they shouldn't be.

"What deal? Do you see anyone soaping up my ass?"

"That guy rubbed your feet with towels, and I figured this was part of the deal."

"I still have no idea what deal you're talking about. Scraping dead skin from my feet is different from SOAPING UP YOUR ASS! You could always say, NO!"

"I didn't know. It's a foreign country and all."

I've visited a few saunas but never had an experience like this. Some toilets in the karaoke had over-ambitious bathroom attendants who snuck up from behind to give you a shoulder massage when at the urinal. I found that to be infringing and told them no thanks.

Here, I helped Duane thank the guy for whatever service he was supplying. Perhaps it was dude night at the sauna, or we had chosen the wrong one.

A day later, my friend Jack picked us up in his jeep; we drove down to Leshan and headed to the best three-star. He married a local gal who ran a bar, and they became friendly with the cops. Jack invited them to dinner. He selected an open-front hotpot place on the way to the bar street off a dirt road. I saw nothing I craved on the menu. They had lots of animal parts such as intestines, stomach, and liver, but they didn't have shaved lamb. I hated it when a restaurant only had innards. This was Sichuan hotpot, not Beijing Mongolian.

We drank beer until the police showed up, then switched to *baijiu*. The top cop was the most boisterous. It thrilled him to be eating with two Mandarin-speaking *laowai*. Jack mentioned we studied at Beida with Big Mountain. He concurred it helped to start conversations.

When dinner ended, we arranged to relocate the party to Jack's wife's joint. The top cop wanted me to ride shotgun in the police car. The nightclub was only ten minutes down the road, but we got liquored up. I asked him if he was good, and he said, "Do you want to drive?"

I wasn't stupid enough to say yes to driving a police car while lit, so I gave him the honor.

We sang and drank with the cops until the early hours, and then Jack sent us to the hotel. It turned into a fun evening. I preferred to stay, but we had a schedule.

The following morning, we returned to Chengdu and flew to Fujian to experience some factory meals, followed by karaoke with Zhang Bo and the QC posse. I wanted Duane to witness how much of a karaoke star I was. In front of the darkly lit dancefloor, I sang "Don't It Make My Brown Eyes Blue," my best song at that place. It was a better choice than "Billie Jean." And, of course, I sang Mandarin and Taiwanese for the ovation.

Duane was beat and didn't want another drink when we reached The Hai.

"How do you continue to do this week after week?"

"I guess it's in my blood. Sometimes it kicks my ass, but I'm back in the game a day later. No other way to do it."

It was one hell of an introduction.

V

After establishing my special ability, friends requested me to be the best man at weddings to manage heavy consumption, similar to mine. I became the best man at four ceremonies, and due to my language skills, I made speeches to entertain the Chinese relatives. Hell, Louis, the owner who refused my entrance, asked me to be the best man at his wedding. Dig that! I loved a grand party, and his blowout occurred at the Four Seasons. He fitted me for a traditional Chinese suit. It turned into an expensive affair.

I also attended Paul's wedding in Australia in 2000. Initially, I planned to pass because flying to Brisbane for a banquet seemed a bit much, but Paul reminded me I flew to Tasmania to join a Hashing event in February of the same year. If I could go that far to drink and run, I should be able to attend his wedding. He had a point. I booked a trip with an American guy I worked with. We aimed to travel and hang around the Gold Coast for a few days. That sounded amazing, considering the non-existence of a similar thing in China.

We rented a car, and Steve took up the challenge of driving on the wrong side, similar to Hong Kong. On our way out of customs, we bought extra-large bottles of Blue Label Johnny, Jameson, and Absolut at duty-free to consume as we attempted to locate perfectly cooked steaks. In China, most beef came from Australia; we assumed it would be easy to find huge fillets of quality meat.

Everyone indicated a place to enjoy a great steak, but none had prime, thick fillets. We even stopped by a shop that sold grills, asking for advice. Each time, we were left unsatisfied and moved on to the next place until we gave up and stopped at a Mexican restaurant. That was a HUGE mistake, and we walked out. What were we thinking?

A good steak was not in our future, so we hit the bars with our excessive expat boozing habits. We both missed the variety of food and beverages and prepared to devour all in our path. The bars had all sorts of ales on tap—excellent stuff, and I wanted to try each. It was relieving to consume an alternative drink besides *baijiu*. One pub had a breath-analyzing machine to measure alcohol content before driving. We competed to out-drink each other to determine the highest score. Yeah, we turned into wild beasts roaming free.

Before the trip, I had problems with Steve. He had shown increasing animosity towards me, and those feelings came out after hitting the bottle. Paul questioned if it was a good idea for us to travel together, drinking heavily. I said we would be fine, and we were. Steve was okay until his inner Mr. Hyde appeared.

The day before the wedding, we checked into a posh hotel and joined the others. We spent the afternoon with them before the party moved to a different bar. I accompanied them while Steve returned to the hotel. He had too much and tapped out. When the wedding party called it a night, I grabbed a large sub from the pub to take back to the room I shared with Steve.

I got back around eleven and saw him scanning through the phone book.

"What are you looking for? Ordering a pizza? I bought a sub we can share."

"No, I'm looking at escort services."

"You might need to get a separate room. I want to sleep."

"Do you think you're better than me?"

"I don't know what you're talking about. We have to rise soon for the all-day wedding in a few hours—the reason we're here."

"You always think you're better than me."

Mr. Hyde had arrived at an inconvenient time. I felt good, but he looked angry. I said,

"You have a problem with me and think you're so tough. Why don't we see how tough you are? Let's sit at the desk and finish that bottle of whiskey, shot for shot, and see who is the last man standing."

In hindsight, that was the wrong thing to say. I hoped a few more shots would mellow him out and incapacitate him. Instead, it added fuel to the fire. He outsized me, and I didn't want to fight, but that was not my choice.

We started with the shots, and he grew angrier. I knew it irked him that when he said a Mandarin phrase a few times, I repeated what he said with better pronunciation to make it clear. Then the locals told me, "YOU speak Chinese well." That kind of thing can sting students of the language. He was also upset that I gave him tasks to complete. I reminded him I was the quality manager for all areas, and *I interviewed him for the job!* It was my responsibility to tell him what to do. Sometimes, our closeness obscured the boundaries of command. He had a lot of grievances he needed to deal with. But he kept saying,

"Hit me, just once, hit me."

I baited him a bit by saying,

"You're not so tough. You can't even finish this bottle of whiskey. C'mon, tough guy."

I said it jokingly, hoping to lighten the mood, but he took it wrong. The next thing I knew, he hit me in the face and knocked me to the floor. Then he kicked me in the head and body with his shoes on. I attempted to stand, but he continued kicking. This lasted for minutes. That's a long time when someone is kicking you.

He stopped, and I stood up and said,

"What the fuck are you doing?"

"I warned you."

"What do you mean, you warned me?"

I had a fat lip and bruise marks. I tried to talk it out with him now that I knew what he was capable of. After watching *Raging Bull* many times, I recalled the scene where De Niro asked Pesci to hit him harder and harder, but that was just a movie. We sat back at the desk, and I complained I would look bad at the wedding. He said again, "Hit me." I assumed he wanted me to hit him to even things out, so I hit him in the face. Right after, he lunged at me from across the two-foot-wide table.

"Holy shit. This guy is going to kill me."

With his heavier size (250 lbs and over six feet) and his hands around my neck, he pushed me back a few feet until I was against the large window of our room on the twentieth floor. Then he banged my head on the glass like he tried to break it. He made several attempts until he let go, and I fell onto the carpet. Before I got up, he kicked me again.

I could do nothing until he ran out of breath and quit. Except for the one punch he requested, I avoided fighting and ensured it was one-sided. He should bear full responsibility. I was trying to prevent people from assuming it was a drunken brawl. There would be no way we could work together after this.

When the second beatdown ended, I repeated, "What the fuck?" He wore himself out with the alcohol surging through his veins. He was breathing heavily, lying on his bed. I had a fat lip, a black eye with blood taking up the white in my eyeball, and bruise marks on my face, neck, and body. He whipped the shit out of me, and I took it. I was proud, angry, and upset. I walked out of the bathroom and was relieved to see he passed out with his clothes and shoes on. In my mangled state, I was too wired to sleep and an emotional wreck, so I drank the whiskey to ease my nerves.

"I'm the last man standing, so I'm the tougher one." He turned me into Bukowski's *Barfly*.

I considered changing rooms in case he strangled me in my sleep, but why should I shell out a couple hundred dollars for a possibility? If it happens, it happens.

Sonny arrived the following day and showed up at our room at 8 a.m. When I opened it, he said,

"Holy shit. What happened to you?"

"Ask Steve."

From the look of it, he woke up and remembered little but still had anger and said he would beat me again. I was crystal clear. That happens when you receive a beating. You remember it. Sonny called room service and ordered a raw steak. That sounded cartoonish, and I didn't think they would bring one, but I would try anything.

Finally, I would have that steak I had been searching for.

I slapped the raw meat on my eye and left it there for an hour, hoping it would do something. My hands shook too much from the beatdown and the booze to fix my tie, so Sonny gave me a hand.

I joked about it by saying, "The first rule of Fight Club is you don't talk about Fight Club." But it was difficult to laugh about a tragedy that had only happened to me.

Sonny lent me a pair of sunglasses, which I kept on for the entire wedding, even at night. Steve also wore shades. It was a friendly gesture, but more was needed.

The day after his wedding, Paul and his bride accompanied me to the doctor to get my head scanned for damage. The physician asked how it happened.

"A drunken coworker beat me."

"Did you press charges?"

I never thought about that, but I wanted to put it behind me.

After assaulting another coworker, Steve had to leave. He had value, but that wasn't enough.

It took four weeks for my eye to return to normal. I wore sunglasses except for when going through customs. I did the right thing, and my career continued because of my restraint, but it was hard to take a beating like that. It made me angry for a long time, especially when I had to explain why I didn't fight back.

Never again would I put myself in that situation.

CHAPTER TWENTY

MOSCOW: JUST GIVE THEM MONEY

For the CNY break in February 2001, I wished to travel outside of China. I spent my previous holidays in Putian and Hong Kong. If we wanted to go anywhere that would accept a mainland passport, we needed to book three months ahead. Before, few locals traveled during CNY. Everyone returned home. Flights leaving were light on passengers. Now, the masses filled the planes.

A possible choice was Moscow. Since the PRC and Russia were pals, Debbie should have no problem. I might be the one with the issue.

"Why can't we go in the summer?" She asked.

"That's the peak period. Fewer tourists go there in the winter, and that's the best time to get the full Russian experience. Bowls of hot soup with rye bread and lots of vodka."

The more I thought about it, the more I desired to go. She was not as eager.

"Perhaps we shouldn't travel because of your health."

"I'm fine. I fly every week. Plus, won't it be better to visit when I can't drink? I will take what I can get, but trips such as this should be experienced to the fullest."

I could see myself drinking moderate amounts, but not my factory dinner amount. For me, sitting with a couple of dudes finishing a bottle, having a few smokes, and enjoying the crisp weather of Moscow was the thing.

I convinced her it wouldn't be colder than Beijing, so she got on board. We needed a Russian citizen or organization to vouch for us to secure the visa. The easiest way was to book a hostel, and they would fax a guarantee letter. Once again, I relied on my Lonely Planet to locate a place. The guesthouse requested $50 for a deposit. I wired it, and they sent the letter. We collected our documents and headed to the Russian Consulate, on the north end of the Bund, in a Baroque and German Renaissance building. When it opened in 1917, the Russian Revolution started, so it closed. It opened and shut several times over the decades. Eighty years later, it still operated with an enormous satellite dish out front. They had better TV.

The consulate started its service at 9:00 a.m., and we planned to arrive before to queue. The U.S. Consulate had a line that wrapped around the entire complex. It was so stretched that a racket of place savers charged for waiting—space scalpers. I doubted the Russian line would be that extended, but we left early, anyway.

We rode the Yanan Elevated Road to the Bund and across the Waibaidu Bridge. The consulate was on the corner with no wait. Two soldiers stood outside, and my wife asked where to apply. They directed us through the guard house to a building.

As we strolled on the grounds, I recalled the 007 movies. Currently, I was in the adversary's home and couldn't wait to see what Russia would be like if they let me in.

The visa office was smaller than my living room, with two windows: one to submit and another to pay. Of course, we didn't have the forms filled in correctly and had to redo them. My wife talked with a guy filling in his application about what he did in Moscow. She asked too many questions. I tried not to listen.

On this occasion, it turned into a positive thing. He would be there at the same time. He told Debbie to call him, and he would pick her up to celebrate New Year's Eve.

"No Chinese should spend CNY without other Chinese."

I assumed I could tag along, and he wasn't hitting on her.

While we redid our forms, three more people showed up. The room sat silent. I almost fell into a trance. I worried they would trouble me because I had a thick (an inch with pages added) passport with stamps from all over. A lot of officials over-scrutinized my book. Also, our hostel only guaranteed the days we stayed. We'd hoped the visa office would issue two-week visas. I let my wife go first. If she had problems, I would have complications with my Yankee passport. They received her application and charged less than I had to pay. I stepped up, and the agent reviewed my paperwork. I felt relieved once she passed my documents to the money lady. She instructed me to retrieve it after lunch. What the hell? My wife received hers right away.

When I came back, I noticed my visa expired a day before our departure. The agent said it would be okay as nobody paid attention to it. I knew better, so I asked again. With more pleading, she fixed it with a pen and a chop. Meanwhile, Debbie got a visa for a month.

Yeah, friends indeed!

We flew for ten hours, a little shorter than going to Los Angeles. Aeroflot, the Russian airline, was the only option. They had a departure that arrived at dinner. That allowed us to go from the airfield to our guesthouse before midnight.

Our flight departed from the brand-new Pudong Airport before it closed for the evening. We breezed through customs. That was a gift, but empty airports seemed eerie.

"Who goes to Moscow the day before Chinese New Year's Eve?"

Big Russian dudes, that's who. My wife was the sole woman beside the flight attendant and was apprehensive.

The plane was Russian-built, a gigantic beast we boarded from the belly. They sat us in the same area, five rows apart. The duty-free cart came out as soon as the aircraft reached cruising altitude. It seemed odd they tried to sell perfume, cigarettes, and alcohol with ten hours until arrival. But it wasn't for arrival.

The cart stopped at the Russian dudes, and they purchased bottles of vodka and cracked them open. They flipped over a row to face each other while playing cards. I wanted to join for shots, but it was better to be on my toes if something happened.

They stayed engaged with their cards and never approached but became over-excited occasionally.

Once things looked okay, I had a separate issue to deal with. We bought ski pants and jackets at the Rainbow Market in Beijing. I also purchased heavy boots with a fur lining. We prepared for Arctic cold, but the plane was hot, and they wouldn't turn the heat down. I sweated so much that I desperately wanted to disembark.

That may be the point.

Finally, we touched down at Moscow's Sheremetyevo Airport. The plane parked away from the main building, and we walked down the stairs to board a bus. Similar to the Chinese bendy coaches, the Russian-made ride was a refrigerated steel box on wheels with a tilt-a-whirl in the center that spun around when the vehicle turned. It shocked me that Russia made everything. I was used to Made in China. The country just started to get saturated with mainland goods. They had a way to go.

The airport stood empty, with no line at customs. I was the only traveler held up. Everyone else waltzed through with a quick stamp and no questions.

The agent flipped through my never-ending passport while asking, "What is the purpose of your visit?" and "Where are you staying?"

I thought I would have a problem with the visa, but he didn't ask. It would appear Russia had more flexibility than China.

The agent told me always to carry my passport, then stamped it and released me.

I underwent stress for nothing; I only tried to visit, not overrun it.

Our flight was the last, and the airport closed at 9 p.m. Few people hung around. It seemed safe to leave Debbie at the customs exit while I changed money and found transportation. In Russia, I would draw less attention than with my Asian spouse next to me.

Taxis waited, but the idea of driving off into the dark with a random Russian driver set off alarm bells. There had to be a safer way. The airport staff said,

"Walk out and go right. Keep going until you find a bus stop."

If we went outside, we wouldn't be able to reenter. We had no choice but to take a leap of faith. Once through the doors, we were fresh meat for the taxis and anyone else looking for a mark. We kept going until they lost interest. They weren't pushy. It was too cold. We continued for ten minutes through the snow to reach the only source of illumination, a beacon we hoped would take us away. Three others waited with luggage. It looked as if we had found the correct place.

The minibus pulled up, and I asked if it was headed toward the subway by showing him the map like a tourist. He said yes, and we boarded. I paid him by holding shrapnel (coins) in my hand and letting him pick the ones he wanted. It seemed reasonable. We were at the mercy of strangers now. I had a hard time being so helpless. I wished to say something, and only Chinese words popped into my head. Mandarin controlled my brain.

For an extended period, we saw nothing. It was a profound change from The Hai. Eventually, houses appeared, and then Moscow. We were far from downtown and even further from our hostel. The bus would drop us off at the northernmost subway stop, and we had to transfer to the southernmost.

When we reached the station, the driver signaled to exit. We located the ticket office, and I focused on buying tickets by consulting my guidebook and bending down to communicate with the lady on the other side of the hole (like in China). Right away, I realized everyone would assume I was Russian and speak Russian.

The police had another opinion. They thought I looked suspicious. Often, the cops (in pairs) approached me, or they would pull me out of the crowd. When they did, I would say,

"*Tourista, Tourista!*"

I assumed it meant tourist and not "*Terrorista, Terrorista!*" They scrutinized my passport but never my wife's. It turned into wise advice to carry it.

I drank with some guys in a bar and told them about my predicament. They said I looked Georgian and not the Atlanta one. Now, it made sense. My North Face jacket and scruffy beard did me no favors.

I purchased the tickets, and we followed the flow down the escalator. Moscow had grand stations with chandeliers, gigantic domes, decorative archways, and extensive mosaic tile work. The escalators traveled deep down, three floors, non-stop. The depth had to do with protecting the system from bombing. However, the long trek down turned vertigo-inducing. I could understand how difficult it would be when sloppy. A Weeble Wobble would need to grab the handrail for dear life.

We got in the only open car. With the luggage off my back, I attempted to identify the transfer stops. Few others sat on the train, but I stayed alert.

Look no one in the eye, but don't take your eye off them.

As more boarded, it was clear this town (country?) had a booze problem. I noticed quite a few guys struggling to walk. I had been in the same situation a handful of times. Here, it seemed like an epidemic. Day and night, someone wasted rode on public transport. I heard the police patrolled the parks during the winter to ensure the drunks wouldn't pass out and freeze to death.

I thought I had recovered from whatever ailed me, so I gave myself the green light to have a few. Anything more, and I ran into the possibility of tossing everything up. With all the potential dangers, I had better avoid Moscow's nightlife. Besides, I lacked *guanxi*, which acted like a force field.

After an hour, we reached our stop. Finally, this leg had ended. Once I deciphered the Cyrillic alphabet, the subway became easy to navigate. The hostel's directions indicated it was around the corner from the stop. My travel guide advised to buy bottles of water to drink. Fortunately, a kiosk remained open. It was no larger than a photoshop. An old lady stuck her head out. I put up two fingers while asking for "Two *vatas*." She asked something, but I repeated the same. Then, she gave me two bottles. That worked well. I showed her the hostel's name, and she pointed to a building. My boots had no traction, and I slipped every few feet but righted myself. I carried two large glass bottles, my laptop, and a full-sized backpack. If I took a spill, it would be disastrous.

The buildings appeared identical, but we stumbled upon the correct one by wandering in the dark. After checking in, we went to our room, a sizable concrete box with a pair of military beds and a small TV with Russian channels. It was definitely a hostel, similar to horror films I had seen. They held our passports and would return them in the morning. We couldn't leave, typical of slasher flicks. But I felt relieved to be at our destination. The hangout area was in the lounge. It reminded me of my days at Chung King Mansions, with travelers, sharing tips, drinking, and listening to Euro techno or The Scorpions. I would have dropped my bags and returned to partake, but not that night. I took a hot shower because I was beat. The showers were communal, so it was wise to choose an off time. I never forgot the importance of timing after Putian.

The warm liquid was medicinal. When I tore myself away from the healing fluid, I had to return to the room to get water to brush my teeth. I twisted the cap, and it produced a fizzing sound. Then I realized the lady asked if I wanted "Gas" or "No gas?" I acquired soda water. It paired with vodka but was not suitable for brushing. I switched to boiled tap instead.

Upon entering the room, I propped a chair against the door in case someone paid us a visit. Even as tired as I was, something prevented me from sleeping. My body functioned over time, dealing with multiple disorders, and life caught up with me. Around 3 a.m., I managed a little shuteye before sunrise.

The next day, my wife called the guy. He said he would come to pick her up for dinner. I didn't relish the idea, but I warmed up to it, considering they might show us things we wouldn't see on the tourist trail. What kind of celebration would this be? A Chinese New Year's Eve party in Moscow? Let's do it.

During the day, we visited key sites, such as the Kremlin, St. Basil's Cathedral, and the Tomb of Lenin. I had viewed an embalmed Mao many times and was eager to examine how the older Lenin held up (not well). Like Beijing, we did an enormous amount of walking. I was fatigued and reconsidered the dinner, but we couldn't cancel. They were on their way.

"Okay, we can go to a restaurant and be back by eight for another sleepless night."

They showed up and guided us onto the subway in the airport's direction.

"The restaurant seems far."

Zhang, the guy we met at the consulate, said,

"Oh no, we are taking you to our apartment."

They lived in a worker complex that housed mainlanders, a real Chinatown for the traders doing business between countries. I yearned to experience what this place was like. I pictured a ghetto with room after room of individuals crammed into closet-sized spaces, close to what it turned out to be.

It was fortunate they piqued my interest because their dorm was on the other side of the city. I should have figured it would not have been downtown. And I felt terrible they traveled south to pick up strangers. We had to see this out.

On the way, I got stares traveling with three Chinese and speaking Mandarin. Everyone expected me to be Russian, so why did a Russian speak their strange language?

I had my guidebook, but we relied on these dudes because the dorm fell off the map. We accompanied them through housing complexes similar to those in America's inner cities, with low-rise buildings surrounding an open area. It was too cold to worry. We needed warmth.

They directed us to a door in a lengthy building with a huge flap covering the entrance to keep the cold out. Zhang held the flap while his friend entered, followed by Debbie and me. A small guard's booth watched over the entrance. When the soldier noticed a non-Chinese, he shouted in Russian. I got scared.

Zhang replied in broken Russian while nudging me forward and telling me to keep walking in Chinese. My instinct was to stand still. I didn't need to see the dormitory that badly. Zhang shoved me and repeated something to the guard. Then he pulled out 50 rubles (about 50 cents) and handed it to him. That was it. I continued without turning. Zhang's friend said,

"The best way to deal with Russians is to give them money."

That sounded familiar.

Inside were shops selling products imported by trading companies, money wiring, long-distance telephone, vegetables, a tremendous quantity of rice, and cooking ingredients. The living quarters were upstairs. As I followed Zhang, I avoided the trash. I never understood why individuals destroyed their surroundings. The rooms were clean. Why did they have to mess up the outside? The same thing occurred in the factory dorms. Why kick in the door to the toilet stall when you lived there?

Zhang resided with eight people in a space smaller than my kitchen. They alternated using the bunks when somebody departed to China or worked. Zhang surprised them when he brought me back. I assumed he only informed them about the woman he met, not the Russian guy. Everyone gazed at me with suspicion. There wasn't a lot of love between the Russians and the Chinese, after all.

My wife did the talking while I sat squeezed on a stool. Their room was barely big enough to fit a square folding table. They used a communal kitchen down the hall. However, I had lost my appetite after noticing how little care they took to maintain a sanitary environment. Instead, I drank beer. They offered a local dark brew in a jug, but they weren't a boozing bunch. They survived on almost no money and saved everything. I didn't care for them to overextend, and I wished to give my liver a rest.

News got out that a Chinese-speaking Russian was in the house. People celebrating showed up to *ganbei* with the circus monkey. They spoke Russian to me and waited for a reply. Of course, they shit themselves when I spoke Mandarin. A Russian that spoke Chinese??? Then I announced I was an American. Now, they could complain about the Russians in *Putong Hua* (Mandarin).

I enjoyed the attention but remembered I had a limit, or I would be forced to dispense of the evening's black beer in the toilet. Zhang and the family were tired of the disruptions and didn't want to share their Russian American. They closed their door to continue watching the CCTV Chinese New Year's Eve Evening Gala on satellite. We left China twenty-four hours ago, and now we watched Chinese TV in a closet in Moscow. It seemed we had never left.

Following the rapid succession of *ganbeis*, I needed to take a leak. Zhang led me to the washroom. There, I discovered an example of ingenuity. Russia lacked squat toilets, but that was the preferred *modus operandi* in China. How to solve the problem? Easy, stack concrete blocks on the sides of a sit-down toilet and cement them together. Wala! A platform for squatting.

Zhang left me, and I knew the way. As I headed in that direction, I asked people what they did and to let me check their ID cards. That line of questioning made the Chinese nervous. They assumed I was a spy.

I pulled the same prank on tour groups visiting the museum where I worked. Chinese-speaking tourists passed by, saying something about Americans, and I responded to them in Mandarin. It shocked the hell out of them.

That was playful but not as hilarious as when the Russian police checked my ID. That was not that fun at all.

We sat in Zhang's dorm for an hour before the conversation got around to what kind of business I did. Their relatives manufactured shoes in Qingdao, and they recognized the factories and people I mentioned. When the topic moved on to footwear, I headed for the exit before they introduced a factory. Besides, we had the journey to the hostel, and I had a headache.

We never contacted Zhang again but were thankful to witness a different side of Moscow. You needed to take those opportunities when you came across them.

We finished our time in the capital before going to St. Petersburg and then back to The Hai.

Many things about Russia surprised me, like the domestic production of everything, the massive amount of stairs, and the high food cost. We had a few meals at McDonald's, where we paid for ketchup. Pay for ketchup?

Russia turned out to be an actual hardship posting.

CHAPTER TWENTY-ONE

SHANGHAI: DOWN BUT NOT OUT

I finished a long haul to Sydney in February 2000 and had nosebleeds that would not let up. My self-diagnosis concluded that the air pressure caused my nose to drip, but the bleeds refused to cease.

Past checkups warned me that my blood pressure and weight were over the limit. Eating and drinking for three hours, then sitting in a car for four, adds pounds. Although I ran once or twice a week, my friends begged to differ that what I did was called running,

Towards the middle of the year, I had trouble sleeping. That seemed normal, considering I traveled weekly and answered phone calls from the U.S. as late as midnight.

I often took calls during a rousing singing session. It was times like those that made me despise the invention of the mobile phone. Picture being in the karaoke, creating *guanxi*. Perhaps you sang or engaged in a liar's dice showdown, and your phone vibrated. When that happened, I asked myself, "How do I find a quiet place?" There was rarely a peaceful area to conduct a call within a hundred feet from a karaoke hall. You never wanted to make the mistake of thinking the current song was mellow; it should be okay. Not a brilliant idea: You might scramble for any space that provided shelter from the noise while people on the other side of the world, drinking their morning coffee, listened to the madness over a loudspeaker. Even if your fellow crooners paused, you had other music coming through the walls. If you neglected to blast your tunes, you threw off the balance and endured everyone else's songs. I sang horribly, but I knew it. Others never acknowledged and shouted into the microphone. You couldn't critique if your ears rang. It was better to go deaf to music you enjoy. That's why I played my CDs.

In The Hai, I hung out with expat friends to keep in touch with happenings in the city and to shoot the shit. Those late nights spent bar-hopping disrupted my sleeping schedule as well. But even when lit and exhausted, I found it difficult to sleep. I tossed and turned until I dozed off at 3 a.m. During the day, massive dark rings formed around my eyes, like a panda, and I couldn't keep them open. It became impossible to stay awake in meetings. I needed to continue moving and thought this was a phase; it would pass, but it didn't.

October of the same year, I traveled to Koh Samui, Thailand, with my wife and a couple we met on the Hash. Soon after arriving, I sensed pain in my ankle. It turned tight and swollen. Whenever the slightest thing grazed my foot, I endured excruciating agony up and down my nervous system. I had a similar tenderness in my big toe, but this was my ankle. Despite this, I refused to let it destroy my vacation. I carried on consuming seafood and drinking beer, which I discovered was the worst thing. A week later, the pain dissipated.

I learned the ache in my foot was gout. If you have suffered from it, you know it is one of the most painful problems. A buildup of uric acid in the joints that forms sharp crystals caused it. I read it is genetic, but eating a rich diet doesn't help. Somehow, I knew I would not get away unscathed from that *foie gras*.

But the gout wasn't the worst part. We almost missed our flight because international departures relocated to a new airport in Shanghai. We showed up at the wrong airfield. Luckily, we had a speedy driver and made it before check-in closed.

Next, the couple we traveled with left their bag with cash and passports in a Bangkok taxi.

Rule #24: Never leave a taxi before ensuring you have everything.

That mishap would have derailed the trip, but following **Rule #24**, I checked the taxi and avoided a disaster.

No, the absolute worst thing that happened was unavoidable and unexpected. We walked down the main street in Koh Samui when we bumped into another Shanghai hashing couple. They came to Thailand to marry and to avoid the red tape in China. That evening, we dined and bar-hopped. My wife returned to our bungalow, and I drank with my friends until 1 a.m.

When I returned and reached for the lobby front door, I found it locked. As I attempted to enter, a Thai dude approached from the road. I assumed he worked for the resort. He asked if I required help, and I said, "Yeah, the door is loc . . ."

Before I finished, he rushed over and extended his hand to grab the handle, but he grabbed my crotch and ran away laughing. It took a few seconds to compute.

"Did that guy molest me? How did he do that so fast?"

I had a moment of clarity and figured out that because our hut sat on the beach, I didn't need to enter through the lobby. Live and learn.

A couple of months after our Thailand trip, my body rejected liquor. Now, I had a serious situation. I was accustomed to tossing up my yellow stomach acids in the morning on heavy nights, but it became more regular, like brushing my teeth. Then, I expelled the smallest amount of booze after I went home. I hadn't done that since I was a teenager. Something was broken. I dealt with sleepless nights and gout, but no alcohol? No longer would I be capable of having factory meals or living an expat life.

I needed to get this checked out but refused to visit a mainland infirmary after my experience. How would I find the right doctor in Hong Kong? It was easier to focus on my job rather than to do the research to locate a qualified doctor. Thankfully, Debbie thought of an easier way and talked me into seeing a Traditional Chinese Medicine (TCM) physician. She said my *Qi* (circulating life force) fell off balance, and Chinese medicine would fix that. It sounded plausible, so I agreed to go.

The TCM doctor requested me to stretch out my arm while he placed a finger on my wrist and asked me to stick out my tongue to check the color and texture. He prescribed many Chinese wild herbs, which we bought at a TCM pharmacy. We handed them the prescription, and they gathered the weeds from the back room, a garbage bag, or more, depending on the length and type of medication. Then, we took them home and boiled them in a large clay pot for several hours to create a thick, black concoction. Some pharmacies sold individual medicine packets for people who travel. Otherwise, you needed to fill water bottles with the elixir and hope they wouldn't leak in your luggage, or you ended up with tie-dyed clothes—not the good kind. Often, customs examined my bags. In China, everyone could smell that it was TCM. The medicine gave off a unique herbal odor that you never forgot, similar to *baijiu*. Customs let me pass as if they felt sorry that I had to drink so many doses.

"You drink two pouches a day for months, and you'll improve." It seemed long, but I tried it. I guzzled those pouches of molasses water despite hating them.

"Add some sugar. That will make it sweeter."

The sugar never tamed the bitter flavor, but I persisted. Meanwhile, I experienced pains in the center of my chest on a regular trip to Hong Kong. They weren't stroke-type aches but deep-in-the-bone agony that never receded. I attempted to soothe my frame with hot baths while asking the front desk to recommend a clinic. They directed me to a pediatrician who did little for me except prescribe pain and sleeping pills. He didn't even measure my BP correctly. As a result, I kept on traveling, drinking TCM, and hoping for magic.

My health issues became more evident to others when I dropped pounds at an abnormal rate and developed bruise marks. I assumed I bumped things while sloppy, but they showed up in places such as the back of my leg. I wasn't aware until someone told me.

The final straw was my eyesight. In April 2001, I noticed my vision had lost focus. I wore glasses and assumed I required a new prescription. Debbie accompanied me to a clinic in Shanghai to examine my eyes. They had a foreigner department. It sounded okay, so we headed over.

When the doctor examined me, he noticed something and led me to a room to measure my blood pressure. He discovered my BP was 240 / 160. That explained why my nosebleeds wouldn't stop—the blood looked for a release.

The physician admitted me. I might have been the initial foreign patient, but that was an acknowledgment I didn't want.

Considering I came in for an eye exam, I was unprepared for what happened next. For a day and a half, they hooked me to multiple IVs, jammed cotton up my nose to stop the bleeding, and took loads of blood tests. They said several of my organs were failing. Wait a minute, I came in from the street, and now I could be dead in a few days?

If that doesn't cause you to pay attention, I don't know what will.

They decided that only an H. K. trauma center had the ability to treat a life-or-death case similar to mine. With my extremely high blood pressure, they cautioned that the altitude of a commercial flight might cause a heart attack. I was a ticking time bomb and didn't know it.

My SOS Insurance covered airlifting me out of any situation, and they did. The consulate, SOS, and my office completed the paperwork in a few hours, and they sent me to the airport.

The orderlies strapped me to a stretcher with a fake bearskin to keep me warm, but it was April. They also secured my arms, preventing me from scratching my face for over four hours. That was torture.

Next, they placed me on the floor of a gutted bread truck and anchored the stretcher. While riding on the base of the shock-less vehicle, I felt every pothole in my spine. Previously, I witnessed the trouble ambulances had when trying to break through the gridlock. I felt sorry for anyone inside needing urgent care, and now it was me.

As we rushed to the airport, I wondered how I would go through customs. Would they slide me through the X-ray machine or pat me down? What kind of plane would we take?

I had questions that would soon be answered.

We drove onto the tarmac and stopped. From my vantage point, it was hard to see, but we had the proper license plate or sticker to cruise through half a dozen checkpoints. It impressed me.

They slid me out and loaded me onto the jet—like Hannibal Lecter. I held my passport in my hand, and an agent came on the plane, stamped it, and we took off. The pilot said we flew at a lower altitude, but I didn't experience any difference. They kept me strapped down until we reached Hong Kong. The flight seemed great, but it would have been enjoyable if I wasn't on my deathbed.

We arrived three hours later, and they did the handoff to the H.K. paramedics. Once in the ambulance, I looked forward to decent health care—after they figured out which hospital to go to. From what I heard, the driver got lost. Shouldn't he know? He explained there was a last-minute change as only one hospital would admit me, and he had never been there.

Was that supposed to calm me?

He sent me to the correct place, and they wheeled me into the ICU to determine why my organs had shut down. The drugs reduced my BP, and I slept some. It was challenging to get shut-eye in a hospital with lights and noises all night. Then I had the blood pressure cuff on my arm inflating every thirty minutes, nurses taking blood starting at 5:30 a.m., and IVs hooked up to both arms.

Two days later, I stabilized and changed to a regular room. The doctors had no idea what ailed me. They ordered every test, including a spinal tap, for which I signed a release of responsibility. It was standard but alarming.

I continued to have problems with my eyesight and lost it. If I couldn't see, what would I do? Even when stuck in bed, I worked, but there would be no way to read emails without eyes. This was disastrous.

Before this sudden dose of reality, I thought they had overreacted. How could I be facing life-threatening problems at thirty? For the first time, I got worried. I had a lot of stuff on my plate, like the new position I had taken in Hong Kong, the two-year rental agreement, not to mention my life in The Hai. What would I do if I became blind? The optometrist told me my blood pressure threw the retina off focus. He had never seen such a severe case except in textbooks.

Despite performing the tests, they were unable to identify the root cause. They hoped it was as simple as controlling my BP, and it worked: my organs returned to normal, and my eyesight slowly recovered. Everything began to rebound, and I had thought about the future. I asked the physician if I could drink since my liver was fine.

"It isn't wise, but if you do, drink something clear, such as vodka or gin. Stay away from beer."

That sounded promising.

But wait, not so fast; my kidneys still teetered on the brink. The doctor planned to do a biopsy. They would open me to remove a slice and do more tests. Since I lacked sufficient red blood cells to operate, they administered transfusions. The blood bags were freezing. When that cold liquid hit my warm veins, it felt like razor blades zigzagging their way up my arm and freezing my hand until numb.

During the third transfusion, another doctor came in and said he was Dr. Wong, assigned to me by my insurance. He planned to move me to an approved place, not what was best for my health. He called my insurance company, who informed me I was in a private hospital because no one would accept me. Now that I had improved, they wanted me to change to the cheaper public hospital. Nobody informed my current doctor, so I told her I had to leave or wouldn't be covered.

Dr. Wong gave me the hospital's address and said I should head over without stopping. I could walk short distances at a slow pace, and my sight had returned enough to see shapes in black and white. My wife completed the paperwork to fly to Hong Kong to help me move over after I grabbed clothes from my new apartment, which I had not even unpacked. Before I caught a cab to the public infirmary, I made a pit stop at an American diner. For two weeks, I had eaten bland mush. What would the next hospital be like? This might be my only chance, so I ordered a plate of nachos and clam chowder, pure fatty comfort food with lots of salt. I still didn't accept my illness, and the meal skewed my blood test, but it was worth it.

Dr. Wong told me if I kept my BP low, all my organs would return to normal, except my kidneys.

"When your kidneys are damaged, there is no way they can recover. You should prepare for a fistula to be implanted into your forearm for dialysis. It takes six weeks to be ready for use."

Slow down, doc; no need to jump the gun; I would rebound on my own. And everything turned around, including my kidneys, to a point. I lost about thirty percent of the function, but you can live on one kidney, right? That was true unless both your kidneys were down thirty percent. I aimed to be the miracle case that recovered. I did, but not until after a relapse four months later.

II

When they discharged me, I weighed less than I did in high school and vowed to keep the weight off. My wife served me Chinese herbs and traditional health foods, which I refused. Eating to live was boring, not to mention impractical.

I took it easy for a few weeks, and my sleeping and eyesight normalized. My eyes corrected to where I no longer needed glasses, the only positive thing to come out of this situation. Once I felt close to a hundred percent, I rejoined the social scene and factory meals.

Then came the relapse.

In August 2001, I joined a weekend Hash trip to Guilin, Guizhou (Southwest China). The day before, I came down with a fever. I had slight fevers in the past, and they subsided after a day. A decent night of boozing did the trick. We would do plenty on this excursion.

On the day, I still had a fever and a massive headache. The best thing would have been to stay home, but I had prepaid. I thought I could stick it out for forty-eight hours. I realized I had made a mistake when we landed. During the flight, I turned pale. My lungs had fluid building up, causing a bubbling sensation when I exhaled. These were grave signs, but when the bus we hired stopped for a toilet break, I noticed my urine was dark reddish-brown. Now, I regretted going on this adventure.

We stopped at a small town to stay. The organizers arranged a grand bash at a night market, the type of party I thrived on, but I couldn't eat or drink. I headed back to the shite guesthouse to rest. Our running group occupied the entire place, and Hashers partied all evening. Some individuals possessed the ability to booze it up the day before and run a half marathon the next morning. I was not one of those runners.

The following day, we rented longboats to navigate the winding river deep into the mountain range. I didn't know where we would crash until we arrived, and the organizer announced we would sleep on the floor of the villagers' homes. It was a strenuous exploit for a healthy person, not to mention an individual in my state.

I considered walking the trail but turned back. It was a dumb idea to try it when I barely had sufficient stamina to walk on flat land. Besides, nobody would notice if I stayed in the village.

My stomach had been empty for two days, but my body refused food or water. I needed to try, so I checked out the villagers' outdoor kitchen. They put the ingredients in large buckets on the ground. I lost interest when I watched a pair of wild dogs stick their heads into the food.

While waiting for the runners to return two hours later, I sat in agony. Then, there was the usual hour or more of jokes and stories from the run. I wanted my sleeping arrangements and hoped they would wrap up soon.

We finally received our marching orders when dinner finished. The organizer advised us to grab our gear and follow a villager. Each led three or four people to sleep on their floors. I didn't mind doing stuff like this when I backpacked, but not now.

Despite having a bed, I was unable to doze off. If I laid down, the fluid in my lungs blocked my breathing, so I got up and walked outside, or I would wake everyone. Instead, I startled the roosters, who woke everybody up anyway.

All I wanted was to return to town and register in a decent hotel before the evening trip to Hong Kong. That would not happen. The buses drove away from the city to another scenic site for a run before the flight. There was no way I would consider a trail. I stayed on the bus with bone, muscle, joint, and nerve pain. I attempted not to move for three hours until everyone returned. Then, we drove to the airport to sit for three more. It was misery on top of misery. Never had I been in so much pain. Everything hurt.

I reached my Hong Kong apartment late on Sunday and attempted to eat a sandwich. My jaw clenched, confirming my body rejected even light food. I gave up and tried to sleep. With the bubbles in my lungs, I had to stand up every half hour to breathe. I did this a few times until I dozed off out of exhaustion.

I needed to head to the emergency room.

The next day, I returned to the public hospital that had treated me four months ago. They had my history, so it would be easy to see someone. After a blood test, the physician told me I should admit myself within twenty-four hours, either in Hong Kong or Shanghai, but I had to do it fast. He informed me my kidneys had failed. If I neglected to do something soon, I would die. It was my second death warning. He said I would be in for an undetermined amount of time. It shocked him I still walked the earth.

With no family in H.K., I flew to The Hai, and Debbie met me at the airport. It was a race against time; the sand in my hourglass rapidly drained; I felt myself getting weaker. When I arrived, the plane parked at the farthest gate, making my trek to customs seem like a marathon. I walked slower than the other passengers, barely able to lift my feet. If healthy, I would be the first off, passing everyone. I knew the airport like the back of my hand, and I had no time for slow travelers. Now, I was last. I had just enough strength to make it out and hand my carry-on to my wife. It required too much power to pull my bag with the lightning-fast wheels.

We returned to our apartment and planned to go to the hospital in the morning. They would do nothing for me if we went straight there. Better to enjoy a last night at home.

I packed my stuff for a few days and grabbed my computer. I learned from my previous hospitalization and hoped for a phone jack to download emails. There would be a lot of downtime lying on a bed. I might as well work. That way, I didn't have hundreds of emails to delete, file, or answer. Every day I couldn't log on would increase my stress, knowing my emails multiplied like gremlins, and my mailbox would bounce messages.

My wife accompanied me to a well-known public hospital near the Bund with a famous kidney specialist who had treated me before. The socialist hospitals were dirt cheap, dank, lax on services, and packed with patients. They all looked the same. The level of experience or the number of PhDs was the difference.

Private clinics popped up near foreign neighborhoods but wouldn't treat major problems.

Debbie worked on getting the paperwork sorted. She called ahead to ensure they had a bed and would take a foreigner, but the person in my space refused to leave. I learned that possession was everything. If you had the bed, you could stay if you paid. You might ask why someone would want to stay in a hospital. I asked the same question. It was an insurance scam; government insurance paid the bill, including meals, for as long as you stayed. Some enjoyed it more than going home. Why not stretch it out?

The facilities lacked the same high quality as Hong Kong but were first-class in China. I tried booking a room on the VIP floor with TVs and a bathroom. It was similar to living in a two-star. They called it "hotel-style service." I didn't appreciate the difference until I saw the regular ward. They loaded them with patients with zero privacy. You also provided nursing duties such as changing bandages and dealing with other messy things, not advised for the queasy. People brought their pans, hot water bottles, and stuff to use while caring for their friends or relatives. How would I heal with other families, cooking noodles and eating sunflower seeds? I would have to go elsewhere if I couldn't get on the hotel service floor.

As luck would have it, they found me a single with a bathroom, but they used half the room for storage. Nurses would come in to retrieve supplies. Still, it was a single: no instant noodles, peculiar smells, or non-stop chatter. I would pay extra to snag the bed before somebody stole it. They had no idea what to charge for a deposit because everybody else carried government insurance. They decided on 10,000 RMB ($1,300) cash. If I surpassed it, they asked for more before they cut services. They didn't mess around.

We gave them the deposit and took the elevator up to the room, where they handed me the prisoner's clothing to change into. The bathroom looked horrible, but it was mine. I would have forked over double for a private commode. Other hospitals lacked individual bathrooms, and patients used public ones. Those toilets were squatters and reeked. I wouldn't have had the energy to squat and did not desire to listen to individuals hawking into the urinals or on the floor. Guys smoked like chimneys in the restroom, too. I had terrible experiences giving urine and stool samples at these places.

The doctor asked, "Why did you fly back?"

He thought I was crazy to travel when Hong Kong had superior health care. I knew that, but I required help to navigate this whole thing. I became accustomed to the bizarre and common sense questions. Everyone remarked it was strange that I picked China to have this disease. I replied, it just happened.

He ordered blood tests, and I waited. An hour later, he came back with the news.

"Your kidneys have shut down, and you need emergency dialysis or will die."

I failed to understand what dialysis meant. He explained they would insert pipes into a central vein in my neck. The lines coming out would be six inches long, one for blood to exit and another to enter after a spin cycle. He told me they would tether me to a blood filtering machine for four and a half hours, three days a week. I said okay. What choice did I have? Where would I go? They insisted I sign an agreement that relieved them of responsibility for my death since I had walked in that way. It's a hospital! That's where sick people go. The doctor said I could enter into cardiac arrest at any moment. Once again, the seriousness of the situation ratcheted up. I developed my own DEFCON system: "a Five" for minor incidents and "a One" for near-death. This turned into a One-plus. The speed was telling. I had never seen physicians react so quickly in China. After I approved, they put me on a gurney and wheeled me into surgery. I lacked a clear understanding because I understood only eighty percent. My teachers neglected to teach the medical lesson. I trusted my wife would ask the right questions.

The pipe insertion finished after thirty minutes. They made an incision, then threaded it until securely lodged. I was awake and sensed them inserting and pushing. It wasn't painful, but I had anesthesia. Next, they delivered me to the blood room. There were twenty chairs with individuals connected to cyclers, with no empty seats. They squeezed me in because of the urgency. Otherwise, I would be out of luck. Dialysis patients who lived nearby booked the seats. The nurse told me if I planned to remain, I had to locate another infirmary. There was no sugarcoating my situation. It all happened so fast, but I was too weak to think about it.

After the treatment, they dropped me off in my room at 10 p.m. I remained alone in the dark with IV drips inserted into both arms. My mind began to process all the information from the morning and afternoon, and I assessed what I needed to do. My life, career, and everything I had built were in jeopardy. I would show them by getting well. There was more living to be lived, places to visit, and a family that had to be started.

I would not perish in a bed in Shanghai.

The next day, the doctor discussed inserting a permanent channel in my forearm, as the H.K. physician suggested. The collar connection was temporary, and no one wanted those red and blue lines sticking out of their neck forever. Despite this, I waited. My body would recover after a couple of sessions of dialysis. If I rested my kidneys for a week, that might kick-start them.

He informed me about a separate option. Instead of a duct in my arm, I could do Peritoneal Dialysis (PD). Again, I got lost in unfamiliar medical Mandarin. He explained PD worked through a pipe inserted into my abdomen. I would connect my line to a 2000 ml bag of solution (about half a gallon). The liquid filled the thin membrane that contained my organs, staying in for up to four hours before draining and refilling. The entire process lasted forty-five minutes. Somehow, the solution would remove the waste in the blood and excess water. I should exchange every four hours for the best results, even at night. I liked I did not need to use a blood machine, but exchanging every few hours? How would I get things done?

Anyway, I would rebound, so it didn't matter. Just in case, the doctor led me to the PD area to meet patients. Everyone appeared unhealthy and yellow. As usual, anyone I talked to said, "You speak Chinese well." My language abilities were the least of my concerns.

I barraged people with emails while waiting for treatments. If things ran smoothly, I wouldn't receive phone calls. Sometimes, I watched TV, but I only had local channels. However, I caught a shocking event when I flipped stations one evening—a news broadcast. At the end, the female newscaster said,

"Two airplanes have hit the World Trade Center Towers in New York, and a tower has collapsed. Whatever happens, have a good sleep tonight. Goodbye."

That was it. Was she talking about THE WTC? If so, shouldn't it be breaking news with live coverage? Nothing. I attempted to hook up to my ADSL dial-up but had a slow connection, and websites wouldn't load. As I lay alone with the pipes connected, I wondered,

"What terror is happening in the U.S.?"

It was 9/11, and I will never forget where I was when the planes hit—in a Shanghai infirmary, dealing with my own horror.

As the situation unfolded, I did seven blood-washing sessions, and the waste level returned to normal, partly because I ate little. Before I arrived, I planned to follow all instructions, including eating the food. The H.K. hospitals had acceptable nosh and an extensive menu. In China, you ate what they gave you. Those Chinese airplane meals now seemed like fare for kings. In the infirmary, they brought me a tray that sat on the table, waiting for me to finish dialysis. Cold, sticky rice, flavorless vegetables, and seaweed broth were not the meal I wanted after getting my blood sucked out. Luckily, a few months before my downfall, the first Subway restaurant opened close to the hospital. I begged Debbie to pick up a couple of foot-longs to store in my mini-fridge. Those sandwiches helped me through that time. Without them, I would have starved. My in-laws worried I shouldn't eat cold items and brought my toaster oven from home. I assumed the hospital might not allow it, but nobody cared.

When in Rome, as they say.

Since my vitals looked promising, I requested to fly to Hong Kong for further treatment. They agreed only if I signed something saying they would not be held responsible for my demise. It was the same form they gave me when I arrived. It absolved them of any mishaps because of my unknown ailments upon arrival. I'm sure it pleased them to see me leave; I would be someone else's problem. Sick foreigners were a liability. If I died on their watch, there would be much paperwork but no responsibility.

We paid and left. Except for the slammer, nothing felt better than leaving a socialist hospital after two weeks. They wrapped my pipes in thick gauze and covered the hole. It looked as if I wore a white ascot. It should have been all right to fly, but I consumed extra BP meds just in case.

The next scheduled blood cleaning should occur in three days. The clock started as soon as I unhooked from the machine. I figured I would be okay for five days. My self-prescription was to stretch out the treatments to wean my kidneys off dialysis. None of the doctors supported my theory.

At this moment, I considered flying to the U.S. Then I thought about the cost of medicine with no insurance and stayed in Asia.

Upon landing, I contacted the negative Dr. Wong, who scheduled a dialysis appointment. I waited for him to say the Shanghai doctors were quacks, but he agreed with them: I required a pipe. That was not comforting.

I met him at the ER to receive my life-sustaining filtering. He showed up, and it seemed as if I had interrupted his tennis game. He connected the pipes and left. The machine was in an isolated room for emergency dialysis. Doctor Wong rented the facilities. He did not belong to the ER.

Not long after, I experienced wetness. I sweated a little, but it shouldn't have been that much. When I took my free hand and reached around, it came back covered in blood. My pipe loosened, and my juice poured out. I rang the emergency button to get someone's attention. The nurse called the physician. Meanwhile, more trickled out. I drained but didn't refill.

Dr. Wong looked perturbed he had to return while I was upset about lying in my blood. He said they did not insert the line correctly, and my vein had partially closed.

"This is a problem caused by Shanghai, not me. I might fix it, but this connection can only be used once more. After that, you will require an additional temporary line until we install your permanent one."

Fine by me. I only required one more cleaning. Besides, the charge in Hong Kong cost nearly what I paid for fourteen days in the socialist hospital, including the surgery. I would be broke at HKD 10,000 ($1,300) per treatment three times weekly. In addition, I had to pay for another tube insertion. The fee alone was an incentive to will myself to recover.

On the bright side, when I asked Dr. Wong if he thought Chinese medicine (TCM) would help me. He replied a firm no. That was what I wished to hear. He supported my case to stop drinking it. I questioned whether the toxic combination of strong herbs contributed to the rapid decrease in my kidney function. From now on, I would no longer drink it, and I had a doctor's consent.

For two weeks, I worked in the office. I wrapped the lines around my neck like a snake and got better at hiding it under my collar. After my last cleaning, my test results held up. That was proof the old boys worked but at a decreased rate. It was a good thing, too—the pipe became unhooked again. The hole could have caused an infection in a major artery in my neck. Not cool.

My exceptional doctor was skeptical about my healing.

"You should still prepare to insert a fistula. This rebound won't last."

Even with the positive news, he had to go negative on me. Never mind, I was a medical miracle and had to stretch it to show him. I also yearned to return to my everyday life. Nobody explained why I became deadly ill twice in four months or why I recovered. Sure, my blood pressure ran super high, but what caused it? The lack of exercise? Flying too much? The booze? Chemicals in the factories?

Perhaps it was all four.

Following the second bout with disaster, my function decreased to thirty percent. It was enough to keep chugging along, and I slowed down for a year. My weakened state made me prone to other problems, such as gout, but I didn't require dialysis. The longer I went without it, the more I felt I had special healing powers. Nothing would stop me.

And so I continued on my journey.

III

My wife searched everywhere for a remedy. Western medicine had no cure, but Chinese medicine knew no bounds. She searched for the right combination of diet and TCM to prevent me from relapsing. Then, she eliminated all my regular meals and replaced them with porridge, vegetables, and other traditional foods. That turned into a week of arguing.

The most significant change I made was to stop drinking beer. Previously, I consumed gallons of the stuff at the pub and on the Hash. I played on a darts team and downed eight or nine pints with a few shots of Jaegermeister each Tuesday night in The Hai. I hit it fast and hard because Debbie set a curfew. She was aware of what time it ended and called to ensure I wouldn't get sidetracked by my non-married friends.

One of the hardest things to do was to kick the cigs. Try going cold turkey in a country of addicts—a real challenge. I was a well-known smoker. Factories and my employees saw me inhale packs at meals and banquets. Everyone did. Smoking tapered off by the 2000s but was still a part of business, and it took me a few years to quit for good.

I also agreed to try the TCM cures my wife researched. Not only did I drink the black oil, but I consumed a crunchy powder mixed with water. Next, she convinced me to visit a traditional clinic in Changchun,

Northern China (a three-hour flight) during CNY 2002. They had a ski resort, and I wished to see what skiing looked like.

It was wintertime with a fierce wind. Instead of doors, all buildings hung heavy insulated flaps to block the gust. We shivered in the old socialist hospital while waiting for the doctor/boss to see me. He had his own TCM recipe that he manufactured and sold worldwide. When we walked into the examination room, we interrupted his chain-smoking habit, which was not a great sign. He performed a blood test to compare after a week. I told him it meant little because I had eaten a massive lunch. The food would throw off the tests and make the medicine appear to be doing something.

His cure consisted of the same crunchy powder the Shanghai specialist gave me. In addition, he prescribed a golf ball-sized tootsie roll and not the type the Xinjiang guys pushed. After I swallowed the drugs, the nurse had me lie on my stomach. She placed two electric pads on my lower back to send shocks to stimulate my kidneys. It sort of made sense, and I didn't find it too painful. IV drips were the last part of the treatment. The whole routine had to be done twice a day.

Between my morning and evening visits to the clinic, we scoped out the ski resort. I wanted to learn how to ski, but no mountains were near Chicago. Perhaps this would be affordable, and we could fly back for skiing, not the shock sessions.

Similar to many things, it sounded better than what it turned out to be. People smoked while skiing; they stepped on others' skis while crowding the lift because nobody waited; mothers pulled down the pants of their youngsters for them to pee, front and center. It was street life transported to the slopes. China needed at least ten years to work out the problems.

It would be wise to return a decade later if I was still alive.

I finished the treatment but didn't notice a difference. My labs improved slightly. Even though I thought it was useless, I bought a month's worth of drugs and gobbled them down with no noticeable change.

By now, my wife had talked me into taking Chinese meds for over a year. The doctor said to consume three 12-ounce pouches a day. If I had to take a four-day excursion, I loaded my bag with medicine. As the trip proceeded, my suitcase got lighter. But when I joined factory meals, I lacked the motivation to heat an herbal pouch and slam it when I returned to my room. Then, I lugged around the medicine and came home with the same amount.

Yeah, I did not enjoy the TCM experience, and my situation stayed the same. There was no reason to continue, but I tried it again every time my health dipped.

Meanwhile, I reduced my drinking to a glass per meal for six months and avoided social events and factory meals. When I felt confident enough to join the dinners, I slowly relaxed my one-drink rule, and soon, I was back to the level I was at before I got ill. This time, I drank on fewer days but much harder. I became a binge drinker.

IV

The first reported case of SARS (Short Acute Respiratory Syndrome) happened in Southern China in November 2002. Children, seniors, and individuals with compromised health systems became the most vulnerable. Individuals worked from home, stopped traveling, and used serving spoons instead of digging in with their chopsticks during group meals. Most citizens wore face masks, which wasn't strange for Hong Kong. They became commonplace after the bird flu outbreak (1996). People wore them to prevent the spread of colds in the office and to block bus fumes when waiting at the stop. After the SARS outbreak, everyone followed the government's advice because it was in their best interest.

Infection began with a fever, so airports installed heat sensors to catch visitors arriving with the virus. If you were red hot on the screen, you got quarantined. I had a decent chance of catching a cold while traveling but needed to avoid setting off the sensor to keep flying.

When hungover and on a morning flight, I had allergy issues, sneezing multiple times until my system normalized. Often, I mentally cooled myself off to pass through the sensor—not sure if it worked, but they never stopped me.

Once on the plane, I couldn't cough or sneeze, or people would flash dirty looks. It was serious stuff. If they located a sick passenger, the authorities quarantined that person and the individuals in the surrounding rows. The most uncomfortable situation happened when I was on the verge of a cold and had a scratchy throat. I carried a bottle of water to ease the coughing, but when I forgot, I held it. Have you tried to hold back a coughing fit for thirty minutes? I teared up, sweated, and had difficulty sitting still. It sucked, but these precautions prevented the disease from infecting more.

Hong Kong addressed the problem head-on. The local newspapers even published a daily death count. China downplayed the danger. Citizens read about the virus but weren't advised of the risk. It was a Hong Kong and Southeast Asia issue.

At the beginning of 2003, China finally acknowledged the spread and examined anyone arriving from Hong Kong or any other country that had reported SARS deaths. First, it started with a revised health form that asked where you had traveled over the past six months and if you had touched any birds (poultry). They handed out forms before, but I don't think anybody looked at them. Sometimes, the airport never bothered to have a person to collect the papers. Now, things were serious. They checked your details, place of stay, and local phone number. Next, customs agents and police wearing hazmat suits took the temperature of everybody on the aircraft before they let anybody disembark. If a single passenger came up positive, they held the entire plane.

That turned into a major hassle, especially on Friday nights. They always delayed Shanghai flights because of the air space controls. Add on the extra time for the health check, the hour wait in the sea of travelers at customs, and the one-to-two-hour ride into town, and the result was a long, sticky day of travel.

With all this inconvenience, I curtailed my flights. Factories asked me to hold off on visits while customers and coworkers canceled trips to Asia and set up video conferencing. We sent packages, but people were concerned they might catch something from the parcels.

Because of the restrictions, I traveled to Shanghai a day a month to pay salaries and rent. A few months into the epidemic, Shanghai quarantined all visitors. If you lived in a flat, they instructed you to stay home for two weeks, but if you stayed in a hotel, you could come and go as you pleased; you only needed to return every night. A five-star opened on the corner opposite my building in a historic gated residence called the Xingguo Guest House. From the outside, you saw little over the walls surrounding it. Once through the gate were manicured green lawns and classical Chinese-style buildings. I joined a Hash run that ended on the grounds a few years ago and desired to take a deeper look.

It felt great to be quarantined. I checked into the hotel, dropped off my bags, and walked across the street to my apartment. I had a combination of the comforts of home and the hotel's luxury. Plus, I didn't have to make the bed or clean. I had room service or could cook. My wife was in the U.S. for her residency requirement for citizenship, and nobody stayed in our flat. Had she been home and I visited, she would have been quarantined after I left. It would have been awkward to return after a few weeks, have dinner, say goodbye, and go across the street. That would be perfect for me but not fantastic for her.

But with her away, I explored nightlife without a curfew. For the first time since I moved to The Hai, no one policed me, but only for a night a month. I used my time wisely.

A friend tended a small bar about a mile from my digs. It was the perfect location for my local watering hole: not too far, but far enough. The joint squeezed in a pool table, two dartboards, and a bar top with a few stools. Depending on where you stood, you might get hit by a stick or a dart. It was owned by a Kiwi, who drank harder than anyone. He was proud that he got banned from ANZAC celebrations for being drunk and disorderly and posted the letter on the wall. His co-owner enjoyed taking bites out of pint glasses! It was a rough place that drew a heavy drinking crowd.

One evening before quarantine started, I grew tired of listening to the same Kid Rock and Black Sabbath mix. I told my friend I would run to my place, grab two CD books, and return to handle the tunes while he tended the drinks. I came back in twenty minutes and sat behind the bar, selecting music from the four hundred CDs I brought, or I took requests. For my effort, my friend hooked me up with pint-sized glasses, half vodka and half soda. Whenever my glass was low, he filled it to the top. People requesting songs bought me shots. This continued for five hours until 3 a.m. The bar was closed, and only the hard cores remained. I drank so much that I no longer felt drunk, but my legs turned to rubber. Before I lost complete control, I needed to escape.

I got my shit together and made it into a cab. My brain was clear, but my mouth didn't want to make intelligible sounds. A simple "go straight" in Chinese became impossible to pronounce. Instead, I pointed ahead. It was a five-minute ride, but I wanted it to be longer. I knew I would have difficulty getting out and maneuvering up the four marble steps (with no railing) at the entrance to my building. Four times in my drinking career, my legs gave out on me. Two of those, I had to climb up these four steps. I used the CD books to balance out like on a tightrope. The stairs were accessible during the day but transformed into an ironman course after a gallon of vodka. Step after wobbly step, I maneuvered my way over that obstacle without falling or crawling; it took a while.

The street was empty, but it would have been fun to witness.

Once I reached the door, I remembered I had no food. I skipped the TV dinner on the plane to save myself for an over-the-top meal at the latest culinary experience when I arrived in The Hai, but my flight was delayed. With only vodka swishing in my belly, I required something to eat within crawling distance. I sauntered over to the convenience store with the lights still on.

I attempted to stabilize myself as I strolled into the brightly lit store. In the frozen section, they had *baozi* (buns with meat). I devised the plan to steam the buns and fry them for a crispy side, like a popular Shanghai snack called "*shengjian*."

Yeah, I planned to do all of that at 3:30 a.m.

I paid the clerk, wobbled myself up to my flat, entered, locked the door, boiled some water in the wok, put the buns in to steam, and sat on the sofa.

Then, I fell asleep.

The next thing I knew, a guy was shaking me. When the earth stopped swirling, and I drained the brain haze, I recognized the dude with his hands on me as the doorman. Behind him, I saw another guy with an ax and a large hole chopped through my front door—and it was thick.

While the dude shaking me repeated, he saved my life, I said,

"My door. What did you do?"

Then it hit me. I fell asleep with the stove on. My bad. The doorman told me they knocked and rang the bell several times. They had no choice. Nothing in the living room was burnt, but it reeked. Opening the windows helped little with the heavy air, preventing a breeze. The burnt odor was deep in the walls and curtains. As I got up, the guy kept repeating how he had saved my life, as if he demanded I thank him. I just hoped they would leave so I could inspect the damage without hearing how Superman and his friend had chopped down my door to rescue me. Let me face the fire alone.

Fortunately, I left the cover on the wok, containing the blaze. Except for the buns resembling charcoal briquets, nothing was burned. The whole apartment (and floor) smelled terrible for days. Damn those buns! Now, I had a hole in my door. It was a sobering situation, and I wished to keep this incident quiet, but I figured someone would tell my wife. I wanted to deal with it head-on.

The real estate company handled the details about replacing the door. They said nothing, nor did they come by. Making a replacement would take two weeks and cost $300, a lot more than the door I destroyed in Huaiyin. I didn't care about the charge. I wanted to get it done as soon as possible to hide my stupidity.

They replaced the door as scheduled, and nobody robbed me. The workers came on a Sunday morning to install it. While they worked, I played The Doors to drown out the drilling and sanding noises that exacerbated my hangover. After they completed it, I went to brunch and had champagne and lobster to celebrate. The party never stopped.

As fate would have it, no one informed my wife. I unnecessarily got berated over the phone.

"How did you drink so much that you slept with the stove on?"

That happens when you imbibe multiple pints of vodka and soda.

I should have kept my mouth shut.

V

During SARS, restaurants, hotels, and flights became ridiculously cheap, with everybody remaining home. Debbie completed her citizenship and flew to Hong Kong in April 2003. We then took advantage of the cutthroat prices and booked trips. In two months, we traveled to Ko Samed, Bali, Bohol, and The Great Barrier Reef. All flight tickets went for $50 one way. We paid two hundred dollars for a three-night stay in Australia, including the flight, hotel, and meals!

In June, we returned to our Shanghai home to discover cockroaches. Months before, I noticed one here or there, but I assumed they would go away. Then they grew up and invited their friends. We found them everywhere, but the most disgusting place had to be the giant water dispenser where we got our "safe" drinking water. For six months, I had been consuming that water on my trips to The Hai! I changed to Evian.

One day, I noticed a large roach crawling away from a neighboring flat and heading toward our door. I killed it, but then I saw another. The hallways were tiled and clean, but we had a highway of cockroaches. Our neighbors left during SARS, and roaches infested their apartment.

It made me happy to know we did not cause the problem. Just a few months ago, I almost set the building on fire; better to have somebody else to blame this on. But once you had roaches, it was impossible to exterminate them. The apartment also held terrible memories of my illness and the SARS period.

It was time to move.

I gave my wife the task of finding a place; rather, she decided I was not qualified. I hated reviewing listings. Half of the time, people still lived in them. It felt uncomfortable walking in on a family while they ate. Occasionally, they knew we planned to drop by, but other times, we caught them unprepared. Property agents didn't care. They focused on the commission.

This time, I desired a flat with easy access to Pudong Airport. I flew weekly to Hong Kong, and they moved all the flights to the Pudong runways. I still hoped for a location near a foreign grocery store, but anything within walking distance would be pricey. Excellent air conditioning became a focus, too; I was tired of part-time AC units.

With my requirements and budget, we still had difficulty. I asked her to check out some of the service apartments in Xintiandi (a growing nightlife district), but they ran from $3,500 a month for a single-bedroom loft to over $5,000 for two bedrooms. Prices stayed stubbornly high despite the supply increasing tenfold. If I wished to make enough to leave, I had to suck it up for a few more years.

So, I lowered my expectations again.

She waited for newer properties to hit the market. The real estate business moved quickly, and individuals bought and sold flats like stocks without seeing them. You could resell an apartment for a profit before getting built. I had friends who worked for businesses before jumping into the real estate gold rush that began around 2000. They spent hundreds of thousands buying historic-lane houses and apartments. That was risky because getting your money out was challenging. However, the value of housing rose so fast that it was difficult to ignore. From street sweepers to grandmas, EVERYONE got into the game, with most individuals owning more than a single residence. People paid in full, and there was no property tax. As a result, they wanted too much for rent or would leave it empty instead of reducing it.

My wife told me she found a two-bedroom (400 square feet) close to a cluster of Western restaurants (three km away) and next to the entrance to the airport highway. A subway station was under construction that looked to be opening. Everything sounded fine except for the lack of a decent grocery store. The other catch was the landlord wished to sell, not rent. I didn't expect to buy a flat, but it was the best place. If we wanted it, we had to agree on the spot, no inspection, no background check: Cash deposit ASAP.

I needed to think about it, but the owner said, "If you want the apartment, you better decide before 2 p.m. because another buyer is coming."

We left at noon and caught a taxi to a restaurant. When we got there, I told my wife to call the agent and tell him we would take it. We had to sign the contract and hand over a small deposit until we paid thirty percent of the total cost! I took losses and depleted my savings because I had no other way.

The more complicated part would be to find a bank willing to lend us the balance of a few hundred thousand dollars. I worked in Hong Kong and traveled to China on business (Hong Kong is a Special Administrative Region but separate in essentially everything). I was not considered a resident of Shanghai and could not purchase. In addition, Debbie did not work. That made her ineligible, but she refused to accept that and began calling banks. I told her she had wasted her time. No one would loan her so much money without a job. Even for "gray area" China, that seemed a bit much. She was undeterred and narrowed the search down to a new bank, closing soon for the day.

On the ride over, I repeated, "This is a waste of time. They'll never give you such a large amount without collateral, especially a half-hour before closing. I will get a loan from Hong Kong."

My doubt in her ability to work the system pushed her to prove me wrong.

"You know a lot about China but don't know how to do things the Chinese way."

She was right. I only dipped my toe into the gray areas. I never wanted to do the backstroke in it. Once you took the dive, there was no turning back. You would always test the flexibility of every law and rule. It became a way of life. For example, almost everyone working should pay income tax or file, but few did because:

1. They didn't earn enough to give to the government.
2. They didn't receive benefits from paying.
3. They didn't want to fund government officials' big dinners and karaoke parties.
4. There were no foreseeable consequences.

Technically, it should be illegal to dodge your taxes unless you convinced yourself based on the above that it was a gray area.

At the bank, I stayed outside, around the corner. My name would not be on the title, and my face would have caused more concern. A half-hour later, Debbie came out. She said she filled in the application, talked to the rep, answered a few more questions, photocopied her ID, and that was it. They approved the loan. I couldn't believe it. There had to be a catch. At some point, the loan would fall through if we lacked a document they required. Nope. She secured it, and we would pay it back. It seemed fair.

The loan came through, and we had a fresh start, but you only knew a place once you lived there. I had my share of experiences, and this turned out to be no different. The owner let us in on two downsides, such as a crack in the concrete wall, wide enough to slip your hand in, and the wind's loud noise. The flat was on the top floor with nothing obstructing the windows. On winter days, the wind rocked the building. At least it didn't topple over as some towers in Shanghai did in 2009.

Something I should have thought about was the elevator situation. Every floor had three flats, and there were thirty floors. That's a lot of stops. It didn't help that people redecorated when someone moved in, and movers held the elevators to fill them with big sacks of demolished concrete.

Lastly, everybody carried their garbage in the elevator to dump it in the bins outside. Living on the highest floor, I saw and smelled what everyone discarded.

Yeah, the elevator turned into a negative, but we (my wife) were now property owners.

CHAPTER TWENTY-TWO

HONG KONG: TIME FOR ME TO FLY

I n the spring of 2000, my company asked me to move to Hong Kong. I would have taken the opportunity had I been offered it six years earlier, but now my priorities were China-based. Shanghai had dining and drinking establishments and playgrounds of exuberance opening all over town. I suffered from a severe case of FOMO (Fear of Missing Out). After the hard times I spent here, I earned a front-row seat to this amazing transformation. This was history. Why would I want to leave? I had considered looking for a new gig and would rather change jobs than packing up.

For the past five years, I have flown to fifteen provinces, auditing factories, inspecting goods, setting up offices, interviewing and hiring staff, and training them to do their jobs. I traveled all year long. My wife gave me a pass during the first few years of our marriage, but lost patience the more I came home exhausted and hungover. As my health declined, I needed less road warrior. I felt the years at thirty. What would forty be like? I required a life similar to the people I saw at the AmCham meetings, with a fancy office and a driver to shuttle me from the company to my five-star service apartment.

About six months after I rejected the position, I got offered it again. This time, I knew I had to accept. I still did not want to give up my home, nor did my wife. Her parents came to visit, and they never left. They now lived with us. I accepted the situation as a tradeoff for being away. But with her parents staying with us, she preferred to remain.

I worked out a deal to have Shanghai as my home and Hong Kong as my office. I planned to commute 1,250 miles twice a week. It was common for individuals to work in China and live in Hong Kong, but I don't think many did the opposite. My company agreed to allow me to fly back and forth until my lease expired. Then we would discuss my relocation. I concurred but didn't plan on changing. As long as everything ran well, everyone should be pleased. How far would they be willing to go to keep the guy happy who made everything run smoothly? In addition, I would save the cost of hiring a manager for Shanghai. They got two for one. My planned schedule was:

Monday: Go to a Shanghai factory and the office.

Tuesday: Take the 8 a.m. flight to Hong Kong.

Tuesday-Thursday: Work in the Hong Kong office.

Friday: Work in the office and take an afternoon flight to Shanghai.

Saturday: Visit Shanghai factories and office.

Sunday: Hash House Harriers.

On top of this schedule, I visited Fujian, Jiangsu, Shandong, and Guangdong offices. I didn't mind the flights if I flew Dragon Air, a Hong Kong-owned airline. They had the only flights competing with the state-run carriers for the Shanghai-Hong Kong route. The price was the same, with contrasting levels of service. A couple of years later, Cathay Pacific bought out Dragon. If I could fly on those airlines, I would travel in style.

Now that I was scheduled to fly to H. K. weekly, I needed a place to stay. Usually, I slept in the company apartment. As more expats joined, we outgrew the office flat, and few things happened in Sheung Shui. Everyone disappeared into their brightly lit apartments once the lonely McDonald's closed for the evening.

At first, I didn't care; I was relieved to have a job and be off instant noodles. When others joined, they desired something near downtown. A prime location for food and restaurants wasn't a bad idea. Considering we stayed for just a day each month, we preferred convenience. Our company wanted us to move close to the office; we compromised and found an apartment in the middle. We moved to Sha Tin.

Sha Tin was a few KCR train stops away, but it had more dining options. I only stayed at this apartment twice. It was a 300-square-foot two-bedroom. Each room was large enough for a twin mattress with a narrow space between the walls. We owned a queen, which filled the entire room. Anyone staying in there climbed in. You had to ensure you took care of your loose items, or they fell into the crack. The toilet was wide enough for an average human to sit down, but you couldn't sit down and then shut the door. It was a tight situation. The kitchen had the same problem. If there was more than a single person, it got crowded.

We had to move six months into the lease when the landlord sold the place. My coworkers pushed for one of the two nightlife districts, Lan Kwai Fong (LKF) and Wanchai (The Chai). I countered that spending loads of money at the bars would be easy if we lived in those areas. It was safer to be close, but not upstairs from a pub. I suggested my old neighborhood of Causeway Bay (CWB). It was only one stop on the subway from the bar streets but distant enough that we needed to go out instead of downstairs. I enjoyed the CWB area for the wide selection of anything. For short-term visitors, it was ideal.

Our Hong Kong staff searched, as none of the expat managers spent enough time in town to inspect flats. I gave them requirements, such as a bathroom we didn't have to back into and bedrooms with sufficient space to close the doors.

We set the bar low.

The CWB flat solved those issues. It had three bedrooms/two baths and gas-powered hot water, while the previous apartments used electric. Without gas, the following individual waited a half-hour for the water to warm up again when someone finished a shower. And don't forget to turn on the heater the night before or there will be no hot water in the morning. It seemed simple until you forgot and woke up hungover, tired, and late for a flight. You better get used to cold showers.

Despite some inconveniences, I was pleased with this apartment. It was a far cry from the gilded towers that banking expats lived in, but we moved closer. Besides, it was an improvement over my first home in CWB, which was important.

Moving to CWB felt like returning home, where it all started. Everywhere I went, I had flashbacks of my unemployed days and how I scraped to get by. Now, I had cash. I could afford to blow ridiculous amounts of coin in Lan Kwai Fong without breaking the bank. In fact, LKF became the location for after-dinner boozing. Partygoers drank, talked, and danced in the narrow streets outside the pubs and restaurants. Taxis snaked their way through to drop off fresh additions and remove those who had too much. It was a festive and amusing atmosphere, with even a Chinese Vegas Elvis (Melvis) walking around, giving impromptu performances. My favorite joint was called Al's Diner. They cooked decent American nosh, blasted rock classics, and sold jello shots, including a flavor with mescal and the worm. It took things to the next level. They offered jello shots all day, but they only made sense after committing to an evening of heavy boozing.

Across from Al's was a Russian pub called Yelt's Inn. When I drank with coworkers or friends, I persuaded them to move between jello and vodka shots. My *baijiu* training turned me into a dangerous drinking companion.

Next, we headed to The Chai for extra innings if my fellow compatriots could keep up. Wan Chai also had people flowing out of bars like The Wanch and Carnegie's. There were various pole dancing clubs with velvet curtains and packed discos such as Amazona, Fenwick's, Neptunes, Dusk til Dawn, Big Apple, and Joe Bananas. Each place drew a particular crowd. Carnegie's had a shot list, which filled both sides of a folded menu. The combinations of alcohol and mixers were endless. I led my companions here for two or three shots before moving on. They offered a type I would not suggest. It was called the Statue of Liberty or something similar. I ordered it after I exhausted my options.

The dude brought a glass of flammable alcohol, like Sambuca, and a glass of ice. I needed to put two fingers into the liquor and hold them up. He would light them while I sang the National Anthem until it became too hot. Then, I would sink my fingers into the glass of ice.

It sounded easy. I dipped my fingers, held them up, and waited for him to find a lighter until I lost my patience and drank the shot. He wanted me to do it right (because nobody else was stupid enough to order it) and gave me another chance. I soaked my fingers, and he lit them. I freaked out and knocked over the glass, thus igniting the counter. Carnegie's often had individuals dancing on the bar top, and they stamped it out. The bartender handed me a second shot and sent me on my way.

Next, I would go for live music at a disco/pub. I stopped by many locations to have a wide selection of venues at my disposal. I always aimed to have a place to entertain; the more exclusive, the better. It gave a sense of adventure or danger, like when I led people through Chung King Mansions to reach a bar or restaurant on the other side.

Rule #25: The entire eating experience, including location and exclusivity, is as essential as the food itself.

Yes, walking through CKM was a culture shock. Most never entered because it looked foreign and risky. Once, I guided Paul and his fiancé through the building to eat Indian. When we passed the last elevator, someone called out, "Randimoolah!" I turned and saw my Nigerian brother, Ramson. It shocked Paul to see a muscular Nigerian dude, who resembled a drug dealer wearing a matching silk shirt and short combo, come up and chat with me. It had been a long time since he had disappeared. He said he had returned to Nigeria. Later, his "brothers" and I store-fronted the 7-11 in The Chai between sessions at the Big Apple disco. It felt like the old days. But after that evening, we never crossed paths again.

I considered it part of my job to find the latest additions to the Hong Kong dining scene (**Rule #16**). I attempted to have options for most cuisines on both sides of the harbor. That knowledge proved helpful.

After working late with a coworker on one occasion, I sent him to his hotel in LKF, assuming we would find a restaurant. I forgot it was Valentine's Day. After calling my wife and apologizing, we tried all my choices, but every eatery required reservations. I dug deep and pulled out an Indian joint in a remote corner. They had a single table in front of the stage. We received a sitar serenade with the other couples. It was awkward, but we had a place to eat, and he never forgot.

Now, you can use your phone—much easier.

Our living arrangements looked to be the proper choice, but the landlord sold the apartment again. The following flat moved us away from the Patterson St. area straight into the throbbing heart of commerce, Hennessy Rd. We requested to be centrally located, and we got our wish right in the thick of it. The ground floor of the building had a gold shop. On the other side were a jewelry and an electronics store. Tourists window-shopped while another group lingered around the multi-line bus stop. Bamboo scaffolding covered the outside, and the steel railings prevented individuals from flowing into the busy Hennessy Rd. It created a bottleneck, packing people into a solid stream of humanity and a pain to navigate with luggage.

Despite having everything we requested, there were additional issues to consider, such as a ground floor entrance and working elevators. Once I broke through and past the steel front door, I climbed up twenty steps in a narrow passageway to catch the elevator on the second floor. The flat was on the eleventh, out of fifteen, with two closet-sized elevators. I could deal with the hassle for two days a month. But one day, I noticed an announcement stating both lifts would be down for six months or longer. The owners planned to install new elevators. When I saw the sign, I flipped.

"I need to carry my bags up eleven flights of stairs?"

If I wanted to eat, I had to go down, fight through the crowd while carrying as many things as possible, and climb up again. When I reached our flat, I would be drenched with sweat. I did this a couple of times before I switched to a hotel.

I moved to the Royal Pacific.

From 1994 to 1997, I stayed here when I traveled with someone by ferry to China. The dock was downstairs. It was a real luxury back then because I crashed in hotels further down the comfort scale. Many customers and coworkers chose the Royal Pacific, making it the ideal option for business meals. I preferred the Swiss Chalet. There was nothing similar to fondue or any cheese on the mainland. They also served steak tartare. I thought twice when I caught them pushing a cart beside our table with raw beef and eggs. But, once the chef mixed it and put it on a square of toast, it tasted amazing. Ironically, I hand-carried canned soup while I ate fondue and tartare in H.K.

For something lighter, there was a McDonald's in the connected mall. It may seem obscene for such delight to be given to fast food while staying in one of the best foodie locations in the world, but I can't emphasize how satisfying it was to have something simple, easy, and fast. Nothing soothed a hangover better than an Egg McMuffin and crispy hash browns, while the orange juice calmed an angry stomach. Sometimes, I felt so dehydrated that I craved the sugary water like a crack fiend, and my cells absorbed the liquid with glee. It was the finest morning meal to devour on my way to the airport or on the ferry.

In 1998, our contract ran out, and we moved to the shadier east side of Kowloon to stay at the Grand Stanford. The hotel was within walking distance from a Ruth Chris steak house, which became the go-to restaurant for treating overseas staff. I gained an education about how to order gourmet food and wine. We also had customers that requested Japanese, top-notch stuff in Hong Kong, and it was even more enjoyable when someone else paid for the experience.

Then, in 1999, Morton's opened. When I attended a Las Vegas trade show, I heard about Morton's, but I wasn't important enough to be included. Now I was. I grew excited about eating there until it turned into overkill. A few months during the next two years, I had dinner here twice a week, and the dinners started near nine o'clock. That was a terrible time to devour a steak the size of your head, followed by garlic potatoes, buttery mushrooms, lobster bisque with cognac, a couple of bottles of red wine, and half a pack of cigarettes. But I couldn't help myself. No way would I be the only one ordering salmon or, worse, a salad unless a 12 oz fillet chased it.

This was Morton's! I never wanted to refuse a sumptuous feast and put my body through torture.

Two years later, I skipped some dinners as my health deteriorated and the heavy meals became too much.

When I started flying to Hong Kong every week at the end of 2000, I needed to secure affordable housing. I had a friend who managed a hotel on Hong Kong's Gold Coast, deep in the New Territories. The resort was close to my office but far from downtown. It didn't feel like Hong Kong or China, with a big outdoor pool and palm trees.

I arrived from Shanghai at noon and would go to the hotel for lunch before the office. Shanghai was cold, and I wore too much, so nothing looked more soothing than the chlorinated, sky-blue water. Either I could eat lunch or soak on a sunny day. As hungry as I was, I picked the pool. But after struggling to get out and showing up at work sunburned, I forced myself to head to the office from the airport to no longer tempt myself.

It was wise to get the job done first.

My friend ran on the Hash four times a week. When I arrived, he dragged me to the run of the day. We followed it with excessive drinking in The Chai until two or three in the morning before traveling back to the Gold Coast, over an hour by minibus. I lacked the patience to maneuver the bus system and grabbed a cab costing $50-a pricey way to end an expensive evening.

I moved when my friend took another job and found lodging downtown. The Lucky Shamrock operated on the busiest street in TST. They charged HKD 300 a night ($38), and I stayed three nights a week. There wasn't much else to say about the place. It had dimly lit rooms with pink walls and bathrooms as small as possible without combining the shower, sink, and toilet. I pictured all sorts of horrible events in this building but endured it for three months before relocating. I became very ill and had problems sleeping, which worsened my stay. It was time to move to Causeway Bay, and I would approve since I would live here every week.

I settled on a two-bedroom behind the Sogo Japanese department store. The timing was fortunate. After moving, I got air-freighted from The Hai to the H.K. ICU for my initial round of kidney failure.

II

It was tough to avoid boozing without people thinking I had an ulterior motive or something displeased me. I was Mr. Thunder, the Weeble Wobble, who out-drank everybody at the table. Why would I not be drinking? I got that impression from the individuals on the front lines. If I refused to imbibe at dinner, everyone refrained. Sometimes, they might continue without me, but often checked to see if I had changed my mind. The party waited, begging for me to lead the charge. I enjoyed that role and had difficulty opting out.

I had the same problem with cigarettes. Factories gifted me sticks for holidays, and people tossed them at me during visits. I was the odd man out if I didn't smoke.

"Here you go, Mr. Thunder. Smoke up."

When visiting multiple factories in a single day (sometimes ten), I inhaled a pack or more. I tried limiting myself to only a cigarette, but it proved challenging. I cut back, and my friends hazed me. They said going cold turkey would be bad for my body.

"C'mon, have a cigarette. You know you want one."

The only way to break it off would be to avoid the factories and social events. But I had to quit. If I wished to live a healthier lifestyle, I needed to choose. My chest burned when I ran. I put my lungs through agony. I'd go the distance if I survived the initial twenty minutes. If not, I walked to the start and waited for the others to finish. That was the wonderful thing about the Hash. It turned into a party on a boring Sunday, and exercise was optional.

My running never reached marathon status, but a 10k grew more manageable, and my lungs hurt less after I kicked the habit for good (2005). I decided I no longer smoked and stood by it.

After a prolonged abstinence and willpower, I felt rehabilitated. I weaned myself off beer and introduced wine to my meals. The smaller amount of fluid with higher alcohol content put less stress on my kidneys, but I didn't do my liver any favors. While attempting to limit my drinking, I worked as much as possible in the office. If I stayed away from the dinners, I was safe. But on every occasion that I pushed my limit and came out okay, my confidence in my healing powers grew.

I got my mojo back.

An increase in my dietary options followed my reintroduction to alcohol. I shopped at the wide-ranging, high-end supermarkets, buying choice steaks, lobster, scallops, and tiger prawns. To cook this array of proteins, I used an indoor grill. I didn't have to worry about the odor drifting through the hallways of our multicultural building. Next to me lived an Indian family, and the curry fragrance trumped others. I bought a bottle of red and one white to accompany my feast. Soon, I upped it to three bottles. I drank through two but avoided the bars, so I purchased a third. It wasn't my purpose to drink gallons of wine. I was thirsty and bored, and it went down quickly.

Months later, three bottles would no longer do it. When I finished the third, I debated going out for vodka sodas in The Chai and lost that debate.

By the time the SARS epidemic was in full bloom in 2003, my wife stayed with me in Hong Kong after returning from the U.S. While she remained in H.K., my Wednesday night feasts got put on hold. I encouraged her to join the Sunday Wanchai Hash. It was a great way to see the territory, make friends, and have drinks.

During this Hash, I met a couple of guys from a group called The Royal Southside (RS2H3). I ran with them in 2000 (including a Haggis run). RS2H3 was a men's only, running on the south side of Hong Kong Island, a perfect location from where I lived. They had a reputation for pushing things to the limit and transforming back into gentlemen the next day for work. Yeah, I wanted to hang with these guys again.

The dudes I met, Camel and Small Bone (everyone had a Hash name), often ran with the Southside. Small Bone gave me the location for the following Thursday run, but I doubted I would make it because of the logistics of navigating through the commuter crowd. I had to return to my apartment, drop off my laptop, and then travel to the middle of nowhere for an event starting at 6:30. It took an hour and three subway changes to reach home. Because of that hassle, I needed motivation to venture back out, and my wife provided it. I became accustomed to having a few days every week without her company, and now we lived together full-time. She remained at home while I worked, and the last thing she wanted would be for me to take off at night. But I required at least an evening out, so I joined the Royal Southside.

What I remembered about them was the hard-drinking they did. After each run, they ranked on each other while shotgunning beers. They drank half and full cans for each down-down and smashed them on the ground to show completion.

If you were a visitor or disliked on an evening, they selected you to be the Amah. The Amah prepared the down-down drinks and drank anytime someone in the circle told him to. Depending on the number of penalties, it could be a grueling job.

I showed up for a run from Sha Tin, where I lived before. I thought I knew the area but discovered there was more to the place than the air-conditioned shopping mall. Usually, the Hare laid chalk markings outside the train station to direct you to the start. Sha Tin Station had a dozen exits. As I feared, I had trouble finding the markings and arrived when the runners set off.

During the first few minutes, I kept up. We cruised through a small village with lots of barking dogs. I had a flashlight but didn't need it; enough light seeped out of the windows of the homes to brighten the path. But then, the trail moved away from the houses and towards a mountain. I was screwed.

Falling behind on countryside runs was the worst thing I could do. If nobody closed the checkpoints, I would get lost or take a long time to locate the route. Thankfully, someone did initially, and I heard the runners calling "On, On" in the distance. I was still confident I would find my way through. In retrospect, I should have turned around. Instead, I took on a more significant challenge than I could handle.

As I followed the runners' direction, I fell far behind with nothing but wilderness. I continued up the path to the top and lost the trail again. There were a few options, and I tried each until I spotted the markings. I felt good about my progress, assuming there was only a single mountain and I would be descending. Then my flashlight died. I cursed myself for buying one at the fake market. I shook it to produce enough light to find the chalk at each intersection. My shirt got so soaked with sweat that it weighed me down.

Shanghai was flat, with street running; I wasn't used to the mountains. Plus, I had weak kidneys and no water. My calves burned after the climb, and I lost all hope when I realized the trail headed up a second mountain. I swore I would never do a run like this again.

More than two hours later, my hell trail ended, just in time for down-downs. They handed me a beer as I crawled back. I needed water, but it was cold, and I didn't have to slam it. The group no longer drank as hard as three years prior.

Expat living did that to you. Guys quit drinking and smoking, only to return. I was not alone in my attempt to control my vices.

The circle ended at 10:30, and they talked about going for dinner in The Chai. My wife gave me a curfew and called me home. She considered anything after 10 p.m. late. I had to wait until she returned to The Hai before joining the gents on the On On after the On On (the party after the party).

The more I ran with the group, the harder it became to avoid beer. Instead, I picked up pints of cheap vodka called King Richards as my penalty drink. It had a medicinal flavor but paired well with the sweet orange soda at the runs. I poured out half of the soda, filled it with vodka, and sipped it.

When the beer ran out, we piled into cabs to The Chai for Malaysian or a kebab before heading into the basement nightclubs. We grouped into cliques by country: the British, the Aussies, the Yanks, and everybody else, such as the Germans. I hung with the "Mercans," which included Camel and Small Bone. They were over six feet, which made me the short guy squeezed between two tower-sized dudes in the rear of a cab.

Our first bar of the evening would be Neptune's. The club was downstairs with a wall of mirrors along the staircase, which I assumed were installed to give people a last look before bringing a friend home. We bypassed the doorman with running gear in tow. I'm not sure he knew us, but we walked in as if we owned the place (**Rule #9**) and never paid the cover while others, like the American sailors on leave, negotiated.

Small Bone had a favorite location he perched from. It was an open spot in the corner. From there, he could assess the situation on the dance floor. Later, that area became known as Club Small Bone, the "club within a club." If you told somebody you were headed to Club SB, they knew where that was. We took turns buying rounds until the hardcores moved on to the next stop.

Leaving Neptune's, we strolled down the street to a larger place called Fenwick's, a basement nightclub popular with the suit crowd. It was a little classier than Club Small Bone, but only marginally. Some nights, you might catch individuals doing blow on the tables in the darker areas. Typically, two hundred people filled the venue. One thing I enjoyed was the semi-secret entry. A bouncer would let you in if you walked down the back stairs and knocked. It impressed guests when I led them through this entrance, especially when stepping out of Firehouse across the road.

Fenwick's and the other discos did not have "pole girls" dancing around in skimpy bathing suits like many clubs in The Chai, but women outnumbered men. Most of the ladies traveled on tourist visas from all over Asia and as far as South America. Sometimes, the H.K. police cracked down on tourists, overstaying their visas and doing other nefarious things. They blocked the exits, turned the lights on, and halted the music. You carried on drinking and talking as usual if you were a white dude (even dressed in shorts and T-shirts like my running pals and me). It felt colonial. I never showed my passport, which I neglected to carry when running.

They checked all the women, then the band started up, and the disco lights went into motion. As if someone said,

"Now, get back to work. Business as usual!"

And it was a great business. The women received a cut for every drink a customer purchased for them, and the bar gave them watered-down beverages. That way, they worked longer without getting drunk. All the discos had a similar setup. These "tourists" filled the nightclubs, making them look busier on slow nights. They weren't the prime customers and had fewer rights on the patron scale.

At Fenwick's, I had a table I declared my own. My table had access to the exit if a fight or fire broke out and was within view of the band. If I arrived and "tourists" happened to have taken up my spot, it was no problem to ask them to relinquish it. They understood the scale and got up, saying nothing. It was a matter of economics. I sometimes paid $100 to sit there with all the drinks I bought.

Rule #26: Too much local culture is not suitable for people not living in Asia.

As an expat, you grew accustomed to unique situations and behaviors you would not get away with back home. I realized that certain environments would be less understandable to the uninitiated. So, I rarely introduced coworkers from the U.S. to these discos. It would shock most to enter a club with a couple of hundred people and notice that seventy percent were women of every color. Despite knowing this, I made a mistake when out with visitors and a guy I worked with named Scott, a well-known swinger. We drank at dinner and in LKF after. My coworkers wished to dance, and I questioned Scott if he thought they could handle The Chai. He said yes, and against my better judgment, we took them to Fenwick's. It was as bad as I thought it would be. Sure, everyone enjoyed the disco and the trays of Kamikaze test tubes I bought, but it was too much local culture. Scott provided a case example of why so many women packed the club. We all sat at my table, and while I ordered drinks, Scott got up and disappeared before returning with a young lady from the Philippines. They sat down to talk and do some shots. He never introduced her, as if it wasn't peculiar that he had a strange woman on his lap. Between the loud renditions of Western classics, my American coworkers leaned over and asked,

"Who's the girl?"

"Don't worry. She's his girlfriend, not a working one."

I had seen the girl before. Most likely, she was open for business, but that settled the issue. Later, he melted into the crowd with his girlfriend. Scott returned after twenty minutes and sat down with a Thai girl. My coworkers asked me,

"Who is THIS girl?"

"I wasn't clear, but the first was his ex. This is his new girlfriend. I can't keep up."

It held for a while, but when Scott stood up again, I figured we should end the evening before he came back. Simultaneously, a guy chatted up my female coworker, and he thought she might be working. We had better leave before he asked her how much.

By the time I flagged down a server, settled the bill, and maneuvered through the people, we ran into Scott, leaving with a THIRD girlfriend. I gave up. It proved my rule: no matter how badly my U.S. coworkers desired to go to a disco, it was best to stick to the pubs and places without the "tourists."

Often, when I escaped from the bars in the early hours, I stopped by the twenty-four-hour supermarket. I found it easier to buy groceries and hand-carry them twelve hundred miles to The Hai instead of going to a grocery store in an expensive mall at home. I bought durables such as oatmeal, cereal, chips, etc., and bottles of wine for the following Wednesday.

For years, I did this until once, I purchased my stuff and paused to pick up cigarettes at a newsstand. While I waited, I put my bags down and looked at the magazines. When he sold me the smokes, I noticed my things had disappeared. I was drunk and off guard, but it happened quickly. I thought the shop owner had distracted me while his friend stole my groceries and argued with him. He yelled at me in Cantonese.

"Crazy *gweilo*!"

It wasn't the proper moment to chat with the po-po, so I forgot it and left. It was late, and I had a flight in a few hours.

I returned to my apartment and found my bags inside the doorway. It appeared I had a lapse of memory and must've taken them home AND THEN went out to buy smokes. Wow! How did I forget? I felt embarrassed about arguing with the guy and crossed the street to avoid him.

Rule #27: Don't buy groceries after drinking. Go home and quit consuming so much vodka.

Friday mornings, I showed up at the office with my bags by 9:30 a.m. I headed to the airport at noon and took the 2:30 flight. I flew this route for four years.

My daughter was born at the end of 2004, and I wanted to see her as much as possible. I switched to the earliest plane because the 2:30 was always delayed with the increased air traffic to the mainland. It was a two-and-a-half-hour flight, and I touched down as late as 7:30 p.m., reaching home by ten. If I preferred to play, I had to pay and get my ass up at 5 a.m. to catch the 8 a.m., giving me three hours of sleep on Thursday.

I reeked of booze during those early mornings while going through customs with the 'baby folks,' picking up an adopted child from China. A Northwest (later Delta) flight departed at the same time, filled with Caucasian couples, each with a Chinese baby. It was strange to witness, but it became routine, and I had to beat them to the customs line before they slowed things down. They were eager parents and brought loads of baby stuff. On those hungover mornings, I was in a rush and repeated,

"Gotta beat the baby people. Gotta beat the baby people."

Then, I rushed to the Dragon Air lounge and ate the sticky steamed shrimp dumplings, *siu mai*, cereal, a cappuccino, and sometimes a shot or two of vodka to steady myself. Nothing unsettled or disgusted people more than seeing someone reaching for shots at 7 a.m. My gate was visible from the second-floor lounge, and I waited for the others to get on before I boarded. After I sat, the air hostesses brought a tray of champagne and a special cocktail. I had to decide if it would be a liquid Friday, a three-or four-day bender, or if I would control myself and arrive only slightly smelling. Most of the time, I chose the liquid route or passed out from exhaustion.

Although I pushed it to the limit on Thursdays, the Hash was a necessary break and provided an option for relaxing besides my Wednesday night feasts. The meals still happened, but only for some weeks. The big problem was the painful hangovers from the wine. Then, I had a few hours to finish work and get to the run. In the beginning, the runs sucked while the remnants of the wine escaped through my pores, and my lungs ached from all the cigs.

After the run, I did it all over again.

With my other business entertainment taking up more of my precious stay, I gave up my Wednesday feasts and joined the Thursday run less. I made up for it by doing the tours.

The Royal Southside would embark on a trip to Southeast Asia twice a year. These expeditions coincided with a send-off for a longtime runner. A Tour Master would lead the group to a designated city and arrange the details. We would spend three days eating, drinking, and running through stunning backgrounds before returning.

When I heard about tour, it sounded terrific. I could check off countries I aimed to visit, and someone did the planning. Since my wife remained in Shanghai, heading anywhere for a three-day holiday was challenging. Hong Kong had hundreds of flights to any destination. I simply needed to show up and pay.

On my premier trip, I traveled to Bangkok. I had visited with my wife and our friends three years earlier when I got molested. We knew nothing about the city and relied on my Lonely Planet and taxi drivers. Naturally, we were curious to see the famed Bangkok nightlife. We found ourselves down a street with both sides, inviting us to view unbelievable bodily performances beyond the velvet curtain. We picked a place to take cover from the steamy weather. Inside, a performer in the middle of the floor was deep into her act.

I will never look at ping-pong balls, razor blades, coke bottles, and balloons the same way.

The eating and drinking in Thailand were always magnificent. I enjoyed new foods and learned from the insiders. The Hash had plenty of "Bangkok Hands." I was out of my element and took a back seat.

We arrived on a Friday night and had a sumptuous dinner, followed by hours of barhopping. The following morning, I checked out the streets before the noon run. The hotel served breakfast, similar to a Chinese three-star. I desired something adventurous. Almost across the alley was a noodle and rice joint. The fragrant aroma of fresh Thai drew me in. Inside, one of my fellow Hashers named Mr. Whippy was sipping a brew at 9 a.m. What a novel thing! I attempted to save myself to improve my chances of running, but that would not happen. The ice-cold beer slid down my throat so well in the Bangkok heat. We continued ordering, and they kept bringing them. For the next few hours, we exchanged stories and jokes until our group pulled us out to start the run. We drank through eighteen tall bottles with the help of other Hashers. The others stopped by but kept their distance. It was easy to drop everything and hit the bottle on days like this. Fortunately, the run transformed into a pub crawl as the rest had rough mornings and planned to skip the exercise due to the heat.

We drank at three bars on the way to the park. Once there, you could follow the path around or sit at a table in the shade and drink more cold beer. I took the obvious choice.

In the morning, I felt invincible, but now the alcohol had caught up, and it wasn't even 3 p.m. We planned to hit a bar to watch a soccer game. My ability to survive until then dwindled. After the "run," they served me plenty of penalty drinks for being the thirsty Hasher on my first tour. That did not help.

At the bar, my legs started to give out. I had to leave before they turned to rubber. I already experienced that situation. Ultimately, I looked like a blow-up figure waving in the wind in front of a car dealership. I had to return to the hotel, but I feared leaving the safety of the bar stool. Except for my legs, I was fine. I think my body removed my limbs from under me to say, "It's time to go."

I slid off the stool and headed for the black curtain, saying nothing. The sun's brightness hit me as soon as I found the opening. It was the shock I needed to give me the strength to make it home. A taxi was out of the question. I couldn't recall the address or name of the guesthouse; however, I had a general idea. Eventually, I found it and stayed in my room until the pub crawl the following morning. Besides a severe case of the shakes that affected me for days, I enjoyed the trip. Overall, I joined tours to Manila, Phnom Penh, Siem Reap, Yangon, Koh Samui, Hanoi, Vientiane, Macau, and Shekou. They turned out to be great excursions.

III

The years following SARS were an excellent opportunity for real estate. I moved into a three-bedroom flat, twice the size of my previous place, a street over. The apartment had everything, but the streetlights shined right into my room. On weekends, I listened to drunken teenagers while they waited for taxis. Their voices bounced off the tall buildings on both sides. But, the location and price were too good to pass. A flat this size would have cost an additional $2K a month before SARS.

Two years later, the landlord sold the apartment, and I moved once more. My property agent specialized in Causeway Bay apartments and found a three-bedroom with a balcony for a higher price but guaranteed the landlord would not sell. They were an elderly H. K. couple surviving off the rent. When I met them, they said an expat executive had stayed before, and they knew all about the living habits of foreigners; they understood us. I had no idea what that meant, but I signed the lease.

The following year (2007), Debbie and our three-year-old daughter came to stay for a month during the Chinese New Year holiday. My lease didn't specify how long guests could stay. Considering it was my spouse and daughter and the biggest holiday of the year, who would disagree with my family visiting? The landlord, that's who. The old lady phoned and said,

"Someone (the doorman) told me you have a pregnant woman and a child living in the apartment."

"It's my wife and daughter."

"You are violating the terms of the contract by having people not listed staying there. I am calling my lawyer, and you will hear from him."

"Are you fuckin' kidding me?"

My wife planned to give birth to our second child in Shanghai. She even had a plane ticket to return in a week. We didn't need an anchor baby when our son (we found out the sex through *guanxi*; it was illegal for doctors to tell) would receive U.S. citizenship because both parents were citizens. Nope. Wicked Wong called her counselor. He sent me a letter to meet and billed me $500. Not only did she sue me, but she charged me for her lawyer. I met them at the law office and explained my side. My lawyer friends said it was hard to fight landlords. Although I had a good chance of winning, it would suck up time and money. Better to settle.

The landlord gave me the option of paying an extra HKD 1,500 ($200) a month for my family to stay, or they would have to leave within three days. It was such a stupid waste. I sensed the resentment towards Chinese from across the border when Wicked Wong said, "Your pregnant MAINLAND wife. . ." There was an increasing animosity towards mainlanders as they flooded H. K. on tours. That was not us. My wife and daughter flew out as they demanded, but that wouldn't satisfy Wicked. She needed to build a sturdier and higher balcony wall if I had small children in the apartment again. Did she think I ran a pedophilia ring?

"Why did no one mention the balcony was not sturdy?"

I never stepped onto the terrace in the year and a half I lived there, and her plants died. It still would have been nice for someone to warn me. Now, she wanted workers to re-concrete the balcony and build a higher wall. She requested a reasonable time for laborers to enter. I reminded her I worked in Hong Kong for a short period, and her project would need to be spread over months. She called my office and complained to my staff about how unreasonable I was. It became a problem until I told her to stop harassing them or I would refer the issue to the police.

It took over two months to complete. My lease was almost up, and I had prepared to move. I still lived on the same street and ran into her for months. Every time I saw her, my blood boiled.

My next apartment was a downsizing. The rent prices had rebounded from the lows of SARS. I also contended with a new group that hadn't been here ten years prior, the mainland Chinese. In 2003, the rules for visitors were relaxed. The cross-border population increased as the RMB strengthened and became easier to use. Hong Kong turned into an insurance policy for individuals who enjoyed superb Chinese cuisine and excellent schools without traveling to the West. Tourists converted huge amounts of RuMBas into HKD or USD. It was troublesome to do that in China. They bought property and priced me off my block.

I told my agent to find a no-frills, two-bedroom with identical requests, but I needed a hassle-free landlord and a lower price. I no longer had expat coworkers to share the cost. During the past twelve years, I collaborated with thirteen Americans and was the last remaining. Expat jobs got harder to come by as locals filled those positions for less.

We worked ourselves out of jobs.

The apartment's location was great, and the lobby appeared expensive, with marble tiles and bright lights. I passed by every day. It surprised me I could afford it. And then the elevator stopped at my floor. They painted the walls the most miserable shade of greenish/blue.

The place she showed me was on the right. We exited the elevator, and my eyes followed the white light to the left. Then I turned to the right, and there was no light but what came through the open window at the end of the hall.

The other flat on this side had a wooden door with a padlock. It seemed as if they tried to keep something in. My apartment had what I asked for on a tiny scale. I got spoiled by rooms down a hallway away from the living room. This was not that. When I opened the door, I stood in my bedroom. The dining table had space for one. All the windows looked out onto the kitchens below, with pipes bursting with steam and food smells. The agent reassured me I could play loud music, but returning to this flat after work felt depressing and worse when I suffered from medical problems.

Another issue was mold. In the past, I endured the excessive humidity of Hong Kong, but this place took the problem to a new level. I returned after being away for three weeks in February (the rainy season), and the walls and sofa bloomed with black mold. That morning, I flew in and worked all day at the office. I headed back to my apartment at 8 p.m. and spent the next couple of hours wiping the mold off before it got me in my sleep like a Stephen King story. My sheets and clothes always appeared wet, but that was life in jungle weather.

Something about the black mold seemed more horrific than the damp sheets.

IV

As manufacturing costs rose, we required cheaper factory options. I flew to Vietnam, India, the Philippines, and Indonesia, looking for suppliers. The vendors we worked with at these places did not entertain on the level of the Chinese. Some had religious restrictions on alcohol, or the local cuisines could not match what China served. That was fine as I attempted abstinence again. A break from the feasts did me well.

Often, I met up with Chinese factory friends to reminisce about the old days and to tie on a couple. More factories that used to imbibe wine now drank Scotch—dinners comprised two or three bottles of Chivas or Johnny. I tried to control the filling of my glass, but at some point, I would concede and purchase my ticket for the whiskey train.

Because of my health issues, I reduced my drinking to a minimum when I could. It became a constant battle with my alter-ego, Mr. Thunder, who never wanted to say no. Besides wanting to avoid gout, I required the energy to go out with my kids on the weekends. Returning drunk or hungover left me tired, which was unfair to them. After going at it hard for as long as I could remember, my hangovers were crippling unless I started boozing again. It took two days to recover now.

When I managed another part of the business, my commute shortened to just over the other side of the harbor in Tsimshatsui (TST). In the morning, I followed everybody else on the subway like sheep. It was a well-oiled machine. You had to keep marching forward to hop on the escalator down to the platform.

Then, I transferred with the mob exiting and waited thirty deep for the next available train to wedge myself on. Once through the harbor tunnel, I rushed to get off while more commuters forced their way on. Then I got sucked into the river of individuals heading out of the station and onto the fast-moving human escalator towards the high rises.

Downstairs from my office was a glitzy mall with high-end fashion brands. As the economy turned from bad to worse during the financial crisis of 2008, stores closed or moved to cheaper districts. Commercial rents dropped. Everyone slashed costs and reduced staff.

This new job allowed me to work with different vendors in Hong Kong and Taiwan, who expanded my eating and drinking options. They had a history of working with foreigners and provided as much comfort (and alcohol) as possible. They knew how to order whether the cuisine was Italian, Japanese, or both (Aqua). I still had an addiction to filling in my mental Rolodex, and soon, I advised the suppliers on which restaurant to take people in my company. I loved eating with these factory owners because they drank any liquor paired with the food. If it was Japanese Omakase or Nobu, we downed sake served in long, hollowed-out bamboo pitchers that only had a bottom if I paid. If we ate Western, we had smooth-tasting red wine poured into decanters and lots of it. Chinese seafood at Lei Yue Mun would be white wine unless I were the only customer; then, it would be *baijiu*. And we always started with two bottles of champagne to get things going—nothing like ordering Dom Pérignon to start the meal.

The feasts were an introduction to the lifestyle of the wealthy, but they came as my health continued to falter.

I finally reached the top of the food chain but barely hung on.

Once we completed dinner, the next stop would be Lan Kwai Fong or Sevva, an outdoor terrace lounge on the twenty-fifth floor with amazing views.

Sometimes, we finished dinner off at a Scotch bar I found in a hotel in TST. They had a menu of about fifty single malts and blends. My factory-owner friend ordered them one after another. When we finished five types, we helped the others in our party to drink theirs. You can't leave $30 glasses of Scotch lying around.

I had big dinners five or more times a month. It sucked joining these over-top meals and returning to my slasher film apartment. When the rent prices decreased in 2008, it was my opportunity to upgrade. I needed a flat I didn't feel like killing myself in and where I could get some sleep.

My agent located a place in a quieter section of CWB with a Rolls Royce and Aston Martin dealership downstairs. It was nice to have something to remind me why I put myself through this.

The location was on the way to HK Stadium, where the Rugby 7s international tournament was held at the end of every March. I joined the Sevens in 1997 and every year after for sixteen years. It turned into a sporting event, a rock concert, and a college party rolled into one. My knowledge of rugby was nil. Instead of watching the games, I focused on my boozing. People took a lengthy lunch on Friday to get ready. Then, there were two and a half days to continue the celebration until exhausted and alcohol-soaked on Sunday night. Most headed to Wanchai, but you had to be a real pro to do that if you began drinking at ten in the morning for two days (or four if I commenced on Thursday). Luckily, I had a short walk to my apartment to crash.

Even though I dealt with the light problems as before, things improved after putting up blocking curtains to weaken the beams. The noise was non-stop as mini-buses and taxis flew around the corner all evening. These were the drawbacks of convenience and location.

Everything else about the apartment was fine. The landlord never bothered me, and I didn't trouble her. I enjoyed it so much that I stayed for four years until I moved out of Hong Kong in 2013. Later, I stayed at the Langham Hotel across from my office during my monthly visits until my last in March 2015.

I never imagined staying for twenty years when I arrived with a backpack, but it was an adventurous twenty.

CHAPTER TWENTY-THREE

SHANGHAI: IT HAD TO END SOMETIME.

From 2004 to 2007, I flew 130–150 flights a year within China and a growing number of countries. I earned top-tier status on two of the three airline groups and had lounge access in every airport. My Priority, Platinum, and Gold card collection for airlines and hotels was impressive. This privileged traveling increased the speed and ease of being an everywhere man. It was the business career I had aspired for, and now I lived it.

I passed through H. K. Airport, so often I received an escort to my gate. A guy drove me in a golf cart after clearing customs and consuming my made-to-order omelet and cappuccino at the first class lounge. It was the pinnacle of being a VIP and a godsend for a person living with gout. Since it was crowded, the driver honked to instruct travelers to move. They turned, either scared, curious, or angry. "Is he someone famous?" During these times, I didn't want to be the sole jackass sitting in the cart. But I got over it and assumed everyone would take the escort. When my car pulled up to the gate, the gracious air hostesses assisted me with my luggage and guided me to the plane while the other two hundred passengers waited. That was the shit, and I became spoiled.

But I had kids waiting for me, doing things without me. I missed out on a special time and attempted to curtail my flights outside my Hong Kong to Shanghai route.

Besides reducing my trips, I struggled with clean living to be here to watch my kids grow up. I thought I had healed myself, but my blood tests told a different story. In addition, my nagging gout problem became frequent, and it moved. One day, I might wake up with it in my big toe, making walking painful beyond imagination. Who knew that an irrelevant toe would cause havoc throughout my entire body?

A few days later, my other big toe might join the party. I mustered through it and bit my bottom lip as I moved. Often, the anguish was so intense that I felt I would pass out after arriving at my destination. At night, I gobbled sleeping pills and NSAIDs (non-steroidal anti-inflammatory drugs) to reduce the swelling in my joints. I appeared older than my age as I gingerly lifted my feet, careful not to bump the slightest crack in the sidewalk. Damn gout!

Sleeping pills were ineffective, and I nursed my pain all night. When that happened, I soaked in warm water to soothe the suffering, but the throbbing and redness returned as soon as I got out. After an hour, I jumped back into the shower. Some nights, I took three or more to tire myself out, but my eyes never closed. I watched DVDs until I dosed off. It was not enjoyable to have excruciating agony as the last thing I remembered before the sun hit me in the eye to wake up. I was exhausted and arrived at work with dark rings, eye bags, and limping, but I had clean skin. Actually, I flaked from those showers. Little pieces of dead skin fell off like dandruff if I scratched my arm. I carried lotion to prevent from leaving a trail.

Two weeks after the initial pain, the gout would go away and reappear in a different spot. If it bloomed in my ankle, it would swell up, making it hard to flex my foot or put my shoes on. The more I walked, the worse it got. I constantly rubbed my feet to relieve the misery to think.

Once, it occurred in both knees. Try going up or down stairs when you can't bend your legs. Going down was easier if I stepped on the edge and leaned forward while stiff-legging to the next stair, similar to Frankenstein. I perfected this walk, but I was careful not to over-guess the edge or I slide down on my spine.

Through it all, I traveled and covered enormous distances. When visiting factories, I navigated the meal to avoid worsening my suffering. Beer and seafood were off-limits, as were tofu and lesser-known causes, such as cauliflower and spinach. A business meal became a minefield. Ironically, many had their own gout stories, yet they never ordered non-gout-causing food or gave me a pass on the drinking. Everyone had a remedy, but it had to wait until after the meal. The booze helped me forget about some of the pain but never fixed the mobility of my joints. I was left with red-hot, throbbing feet that sent shock waves up and down my nerves.

Time to start the showers again.

I tried everything Debbie searched to cure gout. Meanwhile, I saw the same crappy H.K. doctor who had left me to lie in my blood. He did little for my kidneys besides issuing blood pressure meds, and he prescribed name-brand drugs costing me $500 a month. I paid full price but didn't notice an improvement, with my BP still at 200/120.

The doctor requested blood tests every six months to ensure my kidneys functioned. I did the first couple in Hong Kong, and they ran $300 a test. In China, hospitals charged $10. In addition, I had multiple places nearby to get tested, like the local public health clinic in the alley or the crumbling socialist hospital down the street. Sometimes, my seventy-one-year-old mother-in-law requested kidney blood tests for me. She checked on something and asked the doctor to complete the requests. They didn't care as long as she paid.

I never noticed until I heard my wife say something about the gender mix-up when I showed up for the test. The receipt said I was a seventy-one-year-old female, which looked strange when I stuck my hairy arm through the window. Debbie persuaded the nurses to accept the receipts. I caved and returned home without the test when I tried.

Once a year, Dr. Wong did an ultrasound. He did routine checks before finding a quarter-sized shadow on my left kidney in March 2007. He called for a CT scan, but it wasn't conclusive. Then, he ordered an MRI, and I booked an appointment to see him. I entered the doctor's mini office/examination room and sat on the stool beside his desk, waiting for the verdict. He had the report and said,

"Well, it looks clear. You have a malignant tumor."

Just then, his cell phone rang, and he answered it.

Really? Did he tell me I have cancer and take a phone call?

And it was about a parking space in the building he lived in!

He got off and told me I had two options: take a PET scan for a sharper image or arrange surgery to remove my left kidney and plan for dialysis. If a PET was the clearest, why not do that first? Because it cost $2,000, lasted several hours, had multiple shots, and most insurances refused to cover it while the CT was under a couple hundred, and an MRI ran $1,000.

The surgery seemed extreme.

"Are there other possibilities?"

"You could find a specialist to cut the tumor and the surrounding tissue out while keeping the kidney intact. You would still need to do the PET scan so the surgeon can see what he is cutting, and there is no guarantee your kidneys will work after."

"Are there Hong Kong surgeons that use minimally invasive technology?"

"Possibly, discuss with the specialist."

"How large will the opening be?"

"About four inches if it is minimally invasive and seven if it is open surgery."

WHAT??? I was expecting it to be two inches. We had different definitions for minimally. As daunting as it was, I chose the slice-and-dice option over complete removal. He handed me the name of an urologist/surgeon. They did both jobs.

I left the doctor's office, trying to figure out what the next few months would look like. Was this the end? What if the surgeon couldn't save enough function? Should I move to the U.S.?

Once again, I had unanswered questions.

I called the urologist, and his assistant arranged the scan. Two weeks later, I followed up to hear the findings. I endured sleepless nights but got used to that. I had slight, burning feelings in the location of my kidneys. It was hard to tell if they were real or imagined.

When the time arrived, I flew to Hong Kong to learn about my future. As I waited, I kept thinking, "Everything will be okay. How could

I have cancer?" Then it was my turn. I put down my Blackberry and walked into the examination room while the doctor stood up, shook my hand, and asked me to sit. He made small talk and then got down to business.

"You have two tumors that need to be removed."

When he said that, it felt like a load of bricks had fallen on my chest. This was the last test. Now, I had to face the consequences: not one, but two tumors!

"There are also two tumors in your right kidney, but they are not cancerous . . . yet."

What a pleasant surprise.

"Can you save the kidney and cut out the tumors?"

"I can do that."

"How big will the scar be, and how long will I stay in the hospital?"

"The scar will be twelve inches, and you will stay for ten days."

Twelve inches??? He showed me from front to back. He needed an enormous gap to reach his hands inside to have more room to work.

"What happened to minimally invasive?"

He only required a four-inch incision if I wanted him to remove the kidney.

"No, let's do what we need to."

He scheduled the surgery for the end of April, the start of a week's holiday in China, and right before my wife planned to give birth. If the procedure went well, I would fly back after being discharged.

As if it wasn't challenging already, the PET showed a blocked artery leading into my kidneys. The doctor suggested an angioplasty. A specialist would feed a pipe through a vein in my thigh until it reached the stoppage. Then, he would pump a balloon at the tip to insert a stent. It was a lot to take in, but I decided on the spot and scheduled both.

The angioplasty turned out to be no big deal. I got admitted, and the hospital charged me an HKD 50,000 ($6,400) deposit. It was an outpatient operation, but they checked me in. Within five hours, I was released. They let me leave upon paying the HKD 80,000 ($10,300) bill.

The kidney surgery was a whole different ballgame. I packed a bag and rode the tram to the infirmary. It stopped in front and was as slow as I could go without walking. I had to save up to pay these enormous bills, and I wasn't in a rush to be cut in half.

I checked in, and they charged an additional HKD 50,000 deposit. This surgery would use up my credit. To avoid this, I opted for a semi-private room with six beds and no privacy beyond a curtain. This hospital was ten times better than across the border. They provided multiple English channels, a decent food menu, and a motorized bed.

Not long after I completed signing the papers, the doctor showed up suited in operating blues, ready for some slicing. He drew marks on my body while explaining the procedure as if I was a cadaver.

As he walked out, he said, "Don't worry, you'll be just fine." He seemed calm. My greatest fear was not waking up after being anesthetized for five hours. That's a lengthy time. And just like that, they put me on a gurney and wheeled me around several wards until I arrived at the operating theater. They slid me onto the table, put the oxygen tubes in my nose, and I waited for the anesthesiologist to inject the sleeping potion. And then . . . I was out.

Five hours later, I woke with a gasp, coming up for air. The bright light of the operating room blinded my vision. I had an immense ache on my left side, which was wrapped in gauze, similar to an adult diaper. While in a daze, they lifted me onto another gurney and sent me to my bed. I tried to lift myself to slide over, and I had my first taste of EXTREME PAIN. Even with the drugs, I felt sliced in half, like a magic show gone wrong.

My lungs filled with fluid, forcing me to cough and shoot lightning pains through my nervous system. And then there was the catheter. When I touched the pipe, I wondered how did they insert it. I should have been worried about how they would remove it.

They locked me in, but I couldn't move without causing excruciating torment. The doctor reassured me he had inserted staples instead of stitches and said I shouldn't be concerned about tearing them open.

For ten days, I aimed to get well enough to be released. I grew concerned I would run out of credit and needed to check out before that happened.

In between the BP and blood tests, I answered phone calls and wrote emails. I practiced getting up because I hated using bedpans. My labs had to show my kidneys worked before they discharged me. Every day, they improved until I reached the same level as when I walked in.

Lastly, the doctor removed the catheter.

"Brace yourself. This is going to hurt."

Typically, doctors said, "This will feel like a pinch," or "This won't hurt at all."

What the hell then, "Whip!" The agony from gout and being sliced in half was surpassed by the sheer pain I experienced while the catheter was pulled out. I lost my breath but didn't scream out. Instead, I choked on my own air. That shit HURT.

I returned to my flat (after paying the HKD 280,000 ($36,000) bill) broke and broken. Every task exacerbated my torn muscles. When I coughed to clear the fluid in my lungs, the pain felt like a knife in my side. I required nourishment but resembled a dead man walking with little energy and ghastly pale. To prevent causing myself more pain, I ate what was in the apartment, canned soup. Once again, I dined alone on soup.

Clearly, I needed help, so I flew back to The Hai. The doctor said the air pressure wouldn't affect the fourteen-inch gash, and the staples would hold. It turned into a slow and painful journey, but I had extra motivation: My wife would give birth any day. She planned to have a C-section and waited to pick an auspicious moment. Since I came through, she booked her operation a few days later.

Things looked up with a baby boy's arrival and my tumors removed. My color filled in, and I continued my usual flying schedule. I stayed away from booze and had already quit smoking. My running increased to 100 kilometers a week. After I stopped the cigs, jogging became more manageable, but not as much as I had hoped.

As time passed, everyone, including myself, forgot that I had considerable chunks of my kidneys sliced out. On each occasion I exceeded my self-imposed limit, and my tests remained stable, I pushed it further. I was addicted to exceptional food and choice alcohol, not heroin. They were bad for me, but not the same type of vice. No matter how hard I attempted to avoid it, someone enticed me with a glass of wine or Scotch. People figured I had returned to normal if I gave in a little. I even fooled myself into thinking I could drink like the old days, but less often.

China grew seriously rich, and it showed in the quality of everything at the restaurants. Even the smaller towns joined the rush to modernize. In the past, it impressed me when I ate at a rustic joint, and they served Diet Coke. I called it a "KFC moment." When KFC came to town, long lines formed. It became a celebration, and nothing pleased me more than discovering one in the hinterlands after a *baijiu* bender. I knew that life would change in surprising ways the next time I visited that city. Now, things had moved to the other end of the spectrum. If you asked what they offered to drink, the server would list Western and Chinese beverages to pair with your steaming bowl of bull penis soup.

Unfortunately, there was more bad news about my health. Before my CT scan in 2008, I felt my kidneys burning in my back again. I predicted a poor diagnosis, and I was correct: the two tumors in my right kidney needed to be dealt with. I also had other unremarkable nodes in both. They had the potential to turn into cancer.

The doctor wanted to try a different approach.

"We can't keep doing open surgery on you every year."

I agreed as I had difficulty recovering. I couldn't imagine going through that again. In fact, I almost preferred to ride it out without the operation, but I had to do whatever I needed for the sake of my family.

The new procedure was less invasive. It was a treatment called RFA (Radio Frequency Ablation). This time, they inserted a narrow pipe into my kidney. Then, they utilized a laser inside the tube to burn the tumor. The casing guided the laser to ensure the tumor cells did not spread when punctured. It was high-tech, with possibilities for failure.

The laser-blasting lasted an hour. I exited with a band-aid over the point of entry. My blood tests were worse, but I had enough function. Why didn't they do this instead of open surgery? They weren't sure RFA would work.

With multiple tumors combated and more on the way, it was hard not to think the end might come sooner than I had planned. It made me want to get as much done as possible. So, I traveled to Perth, Australia, and Kuching, Malaysia, for the Inter-hash runs (a bi-annual joint world-hashing event) of 2008 and 2010. In total, I survived six Inter-hashes in Tasmania, Australia (2000); Goa, India (2002); Cardiff, Wales (2004); Chiangmai, Thailand (2006); Perth (2008); and Kuching (2010). In Cardiff, I developed gout in both knees. It was nearly impossible to walk, let alone run a 10k. I spent the weekend catching up on emails, answering work calls, and watching my friends get drunk.

For Perth, I used my massive, frequent flier miles to fly business. I arrived at night and was the first off. A customs agent stood before the booth and asked to see my passport.

"What is the purpose of your visit?"

"I'm here for the Hash."

With a population of only 1.6 million, everyone in town should know about a running event attracting 5,000 individuals. Evidently, I met the one uninformed person. She said, "Come with me." As a business class passenger, I thought she was giving me expedited service until I saw we were headed towards the "take all your shit out" lane.

"You realize I was talking about the Hash House Harriers, the running event, right?"

"Take everything out."

She looked through my toiletry, my massive collection of meds, each piece of paper and card in my wallet, notebooks, work papers, laptop, phone, and Blackberry. The longer it took, the more frustrated she got. I worried she would pull out a rubber glove. In the end, she let me go because I had nothing.

I learned that not everybody knows about the Hash.

Next, my close friend from Chicago talked me into flying to Jamaica on a side trip from my regular U.S. visit. Upon finishing the fourteen-hour flight to Chicago, it was a quick seven-hour journey to paradise. We flew down for three days, and I continued on my trip.

Then, I joined my Shanghai friend to travel to Pamplona, Spain, for the running of the bulls. It was a bucket list trip, and I had to do it before my health system crashed. At the time, I suffered from sciatica with pain shooting from the middle of my back down my leg. I didn't plan on running, but you will run when you have bulls the size of compact cars chasing you. And I did, two days in a row.

For business, I flew to Paris once a year for a meeting. While there, I took advantage of the museums, food, and wine. I woke up early due to jet lag and ran in different parts of the city. I quickly became familiar with the streets. But Paris was a tough city to navigate as a sufferer of gout.

Future trips would be challenging, and I was glad to see as much as I did.

II

2007 and 2008 turned into tough years with health problems, surgeries, and a stock market crash. At the same time, the Middle Kingdom was not showing signs of slowing down. Everything marched forward.

As development increased speed, more apartment buildings entered the market. Our two-bedroom grew too small for two adults, two kids, and in-laws. I enjoyed my free space in Hong Kong but desired something spacious back in The Hai and looked for a four-bedroom before we got priced out. A flat of that size would cost 6 million RMB ($1 million). It seemed cheap when China was awash in cash. Locals threw around high dollar values when talking with friends and family about the apartments they purchased. Everyone stashed bricks of RuMBas somewhere. I, unfortunately, did not have piles under my bed and needed to gather all my assets.

I depleted my bank account until my insurance company reimbursed me for the surgeries. If I sold stock, I would take a forty percent loss after the crash. To purchase the place we looked for required a few hundred thousand for a down payment. That was the value of the flat we lived in.

Ten years ago, I objected to transferring a single dollar over for fear of being unable to take it out. Now, I moved most of our savings to ride the real estate wave and have a better quality of life. Plus, I was tired of smelling everyone's garbage in the elevator.

My wife dug out her list of agents and made calls. We focused on the Bund area. A grocery store was high on the checklist again, but I knew where all the best supermarkets were, and we couldn't afford anything within walking distance.

She searched for a couple of weeks before finding a place. I didn't have time to transfer money, but I had to see it.

On the walk over, she said, "The building isn't finished, so expect a mess. It will have a swimming pool and a health club when completed."

The more she told me, the more I thought about walking away. Like my first apartment, I had seen too many "coming soon" notices for malls and clubhouses. That mall never opened. No, I was not interested in coming attractions.

But the flat was a perfect size, right off the southern bridge, crossing over to Pudong and to the airport. That was a significant plus, so I needed to look.

The building was in a small complex with a partially built and three completed high-rises. One of the finished towers housed the families who had their houses demolished to erect these vertical palaces. That building had smaller apartments, and the people seemed angrier. The other towers had larger flats sold at market price, i.e., a lot and rising.

We looked at a four-bedroom with three baths. The agent said we could buy the gray jail cell with bare concrete or a finished unit with five-star amenities. Decorating our current apartment took a measurable amount of trouble, so we chose the completed option. But it was a risk to trust the agent on the quality.

They gave the choice of a top floor or something closer to the ground. The higher up you went, the more the price. We picked the best unit for the cost. The agent agreed to hold it at the existing price until we put down a deposit. We needed to move fast before somebody else swooped in with RuMBas on hand. I resisted putting cash down until we had a guaranteed loan. That disadvantaged us against someone who didn't sweat, laying out lots of dough. I had plenty of concerns. My wife had none. She was fearless in securing the mortgage. A few hours later, she returned with the good news: she found a bank that would loan the rest of the funds. Just like that, she sorted it out and informed the agent. She secured the money, and I paid the mortgage. Our fortune was nothing compared to the cash others walked out of banks with, but it shocked and impressed me. If it worked out and everybody seemed pleased, I didn't need to ask questions.

I just wanted to move.

III

Life near the Bund was great, except my friends hung out at an American pub called Bubba's on the other side of town. The distance prevented me from regularly joining my fellow inebriates. Also, as one of the few with a family, having a social life became harder.

We lived just south of the old Chinese walled city. It was not a destination for barhopping or excellent restaurants but great for sightseeing, picture taking, and local shopping. The surrounding stores were tailors, and vendors sold fabric scraps. Nothing appealed to me, but my in-laws loved that outside our complex, bargaining was the name of the game. Many tourists explored the neighborhood to experience the "real" Shanghai. But when I needed to get home, the crowded streets were not what I wanted as a last-minute obstacle.

I started getting up at 6 a.m. to run the length of the Bund on weekends. I ran from the Nanpu Bridge through the neglected ruins of 1930s wharves that metamorphosed into a yacht dock, a fake beach, and a nightlife destination. Then I passed the Bull on the Bund (a brass bull built to outdo the Wall Street one, bigger and redder with a guard to ensure tourists didn't rub the balls for luck), ran along the river up to Waibaidu Bridge (built in 1906), and down Suzhou Creek. On the run back, I ran on the building side with the obstacles of slow-walking pedestrians. The round trip was twelve kilometers and the best way to enjoy the waterfront.

If running wasn't possible because of the weather, the air, or convenience, I worked out at a health club. My first gym was a garage-sized room with free weights and a smoking section I found down a lane near my "Watermelon Street" flat. I paid 10 RMB a month.

The few health clubs remained inside hotels and cost $1,300 a year. I refused to pay that much and waited for something better.

Every year, AmCham threw an Independence Day party. Fourth of July bashes were essential for all Yanks. The event turned into an opportunity for fellow drunks to carry on until they canceled the free flow. The events also gave American companies entering the market a chance to promote themselves. One such business was Gold's Gym. The investment group bringing Gold's to China used this occasion to give a discount to individuals willing to take a leap of faith that they would open. I grew desperate for a straightforward (and affordable at $250 a year) health club, so I handed over the cash despite my suspicions. They accepted my payment, and the gym never opened. For years, I heard no news, and then, out of the blue, I received a letter telling me not only did they plan to open, but they gave me a two-year membership!

They restored my faith.

Not long after my membership finished, they shut down for good. The space transformed into a massage parlor—a more profitable business. At least I received my money's worth.

In the 2000s, health clubs experienced colossal growth. I joined a gym called California Fitness because Californians were the fittest, of course. Locals discovered the benefits of workout rooms, and they expanded all over the city. Years ago, the Chinese watched us with shock when they saw foreigners running because they didn't understand why we put our bodies through trouble. Weren't we tired from working? Then, more citizens engaged in some form of exercise. I waited in anticipation for the club in my complex to open. They fixed all the landscaping, but the entertainment center took longer. Three years later, they opened the doors to the workout room with three unstable treadmills, a dangerous weight station, a motel-sized swimming pool, a two-person sauna, and a tiny changing room. We paid the inflated annual fee and had the pool to ourselves. But a couple of months later, the price dropped, neighbors inundated the place, and the changing room became a crowded mess of naked elderly men. I passed through this assemblage of nakedness to shower at home. Locals came in to bathe so they didn't have to pay for the water bill. It was common to see individuals strolling around my complex wearing robes and carrying a basket of shower amenities. Even outside residents found it a convenient location to get clean and showed up in their PJs. All-day pajamas were a way of life for Shanghainese. The government discouraged it as backward, but old habits were hard to quit. However, the influx of bathers motivated me to put away my trunks and stick to running.

The more we lived in our apartment, the more shortcomings I discovered. It took them two years to finish an empty tiled lobby with a sofa that became the resting recliner for delivery guys. Every day, the trash had to be brought down in the same elevator that carried people up, similar to our last place. This occurred when I left for the airport at 6:15 a.m. It was the most toxic thing to smell in the morning and on par with the rotting watermelons.

Most Shanghainese chose flats near an outstanding school; that's how prized a spot in a reputable institution was. Shanghai public schools had the highest ratings in the world. Everyone wanted their kids to go to a top one, and it was competitive, even at the kindergarten level. In our area, we had many excellent institutions to choose from. Debbie and her parents researched, waited in line, and shared the info with others doing the same. Everybody used any tool, including cultivating the right *guanxi* to get in. My daughter resembled a full foreigner with gray eyes. She had an easier time because schools desired foreign or mixed-blood kids to appear international. My son looked more Asian and had a more challenging time. The birth year also played a part as 2007 turned into an explosive year for babies.

Around this period, a series of mass stabbings occurred in kindergartens. It was a constant worry for parents. Children were an easy target to take out grievances, such as a lost job or lover. Without guns, knives were the weapon of choice. One guy did it first, then others copied. The government placed a police officer in front of each school when the kids arrived and left, but the cops looked useless and distracted.

Either the situation improved, or they hid the news about other cases.

Shanghai prepared to hold a major international event, The World Expo, and they would do anything to prevent something from tarnishing it.

But before that, Beijing took the spotlight with the Olympics.

IV

In 2008, Beijing held the Summer Olympics. The media advertised this as China's coming-out party. Before the games, everything needed to be cleaned, especially near the Olympic neighborhoods. They built a humongous airport, new stadiums, and high-speed rail lines. Roads and metro tracks tore through the city. When I left Beijing in 1991, they had two subway lines; in 2008, they had eight, with more planned (there are twenty-seven lines now!). They leveled historic districts and replaced them with high-rises. It became everyone's duty to make the Olympics a success, including moving to farmlands, an hour away if your house was in the path of construction. Citizens supported the event, no matter what they required.

Back in 2001, I couldn't wait for the spectacle. Seven years later, China grew affluent, and ticket prices skyrocketed as if numbers meant nothing. The rates at hotels increased beyond an acceptable range. It seemed an event that would be better to watch on TV.

Since Beijing received all the glory, Shanghai felt left out. The city wished to lift its stature on the world stage. The World's Fair was the perfect gala. They would reach a comparable number of countries, and the fair, or Expo, lasted six months compared to two weeks for the Olympics. But it no longer was the jaw-dropping experience it used to be when no one had smartphones. I remembered my days at the Museum of Science and Industry and the World's Fair: Columbian Exposition of 1893 held there. They had inventions people had not seen before. It was an eye-opening occurrence and nothing like the Expo of today.

Now, it focuses on green technology and who can create the most attractive pavilion to advertise why to visit—similar to a travel agency.

For China, it turned into a matter of saving face. They wanted every country to take part. The central government pressured organizations that neglected to sign up. Most countries joined just as they go along with what the Middle Kingdom demands these days.

The U.S. passed, and the PRC considered this a significant snub. America's non-attendance would tarnish it as not worth going. The Chinese government would not allow this. They tried hard to coerce America. For anyone who had the remotest idea about what makes China tick, you knew they would never forget such a loss of face. They would talk about it a century from now. The one person with power who recognized the importance was Secretary of State Hillary Clinton. She persuaded the right people in the U.S. government to agree. Then, she found funding through the private sector. Ultimately, Secretary Clinton got the project off the ground and averted a political crisis.

I supported the Expo since our apartment was on the edge of the Puxi fairgrounds. The government would convert the district into a riverside park after the fair. And having the Expo on our doorstep meant they completed the subway stations, and our neighborhood was beautified. Buildings, elevated roads, and street markings were repainted. It increased the value of our flat.

We anticipated the opening ceremony. This would be a spectacular fireworks display, and we had a front-row seat, with our apartment having an undisturbed view of the river and the Lupu Bridge. I picked up a bucket of KFC on the way through the various security roadblocks. The closer we came, the more police and soldiers we saw. Each looked at me with suspicion. That feeling only heightened as I entered the elevator and pushed the button to the top. Several PLA snipers headed to the roof and hung out on our floor. Their presence made me relieved I did not arrange the Expo bash I thought about having. A bunch of party-going foreigners would cause the police to knock.

Because I lived so close, I envisioned visiting often. There was a lot to see. We received multiple free tickets for residing in the area, and I bought a week pass. After the event started, we kept receiving vouchers from other sources. Everyone handed them out. If they gave away the tickets, they made no money. They were more concerned about attendance. Shanghai required more individuals to attend than before. The record of sixty-four million visitors was set at the Osaka World's Fair in 1970. They needed over 360,000 attendees per day for six months to beat that record. During peak periods, they expected 500,000 individuals.

I waited a month to let the eager ones go first while I waltzed in after the euphoria wore down. Massive crowds showed up when it opened, but then interest collapsed. The attendance dropped to 30,000. This was a gigantic problem for the government but an excellent opportunity for me.

I bit the bullet and entered. I walked around the SOE (state-owned enterprise) pavilions but didn't see the point of waiting in line to hear about oil and gas exploration or the electric grid. The highlight was a large Coca-Cola pavilion handing out Coke samples. Still, I didn't care to learn about the history of Coke.

A half-hour later, I took the ferry across the river to see the much-talked-about international pavilions. That side was spread out, with lots of walking. There were over two hundred exhibits, with about twenty worth visiting. On light attendance days, the lines to enter the popular exhibits were longer than I would have waited for a kick-ass roller-coaster. My Expo experience turned into a bad one. Even though I had a seven-day ticket, I never returned. My wife and in-laws used the remaining passes. They told me about the four-hour peak-day lines and the seven-hour wait for the popular pavilions. I would not queue seven hours for an exhibit about how green Russia or Saudi Arabia were. No thanks. Following the closure, the strange structures were supposed to be dismantled. This requirement only fell on the international pavilions. On my side, the buildings became rundown and overgrown with weeds. Barbed wire fences surrounded the entire area, resembling the aftermath of a war or a zombie apocalypse. I passed through the site daily and reminded myself of my miserable time.

V

My weak kidney function kept me out of the hospital with expanding side effects. I suffered from gout almost daily. It lingered in my joints, waiting for the right moment. I was familiar with it in my toes and ankles, but it moved to my elbows and hands. My hand swelled to twice the usual size, and my skin stretched to the limit. I could barely bend my fingers for six weeks. The only consequence was that it bloomed in my left and not my right. I had to be careful not to bump anything to prevent excruciating pain, and I held my balloon hand under the table when I ate or met someone. If I forgot, I would hear, "Oh my God! What happened?"

I was already explaining why I avoided food and walked funny; I didn't want to explain why my hand had blown up, too.

Then, it appeared in my elbows, enlarging them to where my arms would not bend. Whether I attempted to type on a computer, lift my carry-on bag, or brush my teeth, only when my joints swelled up, and those tasks were no longer effortless did I cherish my health.

Once the swelling subsided, blood got trapped in the bursa, the thin, fluid-filled sac at the tip of the elbow. It had to be removed by sticking a wide gauge needle into the baseball-sized sac and sucking out the blood. I did this procedure in Hong Kong twice, but once, I did it at the local clinic in The Hai. I did labs at this hospital, a low-down place in a forgotten neighborhood, soon to be erased. All the doctor had to do was suck the blood out. And he did, but when he filled the syringe (a big one), he shot the liquid through the air, into the garbage can five feet away, and jabbed the needle back into my elbow to suck more. It seemed unsanitary, but it only cost $1.50 to see him. What did I expect?

I handled gout in some areas better than others. The worst was my feet because I used them often, walking, sitting, or lying down; no position eased the suffering. I limped through airports and around town. All I thought about was reaching my destination to soak my feet for relief. Often, I collapsed as soon as I entered my Hong Kong apartment after traveling all morning from The Hai. My dogs were throbbing, smoking hot, and swollen. The pain went straight to my brain.

Perhaps it's hard for a healthy person to understand the level of torture. You may think, "It's just a foot pain. What's the big deal?"

The agony was similar to being tased or shocked, and it only stopped if I stayed still. That became impossible when sleeping. The slightest touch from a bed sheet would cause agony. I increased my intake to two sleeping pills and an NSAID to no avail. I was so miserable that I returned to drinking the Chinese black tar cocktail, but nothing stemmed **THAT FUCKING GOUT SHIT (TFGS)**. It was constantly on my mind, but I hid my illness to look normal.

In 2010, I turned forty. Despite my ailments, I wished to do something special. Since I had made it this far, I needed to celebrate. The best venue was a private rooftop room at a short-lived Lawry's The Prime Rib in Xintiandi. I invited ten friends to enjoy a steak dinner with four hours of wine and whiskey imbibing. Most of the party moved on to Da Tong Road, a strange underground bar street that had difficulty attracting customers because of the location. It was the government's solution to hide the mayhem of the old bar streets: Banish the foreigners to below ground! We enjoyed eight hours of booze and an evening to remember. Nights like that did not help, but with **TFGS**, sometimes, I felt nothing. I had to wait before I knew if I was in the clear. I might be at another bash by then.

Fortunately, **TFGS** decided not to punish me right after my birthday bender. It was good, considering I booked a hectic flight schedule over the next seven months. I flew to H.K., Paris, H.K., Malaysia, H.K.,

Tokyo, H.K., Seoul, L.A., Cincinnati, Chicago, Jamaica (Yeh Mon), NYC, H.K., Manila, H.K., Hanoi, H.K., L.A., Vegas, three round trips to three China offices and stops back home in The Hai every chance I got. Yeah, I did some mad traveling.

Visits to Hanoi and later to Bangladesh, India, Indonesia, and Cambodia were to monitor production as we moved out of China. In 1994, salaries were 250-300 RMB; in 2010, they rose to 3,500 RMB with a 25 percent increase in the exchange rate. Workers refused to do monotonous labor when they could work in a hotel with air conditioning or as a server in a new restaurant. These opportunities did not exist twenty years ago.

I continued my heavy travel schedule through the beginning of 2011 with off-and-on attacks from **TFGS**. When my birthday rolled around again, I worried about a surprise attack. Unlike my fortieth, I didn't have plans for a blowout. Instead, I arranged a small gathering with Tim, a factory owner friend. I canceled a visit to his hotel (he owned at least one and many other businesses) because of **TFGS**, and I owed him a *baijiu* bash to try his family hootch. Over the years, I drank many types of rocket fuel, but never from an earthen jar; I had only seen these vessels in movies like *Red Sorghum* or *Yellow Earth*. We planned my birthday as the occasion to break out the jug.

He accompanied me to a top hotel in Dongguan, and we followed the server to a VIP room. The quality of everything in Dongguan had improved beyond what I experienced during my inaugural stay at the windowless guesthouse. Now, the hotels and restaurants appeared to be something you would experience in Hong Kong, Vegas, or NYC— very fashionable and expensive. The earthen jar sat on a table against the wall. It looked deceivingly small. My host always showed up ready for the meals either with fine wine or prime sake, and once, he surprised me with a case of Laphroaig: *He brought a dozen bottles of Laphroaig to dinner!*

At my birthday feast was a solid dude who had worked for me for fifteen years. I hired him in Shanghai, and he participated in the never-ending Chuan lunches, bowling parties, and BBQ feasts at my

"Watermelon Street" flat. I knew he could hold his own since I gave him proper training. Tim and his niece, who co-managed the business, had excellent taste in food and liquor and kept up with me. I had to control myself to keep the evil **TFGS** monster at bay. Even with my handicap, I figured we could empty the vessel.

Not surprisingly, I ended up drinking more *baijiu* than I should have. I tried to stick to the vino, but the jar never stopped pouring. We drank for three hours before I called it quits. I found out the pot held four and a half standard bottles. It would have been a bottle per person if we wanted to finish. During my road warrior years, I would not have surrendered. But I had to. I was also required to save room for later.

At the karaoke, Tim called an employee to tag team *ganbei'ing* with me when he reached his limit. It was difficult not to drink when the party rolled on. If I left, it would end.

"No more *baijiu* for me" was my only imperative. I had the *baijiu* burps, and I needed to diffuse the situation. I ordered Absolut, with 40 percent alcohol instead of 65 percent (*baijiu*). Vodka and sodas were easy to down. The karaoke staff kept filling miniature pitchers and putting them on the table. There was plenty, but they opened more bottles (**Rule #2**). I took control to prevent wastage. This was an example of the excesses of China. But I had to call it a night. I agreed to join lunch with a U.S. coworker visiting the factory. I didn't need to be there, but I said I would. No matter what, I wouldn't wimp out and nurse my hangover. All three of my companions had to be at the plant at 8 a.m.! I'm not sure how constructive they were, but they showed up. It didn't help that everyone else stayed close to the factory while I lived an hour away at the "good hotel."

The following day, I arrived at 10 a.m., just enough time to walk the production lines. Then we had lunch. There wouldn't be *baijiu* at this meal. My coworker was not a "China hand," so I didn't expect to have an authentic bash. Fortunately, he was open to drinking some fantastic reds Tim ordered. I required something to take the edge off. Things looked up after a few bottles. Nothing better than being inebriated on a sunny day in Southern China.

I wanted to stay and drink more reds but needed to return to Hong Kong. My factory owner friend also had to go back and gave me a ride. That saved me from sitting in waiting rooms and lugging my luggage while lit. It also spared me the same trouble in H.K., as his driver would send me to my apartment. Usually, we did not exit the car when we arrived at customs on the border. The officers accepted our passports through the window and did a quick look at everyone in the vehicle. After a stamp, we drove a short distance to H.K. customs, and they did the same. Sometimes, we had to get out and walk across, but it still beat the hassle of the bus or ferry.

Back in Hong Kong, Tim wanted to have dinner. I came down from my lunchtime buzz, and I refused to disappoint. We went to his restaurant to eat (he owned his own place) and drink some more. But I had to put a limit on it. I preferred to be reasonably energetic for work the next day and needed sleep.

It was another end to a couple of days on the bottle.

I made an exception for my birthday but knew I would pay for it.

Two weeks later, I did.

VI

At the end of May 2011, I traveled to Paris again. This time, my wife and kids arranged to meet me after the meeting. We would fly to Munich and make our way by train through Austria, Italy, and Switzerland, all in a week. I got excited about the opportunity to watch them experience a new world. However, I woke up on the morning of my flight, and **TFGS** made its presence known. In the days following my birthday bash, I did everything to control my diet, but **TFGS** would not ease up. I sensed an ache in my big toe and ankle. With trains and hotels set, I could only hope for a light version.

I popped an NSAID and slid into the taxi to the airport. The anguish ratcheted up when I arrived. With every step, I further angered **TFGS**, only to receive its wrath the next time I stood on my feet.

Nothing eased the pain, and the air pressure made it more intense. My throbbing foot gave me a fever and cold sweats. For ten hours, I tried to take my mind off the torment by watching movies and constantly switching positions, but there would be no resting with **TFGS**.

When we landed at 5 a.m., it was clear this would be grueling. Ordinarily, I took the train and subway, but I needed to walk as little as possible. I jumped in a taxi and arrived at the hotel at 8 a.m. They wouldn't give me a room until 3 p.m. and forced me to find a place to wait for seven hours. I was inclined not to wander with every slow step, causing damage. My options looked terrible.

The best place to waste time would be the Louvre. It was close, but it would be a lot of walking to reach the entrance. Once in, they had plenty of benches to view the paintings or rest. While surrounded by the most exceptional paintings in the world, all I thought about was soaking in the tub.

As the day continued, **TFGS** grew worse. I returned at three, and they still made me stand by for a half-hour before giving me the key. Then I lugged my bags up the stairs, ironed my clothes, and sent the many emails I had typed on the plane. Inevitably, I received another hundred emails, which curtailed my soaking.

I felt better submerged in the water, but it was short-lived. Regular sleep would be impossible with my body's illness and chemical imbalance. I also waited for a message about the dinner and hoped my colleagues had picked a nearby restaurant. And they did, only fifteen minutes away. As we walked, I did my best to keep up and converse while in severe agony. I hated having to reveal that I had **TFGS**. Often, I told people I twisted my ankle running. That sounded right, but it did not explain why I refused to drink.

During the meal, I struggled to focus while holding my throbbing foot under the table. Fortunately, the dinner went quickly, with my coworkers fatigued. Once someone paid the bill, I hobbled to the hotel and the tub for more restless sleep.

The next day, I lacked energy. It became challenging to remain awake for long sessions. I pinched myself, twisted my fingers, and bit my tongue to keep my eyes open. I wondered why I had difficulty sleeping at night but quickly fell asleep when I needed to be cognizant.

Later, the business dinner on the second day ran over. I sat, trying to avoid drinking more wine with a beautiful glass in front of me. How do you travel to France without imbibing a fair share of vino?

I searched for something simple to eat, but this was Paris. What I thought would be a plain pork chop turned into a bone marrow stew with all the richness you would expect from a French restaurant. It tasted amazing but not the type of meal for a sufferer of **TFGS**.

Two hours had passed, but the conversation kept going. I limited what I said and waited for the lull when people had nothing more to say or the person paying the bill ended the evening. Then, there was the last-minute offer for dessert or coffee, which added another half-hour.

My mind dreamed of the moment I would return to the comfort of the tub, my bed for the evening. I needed to be at the airport at 5 a.m. to meet my wife and kids to catch our 7 a.m. to Munich. That was in six hours. There would be no chance for nocturnal healing tonight.

At last, the meal concluded, and we squeezed into a cab, giving me no space to relieve my foot during the half-hour ride. I could barely get in and out. By the time we reached the hotel, I had four hours to soak before going to the airport.

It was a terrible way to live.

I looked like a mess when I met my family in the transit lounge. They brought pills from home, and I gobbled them down to no avail. We were about to fly to the biggest beer-drinking area in the world, and I was in no shape to take part. At least in Paris, I could sip wine, but there would be nowhere to hide a gigantic stein.

The flight lasted an hour, about all I could handle. Upon arrival, Debbie had a close friend from Putian living in a suburb near the city, picking us up in her car, which amazed her: Here was her classmate, driving her own vehicle in Germany. I think that motivated her to get a driver's license.

I met Jackie when she helped me find my Putian apartment with the friendly neighborhood pig. Later, she changed to the footwear business, worked for a German brand of athletic shoes, transferred to Germany, met a German, married, and settled down. She had a great job, a car, and a home in another country. Bravo! She lived the dream.

Jackie drove us to her house to stay for a night.

"But first, my husband is meeting us at a beer garden for lunch."

Oh shit. What do I do? It was a 'damned if you do and damned if you don't' situation. Usually, I would have been all in. They cooked fresh *Weisswursts* and *Bratwursts*: grilled stuffed animal casings, with the juices waiting to burst at the first fork and knife piercing. They served rabbit pate with liver, giblets, and white asparagus soup prepared from local vegetables in season; some amazing gastronome stuff and the worst things for someone struggling with **TFGS**.

When I visited Munich during Oktoberfest in 1999, I ate huge, crispy pork knuckles and drank massive amounts of ale. That was the way I devoured anything different and delicious. Now, I avoided most things, but I couldn't say no to this array. It was why I had **TFGS**. Even with it, I ordered a beer. Of course . . . it was a beer garden!

My pride would be the end of me.

Soon, both of my feet suffered from **TFGS**. They had turned purplish and squishy because of the blood collection and the subsequent nerve damage to my calves, real fire, and pain. They tried to burst out of my shoes. I didn't expect to have **TFGS** when I packed my bag, so I only brought business clothes. My wife carried my more comfortable backpacking wear.

Upon arriving in Paris, I wrote her an email describing the best **TFGS** shoes she needed to bring. I wouldn't leave anything to chance in case she might pick the wrong pair. This was an emergency. During extreme situations, a beach shoe called Sanuks became THE ONLY footwear I wore, with soft rubber soles and a loose construction.

Thank God she carried the correct ones, but she stored them in her checked-in luggage. When I saw her at the airport, I had hoped for a change; my dogs expected it. If I knew we planned to go to lunch after arriving, I would have unzipped her bags and searched for them, but I wanted to save time. The most important thing was to soak.

Jackie's house was compact and vertical, with three levels straight up. She set us up on the top floor. I barely had the juice to make it. Once there, I didn't want to go down. Hell, I started my journey at 4 a.m., after three hours of restless sleep, but I reached this tub in a home in Munich. Why would I go anywhere else?

I planned to soak, pop another NSAID, and attempt to sleep.

My chances of passing out looked good after little rest over three days. Even if my eyes refused to close, my body was so exhausted that it would force my eyes to shut.

I slept, but I had no luck with the magic cure. Without my shoes, my feet expanded at will. My right blew up as if I had elephantiasis. My left experienced **TFGS** but was in the beginning stages. It was too early to tell if it would destroy me, similar to my right. NSAIDs provided scant comfort with lasting damage. It was a Catch-22: They helped me sleep but killed my kidneys.

The more I popped, the closer I got to the end, but I was desperate.

Jackie sent us to the train station for the next leg the following day. She had gifts for our kids, but I refused to carry the extra weight. We said our goodbyes and traveled to the other side of Munich, the neighborhood I stayed in during Oktoberfest twelve years ago. Having lived in China for so long, it shocked me to see nothing changed during that period. The hotel was beside the subway entrance, an easy journey if I didn't have bum feet. A short jaunt now took longer, and the weight from the backpack put more pressure on me. I compensated by leaning on my left foot, and soon, I had unbearable pain in both.

We reached the hotel before noon, and I fretted they wouldn't give the room until 3 p.m. Perhaps my miserable appearance prompted sympathy, or Germans were more flexible than the French; they handed over the key without the wait.

Inside the room, I headed for the tub. My wife and kids wanted to explore, but I barely made it from the bed to the bathroom. Sightseeing no longer interested me; I was in too much agony. Any movement caused more anguish, fever, and sweat. Meanwhile, my BP remained in the 200 range, and my skin felt parched and itchy from the baths. There was no way to win this war, but we didn't come this far to stay in a hotel.

I bit my lip and dealt with it as we ventured out.

In the end, I made it through a week of traveling around Europe before arriving at our destination of Bern, Switzerland. Jackie's husband worked there and kept an apartment. He allowed us to stay before we took a train to Paris for the plane to The Hai.

I couldn't believe **TFGS** would not let up during the entire week. On the one hand, it was a grand adventure with my family, but it also transformed into a week of twenty-four-hour non-stop throbbing hell for me. I missed out on the culinary delights because food frightened me, unlike my Chinese alter ego, Mr. Thunder. That guy ate and drank everything in his path while I was a quivering mess.

I felt a sense of victory when I boarded the plane. I avoided letting **TFGS** stop our European holiday. All I needed was to get through the flight, walk the vast distance from the gate to customs in The Hai, wait in the taxi line for an hour, and take an hour's ride home.

And that would be when I could rest in my own bed and tub.

Once airborne, the air pressure worsened my suffering beyond what I thought was the maximum. The throbbing, swelling, and burning were amplified. The nerves sent constant shocks to my system. I rubbed my feet the entire time. It turned into the worst flight in my life, period, and I counted each minute and stared at the video path for ten hours.

I prayed for the plane to move faster.

Finally, the wheels touched down, and I had my bags ready. The aircraft taxied to the final gate, which increased my hobbling. The entire plane passed me on the way to customs despite being the first off. I walked as slowly as possible to keep my temperature down to pass through the fever meter.

We picked up our suitcases and separated the crowd waiting at the exit with the luggage cart I leaned on to glide. Once through the doors, the hot, thick, and sticky air hit me in the face, but this time, I didn't mind. I was happy to be getting closer to my bed.

We reached home, and I dropped the bags, turned on the A/C, closed the curtains, and crashed because of the immense strain, particularly the last fourteen hours. In case my body forced me awake, I downed a few sleeping pills. I rose after a deep sleep. My body screamed for healing, and it broke down.

When I awakened, I pulled the sheet to see if I still experienced pain. I did, and it stayed with me for a month. I had minor swelling in the morning, making it the best time to wedge my shoes on. Afterward, I needed to wear them all day, or I squeezed my mushy purple dogs in with a shoehorn again.

I suffered from severe cases of **TFGS**, unrelenting for the next eight months, and each bout lasted longer. It was Brutal. If I woke early for a flight, I had to decide if I wanted to suffer through the trip or cancel and go when I had less torment. But there were fewer periods with manageable suffering. Some days, it was too unbearable even for my high tolerance. I would have set off the heat meters, anyway.

My wife found a TCM clinic in Shenzhen run by a specialist with a practice in the U.S. He had received great reviews from his American patients. Usually, they said they were a stage four or five (out of five) on the kidney failure scale, and his medicine brought them back. It seemed encouraging, but I had heard it before. I suspected I had no more chances and became determined to visit this doctor and follow his instructions.

On the day of my appointment, I did not want to contemplate the two-hour journey to the doctor's office on the other side of the border with **TFGS** nagging me. It was a tremendous amount of walking, but I survived.

I surprised the doctor by tracking him down in China. "You speak Chinese well," was the farthest thing from my mind when my spongy feet were on fire with nerves like live wires. He glanced at my tongue, held my wrist, and gave me a TCM prescription. I took it and gingerly made the journey back to Hong Kong. If you wish to challenge yourself, try marching up and down stairs with a severe case of **TFGS** for two hours, non-stop. It was a lengthy walk, and I FUCKING HATED

MYSELF for every step. The only motivation keeping me going was knowing that each shock carried me closer to salvation.

We bought the herbs in The Hai and stewed them for four hours, producing the dark brown elixir I consumed three times a day. This doctor's formula tasted no different from the other motor oil I gulped. My wife and in-laws brewed the drink in Shanghai, and I attempted to stew it in Hong Kong. I made it once without a problem. Then I cooked it after coming back from a big evening. That was a horrible idea.

After I started the brew, I laid down (you can see where this is going). I set my alarm, but it never rang. Miraculously, I woke up as the pot was burning. It appears I had a guardian angel keeping up with me.

For two weeks, I drank the elixir with no improvement. It was March 2012, and I joined a tour to Thailand with the Hash. There would be lots of beer drinking and seafood eating, but not by me unless **TFGS** cleared up. It had attacked me hard for more than a year, so my chances for a recovery did not look great. I grimaced through it, poured my witches' brew into a couple of thermos bottles, and packed them in my luggage, hoping no one would think it was suspicious to travel with a bunch of liquid-filled containers.

After all I had been through, I needed a rest. I planned to avoid the run and float in the shallow waters of Koh Samui and maybe get some solid sleep. Floating had the same effect as soaking. I would be weightless, with no pressure on my feet. It was the perfect cure.

My hopes were dashed when I stepped onto the sand. Since I had no firm footing, each step flexed my ankles and toes. I would have preferred walking on nails. Once I started, I couldn't stop, or my feet burned. One step, pain, wait for a few seconds, burn . . . take another step, pain, wait . . . burn. Repeat until I reached the water. I floated for hours and never wanted to leave.

When my group prepared for dinner, I mustered the courage to race to the nearest chair before I passed out from the pain. The rest of my stay was no better. At least I didn't get molested. I would have been an easy target as a gimp.

I chugged the molasses water and returned to the clinic to tinker with the formula. It was hard to go every two weeks, so I asked for a lengthier prescription. Besides, what improvements could he make? Why not give me the most potent medicine for a person suffering from relentless **TFGS**? There should be a mixture that worked best, right?

Soon, I would no longer need his recipe.

Things were about to go south for good.

VII

After my last trip to the TCM specialist, my movements became sluggish, similar to being stuck in quicksand. The most straightforward tasks turned energy draining. The last time this happened, they checked me in for kidney failure, but I hoped it was a false alarm.

My optimism disappeared when I couldn't sit up or turn over one morning. It seemed as if an invisible weight held me down. I grew frustrated and required help to stand up.

In the past, I had problems standing because of sciatica. That pain shot an electric current from my waist down a nerve in my leg, and I straightened my backbone as if twice my age. All the planes, trains, ferries, and automobiles I had taken over twenty years and the rock-hard beds I slept on took a toll. To treat it, I went to a TCM ward twice a week to lie down while they placed hot pouches of herbs on my lower back. It was enjoyable, and I dozed off on the table, but it did nothing.

Then I switched hospitals, and the next one strapped me to a machine for thirty minutes that stretched me like a medieval torture device. After, I flipped over, and they electro-shocked my ass cheeks for an additional thirty. Holy shit! The first jolt was a surprise. "Bzzzt!" It felt similar to sticking my finger in a live socket, but it was my ass. The nurse turned a dial to alter the strength of the shock and the number of seconds between each. It varied depending on who hooked me up. As torturous as the treatments were, they didn't cure my ailment.

But my predicament appeared worse than a case of sciatica.

My wife dragged me in for a blood test. After giving a sample, I strolled out to buy groceries. Even in this miserable state, I took advantage of being near a foreign supermarket. The walk used to be five minutes, but now I required twenty.

When I reached the store, my wife called my cell. I avoided answering it: I knew it concerned my labs. And it was terrible news. My creatine level (the waste in your blood) was above 2000; an average person with functioning kidneys had a standard of below a hundred. Suddenly, it didn't seem necessary to fill my grocery list.

It was time for emergency dialysis. I survived more than one close call and would do it again. In fact, I experienced a precarious state every minute with a life-threatening BP.

My wife assured me the place I did the blood test had excellent kidney physicians. She still called around to find a better infirmary. The hospitals I visited before lacked empty beds. That was the problem when you lived in a country with 1.4 billion people. So, I stayed put.

The staff led me upstairs and arranged a single. I shared it with storage again, but it was better than the public ward. I lacked a bathroom, so I would be required to squat. That was a considerable obstacle.

While Debbie handled the details, I sat on my bed and looked out the window at Huaihai Park. Waiting for what came next, I watched individuals enjoying the sunny weather. That used to be me, going about my day without a care in the world. My freedom would soon be taken away, and I regretted the time I had wasted.

Despite having a shite room, I was grateful they gave me a bed until the hospital decided they had made a mistake: they didn't have approval to accept foreigners. Really? That seemed like something they would know right away. Why did it take so long to decide? Perhaps an administration head concluded they didn't want the risk, so they kicked me to the curb.

I was a very sick man with nowhere to go.

We tried a famous hospital on the Pudong side as a last resort. Patients came from all over to fight for a coveted numbered ticket to see a specialist. No ticket? You needed to wait until the following week. Most doctors saw twenty patients during their office hours as an obligation to the government. People had a few minutes to explain their situation before being nudged out. My in-laws usually lined up for me, but I headed to the emergency room this time.

The ER was packed with individuals and looked similar to a mash unit. We registered and waited for hours to be evaluated to see if I had passed the threshold of being deathly sick. With no capacity, it was a high bar, and I failed. They told me I was not close enough to death to be urgent in China and come back when I deteriorated.

That was Friday night. On Saturday, my slowness transformed into barely any movement. The weight grew heavier, making breathing harder. I felt I would have a heart attack at any moment. I needed emergency treatment.

Once again, my wife scrambled.

With no option, we planned to show up at a reputable place and take our chances. I grabbed my stuff and slowly headed downstairs to the taxi. I lifted each leg an inch or two off the ground to walk and had difficulty bending down.

Things worsened by the hour.

We arrived to join the wait at the ER. The reception nurse reviewed my blood tests, but I wasn't dying enough for this hospital, too. I leaned on my kids like crutches to walk, which seemed severe.

I sat for an hour before I saw a physician for a few minutes, and he ordered an EKG. They helped me lie flat, which should have been a warning sign. I felt as if rigor mortis had set in. My legs and arms moved on their own. I no longer controlled them. The test showed my heart worked well, but something else was wrong. Really? They recommended a series of IV drips.

We took the prescription and shuffled over to the drip room. There, we found row after row of sick individuals sitting in chairs hooked up to IVs, dozens of them. I couldn't stand without resting on something, but before I snagged a seat, we waited two hours to receive the medicine.

After Debbie reached the front of the line, I commandeered an open seat by strategically standing over someone with a drip almost empty and no refills. I knew how to play the game and prepared for my turn. What shocked me was the length of treatment: Twelve hours!

I would be stuck overnight in that disease-filled recliner.

Sitting there, I wondered why they put more fluid in my body if I suffered from kidney failure. Wouldn't that complicate the issue? I lasted an hour. I told Debbie I would rather lie at home while she attempted to get me into a proper hospital. If unsuccessful by Monday, I would fly to Hong Kong.

Two days later, we returned to the emergency room at the Pudong campus. A gridlock of taxis, bikes, pedicabs, and other riff-raff blocked the entrance. It forced us to disembark a hundred feet from the gate. When healthy, I preferred to walk, but now, a hundred feet seemed as challenging as a 100k. While I moved as if I wore gravity boots, my wife rushed ahead to start the registration.

By the time I made it to the entrance, I was exhausted and collapsed on the nearest uncomfortable plastic chair. With all the ill patients surrounding me, if I didn't arrive sick, I would be.

My wife found me and said there were no beds. She decided to try a secret VIP ward hidden in a building on the campus and headed over. She lifted me, and I possessed just enough juice to shuffle over in thirty minutes. I walked into the lobby and sank into a big leather armchair. The first floor stood empty besides a pair of recliners and some fake plants. From the outside, you wouldn't know this was a hospital. They only served connected locals and kept it low-key.

The longer I slept in the armchair, the more I realized Hong Kong might be my only choice. The walks were far between here and there. How would I manage? Would they allow me to fly? Did I miss the window of opportunity?

Finally, Debbie returned with the good news. After a long negotiation and a slight greasing, the VIP hospital agreed to admit me. Thank God. I didn't know what kind of health care I would receive or how much it would cost, but I had a place willing to accept me. That was a huge win.

She assisted me to the top floor, a special ER for the privileged. This room only had two patients lying on high-tech beds, no bleeding sufferers in the hallways, or families eating sunflower seeds. I had never witnessed facilities such as this in China. The bed they gave me was so new that they kept it wrapped in plastic. It looked similar to a museum piece. Do not touch! Why did they leave me dying when they had an empty bed?

It would have been worse if I croaked in the lobby.

We paid the deposit and signed the papers, relieving the hospital of responsibility. Then I changed into the lockup clothes while waiting for someone to whisk me into the operating theatre to insert an emergency dialysis pipe. This was not my first rodeo, and I assumed they would insert a tube in my neck. This doctor decided to go in through a major artery in my groin. He thought my neck vein might be closed and avoided it. I had no choice. I was an invalid who could no longer move my limbs and wouldn't have made it to Hong Kong.

As they wheeled me down the hall and into an elevator, I tried to gauge where they were taking me by following the ceiling tiles. The elevators were dual usage, so random visitors used the same lift, looking me over, trying to guess what ailed this foreigner. It was annoying.

The procedure of inserting the tube went quickly. After which, I had two six-inch pipes dangling from my crotch. Then, they sent me to the dialysis room in the public ward. Even the exclusive cadre VIP hospital did not have blood machines.

They made the booking and wheeled me outside, where I waited for a bread van to pick me up. It was evening and chilly. I had multiple layers of heavy blankets piled on top, adding to the weight on my chest. It felt scary when your brain signaled your arms and legs to move, but they refused. I kept trying, but it didn't happen, like when I drank too much.

The van arrived, and the staff lifted the stretcher and slid me in to join the rest of the people too lazy to walk. I couldn't see anything but blurred lights as the minivan maneuvered through the dark campus. I was aware this van lacked shocks and braced myself for the jolts to my bones when we hit the speed bumps, which should not have been necessary. There wasn't enough road to accelerate, but that didn't stop individuals from trying. The minivan stopped to allow the healthy ones off until we arrived at the final destination. They off-loaded and wheeled me into another elevator, taking me down to the blood machines in the basement.

People treated me with equal measures of shock and curiosity. "Why did this hairy beast choose to have kidney failure in China?" I wish I knew.

They weighed me, and I waited for the nurses to flush out the pipes before hooking me up for four and a half hours. Twenty machines churned away, giving individuals life for a few days. The room was silent except for blood pumping in and out of people's bodies. Occasionally, a patient had an adverse reaction and vomited or cried out from being miserable. I played my iPod and passed out. It sucked being the youngest, hanging with seniors who had already lived most of their lives. I'm sure they desired more time, but I required more. I was only forty-one.

When my spin cycle finished, they trucked me back to the soft ER bed. With clean blood circulating through my body, I slept for six hours before the nurse arrived to take samples at dawn.

It took two spin cycles in the ER to stabilize me before a standard room opened. I grabbed it before another VIP did. With a few empty beds in the entire city (population 26 million in 2012), patients fought for each. They agreed to let me stay until the weekend before transferring to gen pop, but possession was all that mattered. The accommodations resembled a three-star. I had a motorized bed, a flat-screen TV, a refrigerator (plugged in, too!), a sofa for guests, and **a private bathroom with a shower and a sit-down toilet**! Holy shit!!! After all the abysmal hospitals, I would finally be treated humanely, so much for the communist ideology of everyone being equal. People with the *guanxi* to receive these high-end services lived a better life and averted death.

I paid cash for the privilege and at a higher rate. If I could find the right recipient, throwing RuMBas at the problem would open more doors. Compared to the U.S., $200 a night was a bargain.

The public ward ran $30 a day, and you received a hard bed with no privacy.

Why would I want to subject myself to that?

The room was suitable, but the fare was lousy. They brought me a set meal of a cold *baozi* (cabbage and mushroom stuffed steamed bun) or plain congee for breakfast and the stir-fry of the day for lunch and dinner. They served the food at 7, 10:30, and 4:30. Even then, it showed up cold. I picked through the meal and filled up on Subway.

During the second week, I gained use of my legs, but it took practice. How was it possible that they had deteriorated so quickly? The hospital built a garden on the roof of a connected building, and they encouraged me to stroll. I attempted to increase my distance to show them I could heal my body, similar to ten years ago, but I only fooled myself.

While I thought I had improved, the physician told me the terrible news: my kidneys had failed for good. I had to choose between hemodialysis or peritoneal dialysis (PD). I didn't understand the repercussions of each treatment or the benefits. But I had to decide, or I would miss the operating room (OR) cut-off and be forced to stay an additional week on top of what I needed. I wanted to avoid that, but I remembered it took four weeks of blood cleaning to kick-start my kidneys last time.

"How about I wait a week to see if they turn on again?"

"For sure, your kidneys will not work."

That was hard to accept, but I figured she might be right. I searched the internet for the pros and cons of both treatments. With red and blue pipes dangling from my leg, I wouldn't be able to get a second opinion, nor would any place accept me. These were my options.

I said I would do PD, allowing me to travel and independently manage my health care. It appeared to be the most suitable option but had its own complications. For one, it required me to pour 2000 ml of a solution through a pipe they would insert into my belly every four hours. Before each fill, I would connect a drain bag to remove the waste fluid. If it worked, I should exist.

After I confirmed, they arranged a time and sent me to the OR. The equipment looked new, with plastic bags covering everything. My wife said the doctors at this VIP hospital were the most skilled, and only the top PhDs with *guanxi* snagged jobs in the elite public hospitals. I prayed the doctor had plenty of field experience. I also hoped she wouldn't leave a messy scar or insert the pipe wrongly. There was a lot to consider as I lay awake during the surgery. They covered my face, but my eyes were open, and I sensed her cutting into my abdomen.

Just before she implanted the duct, she showed me it was sealed in the original packaging from the U.S. She even opened it before me. The surgeon knew China's reputation for copying things and wanted me to witness she didn't put a faulty line inside me. That would have been more reassuring if I wasn't aware that China copied packaging to perfection, too.

The surgery lasted an hour, and they wheeled me to my room to practice the fill-and-drain process. I hung a 2000 ml bag on the IV pole and let the solution expand my stomach. They warmed the liquid, which I found was essential. I frosted my insides when not at room temperature (especially during the winter). I also had to push the air out of the pipes, or bubbles rose internally to my shoulders, and the pain was unbearable. There was a lot to learn.

Dialysis patients practiced strict liquid control; the more I drank, the more I had to suck out. At some point, I would intake too much, causing my legs to balloon up and my heart to take on more pressure. It was already struggling with the high BP.

How do I visit factories or have a dim sum lunch without drinking loads of tea? Do I need to quit and leave China? I signed for the company leases and office registrations in Hong Kong and Shanghai. How would I disentangle myself? The doctor told me I could travel, but do I have to lock myself in an airplane toilet to drain and fill? How would I get fluid bags in my carry-on?

I had many thoughts going through my mind as I sat alone with an IV needle jabbed in both hands and pipes coming out of my abdomen and crotch.

They had me fill and drain four times to ensure the duct worked. My stomach swelled as the sugar water filled my insides and deflated when I drained. I would have to do this several times a day. The IV pole became my best friend.

That first night, I went to sleep thinking my entire career was over. Everything I built had fallen apart, and I might no longer provide for my family. I lacked a solution for dealing with the things on my plate.

I figured my down-and-out days in H.K. were rock bottom, but this situation broke through that floor and set a lower one.

With everything crashing down, I prayed for direction. You can't help but pray. I blamed nobody, nor did I ask why this happened to me. It was clear my kidneys would fail. Now, I needed guidance to navigate.

My thoughts weighed heavily on me as I tried to sleep.

The following day, something was different. I still had the pipes, but it seemed as if a colossal weight had been lifted. I stood up to open the curtains, and it was blue and sunny—rare for a city with hazy skies. Peter Gabriel's "Don't Give Up" randomly shuffled on iTunes, and I experienced a moment of extreme clarity. The day before, I had dark thoughts, but it appeared someone had removed those obstacles and the despair. Suddenly, I knew how to deal with my situation. I felt lighter. It turned out that the power of prayer worked. I didn't ask to be healed; I required guidance.

For that, I am forever grateful.

First, I had to remove the pipe from my thigh and escape from the infirmary. The doctor was reluctant to remove the bloodlines until I did two weeks of tests. My stay at the hospital lasted for a month.

With lots of downtime, I did emails and made calls. My staff brought me documents to sign and chop while I worked on rehabilitating my legs. Thirty days ago, I thought I might never step out and would die in a chair in the lobby. When I passed the recliner on my way out, I felt a sense of triumph. But it was too early to say goodbye.

It wouldn't be the last time I saw it.

Immediately after discharged, I booked a flight to Hong Kong to test-drive the drain-and-fill process while on the road. The biggest annoyance was hand-carrying the solution. I needed four pouches per day or twelve for a three-day trip, but my rollaboard suitcase fit ten, with no space for anything else.

They subjected me to a thorough hand inspection with my suitcase full of five-pound liquid pouches. Security called me to the luggage room and asked me to open my bag before they swept it for explosives. Everything was labeled in Chinese, but I prepared to whip out my pipe at a moment's notice. That turned out to be unnecessary. Perhaps it had to do with the number of patients using PD in China with few blood machines available.

For the next few weeks, I tried to hide my condition and act as if the complications were behind me. But I lacked an understanding of how to lead this new life, while my alter ego, Mr. Thunder, refused to get off the merry-go-round that nearly killed me. He was invincible, and people expected him always to be ready and willing. I realized I could no longer live up to my created persona, but I kept trying.

When my staff and others filled my cup with tea, wine, or whiskey, I was incapable of saying no, even though I knew I should. Likewise, I had trouble breaking my habit of enjoying a cappuccino or passing up on the fruit, soup, and other water-soaked foods being served to me. I was embarrassed and refused to admit I had a problem.

Anything I ate or drank weighed me down. If I overdid it with liquids or consumed over three glasses of alcohol when my reputation preceded me, I expelled that booze in a few hours. It was as if I sent the liquor to a holding station, waiting for the right moment to discharge because my body would not dialyze so much. It pleased me to release the pressure, but I wasted good whiskey.

I missed treatments when I traveled and never caught up. Waste and water gathered in my body, going straight to my limbs and causing them to expand to twice their standard size. I couldn't bend my knees to sit in a car because they were inflated.

My feet exploded out of my shoes; my pants and shirts—once baggy, became tight. I shed my skin like a reptile and woke up each morning, pulling long, stretchy pieces off, not a few flakes. I was bloated and had difficulty lying down because fluid had collected in my lungs. My BP remained in the 200 range; nothing brought it down past 170 for years. I accepted I might never reach a reasonable level.

A month out, I was back in. This time, I tried H.K. I took a risk flying with my super high BP. I didn't want to have SOS fly me out. Instead, I popped extra pills and boarded a commercial flight. My wife called ahead to let the doctor (a new one) know I was coming in hot.

With a flying time of two and a half hours and the additional two-hour delay on every plane leaving The Hai, I looked at arriving at 8 p.m. Once processed, they gave me a bed and hooked me to an automated PD machine for eighteen hours. It drained and filled every other hour.

After finishing, the cycler sucked out 3500 ml (a gallon) of excess water. The hospital did not expect that much. They connected me to drain bags that were too small, and my fluid overflowed.

Because of my high BP, they strapped me in and slapped a warning at the end of my bed that I should not stand. The nurses took that labeling seriously. I had to move before my 5 a.m. blood sample and pill swallowing, so I undid the straps and maneuvered the sidebars enough to pick up my shoes and bag.

Even though it was my fluid, I didn't want that oily mixture on my stuff.

The following night, they ensured they set it up correctly. Also, I produced less water with each marathon-sucking session. The more liquid they squeezed out, the more my BP dropped. I figured I would be in for three days, but I did seven. They stabilized my vitals and returned me to an acceptable sick. However, the clock started ticking when I disconnected until I began manual treatments in four hours.

Securing a machine would be the only solution to my dilemma. The nurse said, "Sure, no problem."

She showed me the dialysis ward, explained the process, and said they would send the liquid to my flat. Everything sounded great. The catch was that I had to be a permanent resident, but I was only temporary, therefore ineligible. China did not sell machines or rent them. Luckily, the H.K. hospital offered to help me buy a device from

Singapore. I paid $18,000. No matter the price, I required one, perhaps two. It seemed the only way to remain out of the infirmary and alive.

The Hong Kong hospital put me back on my feet, ready to board my first international flight to Paris. A month ago, I wasn't sure I would make the trip, but now I felt strong. I wanted to show overseas coworkers I remained alive and well. They heard bits and pieces. I learned before that when you were weak, individuals took advantage. It amazed me that people assumed I wouldn't notice.

My BP improved to 190/118, so the trip seemed doable. I planned to fly on the overnight flight, arriving the following morning. It was a brief excursion of two days: one to get my dialysis set up and one for meetings. I squeezed out most of the excess water to compensate for missed medications during the long haul. Actually, I missed an entire day because the hotel would only give me the room at 3 p.m. again.

Once I received the key, I rushed to fill. I lacked an IV pole and searched for something sturdy to sustain the weight of the drip bag. My best option was the bathroom shower rack. I sat on the rim of the tub for an hour while filling and repeated this every three hours until the meeting the next day. During the conference, I skipped treatments, so I had unused fluid bags to carry home, but I got by unscathed.

Three weeks later, I was back in the hospital on the cycler for two days of eighteen-hour shifts. This became routine until I picked up my machine four months later. Thirty days was as long as I could last until my legs inflated and my lungs filled with fluid.

Then I returned to the infirmary.

My apparatus arrived in Hong Kong in August 2012. Before allowing me to take it home, I had to undergo extensive training. Because they tethered me to the cycler many times, I knew how to run it. I should be in and out in a day. That was not the case; they kept me for three, reduced from seven. I complained daily and got more anxious as they refused to let me leave. They wanted to ensure I would be careful. It was apparent with A FUCKIN' HOLE IN MY BELLY! They didn't need to push the point. My habitual complaining caused them to release me.

Life would be perfect now that I owned a machine.

VIII

I avoided most business meals and parties for several months. When I joined, I sipped wine because I knew I had a built-in circuit breaker that prevented me from downing over three glasses.

That didn't stop me from testing that limit with the same results. It was never immediate, which gave me the false sense I could drink without payback, but I would spout all that single malt and red wine down the drain.

I continued flying between Hong Kong and Shanghai and other destinations. Since I spent more days in The Hai, I moved my machine there and did drip bags in Hong Kong—four to five exchanges a day. Even though I had my own office, it would have been work carrying cases of fluid in. Once I drained, I had a five lb. drain bag to dispose of. Dragging it through the office to the toilet wouldn't be optimum. Instead, I went home. My schedule looked like this:

7 a.m. Drain and fill (45 minutes).

8 a.m. Endure the 45-minute commute.

12:15 p.m. Start the 45-minute trip to my apartment.

1 p.m. Eat while draining and filling. Pass out for 15 minutes.

2 p.m. Make the 45-minute return to the office.

6 p.m. Get through a final 45-minute commute.

7 p.m. Eat while draining and filling.

10 p.m. Drain and fill.

3 a.m. Drain and fill.

7 a.m. Drain and fill.

It was a hard life, made worse when I suffered from **TFGS**. My feet killed me because I missed treatments. I had to either move back to the U.S. or continue through the anguish. I considered moving when I returned for the first time since the change. To stay more than a few days, I ordered fluid from the supplier, who delivered it to the U.S.

I got in to see a nephrologist at UCLA days before returning. My BP was still beyond control, and I worried about having a stroke. The doctor looked at me and said I was in awful shape. He directed me to a clinic that provided me with a few bags of super-strong fluid to drain more liquid. I was grateful for the excess draining, but the side effects were harsh. Soon, I would be back home on the machine.

All I needed was to be healthy enough to get there.

Not long after I arrived, I traveled again and missed more treatments. My ankles grew tight. It felt as if they were full of sand and did not want to move. Then, the nerves in my legs and feet became electrified. The more I walked, the more intense the pain was. The dialysis at night provided short-term relief until I stood up the following morning.

Near the end of May 2013, I prepared to fly to Paris again. I had sufficient experience from the previous visit to make this a smoother one. I also appeared stable enough to travel despite my 198/130 blood pressure. On a good day, I lowered it to 170/118, but most of the time, it bordered on 200. I attempted to decrease it by swallowing multiple pills and doubling down on them. I knew taking an international flight with BP this high would not be intelligent, but I persuaded myself into thinking I would survive. As a precaution, I did extra drains and fills. I flew empty and would fill once I reached the hotel. If I filled before flying, I would absorb the liquid. That would be a terrible start to the trip. With no fluid, anything I ate or drank went to my feet. I wasn't sure how things would end up, but I took a real risk.

Although I ran hot, I passed through Shanghai customs without setting off the alarm. Perhaps it was the high BP or just the everyday mangled state of my body, but my nose ran bloody, and my eyes looked dark and watery. I popped more pills and thought, "What if I have a heart attack on the flight? Is there someone who can start me up? Do they have a defibrillator?"

Once airborne, I counted down the hours until arrival. I felt okay but paid close attention to any changes in my status.

"My heart can take it."

Then, they made an announcement.

"Is there a doctor on the plane?"

Really? Was someone sicker than me? Another passenger had "heart issues." The pilot turned the airplane around to offload the guy in Beijing (I'll bet he didn't have a 200 BP). The dude refused to disembark because he boarded in Shanghai and wanted them to take him there. I was ready to throw him off until the police grabbed him.

"Are you fucking kidding me? "

This added several hours to my ten-hour trip. Not only that but how pissed would others be if we departed and they turned the aircraft around a second time for me? I didn't know if I could last through a new ten-hour flight on top of the four hours I had spent. I swallowed BP pills and hoped for the best.

We arrived in Paris at 9 a.m., and French customs had a problem with my luggage. One suitcase held the ten bags of fluid, and the other had a suit and a change of clothes. They spoke less English than I thought they would, but I attempted to explain dialysis. I exposed my pipe and pointed to the fluid, which was the "Ah-ha!" moment. They let me go to the outside world and away from that plane.

Now, I needed to beg the front desk to give me a room. I wanted to fill and drain twice before dinner with my associates. The only positive thing that came out of the flight being delayed was it ate up time I would spend in the lobby. It seemed all the hotels in Paris had an iron-clad check-in of 3 p.m.

I was a walking sponge. My feet, ankles, and legs became squishy and made sounds when I walked as if I had water in my shoes. When I removed my socks, they left a deep impression on my calves that stressed the blown-up size of my limbs.

Even in my woeful state, I could not check in. I showed up at 10:30 a.m. and would not survive until 3 p.m. I tried to think of a semi-sanitary place to do my fill and drain. A public toilet or a park? It was impossible. I stayed in the tiny lobby and stared at the front desk staff. I told them I required a room to do a shot. They took mercy on me and handed over the key at 11:30 a.m.

I quickly set up in the bathroom. When I glanced in the mirror, I noticed both eyes were bloody. Yeah, they looked scary. I now understood why customs pulled me aside and the hotel offered me the room. I had to give a presentation in twenty-four hours, and would be the focus. The dialysis I could hide, but this was noticeable.

Perhaps the blood would subside after some sleep.

My business partners got held up, and they canceled the dinner. That gave me plenty of chances to drain and fill, and drain and fill, and drain and fill. I did the last fill at 3 a.m. Then, I had the pleasure of sleeping for four hours before doing another drain. The question was, should I fill before going to my meeting? I might be able to leave at lunch. If not, I would risk absorbing the fluid.

I took a chance and filled up—a mistake.

For the rest of the day, I avoided eye contact to prevent scaring my coworkers with my blood-filled eyes. I glanced at the whiteboard for most of the presentation. Then I squinted to hide the red.

The meetings ran over, and I never received that afternoon delight of drain and fill. Initially, we planned an early meal, which became a late one. We returned to the hotel after 10 p.m., way past the limit of four hours. I absorbed half of the liquid with the other fluids I drank. There was nothing left to do but drain and fill, and drain and fill.

What a horrible existence.

IX

In July 2013, I started a new position as Managing Director of Asia, in charge of sales and retail. The job entailed traveling, and that meant more missed treatments. When I took the assignment, I got concerned about this, but they reassured me flying would only be necessary every few months.

I based myself out of Shanghai and no longer flew to H.K. weekly.

After twelve years of commuting, I now lived in one city.

Instead of getting up to trek to the airport, I headed to the office. I established a Representative Office (RO) ten years ago, but it had little ability to do much besides follow up on orders and handle quality control. Now, I had to set up a FICE (Foreign-Invested Commercial Enterprise) to do business. The registration required a year to complete. They always needed a document to be chopped, or they questioned a signature. Our staff begged officials to process things. We lacked *guanxi*, and it slowed the process.

Technically, I wasn't allowed to work in the office until they issued the business license, but I visited and worked there as a visitor (a gray area). As part of the switch from RO to FICE, we had to coerce all the staff to cancel their contracts and sign new ones. Getting everyone to cooperate without asking for more money was no simple task. All employees had two-year agreements as a requirement from the Labor Department to protect them from being fired. It was a headache for companies that followed the law. Foreign businesses turned into soft targets for lawsuits when they let employees go. The Labor Dept. seemed quick to help disgruntled workers against foreign firms. Most of my staff had been with me for years, and I had earned their trust. I also had a vested interest. Since I became the Legal Representative, I had to make sure everything we did was lawful, or the government would hold me responsible. Many firms kept top U.S. management from registering as a Legal Rep because the title assumed too much liability. A CEO could be stopped from leaving the country for a frivolous reason. I accepted the position for the work visa that came with it. Also, the Legal Rep signed all documents. It slowed down the process if we sent them to the U.S.

This office lacked the gorgeous sea view of Hong Kong Harbor, but it was only fifteen minutes from my home—a straight cruise through the haunted Expo village. It was easy to reach with no traffic. Getting anywhere between 7:30 a.m. and 9 p.m. grew challenging with the crowded streets. It got so bad that I rode the subway and stopped going out altogether.

Another benefit was the McDonald's around the corner. Then, a Korean BBQ opened the floor beneath us. Their exhaust system had something wrong, and the smoke drifted into our vents. Every day at 11 a.m., the fragrance of grilled beef would saturate our floor until somebody fixed it. Soon after, an Outback Steak House popped up down the road. I finally didn't need to travel all over the city to find Western fare. When I first arrived in The Hai, there were only three KFCs, including one on the Bund, now a Waldorf-Astoria, and a lonely Tony Roma's. That was it, besides the hotels or the few Western bars. Today, even second and third-tiered cities have Western restaurants on nearly every street. Several years ago, I ran on the Shanghai Hash in the suburbs and ended up at an intersection with a Papa Johns, a Pizza Hut, a McDonald's, a Starbucks, a Pacific Coffee, and a KFC. I don't know if that can be called progress, but I sure as hell would have appreciated a lineup like that in the early days for that necessary infusion of fast food in between the *baijiu*-soaked meals. But not at every corner.

The drawback of the job was the routine. I went to the office each morning and returned home for lunch to drain and fill before heading back. I missed visiting the factories, witnessing the recent developments around China, the adventure of not knowing what would happen on the road, and the strange foods people served me. With my health failing, I couldn't travel as I did in the old days, so this gig was best.

When I flew to Seoul, Tokyo, and Hong Kong for business, I carried my suitcases packed with fluid and did dialysis wherever I found a place. My BP remained in the low 200s, becoming a constant worry. As customary, I doubled up on the meds.

I took a physical for my Legal Representative status, and I scared the shit out of the nurse. He pumped away on the hand-held BP device, and I saw the guy's eyes every time it read 250 over 160. He wrote Emergency Treatment as the course of action, while the other staff at the clinic talked about me as if I were a dead man walking.

I lowered my BP to 180/110 for a business trip to NYC in October, an eighteen-hour direct flight.

For this three-day excursion, I packed two suitcases with seventeen fluid bags and a garment carrier. I dragged these liquid-filled cases through the spacious airports to Midtown. This would be my last trip to

NYC, so I met some college friends for wings and beer, something now easier to get in The Hai but not as good.

When I met up with my fraternity brothers, I came in like a hurricane, ordering shots and bottles of alcohol. Mr. Thunder's tolerance was beyond anything we drank in college, the peak for most. But now, I was a broken man. Perhaps my friends were relieved. Long ago, I realized we partied so much harder overseas. Life seemed a lot more real for my U.S. friends. They had bills, a day job, no expense account, or liquid lunches.

That lifestyle grew foreign. As an expatriate, the party continued forever.

Before I could go anywhere, I needed to fill. This was my schedule:

5 p.m. Arrive at the hotel.

6 p.m. Fill.

11 p.m. Drain and fill.

3 a.m. Drain and fill.

7 a.m. Drain and fill.

8 a.m. Drain.

By the time I walked into the office, I could barely keep my eyes open. I made it through the meetings and rushed to the hotel for a fill before dinner. The restaurant was twenty blocks away, with no empty taxis during rush hour.

I had two choices:

1. Navigate the subway with lots of stairs and lengthy walks.

2. Walk outside in the cool air.

I wrongly chose the second option. The waste buildup in my legs and feet lit them on fire. The nerves in my limbs shocked and jabbed me with needles. Every step sent pain up my nervous system, but I clenched my teeth and continued. Ten blocks in, I was forced to stop and massage my feet. I was in a cold sweat and arrived late.

After dinner, I grabbed a cab to avoid some torment. The following day, I had the same schedule: a day of meetings followed by an evening of draining and filling. I finished all the bags but one. Then I lugged the empty suitcases back to The Hai.

When I reached home, I set up my machine for a night of draining and filling.

X

In May 2014, I took a scan to ensure I didn't have more carcinomas. They found one the size of a nickel. When they injected contrast, multiple tumors lit up, all potential killers in waiting. My Hong Kong urologist told me I needed to have my kidneys removed.

"Okay, perhaps you can use the robot arm to make a small incision and pull them out. You should have that technology by now, right?"

The doctor said since he had operated on my kidneys, they might be sticky and hard to remove. He recommended doing open surgery.

"Open surgery? No way. I can't do it."

I needed a second opinion.

The best place was the VIP cadre hospital. We talked it over with the top doctors, and they held a meeting with other specialists. Most were aware of my case. Now, they had the opportunity to slice me open and take my organs. Part of me would find its way to a lab, where it would sit in a jar labeled "Abbie Normal."

But the doctors got cold feet. They initially said they would do the surgery with only a one-inch scar.

"Great, that's what I want."

They would get back to us after they scheduled the procedure. The longer the wait, the more I thought I had made a mistake. They probably stalled because they realized the risk. The doctors avoided saying they wouldn't do it. That would be too direct. Instead, they said,

"He's a foreigner. Wouldn't he be more comfortable doing this in his own country?"

Sure. Why not go to the U.S.? But how? I didn't have insurance and would need to stay a few months. How could I run the business?

I was in a bind until the obstacles were cleared again, and I knew what to do.

I had to leave China and the job. They were both killing me.

If I required another sign, a car hit me on my way to Sunday morning church. A Catholic chapel built in 1853 was a ten-minute walk through the alleys. I shuffled over with my pain-filled feet for mass and a free cup of cheap coffee. It was calming. Until one Sunday, I got run over outside my apartment.

Hawkers sold stuff on both sides with little room for an automobile, but people never cared about that. They forced through. I limped to the side when a car behind me honked, but I had nowhere to go until the road widened. The guy lacked patience and pushed on ahead when he clipped my leg. Bam! I hit the concrete, and my foot got jammed in the wheel well, pulling me under. He stopped, but I was in shock and needed a few seconds before realizing what had happened. Then I became angry. I attempted to speak Mandarin, but all that came out were multiple uses of the F-word. My pants were torn, and the pain seeped into my foot, but it differed from **TFGS**. This additional anguish replaced my old suffering.

A crowd blocked the alley, with no motorbikes or food carts coming in or going out. Then, a cop showed up and instructed me to get up.

"Really? Is it all you can say? I thought police were supposed to help."

I told him he should leave. That's when my wife arrived to yell at the man who hit me. I called her after the incident. She calmed me enough to get me off the street. Now I understood why locals loved to stay on the ground after being hit. You were free to rant at that moment, and nobody would say anything because you got hit.

"Have both arms and legs where they should be? Then wail away."

Someone provided me with a wooden elementary school chair to sit on while my wife, the cop, and the driver settled the issue. Something wrong occurred, and there should be restitution. Money! I should get some cash, right? First, we had to stop at the police station to file a report. The officer didn't have a car, so we used the vehicle that just ran me over.

We rode to the station, and I sat while the bargaining began. They settled on 1000 RuMBas ($160). "What about my foot?" The pain grew worse. "It might be fractured." With cancer, dialysis, **TFGS**, and other health issues, the last thing I needed was a broken foot. For safety's sake, the guy paid for an X-ray. Naturally, we took his car.

My foot wasn't cracked, but it was too painful to walk on for a few days, which meant a lot coming from me. I endured it, and my wife received the cash.

So that was it. I decided to leave for good. Getting run over on the way to church was the last straw. I knew this day would arrive, but how, why, and when was unclear. Over the years, many friends came and went, but I stayed. I remained for half my time on Earth. Could I walk away and not look back? It's easy when it's a life-or-death situation.

Rule #28: Do not die in China.

I had to go. Decoupling and removing my name from the company would be difficult. Meanwhile, I met with doctors in America to get my kidneys removed before the cancer spread. In December 2014, I had both taken out through a four-inch incision. Each was filled with cancerous nodes; the doctors had never seen anything like it. After the surgery, I was stuck doing hemodialysis for a few months until my abdomen healed enough to attempt PD.

Four months after the operation (on dialysis), I returned to China to complete my repatriation by closing my accounts, selling our apartment, and hiring an international relocation company to move. I arrived so long ago with a backpack and a duffle but was leaving with a hell of a lot more stuff. At the end of March, I boarded a plane from Shanghai to Los Angeles—my last flight after close to a thousand. As I walked through customs, I thought, "This is the last time." I felt sad, but the pain in my feet kept me from dwelling. Besides, this wasn't the same place that had brought me here. I missed the China when I first arrived, the ice-cold, small bottle of Coke on a steamy Beijing summer day. The China, I had to ride my bike across town to tell my friend I couldn't make it. You can still find it in certain pockets, but you have to look hard. It doesn't fall in your lap like it did years ago.

Nonetheless, my China lives here, and I am grateful to have been there.

This is how I lost my kidneys in China.

EPILOGUE

S o that's my story, most of it anyway. I left and never looked back. I have lots of memories, but still no kidneys. My doctors in the U.S. managed to give me a somewhat normal life despite having to hook up to a machine daily for eleven hours and carry fluid for the other thirteen. It's not something I would recommend, but I am alive and can enjoy the fruits of life, such as ice cubes and a sit-down toilet. Every day I wake up without pain with blue skies is another excellent day. If I could do it all over, would I change anything? Not much. It was the journey I was meant to take, for better or worse. Although I no longer drink copious amounts of alcohol (or anything), I can enjoy a glass of Scotch now and then. Things could always be worse, like having gone through life without adventure. What's the point of that?

MAP

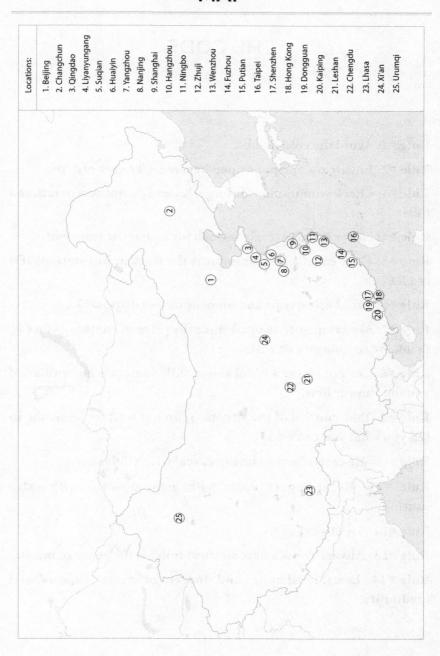

Locations:

1. Beijing
2. Changchun
3. Qingdao
4. Liyanyungang
5. Suqian
6. Huaiyin
7. Yangzhou
8. Nanjing
9. Shanghai
10. Hangzhou
11. Ningbo
12. Zhuji
13. Wenzhou
14. Fuzhou
15. Putian
16. Taipei
17. Shenzhen
18. Hong Kong
19. Dongguan
20. Kaiping
21. Leshan
22. Chengdu
23. Lhasa
24. Xi'an
25. Urumqi

THE CODE

Rule #1: Avoid the cold dishes.

Rule #2: Ensure no one pops open beverages I never ordered.

Rule #3: Check your money for forgeries and do not accept tattered bills.

Rule #4: Never stand up early or rush for a plane or train exit.

Rule #5: Only eat at a restaurant near the train or bus stations if it is a KFC.

Rule #6: Avoid using cups and utensils unless disposable.

Rule #7: Always negotiate in advance the price of anything you eat, drink, or anyone you sit with.

Rule #8: Do not share a hotel room with someone unfamiliar; if you do, shower first.

Rule #9: Take control of the situation; do not wait for someone to tell you what you can't do.

Rule #10: Be careful not to be too casual with students.

Rule #11: Regarding students with gifts, proceed with extra caution.

Rule #12: Trust your gut.

Rule #13: Always know where the best toilet is for peace of mind.

Rule #14: Learn local songs and dialects to create *"Guanxi"* and credibility.

Rule #15: From the choice of hotel to transportation, understand the full itinerary and who handles what.

Rule #16: Scope out the area for the choicest eateries. Ensure the restaurant has items suitable for your companions. A good meal makes people happy. A bad one increases the tension.

Rule #17: If outnumbered, do not start a fight.

Rule #18: Be careful. Someone is always watching.

Rule #19: "Never get off the boat."

Rule #20: Only let your ride leave once you are sure you no longer need it.

Rule #21: Don't *ganbei* with someone drinking a lesser drink.

Rule #22: Never hang my arm outside a car window. Never.

Rule #23: Always close off one side with a friendly and be clear on strategy before the meal.

Rule #24: Never leave a taxi before making sure you have everything.

Rule #25: The entire eating experience, including location and exclusivity, is as essential as selecting the food itself.

Rule #26: Too much local culture is not suitable for people not living in Asia.

Rule #27: Don't buy groceries after drinking. Go straight home and quit consuming so much vodka.

Rule #28: Do not die in China.

GLOSSARY

Baijiu: high alcohol content white spirit distilled from sorghum

Beida: short for Beijing *Daxue* (college) or Peking University

Booze: alcohol

BP: blood pressure

Bread: cash, money

Brogues: a durable shoe with decorative perforations and a wing tip

CCP: China Communist Party

Churrascarias: an all-you-can-eat Brazilian steakhouse where servers bring skewers of meat to your table

CKM: Chungking Mansions

CNY: Chinese New Year

Commode: toilet

Danwei: work unit

CWB: Causeway Bay, a district on Hong Kong Island

Digs: lodgings or home

Dough: cash or money

DPS: Drunk Pilot System

Drop a deuce: a "number two"

Ducats / duckets: cash

Erguotou: a clear, potent spirit with an average strength of 56% or more alcohol by volume

Erhu: a two-stringed bowed instrument

FEC: Foreign Exchange Certificates or foreigner money used in China from 1980-1994

Fifty spot: $50 or a fifty RMB

Fuwuyuan: service attendant or waiter/ waitress

Ganbei/ganbeis/ganbei'ing: to drink a toast until completion or "bottoms up"

Guanxi: relation or relationship that can be used to get things done

Gweilo: Cantonese slang for foreigner translated as "white ghost"

Hash or Hash House Harriers: the drinking group with a running problem

(The) Head: toilet

Heisman: to push your way through a crowd like the Heisman trophy

Hootch/ sauce/ rocket fuel: alcohol

Hua: language or words

Hua jiao: Chinese prickly ash; peppery and leaves a numbing sensation when added to food

Hutong: a Beijing alley with traditional courtyard compounds lining both sides

Jade Garden: "Yu Yuan" is a Shanghai garden built in 1559 and a top city attraction

Jin: a "catty" or Chinese pound equal to approx. 500 grams or 1.1 Western pounds

Laoban: the boss

Laogong: husband or spouse

Laowai: a foreigner; directly translated as "old outsider"

Lei Yue Mun: live seafood stalls in Hong Kong where you take your purchase to be cooked in one of the restaurants

Lit: buzzed on my way to getting drunk

LKF: Lan Kwai Fong, a nightlife district in Hong Kong

Loo: toilet

LP: long-play records made of black vinyl

Mao Wang: Elvis, "The King of the Cats"

(A) Mark: someone easily fooled or tricked

Mashang: immediately; it usually means about an hour

Meiyou Pijiu: out of beer

Mercans: Americans

Nosh: food or a snack

Omakase: "I leave it up to you" is a unique Japanese dining experience. The chef will tailor a several-course meal based on fresh items just received.

Pantones: the standardization of all color shades on paper to compare with when designing

PLA: People's Liberation Army

Po-po: police

PRC: People's Republic of China

Privy: outhouse

QC: quality control or a person who inspects the quality

Qi Gong: a system of deep breathing exercises

RuMBas: RMB (Renminbi) or the people's money

Shiest: to take something from a store or restaurant without paying

Shifu: teacher or master

Shindig: a party

Skivvies: underwear

Slab of smokes: a carton of cigarettes

Slammer: prison

Sliders: White Castle hamburgers

Sloshed: a bit drunk

Social compliance: an extensive list of factory safety and ethical requirements

Souk: an open-air marketplace in North Africa and the Middle East

Suiyi: "as you like" used when drinking if you don't want to consume the entire amount at one time

Swill: beer

TCM: Traditional Chinese medicine

TFGS: "That Fucking Gout Shit"

The Chai: Wanchai, a nightlife district on Hong Kong Island

The Hai: Shanghai

Trepang: a common name for sea cucumber or a similar marine invertebrae

TST: Tsimshatsui, a tourist district in Hong Kong

VOA: Voice Of America radio station

W.C.: Water closet; toilet

Walkman: a hand-held cassette player

Weiya: a traditional year-end party for Chinese companies

Wellies: rainboots

Whiz: urinate

Yanks: Yankees or Americans

Yaogun: rock n roll

Made in the USA
Las Vegas, NV
27 October 2023

79807132R00288